Second Language Syntax

For Clare, Elizabeth and Laura

Second Language Syntax

A Generative Introduction

Roger Hawkins

Blackwell
Publishing

© 2001 by Roger Hawkins

BLACKWELL PUBLISHING
350 Main Street, Malden, MA 02148-5020, USA
9600 Garsington Road, Oxford OX4 2DQ, UK
550 Swanston Street, Carlton, Victoria 3053, Australia

The right of Roger Hawkins to be identified as the Author of this Work has been asserted in accordance with the UK Copyright, Designs, and Patents Act 1988.

First published 2001 by Blackwell Publishing Ltd

3   2006

Library of Congress Cataloging-in-Publication Data has been applied for.

ISBN-13: 978-0-631-19183-4 (hardback)
ISBN-10: 0-631-19183-6 (hardback)
ISBN-13: 978-0-631-19184-1 (paperback)
ISBN-10: 0-631-19184-4 (paperback)

A catalogue record for this title is available from the British Library.

Set in 10/13pt Sabon
by Graphicraft Ltd,Hong Kong

The publisher's policy is to use permanent paper from mills that operate a sustainable forestry policy, and which has been manufactured from pulp processed using acid-free and elementary chlorine-free practices. Furthermore, the publisher ensures that the text paper and cover board used have met acceptable environmental accreditation standards.

For further information on
Blackwell Publishing, visit our website:
www.blackwellpublishing.com

Contents

Figures

Tables

Preface

When researchers first began seriously to investigate how people come by knowledge of second languages, one of their striking findings was the extent to which empirical evidence conflicted with what might be called 'common sense' views of SLA (second language acquisition). For example, one 'common sense' view is that people learn what they are exposed to; but evidence suggested that second language learners often do not learn the properties of the second language they are exposed to straightforwardly, and more significantly sometimes know things about second languages which they haven't encountered in the input at all. Another 'common sense' view is that speakers of native languages as different as Spanish and Japanese will acquire a second language like English differently. But evidence suggested that this is not always the case; native speakers of typologically very different languages often develop knowledge of second languages in the same kind of way. A third 'common sense' view holds that learning second languages in classrooms yields different outcomes from learning them through natural exposure; but evidence suggested there are many instances where classroom and naturalistic second language learners develop similar kinds of knowledge.

Such conflicts between views of second language acquisition which might initially seem self-evident and what goes on in reality have provided the impetus for much revealing work since the early 1970s. This book is an attempt to provide an introduction, overview and critical evaluation of a selection of that work as it relates to how speakers come by knowledge of the syntax of second languages – syntax being those properties which determine how sentences are constructed.

Because our understanding has evolved to the point where there are competing theories of such knowledge, each with its own set of conceptual and technical devices, I have concentrated here on one theoretical approach in particular: the 'generative' approach which follows the work of Chomsky and his associates, and assumes that speakers of a language have an internal mental grammar which productively generates the sentences of that language. From this perspective, the ability to construct such grammars derives from an innate language faculty, at the core of which are principles determining the form that grammars can take. This core is known as Universal Grammar. One reason for concentrating on the generative approach in particular (rather than, say, comparing different approaches) is that it has opened up many fruitful and unexpected avenues of enquiry into the nature of second language acquisition which are worth exploring in some detail. A second reason is that it is not clear, given what we know currently, that meaningful comparisons between hypotheses formulated from different perspectives can be made.

The book starts from the assumption that the reader may have little knowledge either of research into second language acquisition or of specific proposals concerning Universal Grammar. Important features of each are discussed as the text proceeds, including explanations of basic concepts where necessary. However, the aim is also to enable readers to progress to the point where they can evaluate primary second language research literature critically. To this end there are sections in every chapter (excluding chapter 1) where discussion engages some of the more controversial issues which have recently been, or are currently, the subject of debate. These sections are marked in the text by the rubric *More advanced discussion*. Depending on the interests and background knowledge of the reader, these sections could be omitted in a first reading.

While I have attempted to develop a single line of argument running through the eight chapters, each deals with a different topic, so it is possible to read each one independently of the others. Having taught courses on second language syntax both to undergraduates and postgraduates for a number of years now, my experience has been that students new to this area of enquiry find it helpful to have 'cues' to remind them of leading ideas or to locate places where particular arguments are developed. 'Cues' in this text take the form of (a) short outlines at the start of every major section which describe what the section deals with; (b) summaries at the end of longer or more difficult sections reviewing the main points made. To give the reader an opportunity to move from the passive reception of ideas to a more active mode of thinking about the issues involved in understanding second language syntax, at the end of each chapter there are practical exercises or discussion topics. Some of these (particularly in the later chapters) are open-ended, and aim to extend ideas discussed in the text, or to question claims made in the text. For some of these exercises there may be no single straightforward answer.

Acknowledgements

I am grateful to many people for help, both direct and indirect, in writing this book. I would partciularly like to thank Julia Herschensohn, Makiko Hirakawa, Jim Lantolf, Bonnie Schwartz, Antonella Sorace, Lydia White and the publisher's readers for commenting on some or all of the manuscript at various points in its evolution. Their comments helped me avoid a number of errors of interpretation or presentation, with the result that this is a better piece of work than it might otherwise have been.

More generally, the book would not have been possible without the work of researchers around the world investigating second language acquisition. While there are too many of these to mention individually by name, I would like to acknowledge those who, through their work or in my personal contacts with them, have had a particular influence on my thinking about issues in second language acquisition. In addition to those mentioned in the first paragraph: Nives Bazergui, Kevin Gregg, Florence Myles, Teresa Parodi, Rex Sprouse, Richard Towell, Ianthi Tsimpli, Martha Young-Scholten and Shigenori Wakabayashi.

My colleagues in the Department of Language and Linguistics at the University of Essex, while not all interested in second language acquisition, continue to provide the kind of enthusiastic and committed intellectual environment for linguistic research in which writing a book like this is possible. I would particularly like to thank those who form, loosely, the 'acquisition research group': Martin Atkinson, Harald Clahsen, Vivian Cook, Claudia Felser, Mike Jones and Andrew Radford. I am also indebted to the University of Essex itself for allowing me the period of study leave during which most of this book was written.

I am grateful to many students, present and past, who by their interest in and reactions to ideas and hypotheses in second language acquisition research have helped me to clarify my own views and how best to present them to others. I would particularly like to thank Mohammad Al-Hamad, Eidah Al-Malki, Cecilia Chan, Dena Christodoulou, Florencia Franceschina, Judit Kiss-Gulyas, Marzul Hidayat, Maria Karamani, Stano Kong, Sarah Liszka, Cristobal Lozano, Soni Mirizon, Shiro Ojima, Natsumi Okuwaki, Phoevos Panagiotidis, Elena Párraga, Anthony Polentas, Cornelia Sander, Jane Shelton, Emma Thomas, Bee Eng Wong and Manijeh Youhanaee.

The following people have kindly allowed me to use excerpts from their published or unpublished work as exercise material: Camilla Bardel, Tammy Jandrey Hertel and Ana Pérez-Leroux, Josien Lalleman, Patsy Lightbown and Monica Sopher. Finally the author and publisher would like to thank the following for permission to use copyright material in the book: Arnold Publishers, Cambridge University Press, Elsevier Science and Oxford University Press.

None of the above can be held responsible for mistakes, errors of judgement, misrepresentation of the facts or other failings of this work, for which I accept responsibility.

1 A Framework for Studying Second Language Syntax

1.1 Introduction

An important part of learning a second language is learning how words fit together to form phrases, and how phrases fit together to form sentences. The combinatorial properties of words and phrases are known as the **syntax** of a language. Two main research topics are usually identified by those interested in understanding how people acquire the syntax of second languages. The first is to explain how knowledge of syntax develops over time: why are some properties acquired earlier than others, and why do some remain difficult even for advanced second language speakers? This is often referred to as the **developmental problem**. The assumption made here is that syntactic development is best viewed as the consequence of second language learners building subconscious mental grammars, in which representations for some syntactic properties are established before others. Changes in the mental grammar underlie observable changes in the performance of second language speakers over time.

The second research topic is to explain what makes it possible for second language speakers to build mental grammars in the first place. What mechanisms or devices does the human brain make available for such a task? As we shall see, the second language syntactic knowledge that speakers develop appears to go beyond properties they have evidence for in the limited samples of speech or writing they encounter. The problem then is to explain how speakers come to know more than is present in the input, a problem often referred to as the **logical problem** of second language acquisition.[1]

Fortunately for second language researchers, there is already in existence a sophisticated and successful approach to understanding the mechanisms which underlie the human ability to build mental grammars. This stems from the work of Chomsky (1981, 1986a, 1995) on the nature of the mental grammars of mature native speakers. At the heart of the approach is the assumption that the grammars of human languages are all essentially built on the same pattern; that is, there is a **Universal Grammar** which underlies the particular grammars of specific languages. At the same time Universal Grammar allows possibilities for variation between languages in the way that its constructs are realized, but of a limited and specifiable kind. In the 1980s and early 1990s the approach was known as the 'principles and parameters' approach, with principles the universally invariant properties of grammar construction, and parameters the specifications of possible variation. More recently, Chomsky's work has focused on reducing the form that principles and parameters take to the minimal specifications required to allow grammar-building to occur, and the approach has come to be known as a 'minimalist program for linguistic theory' (Chomsky 1995). The goals of the work are nevertheless the same: to characterize the mechanisms made available by the brain for building mental grammars for specific languages. Because a good number of recent studies of second language syntax have been conducted within the framework of the principles and parameters approach to Universal Grammar, that is the perspective that will be adopted in this book.

The aim of the book is to present evidence from the syntactic performance of second language learners to support the view that learners build subconscious mental grammars progressively (the developmental problem), and that they deploy the mechanisms of an underlying Universal Grammar to do so (the logical problem). However, the initial assumption is that the reader has little knowledge either of the principles-and-parameters approach or of current work on second language syntax. Evidence and arguments will be presented in stages, and I will define key notions and assumptions as we proceed. In this chapter we consider what syntax consists of, what a grammar is, and what is involved in studying how second language learners construct the syntactic component of their mental grammars.

1.2   What is syntax?

Section 1.2 describes some of the syntactic properties involved in distinguishing grammatical and ungrammatical sentences.

The syntax of a language is the set of properties which determine the construction of sentences in that language. If a sentence is constructed according to those properties it is well formed or **grammatical**. If a sentence is constructed in violation of those properties it is ill-formed or **ungrammatical**. The examples of (1) are grammatical sentences of English, those of (2) ungrammatical sentences of English (it is a convention in linguistics to mark ungrammatical sentences by an asterisk):

1a George speaks Finnish
 b I wish that Margaret would agree to stop criticizing John
 c Tom often visits Paris
 d Peter gave his sister his stamp collection

2a *George speak Finnish
 b *I wish that Margaret would to agree stop to criticize John
 c *Tom visits often Paris
 d *Peter donated his sister his stamp collection

On the basis of comparing (1) and (2) we can establish, informally, a number of the syntactic properties that grammatical sentences in English must obey:

(1a)–(2a): the first verb in a clause must **agree** with the subject of that clause. The verb must have the ending -s in the present tense if the subject is 3rd person singular, like *George*, and the ending -ϕ for other persons; *George speak-s*, but *I/you/we/they speak-ϕ*.

(1b)–(2b): some verbs **select** infinitive complements with *to* (*agree*: *agree to stop*), others select bare verb complements (*would*: *would agree*), yet others select gerundive complements (marked by *-ing*) (*stop*: *stop criticizing*).

(1c)–(2c): English word order requires that direct objects be **adjacent** to the verbs which govern them (*visits Paris*), and not separated from those verbs (**visits often Paris*).

(1d)–(2d): some verbs allow prepositional phrases to **move** next to the verb, creating 'double object' constructions. *Give* is one of them: *gave his stamp collection to his sister* → *gave his sister his stamp collection*. Other verbs, even those quite close in meaning, do not allow movement of a prepositional phrase. *Donate* is such a verb: *donated his stamp collection to his sister* → **donated his sister his stamp collection*.

The study of syntax involves uncovering those properties of language which are involved in the construction of grammatical sentences in particular languages. Properties like **agreement** (must all verbs agree with their subjects? do any verbs agree with their objects? do any other categories agree?), **selection** (what kinds of complements do verbs select? do other categories have selectional properties?), **adjacency** (what kinds of categories must be adjacent? do adjacency requirements differ in the world's languages?), and **movement** (what kinds of category can move? where do they move from and where do they move to?). Other properties will be encountered as we proceed.

1.3   What is a grammar?

Section 1.3 defines the terms 'grammar', 'generative grammar' and 'mental grammar'.

A **grammar,** in the sense that the term will be used here, is a set of instructions for generating all the grammatical sentences of a particular language. These instructions specify how sentences are pronounced, what their syntax is, and what meaning is to be given to them. The instructions must be sufficiently general to assign the correct specifications to every sentence a speaker has ever heard or read, or may ever hear or read (including novel sentences), yet sufficiently restrictive to exclude all ungrammatical sentences. The reason for this is that native speakers of a particular language know intuitively which strings of words are grammatical and which are ungrammatical in their language. If a grammar is to be a model of human linguistic ability, it must be able to distinguish grammatical from ungrammatical sentences. To take an example, speakers of the variety known as 'standard British English' know that sentences like *My hair needs washing* are grammatical, but would exclude sentences like **My hair needs washed.* By contrast, speakers of one variety of Scots English would allow sentences like *My hair needs washed* and exclude sentences like **My hair needs washing.* The grammars of these varieties must be able to make distinctions like this.

A grammar which is able to generate all and only the grammatical sentences of a language is known as a **generative grammar.** A person who knows a particular language in a subconscious and automatic way, as native speakers do, has internalized a generative grammar for that language; we refer to this as a **mental grammar.** In this book we will concentrate on the syntactic part of mental grammars. Language learners, and in our case second language learners, must construct a mental grammar for the language that they are learning. Part of this task is establishing the correct specifications for properties like agreement, selection, adjacency and movement for the language in question.

1.4   Evidence that the mechanisms which underlie grammar-building are innate

Section 1.4 explains why it is unlikely that language acquisition is determined solely by the sentences one hears (or reads), and why many linguists believe that the principles and parameters of Universal Grammar are biologically determined.

One might wonder if the construction of a mental grammar is not just a question of learning by heart the grammatical sentences one is exposed to, and then creating new sentences by a kind of analogy: substituting different words for those in sentences one has already encountered. Ungrammatical sentences would simply be those one has not encountered. It seems, however, that this 'input-determined' view is an unlikely account of language acquisition for several reasons. One is that native speakers know more about the syntactic properties of their language than is available in the sentences they are exposed to. Input is said to **under-determine** the mental grammar. For example, native speakers of English know that the subjects of embedded (subordinate) clauses can be turned into grammatical *wh*-phrases as in (3):

> 3a She later discovered **who** had written the note
> b **Who** did she later discover had written the note?

They also know that objects in embedded clauses can be turned into grammatical *wh*-phrases, as in (4):

> 4a She later discovered **what** her friend had written
> b **What** did she later discover her friend had written?

Finally, they know that when both the subject and the object are *wh*-phrases, (5a–b) are ungrammatical, and only (5c) is possible:

> 5a *What did she later discover who had written?
> b *Who did she later discover what had written?
> c Who did she later discover had written what?

In acquiring English they will have come across sentences like (3) and (4). Such sentences will tell them that *wh*-phrases can appear at the beginning of main clauses and embedded clauses. But how do they come to know that when two *wh*-phrases are present only a sentence of the type in (5c) is possible? It seems that this is a case where speakers of English know more about the syntactic structure of English than they have evidence for in the sentences they hear when they are acquiring the language; syntactic knowledge is underdetermined by the input.

Another example is provided by the pair of sentences (1d)–(2d) which were used to illustrate the distinction between grammatical and ungrammatical sentences in section 1.2. There is nothing obvious about the sentences in which *give* and *donate* appear that would tell a language learner that verbs like *give* allow double objects, while verbs like *donate* do not. There is no tag attached to *give* saying 'allows double objects' and another attached to *donate* saying 'does not allow double objects'. Learners will come across sentences like *He gave his stamp collection to Oxfam, He gave Oxfam his stamp collection*, and they will come across sentences like *He donated his stamp collection to Oxfam*. They will not come across ungrammatical sentences like **He donated Oxfam his stamp collection*.

But when they are learning verbs like *give* and *donate* what is to stop them from assuming that *donate*, which is very close in meaning to *give*, behaves in all respects like *give*?

The factors which a learner has to establish would seem to be these.[2] Firstly, verbs which belong to the 'double object' class must be (a) monosyllabic, like *give, send, serve*; or (b) if they are polysyllabic, they must either have stress on the first vowel, e.g. *'offer, 'promise*, or on the second vowel, if the first vowel is [ə]: *a'ward, a'llow*. Secondly, for verbs to be members of the 'double object' class they must have as part of their meaning that one of the objects becomes the 'possessor' of the other as a result of the action. For example, in *They awarded James the prize*, 'James' becomes the possessor of 'the prize'. These restrictions rule out double object constructions in cases like the following: *She explained me the problem* (versus *She explained the problem to me*): *explain* is polysyllabic, the stress falls on the second syllable and not the first (*ex'plain*), but the first vowel is not [ə]; *Mary drove Bristol her mother* (versus *Mary drove her mother to Bristol*): *drive* is monosyllabic, but the verb does not imply that *Bristol* becomes the possessor of *her mother*.

Underdetermination by the input of the grammatical knowledge that native speakers develop is one piece of evidence which has led many linguists to believe that the mechanisms which underlie grammar-building – the principles and para-meters of Universal Grammar – are biologically determined. Human beings have them as part of their genetic endowment. A range of further evidence is provided by first language acquisition. First language acquisition has a number of well-known characteristics which are consistent with the view that the mechanisms which underlie grammar-building are innate (see, e.g., Goodluck 1991; Atkinson 1992; Crain and Lillo-Martin 1999):

- All infants with normal abilities have equal potential for acquiring a native language. That is, take any infant, put that infant in any speech community, and given normal exposure the child will acquire the language of the commun-ity as a native language. Such *uniformity* of success is quite surprising given the vagaries in the quality of input children around the world are likely to get, and is compatible with the view that they have stable innate mechanisms for grammar-building.

- Acquisition is *rapid*. Children typically acquire all the major structures of their language by the age of three to three-and-a-half, and by the age of five their understanding of complex and subtle structural distinctions is effectively adult-like. (Obviously at this age their topics of conversation are limited by experience.) Such rapidity would be surprising if children had to build mental grammars on the basis of input alone. It is less surprising if the mechanisms which underlie grammar-building are innate.

- Acquisition is *effortless*. Children do not have to engage in any special learning to acquire language; interaction with native speakers and exposure to samples of language is enough to ensure acquisition. If the mechanisms which underlie grammar-building are genetically determined, the acquisition of syntax should be no more effortful than learning to walk.

- *Correction* (and other kinds of information about ungrammatical sentences in a language) *does not seem to play a significant role* in the development of syntactic knowledge (Brown and Hanlon 1970; Morgan and Travis 1989). Again, if the mechanisms which underlie grammar-building are genetically determined, corrective feedback would largely be irrelevant to acquisition, just as advice about how to walk is irrelevant to the development of walking.

1.5   Investigating the nature of mental grammars independently of other types of knowledge

Section 1.5 explains why the view is taken in this book that properties of the mental grammar can be investigated independently of other mental knowledge. It is argued that syntax is not necessarily designed for making communication easier, and it is shown that mental grammars can be impaired while other mental processes remain intact, and vice versa.

The view taken here will be that the properties of mental grammars can be investigated independently of other kinds of knowledge which might be involved in the full use of a language (e.g., the knowledge involved in drawing inferences, indicating one's intentions, determining the appropriateness of certain kinds of language to context, and a range of other things). There are two reasons for making this assumption. The first is that there is evidence that mental grammars are distinct from other kinds of mental knowledge. Syntactic structure, for example, is not apparently directly reducible to other properties of human psychology. One might imagine that syntax evolved in order to make the task of communicating meanings easier. But this is far from evident. Presumably, when a speaker wants to convey a meaning to a hearer, the important thing is that he or she should do so effectively (so that the hearer understands the intended meaning), concisely (so that the hearer's attention is not lost) and with the minimum of effort (without using more words than are necessary to convey the intention).

Many syntactic properties seem to be quite independent of notions like 'effectiveness', 'concision' and 'economy of effort'. For example, consider adverb placement as illustrated in (6). English requires fairly strict adjacency between verbs and their objects, so that an adverb like *rarely* cannot come between them. To explain this restriction one might initially suggest some principle connected with communication which says that 'the verb–object unit is an important one for conveying the meaning of a sentence effectively, so do not split it with extraneous information'. But if we then look at French, it is normal in French for adverbs like *rarement* (the equivalent of *rarely*) to split verb–object units in that language. Indeed there are systematic differences in the placement of adverbs in English and French, as we can see in (6):

6a   George speaks Finnish rarely
 b   Georges parle le finnois rarement
 c   *George speaks rarely Finnish
 d   Georges parle rarement le finnois
 e   George rarely speaks Finnish
 f   *Georges rarement parle le finnois

Both English and French allow manner adverbs like *rarely/rarement* to appear in clause-final position. But whereas English allows them to appear clause-internally only between the subject and the verb, French allows them to appear clause-internally only between the verb and its complement. Properties like this have to be acquired by the learner of English or French in order to produce grammatical sentences in the language in question, but it is not clear that such properties have anything to do with 'making communication easier', or 'reducing the effort involved in producing sentences', or any such notion.

Similarly, syntactic structure is not directly parasitic on other types of thinking. This becomes clear when the effects of damage to the brain are considered. Some kinds of disorder affecting brain development can result in a person having severely impaired non-linguistic thinking, without apparently affecting their ability to acquire knowledge of complex syntactic structure. For example, Cromer (1991) describes a number of cases of people with spina bifida (a disorder of the spine which increases pressure in the fluid of the brain) who are severely retarded in terms of non-verbal thinking, but who have become 'hyperverbal', suffering from what has been described as 'chatterbox syndrome' (excessive talkativeness). The syntax of the utterances of such people is complex and typically well formed, as the following extract from a conversation between Cromer and the child D.H. illustrates (Cromer 1991: 133):

D.H.:   Like I fell . . . I'm a guide you see and we went to . . . like go to this river to do canoeing and I fell in the river once.
Cromer: Ah.
D.H.:   That wasn't funny; that was frightening. I said I'd never go . . . I said I'd never go canoeing again, and I still go canoeing now. And that's three years later that was. But my Dad's got a canoe and we go canoeing. I threw my Dad in once. Me and my brother threw him in together.

Curtiss (1988) describes several cases of people with severely impaired non-linguistic abilities who appear to have perfectly normal knowledge of syntax. The case of Rick illustrates how good knowledge of syntax can be associated with impaired knowledge of meaning. Rick is a 15-year-old boy institutionalized in a hospital for the mentally retarded in the United States. Here are two brief extracts from a conversation with a researcher:

Rick: She looks like she has blonde hair.
Res: What colour is blonde?
Rick: Black.
Res: Who gets up first in the morning?
Rick: Me.
Res: And then what?
Rick: Cindy gets up third.
Res: Third? Is there someone else getting up?
Rick: No.

Conversely, there are people with normally functioning general non-verbal intelligence who have problems with syntax. Curtiss describes the case of Chelsea, who is hearing-impaired. Chelsea was not diagnosed as such, however, until she was in her thirties and appears to have missed out altogether on learning a language during her first 30 years of life. Acquiring English late has made it very difficult for her to develop syntactic knowledge. Curtiss reports that while Chelsea's knowledge of English vocabulary progressed steadily and substantially, the syntax of her utterances is deviant. Here are some typical examples:

7a   Orange Bill car in
 b   The woman is bus the going
 c   Daddy are be were to the work

Curtiss (1988: 372) concludes that Chelsea's expressive language 'appears, at its best, to be limited to the production of combinations of semantically relevant substantives'; that is, the syntax of her utterances is severely impaired.

The fact that knowledge of the syntactic properties of language can remain intact while other aspects of our mental activity are impaired, and that non-linguistic mental abilities can be normal while our knowledge of syntax is impaired, suggests a **dissociation** between the two kinds of ability. This in turn supports an approach to studying the properties of mental grammars in their own right, as independent objects of enquiry.

The second reason we adopt such an approach is a practical one. Linguistic behaviour in real use is complex precisely because it involves the interaction of knowledge of various kinds. It is simpler, in practice, to restrict attention to these sources of knowledge independently, with the expectation that at some future point, once the properties of each are better understood, connections between them can be established.

1.6   Studying second language syntax

In section 1.6 we make a start on investigating how L2 learners construct mental grammars by first discussing an empirical observation: English speakers learning French appear to have more difficulty in acquiring the correct location for French object pronouns than French speakers do in acquiring the location of English object pronouns. Next the notions 'principle' and 'parameter' are illustrated in relation to the structure of phrases in human languages. Finally, it is proposed that a principles-and-parameters account of phrase structure can help to explain the L2 developmental facts.

If the mechanisms which underlie grammar-building in first language acquisition are innate, and give rise to observable similarities in the way that all children acquire their first languages, a reasonable research strategy for investigating second language acquisition is to assume that the same innate mechanisms underlie second language grammar-building. By applying hypotheses about the principles and parameters of Universal Grammar to observable patterns of second language development, we can potentially confirm or disconfirm their involvement. There are two phases in such an application: we need to collect observations about second language syntactic development, and we need to analyse the syntactic properties they instantiate, asking whether principles and parameters might plausibly be involved. To illustrate the logic of this approach we will consider, in a preliminary way, an empirical observation about the acquisition of the placement of unstressed object pronouns in L2 French and L2 English, and how an account of the facts might be given in terms of unconscious grammar building. Bear in mind, though, that this is only a first sketch; the concepts and descriptive devices used will be refined as we proceed.

1.6.1   The acquisition of unstressed object pronouns in L2 French and English

English and French differ in the placement of unstressed direct and indirect object pronouns. In English they follow the verb, and typically appear in the positions that corresponding non-pronominal noun phrases would appear in. In French they typically appear in front of the (tense-marked) verb. The contrast is illustrated in (8)–(9):

8a   She invited *the Thompsons*
 b   She invited *them*
 c   They will speak *to the interpreter*
 d   They will speak *to him*

9a   Elle a invité *les Thompson*
 b   Elle *les* a invités
 c   Ils parleront *à l'interprète*
 d   Ils *lui* parleront

Native speakers of English learning French as an L2 usually take time, and go through stages in acquiring this preverbal placement of unstressed object pronouns (known as **clitic pronouns,** because they attach or 'cliticize' onto the verb). For example, a study by Selinker et al. (1975) of 20 English-speaking Canadian children around 7 years of age, after 2 years of exposure to French in an 'immersion programme' (where the normal school curriculum is taught through the medium of French), reported examples of postverbal object pronouns in their spontaneous speech like:

10a   *Le chien a mangé *les*
       The dog has eaten them
       (versus the grammatical: Le chien *les* a mangés)
 b   *Il veut *les* encore
       He wants them again
       (versus the grammatical: Il *les* veut encore)
 c   *Je vais manger *des* pour souper
       I am going to eat them for supper
       (versus the grammatical: Je vais *en* manger pour le souper)

Although it is unclear how many such cases there were in the corpus, and whether there were preverbal object clitics as well, other studies have also found postverbal pronouns in the early L2 French of English speakers. White (1996) examined a corpus of longitudinal production data collected by Lightbown (1977) from two English-speaking children (aged five when data-collection began) learning French with native French-speaking peers first at a nursery school and then in a kindergarten in Montreal. She found that for several months before they started to use clitic pronouns they only produced non-pronominal objects and the postverbal non-clitic pronoun *ça*, 'that'.

In a second phase of development, once learners begin to use preverbal object clitic pronouns, it appears that they do not do so consistently. Sometimes they produce utterances with preverbal object clitic pronouns, and sometimes they omit them altogether, as in:

11a   *Le chien a mangé φ
  b   *Il veut φ encore
  c   *Je vais manger φ pour souper

For example, the sample for month 9 in the corpus studied by White shows one of the subjects (Greg) producing 88 non-pronominal objects and 17 preverbal object clitic pronouns, but omitting the object in 15 cases where a native speaker would almost certainly have used a clitic pronoun. Adiv (1984), in another study of English-speaking Canadian children in a French immersion programme, but this time after three years of exposure, found that while 13% of the errors produced by her subjects on unstressed object pronouns were of the type illustrated in (10), the remaining 87% were of the type illustrated in (11). So there is a pattern of development where postverbal pronouns are present in early stages, but once preverbal object clitic pronouns begin to emerge in production they compete with omitted objects.

This pattern of development in acquiring the placement of unstressed object pronouns in L2 French has been found in L2 learners from other first language backgrounds, who begin learning French at different ages. For example, although the studies of Selinker et al. (1975), Adiv (1984) and White (1996) concerned English-speaking child learners of French, studies by Véronique (1986) and Schlyter (1986) have found similar developmental patterns in L2 French with adolescent and adult speakers of Arabic, Berber and Swedish.

In contrast to learners of French as an L2 taking time to acquire the preverbal location of object pronouns, Zobl (1980: 52) suggests that native speakers of French learning English as an L2 (and Spanish speakers learning L2 English too, according to Zobl) take almost no time at all to realize that English has postverbal object pronouns. One does not typically find errors like those in (12) in the L2 English of French and Spanish speakers, even in the earliest stages of acquisition:

12a   *She them invited
  b   *They to him will speak

There is, then, what might be called a 'cross-linguistic difference' between English speakers learning French, who go through stages in acquiring the placement of preverbal object clitic pronouns, and French (and Spanish) speakers learning English, who appear to acquire postverbal object pronouns almost immediately. This is surprising, because a priori we might have expected that the task facing speakers of one language acquiring the other as an L2 would be the same going in both directions. It provides a good illustration of the fact that one cannot explain development in an L2 simply on the basis of a difference in surface properties of the two languages involved.

Is it possible to offer some account of the empirical facts in terms of learners building subconscious mental grammars under the guidance of principles and parameters of Universal Grammar? As a prerequisite to addressing this question, in the next section a principle and two parameters of Universal Grammar involved in determining how phrase structure is represented are discussed. In section 1.6.3 we will return to the L2 facts.

1.6.2   A principle and two parameters of Universal Grammar relating to phrase structure

A view which underlies much modern work in syntax is that there is a fundamental 'sameness' about the structure of human languages, and that superficial differences between them result from a limited amount of variation permitted within this sameness. Sameness in the work of Chomsky (1981, 1986a, 1995), and other linguists who have adopted the principles and parameters approach, is the effect of principles of linguistic organization which are invariant across human languages. Principles define the structural architecture of human language. Variation between particular languages or varieties of language is accounted for by a small number of parameters of variation allowed within the overall design defined by the principles.

The idea can be illustrated in relation to the structure of phrases. Phrases appear to have the same basic structure in all languages. They consist of **head categories** like **nouns, verbs, adjectives** and **prepositions**. Head categories are the core of phrases, and may be modified, optionally, by **complements** and **specifiers**. Some examples of head–complement structures are given in (13) (N = noun, V = verb, A = adjective, P = preposition):

	Head	Complement
13a	stories (N)	[about his past]
	heard (V)	[stories]
	difficult (A)	[to understand]
	in (P)	[the kitchen]

Specifier–head structures are illustrated in (14):

	Specifier	Head
14a	[Joe's]	stories
b	[seldom]	heard
c	[quite]	difficult
d	[probably]	in

And specifier–head–complement structures are illustrated in (15):

	Specifier	Head	Complement
15a	[Joe's]	stories	[about his past]
b	[seldom]	heard	[stories]
c	[quite]	difficult	[to understand]
d	[probably]	in	[the kitchen]

Phrases like *stories*, or *stories about his past*, or *Joe's stories about his past* are called **noun phrases** (NPs); phrases like *heard*, or *heard stories*, or *seldom heard stories* are called **verb phrases** (VPs); phrases like *difficult*, or *difficult to understand*, or *quite difficult to understand* are called **adjective phrases** (APs); and phrases like *in*, or *in the kitchen*, or *probably in the kitchen* are called **prepositional phrases** (PPs). It is easy to see how such phrases combine to form sentences:

16a   We [$_{VP}$ heard [$_{NP}$ stories about his past]]
  b   It is [$_{AP}$ quite difficult to understand [$_{NP}$ Joe's stories]]
  c   [$_{NP}$ Joe's stories] are [$_{AP}$ quite difficult to understand]
  d   They are [$_{PP}$ probably in [$_{NP}$ the kitchen]]

(We will need to look more closely at which categories can function as specifiers and heads in later chapters, but the basic insight will remain the same.)

A strong hypothesis would be that the structure of every phrase in every human language is of this type only. First, it consists of a head X (a variable standing for any of the categories N, V, A, P). The head X **projects** to a phrase consisting of the head and its complement. This is represented by adding a bar to the name of the head: X′ = X-bar. So N′ (N-bar) is the phrase consisting of the N and its complement; V′ (V-bar) is the phrase consisting of V and its complement, etc. A bar-level category then projects to a **maximal projection** or XP (= phrase of type X) which consists of a bar-level phrase and its specifier. So NP (noun phrase) is the phrase consisting of N′ and its specifier; VP (verb phrase) is the phrase consisting of V′ and its specifier, etc. These structures are illustrated in (17):

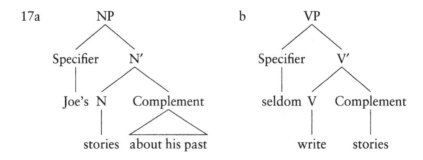

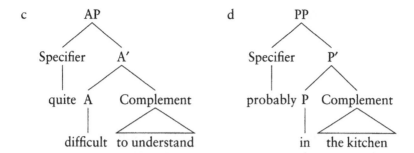

The **X'-theory** of phrase structure, as it is known, is a hypothesis about a principle of Universal Grammar: phrases in all languages are projected from head categories, and (optionally) consist of two higher levels of structure: X' and XP. If the principle can be maintained, it suggests that phrase structure in human languages is of a restricted type.

Notice, though, that in all the cases of (17) the complements **follow** the head category, and the specifiers **precede** the head category. It is the normal pattern in English for complements to follow heads, and for specifiers to precede heads. By contrast, in Japanese, Turkish and Burmese both specifiers and complements precede heads so that in these languages phrases are typically of the form:

18a   Joe's his past about stories
   b   seldom stories heard
   c   quite to understand difficult
   d   probably the kitchen in

In Malagasy, Gilbertese and Fijian both complements and specifiers follow heads (J. Hawkins 1980: 201), which produces phrases typically of the form:

19a   stories about his past Joe's
   b   heard stories seldom
   c   difficult to understand quite
   d   in the kitchen probably

In principle, any of the following orderings could be found in human languages:

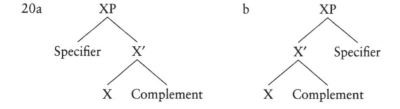

In order to account for these possibilities, associated with the principle that phrase structure projects from head categories there are two parameters of variation:

specifiers may precede or follow X′ categories
complements may precede or follow X categories

Different languages opt for different **values** or **settings** of these parameters. In English, specifiers typically precede, and complements follow. In Japanese both specifiers and complements typically precede. In Malagasy, both specifiers and complements typically follow, and so on.

1.6.3   Applying the principles and parameters framework to explaining the L2 observations

While X′-theory and the parameters determining linear order define the general form that phrases take in a language, some languages also have idiosyncratic ordering in specific cases. In French, for example, the general form of phrases is for specifiers to precede, and complements to follow heads, as the examples in (21) illustrate:

21a   [plusieurs] histoires [sur son passé]
        'several   stories   about his past'
   b   [souvent] entendre [des histoires]
        'often   hear   stories'
   c   [assez] difficile [à comprendre]
        'quite difficult to understand'
   d   [probablement] dans [la cuisine]
        'probably   in   the kitchen'

Unstressed object pronouns, though, which are complements to verbs and should follow them, appear to the left of the verbal head, as we have seen:

22a   Marie [$_{VP}$ [le] reconnaît]   'Marie recognizes it'
   b   Georges [$_{VP}$ [lui] parle]   'George is speaking to him'

One way of accounting for these exceptional cases is not to treat them as true exceptions, but to suggest that unstressed object pronouns originate in a postverbal position. To generate sentences like (22) French has a special syntactic operation which moves the object pronoun into a preverbal location, as illustrated in (23):

23

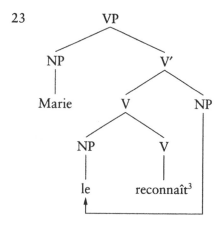

In French, then, there are two properties language learners have to acquire: the parameter values determining that complements follow heads, and that specifiers precede X' phrases, and the operation which moves unstressed object pronouns into a preverbal position.

Now suppose that the operation moving object pronouns into a preverbal position is more difficult to acquire than the values of the ordering parameters. There is some evidence to suggest that child learners of French as an L1 take longer to acquire preverbal object clitics than postverbal non-pronominal complements, which would be consistent with such a claim (Hamann et al. 1996). If a movement operation is more difficult generally for language learners than setting the ordering parameters, this would provide an explanation for why French speakers learning L2 English appear to get postverbal unstressed object pronouns right from early stages of learning, even though their L1 has a different position for them. Postverbal unstressed object pronouns in English are in the same structural position as complements in general; their placement would follow from setting the parameter for postverbal complements. By contrast, speakers of English (and other languages) learning L2 French might initially expect object pronouns to occur in the general position for complements in French: like English, after the head. But this is the wrong location for French unstressed object pronouns, which undergo movement. To establish the nature and extent of the movement operation learners will require evidence from the samples of French they are exposed to, and this takes time.

By applying a principles-and-parameters perspective to analysing L2 performance data, we are in a position to suggest that a particular kind of development is the effect of grammar-building. Obviously the hypothesis is vague and speculative. The definitions of 'syntactic movement' and 'phrase structure' need to be sharpened, and there is a need for further testing, for example by looking at learner behaviour on other types of idiosyncratic phrase structure in other languages, and by looking at how speakers of languages with preverbal clitics (like Spanish and Italian) fare in learning French. But nevertheless it is beginning to move us in the right direction: not only towards collecting empirical observations about second language syntactic development, but also towards trying to explain them as the effect of learners building subconscious mental grammars.

1.7   Acquiring or learning syntax? Second language acquisition in naturalistic and classroom environments

Section 1.7 draws a distinction between 'input' and 'learner development'. It is suggested that learner development is logically independent from input. This opens the way for arguing that type of input has little effect on the course of learner development. However, two qualifications are made: enhanced input can affect the speed of acquisition, and it can affect performance on academic tasks like grammar tests and translation.

It is often assumed that learning second languages in the classroom is different from learning second languages as a result of being exposed to them in naturalistic environments. Some claim that classroom learning is 'better' (see, e.g., Hammerly 1991), others that naturalistic learning is 'better' (see, e.g., Krashen and Terrell 1983). Since we shall be referring to studies of L2 learners both in and out of classrooms, it is important for us to know whether there are differences, and if there are, what kinds of differences there might be.

Firstly, we must be clear about what is being considered when it is said that classroom learning is 'different' from naturalistic learning. A distinction must be drawn between the kind of samples of second language data presented to the learner, or the **input**, and the way that L2 learners respond to that input, or **learner development**. While it may be the case that input is different between classroom and naturalistic environments, it is not necessarily the case that learner development is different in the two settings. Secondly, of course, the notion of 'classroom learning' is not itself a homogeneous one. Some classrooms may be very formal, in the sense that emphasis is placed on the conscious learning of grammatical properties of the L2 via instruction, with reinforcing drills, exercises, translations, and so on. Others may be more communicative, where emphasis is placed on using the L2 naturalistically to communicate speaker intentions, rather than on considering the properties of the language itself. While classroom input to second language learners can be quite different from naturalistic input, and while the kinds of classroom input available can also vary from one classroom to another, the general trend found in studies investigating the effects of input differences is that they have very little impact on the **course** of learner development (with two qualifications which are made below). We shall illustrate by describing two representative studies.

Consider the acquisition of German word order, a phenomenon which has been extensively studied. In main clauses in German, the tense-marked verb, whether it be a 'content' verb or an auxiliary verb, must appear in second position in the clause (known as **verb second**, or **V2**), and any participle, infinitive or verbal particle must appear in sentence-final position. For example:

24a   Johann **kaufte** ein Buch
      Johann bought a book
  b   Heute **kaufte** Johann ein Buch
      Today bought Johann a book
  c   Ein Buch **kaufte** Johann heute
      A book bought Johann today
  d   Johann **hat** ein Buch **gekauft**
      Johann has a book bought
  e   Johann **muss** ein Buch **kaufen**
      Johann must a book buy
  f   Johann **nahm** ein Buch **auf**
      Johann picked a book up

In subordinate clauses, all parts of the verb must appear in clause-final position:

25a   Er glaubt, dass Johann ein Buch **kaufte**
      He thinks that Johann a book bought
  b   Er glaubt, dass Johann ein Buch **gekauft hat**
      He thinks that Johann a book bought has
  c   Er glaubt, dass Johann ein Buch **kaufen muss**
      He thinks that Johann a book buy must

It has been found that the properties involved in these word-order patterns are acquired in the following stages by second language learners whose native languages are Italian, Spanish, Portuguese and English:

Stage I: word order like English, where the parts of the verb are kept together in the middle of a sentence (*Johann hat gekauft ein Buch*)
Stage II: learners separate tense-marked auxiliaries from participles, infinitives and particles in main clauses (examples (24d–f))

Stage III: learners place the tense-marked verb in second position in main clauses (V2) (examples (24b–c))
Stage IV: learners place all parts of the verb at the end of subordinate clauses

Clahsen and Muysken (1986) studied the development of German word order in a group of adult Spanish, Italian and Portuguese speakers, among others, all immigrant workers to Germany, or their children, and all acquiring German predominantly by naturalistic exposure. They found the pattern of development by stages illustrated above. Pienemann (1989) studied a group of ten Italian-speaking elementary school children learning German as a second language both in the classroom and through naturalistic exposure. He found the same pattern of staged development illustrated above. Ellis (1989) studied 39 English-speaking adult students (mean age 20.95 years) who enrolled on an *ab initio* German course in the UK. The kind of instruction they received involved both the teaching of grammar and the communicative use of German. The word order properties of German were introduced to the students in the order: verb second > verb separation > verb final in subordinate clauses. Despite this order of teaching, Ellis found that on a picture description task administered at the end of the first and second terms of teaching, the accuracy order displayed by the subjects was the same as the pattern found in the Clahsen and Muysken and Pienemann studies. The course of learner development in these cases is parallel, although the types of input the learners received was different, going from predominantly naturalistic to predominantly tutored.

As a second example, consider a study by T. Pica (1985) in which she tested the accuracy of a group of 18 L1 Spanish-speaking adults (18–50 years old, learning L2 English) on a number of grammatical items in English:

26a progressive *-ing*:   is eat-*ing*
  b plural *-s*:   apple-*s*
  c forms of copula *be*:   *am* happy, *are* happy, *is* happy
  d forms of auxiliary *be*: *am* eating, *are* eating, *is* eating
  e article: *the/an* apple
  f irregular past: buy – *bought*
  g regular past: talk-*ed*
  h 3rd person singular *-s*: she sing-*s*
  i possessive *'s*:   Paul*'s* beret

Subjects were selected for the study on the basis of whether they were learning L2 English (a) only in the classroom; (b) naturalistically; (c) in a mixed setting where they were both learning English in the classroom and being exposed to it naturalistically outside the classroom. There were six subjects in each group, and data were collected via an individual interview with each subject. Pica found that when accuracy scores on the phenomena in (26) were averaged for each group of subjects, and then ranked in descending order of accuracy, the rankings were highly similar across the three groups, corresponding broadly to the order in (26), where (26a) is the most accurately used grammatical item, and (26i) the least accurately used grammatical item.[4]

From studies like those of the development of German word order and accuracy on English grammatical items, it can be seen that differences in the type of input that learners receive in the classroom and in naturalistic settings does not appear to have any great influence on the course taken by their developing L2 syntactic knowledge. This has led some L2 researchers to assume that 'in principle there ought to be no difference in the learning mechanisms that one assumes for foreign language learning [i.e. classroom exposure] and second language acquisition [i.e. naturalistic exposure] . . .' (White et al. 1992: 351–35). At the same time, this statement needs to be qualified in at least two ways.

Firstly, a number of studies have suggested that learners exposed to formal instruction about the syntactic properties of an L2 develop unconscious knowledge of those properties more quickly than learners exposed to samples of the L2 in naturalistic settings. Although the **route** of development is unaltered by instruction, the **rate** of development may be speeded up (Ellis 1985). Long (1983), in a review of 11 studies comparing naturalistic, classroom or mixed exposure to L2s, notes that 6 of them found faster development in learners who had received instruction than in learners who had not. Ellis (1990: 133), reviewing Long's review and incorporating a number of subsequent studies, concludes that 'it seems reasonable to assume that formal instruction is of value in promoting rapid and higher levels of acquisition', without such instruction altering the course of development.

The second qualification that should be made is that similarity in the course of L2 syntactic development between classroom and naturalistic learners is reflected typically only in situations of language use in which the two groups are directly comparable: usually spontaneous comprehension or production during meaningful communicative interaction with other speakers. Where language use is more 'classroom-like', perhaps involving skills which have to be specially learned, for example in grammar tests, in gap-filling tests and in translation tests, the performance of classroom learners may be quite different from that of naturalistic learners, and may vary even across individual classroom learners. To take an example, Larsen-Freeman (1975) tested 24 adult learners of L2 English on their accuracy on grammatical items like those illustrated in (26), across five tests: picture description, sentence repetition, listening comprehension, reading plus gap-filling, and writing plus gap-filling. Although on the first three tasks the ranked accuracy order of her subjects is very like the order found by T. Pica (1985), on the last two tasks there are different rank orders, for example where 3rd person singular -s is considerably more accurate. In reading and writing tasks classroom learners are apparently able to deploy acquired skills which enable them to increase accuracy in a way which is not intrinsic to their unconscious L2 mental grammars.

1.8   Second language syntactic development is similar in child and adult learners

Section 1.8 describes several studies which suggest that the course of syntactic development is essentially the same in child and adult second language learners, but that there may be differences in the rate of acquisition and in the eventual level of success.

Another issue that we need to be clear about is the effect that starting to acquire a second language in childhood and starting to acquire a second language in later life has on syntactic development. From the available evidence it seems again that the **course** of syntactic development is essentially the same, no matter what age one begins acquiring a second language. For example, take some of the studies we have already considered. In the acquisition of German word order, the stages of development were the same in learners who started in adulthood (the studies of Clahsen and Muysken 1986; and Ellis 1989) and in childhood (Pienemann 1989). In the case of the acquisition of unstressed object clitic pronouns in L2 French, similar stages of development have been found in learners seven to eight years old (Selinker et al. 1975), adolescents (Adiv 1984), and adults (Véronique 1986; Schlyter 1986). In studies of the acquisition of grammatical items like those illustrated in (26), similar patterns of accuracy have been found in children (Dulay and Burt 1973, 1974) and adults (T. Pica 1985 – see chapter 2).

On the other hand, there appear to be two areas where young child learners of second languages are importantly different from adolescent and adult learners. Firstly, in initial stages of acquisition they appear to develop more slowly than adolescents and adults (Snow and Hoefnagel-Höhle 1978). Secondly, in the long run child L2 learners are normally ultimately more successful than older L2 learners; their mental grammars do not 'fossilize' (stop short of becoming native-like) in the way that older L2 learners' mental grammars tend to (Patkowski 1980; Johnson and Newport 1989; Long 1993). These factors are, however, independent of the course of development.

1.9   The nature of the data available to second language researchers

Section 1.9 briefly describes typical elicitation techniques used by second language researchers to obtain data from L2 learners.

Many linguists distinguish between **mental knowledge** of a language and the **real-time use** of that knowledge to understand and produce utterances. All sorts of factors can cause disruption of the understanding or production of utterances which are quite independent of knowledge of a language. For example, one may fail to understand an utterance because it is not heard properly (if there is a lot of background noise, say). Similarly, in producing an utterance a speaker may be distracted by the phone ringing, or by a random thought, with this leading to faulty output. Clearly such temporary interference is not related to the underlying knowledge that a speaker may have about a language, and this has led to a distinction being drawn by some between **competence** and **performance** (Chomsky 1965). Competence is the 'all-time' steady-state knowledge which is the speaker's mental grammar. Performance is the 'real-time' use of that grammar in the comprehension or production of utterances.

Given such a distinction, any observations that are made about how L2 learners construct L2 mental grammars are necessarily made through the evidence provided by their performance. Their mental grammars cannot be inspected directly. Researchers must infer properties of L2 mental grammars from what they observe learners doing in performance. In undertaking this task, researchers have used a range of techniques to tap learners' production of the L2, comprehension of the L2, judgements about L2 sentences, and even the speed at which they parse (i.e. decode sentences) in the L2.

The simplest type of production-based elicitation technique is the observation of unguided spontaneous production. The utterances of an L2 speaker or group of speakers are recorded as they use the L2 in everyday tasks. In guided production the L2 speaker is asked to perform a specific task; for example, is interviewed, or asked to describe a picture, or to retell a story. The aim might be to collect a general sample of language, or it might be to collect samples bearing on specific phenomena (say, accuracy in the use of articles, or the use of the past tense forms of verbs). Other types of guided elicitation task that have been used require speakers to manipulate sentences (e.g. combine two sentences into one, or change one type of sentence into another), or imitate sentences presented to them, or again translate sentences from the L1 into the L2, or the L2 into the L1.

The problem with production data is that they allow the L2 speaker considerable freedom to avoid using grammatical knowledge which the researcher may be particularly interested in. For this reason many researchers have used what some have called **metalinguistic tasks**. These require speakers to judge the grammaticality of sentences presented to them. Such tasks can take different forms. Sentences can be presented visually (i.e. in written form) or aurally (see Murphy (1997) for an assessment of the value of each). They may consist of a list of randomized sentences, some of which are grammatical, others ungrammatical, with speakers asked to record whether they feel them to be grammatical or ungrammatical (often on a scale of grammaticality). Or they may consist of pairs or triples of sentences, with subjects being asked to indicate a preference (which is the most grammatical of these sentences?). The advantages usually cited in support of metalinguistic tasks are that they provide information about learner knowledge in a controlled way (the speaker cannot avoid grammatical properties as he or she can in production); and they eliminate much potential performance interference, because the subject does not have to produce the sentences, merely assess them. The disadvantages of grammaticality judgement tasks are that they are artificial, because they do not engage the speaker in the real use of language; the speaker may wander in attention and respond haphazardly; there may be a response bias (with speakers tending to respond 'yes' everywhere, or 'no' everywhere); and the speaker may be responding to properties of the sentence that the experimenter is not aware of.

In comprehension, typical tasks that have been used are the selection, from an array of pictures, of one that is appropriate to an aurally presented stimulus, or the manipulation of objects to 'act out' an aurally presented stimulus. As for parsing, it is only recently that L2 researchers have begun to use techniques for tapping this aspect of performance, and typically they take the form of comparing learners' reaction times in matching or responding to different types of sentences with the reaction times of native speakers (Eubank 1993; Clahsen and Hong 1995; Duffield and White 1999). For general discussion of methodological issues in collecting L2 data see Larsen-Freeman and Long (1991: chapter 2), White (1989: 57–60), Birdsong (1989), and Sorace (1996).

1.10   Summary of chapter 1

The main points made in chapter 1 are the following:

- A grammar of a language, in the sense we are using the term, is a set of instructions for generating all the grammatical sentences of that language, and excluding all the ungrammatical sentences. A person who knows a language has internalized a mental grammar for that language. The development of syntactic knowledge in second language acquisition is assumed to be the effect of learners building mental grammars (sections 1.1–1.3).
- The construction of a mental grammar involves knowledge which is not available in the input language learners receive, and this has led many linguists to assume that humans have a biologically determined Universal Grammar whose principles and parameters are directly involved in building mental grammars. Mental grammars appear to be independent of other kinds of mental knowledge (sections 1.4–1.5).
- A reasonable research strategy in studying second language syntax is to assume that Universal Grammar underlies grammar-building, just as it underlies

grammar-building in first language acquisition. To test this hypothesis we need to collect empirical observations about second language syntactic development, and analyse those observations in terms of the mechanisms made available by UG. An empirical observation concerning the acquisition of object pronouns in L2 French and L2 English was discussed, and an initial account in terms of principles-and-parameters-determined grammar building was proposed (section 1.6).

- The issues which arise in explaining L2 syntactic development are the same for all types of L2 learning, whether in the classroom or in naturalistic settings, whether learners are young or old (sections 1.7–1.9).

1.11   Exercises

There are two kinds of exercise at the end of each chapter. Those which ask the reader to use ideas discussed in the text to answer specific questions; and those of a more open-ended nature whose aim is to develop critical thinking about the investigation of second language syntax. The latter may question claims made in the text, or ask the reader to extend ideas discussed in the text, or analyse empirical data for which more than one account may be possible.

Exercise 1: Distinguishing 'ungrammaticality' from 'oddity' (sections 1.2, 1.5)

In studying the syntax of a language one needs to distinguish sentences which are **ungrammatical** because they are not generated by the grammar of that language from sentences which are **odd** for some independent reason: they don't make sense, or they do not correspond to what we know as reality. Decide which of the sentences below are ungrammatical by placing a * in front of them, and which are odd by marking them with !

Example: *Where John is going?
            !That spinster's husband is a real bore.

1.   Colorless green ideas sleep furiously (from Chomsky 1957).
2.   Furiously sleep ideas green colorless.
3.   My toothbrush is pregnant again.
4.   Like not you my idea?
5.   The car raced past the police station stalled.
6.   Her snebod wiffled prumely on the orkle.
7.   When we meet her brother will be back home.
8.   The car driven past the police station stalled.

Exercise 2: Determining the distribution of English manner adverbs (sections 1.2, 1.3, 1.5)

The aim of this exercise is to get you thinking about the kind of syntactic properties involved in determining English word order. Study the examples and, assuming the judgements of grammaticality indicated, describe the properties involved in determining the distribution of the manner adverbs (in bold). (You may find it helpful to distinguish the 'content' verbs *speak, ruin* from the auxiliary verb *have* and the modal verb *must*).

1.   She **rarely** speaks Finnish these days.
2.   ***Rarely** she speaks Finnish these days.
3.   *She speaks **rarely** Finnish these days.
4.   She speaks Finnish **rarely** these days.
5.   *She speaks Finnish these days **rarely**.
6.   She has **completely** ruined the carpet.
7.   *She **completely** has ruined the carpet.
8.   She must **completely** have ruined the carpet.
9.   She must have **completely** ruined the carpet.
10. *She must have ruined **completely** the carpet.

Exercise 3: The underdetermination of grammatical knowledge (section 1.4)

In section 1.4 it was argued that the properties of mental grammars are not determined solely by the sentences we are exposed to when we are learning a language. Below are some utterances produced by a child learner of English as a first language called Nina (taken from a database of the utterances of first language learners known as CHILDES – MacWhinney and Snow 1985). How might these data indicate that even children's early syntactic knowledge is not solely determined by the input they hear? (The figures in brackets refer to the age of the child in years and months, e.g. (2,10) = 2 years, 10 months.)

my close it (1,11)	= 'I'll close it'
I seed you (2,1)	= 'I saw you'
my ate outside (2,1)	= 'I ate outside'
no my play my puppet,	= 'I'm not playing with my puppet,
play my toys (2,0)	I'm playing with my toys'
no Leila have a turn (2,1)	= 'Leila can't have a turn'
does it doesn't move? (2,10)	= 'Doesn't it move?'
is this is a dog? (2,10)	= 'Is this a dog?'

Exercise 4: Describing syntactic differences between non-native and native utterances (section 1.6)

In this exercise the aim is to get you thinking about how the syntax of second language learners' utterances might differ from the syntax of the target language. The sentences below were produced by native speakers of French (taken from Sheen 1980). In each sentence there is at least one property which would be different if the same sentence were produced by a native speaker of English. Can you determine what these properties are?

1. She chose a career and not the married life.
2. She fall in love.
3. He knew well French.
4. She is afraid of anything.
5. I had to speak during four years English.
6. It's not as worse as it was before.
7. Being four years in England learned me a lot.
8. I didn't go [there] because it wasn't existing at that time.

Exercise 5: Determining possible L1 influence on L2 syntactic knowledge (section 1.6)

(Material used in this exercise is reprinted with the permission of Cambridge University Press)
The following are typical examples of the L2 English produced by native speakers of Spanish, Greek, Japanese, Arabic and Swahili during the course of development (taken from Swan and Smith 1987). Firstly, try to determine the particular syntactic property of English that each group is having difficulty with. Secondly, on the assumption that these cases reflect the influence of syntactic properties in the learners' L1s, can you suggest what form the property might take in the L1? For example, if a native speaker of French says *I like the classical music*, they are having difficulty with the distribution of articles in English. Where an expression is used generically (to describe a general category of things like 'classical music', 'wine', 'whales', etc.), English typically uses no article. One might guess that French, by contrast, requires an overt article with generic expressions – which is in fact correct: *la musique classique, le vin, les baleines.*

Spanish
1. Maria cans cook.
2. They will can do it next week.
3. Do you can swim?

Greek
1. She is busy to write a book.
2. I must stop to smoke. It's bad for my health.
3. Before to reach home, she ate all the sweets.

Arabic
1. This is the book which I bought it yesterday.
2. The hotel, which I stayed in it last year, was very good.

Japanese
1. We used to live in the big house in suburb of Fukuoka. A house was built of the wood.
2. Oh, that's a shrine; people say some prayers there.
3. I usually spend Sunday by a river; the people who work in office need to relax in some countryside.

Swahili
1. I go to town yesterday.
2. I did go to town yesterday.
3. Did they went to town?

Exercise 6: Collecting data from a judgement task (section 1.9)

This exercise gives you the chance to be an experimental subject in a grammaticality judgement task, and then to think about the kind of syntactic knowledge the task was aiming to elicit from L2 learners of English. Below is a fragment of a grammaticality judgement task (adapted from R. Hawkins, 1987). First do the test, then try to discover the syntactic property the investigator was interested in. (Two of the sentences are random 'distractors'; i.e. irrelevant to the main focus of the test.)

In the following task we are interested in your intuitions about whether certain English sentences are grammatical or not. Read each sentence and grade it on a scale from 1 to 5. 1 means 'is completely ungrammatical'. 5 means 'is completely grammatical'. If you feel that a sentence is completely ungrammatical, put a circle around 1, for example:

   Dog the bone the ate.   ① 2 3 4 5

If you feel that a sentence is completely grammatical, put a circle around 5, for example:

The dog ate the bone.   1 2 3 4 ⑤

If you are unsure, circle 3. If you feel that a sentence is almost, but not quite, ungrammatical circle 2, and if you feel that a sentence is almost, but not quite, grammatical circle 4. Where you circle 1, 2, 3 or 4, draw a line under the part of the sentence which is making it 'feel' ungrammatical. Do not think too hard about this. Your 'feel' for a sentence is more important than anything you may know consciously about what is and what isn't grammatical in English.

1 = ungrammatical   5 = grammatical

1. Mary was opened a door.   1 2 3 4 5
2. Karen was annoyed yesterday.   1 2 3 4 5
3. The accident was reported to   1 2 3 4 5
    the police officer.
4. John was sent a letter.   1 2 3 4 5
5. Billy was bought a lorry.   1 2 3 4 5
6. A door was opened for Mary.   1 2 3 4 5
7. Muriel was walked home.   1 2 3 4 5
8. The police officer was   1 2 3 4 5
    reported the accident.
9. A lorry was bought for Billy.   1 2 3 4 5
10. A letter was sent to John.   1 2 3 4 5

Exercise 7: Making predictions about likely results in experimental studies (sections 1.6, 1.9)

In undertaking research into second language syntax, it is often necessary to make initial predictions about what kinds of behaviour are likely to be found. This exercise asks you to make predictions about the likely behaviour of French speakers learning English as an L2. The French verb *avoir* corresponds to the English verb *have*, and the French verb *être* corresponds to the English verb *be*. However, they have different distributions in each language. Some examples of differences and similarities in distribution are illustrated below.

English	French equivalent
She is 16 years old (be).	Elle a 16 ans (avoir).
We are hungry (be).	Nous avons faim (avoir).
I am afraid (be).	J'ai peur (avoir).
He has gone out (have).	Il est sorti (être).
They have left (have).	Ils sont partis (être).
You have fallen (have).	Vous êtes tombés (être).

She is tall (be).	Elle est grande (être).
They are teachers (be).	Elles sont professeurs (être).
I have resigned (have).	J'ai démissionné (avoir).
He has disappeared (have).	Il a disparu (avoir).

On the assumption that French speakers learning English as a second language will at one stage of development transfer the distributional properties of French *avoir* and *être* onto English *have* and *be*, indicate what L1 French learners of L2 English are likely to say for the native speaker sentences listed below. (In some cases the L2 learner sentences will be identical, in others they will be different):

1. They are thirsty.
2. I am homesick.
3. She has arrived.
4. We have fallen.
5. She is short.
6. They are doctors.
7. We are surprised.
8. They have fired him.
9. Has he gone away?
10. You are afraid.

What sorts of syntactic property might be involved in determining the different distributions of *have/avoir*, *be/être* between the two languages?

Exercise 8: One possible effect of learning an L2 in a tutored environment (section 1.7)

(Material used in this exercise is reprinted with the permission of Patsy Lightbown and Oxford University Press)
In the light of the discussion of the role of input on second language syntactic development in section 1.7, what do you think the implications are of the following case reported by Lightbown (1986)?
   A frequently observed example of staged development in the acquisition of the use of 'content' verbs in L2 English is that learners initially begin with uninflected forms, later add the progressive form *-ing* as the first inflection, later still add the inflection for 3rd person singular: *-s*. For example:

Stage I
She read book.
He open window.

Stage II
She reading book.
He opening window.

Stage III
She (is) reading (the) book.
She reads (the) book.
He (is) opening (the) window.
He opens (the) window.

A study by Lightbown (1986: 267) of L1 Canadian French-speaking adolescent classroom learners of L2 English (who had little or no exposure to English outside the classroom) found, surprisingly, a pattern of development which seemed to conflict with this general trend. When her subjects were in grade 6 (aged about 12 years), and had had one or two years of instruction in English, she found that on a picture description task the proportion of verbs they used inflected with *-ing* was greater than either the proportion of verbs without any inflection, or verbs with the inflection *-s*. But a year later, on the same task, the proportion of uninflected verbs used was greater than the proportion of verbs inflected with *-ing*, which was itself greater than the proportion of verbs inflected with *-s*. That is, these learners were apparently acquiring verb-forms in the reverse order to the pattern normally observed.

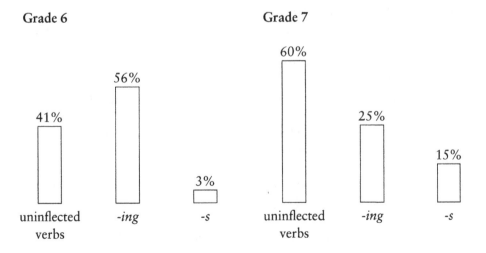

Grade 6

41% uninflected verbs
56% *-ing*
3% *-s*

Grade 7

60% uninflected verbs
25% *-ing*
15% *-s*

In examining the input that learners were exposed to, Lightbown found that in grade 5 and early in grade 6 *-ing* had been introduced, taught, 'practised, drilled, practised some more – not in contrast to anything else, just eleven straight units of lessons on the progressive [*-ing*]' (1986: 267).

1.12   Further reading

There are various readily available general introductory textbooks on syntax which deal with the principles and parameters approach. Four useful sources are the following:

Cook, V. and Newson, M. 1996: *Chomsky's Universal Grammar*. Oxford: Blackwell.
Culicover, P. 1997: *Principles and Parameters: An Introduction to Syntactic Theory*. Oxford: Oxford University Press.
Haegeman, L. 1994: *Introduction to Government and Binding Theory* (2nd edn). Oxford: Blackwell.
Roberts, I. 1997: *Comparative Syntax*. London: Arnold.

For general introductions to research on second language acquisition, the following are recommended:

Ellis, R. 1994: *The Study of Second Language Acquisition*. Oxford: Oxford University Press.
Gass, S. and Selinker, L. 1994: *Second Language Acquisition: An Introductory Course*. Hillsdale, NJ: Lawrence Erlbaum Associates.
Larsen-Freeman, D. and Long, M. 1991: *An Introduction to Second Language Acquisition Research*. London: Longman.
Mitchell, R. and Myles, F. 1998: *Second Language Learning Theories*. London: Arnold.
Ritchie, W. and Bhatia, T. (eds) 1996: *Handbook of Second Language Acquisition*. San Diego: Academic Press.
Sharwood Smith, M. 1994: *Second Language Learning: Theoretical Foundations*. London: Longman.
Towell, R. and Hawkins, R. 1994: *Approaches to Second Language Acquisition*. Clevedon: Multilingual Matters.

The following is an introduction to various approaches to second language syntax, including a chapter on the kind of generative approach adopted here:

Braidi, S. 1999: *The Acquisition of Second Language Syntax*. London: Arnold.

Two excellent texts dealing specifically with issues and theories in the study of L2 syntax from a generative perspective are as follows:

White, L. 1989: *Universal Grammar and Second Language Acquisition*. Amsterdam: John Benjamins.

White, L. forthcoming: *Universal Grammar in the Second Language: From Initial to Steady State*. Cambridge: Cambridge University Press.

The first deals with work up to the end of the 1980s, and the second with current theoretical and research issues.

Notes

1   The idea that there is both a developmental and logical problem requiring explanation in second language syntax goes back at least to Felix (1984), Schwartz (1986). See White (1989) and Gregg (1996) for discussion of this topic.
2   The various properties listed here have been uncovered over the years by a number of researchers: Green (1974), Oehrle (1976), Mazurkewich and White (1984), Pinker (1989).
3   Again, we will need to revise the structural description given to sentences like these in the light of evidence to be encountered in subsequent chapters. The structures assigned here are for preliminary illustrative purposes.
4   T. Pica (1985) is one of a large collection of studies of the acquisition of grammatical items like those in (26) which were undertaken in the 1970s and early 1980s. These are discussed in more detail in chapter 2.

2 The Second Language Acquisition of Grammatical Morphology

2.1 Introduction

In chapter 1 it was suggested that syntactic development in second language acquisition is best viewed as the consequence of learners building subconscious mental grammars, and that a reasonable research strategy is to assume that the mechanisms made available by the brain for grammar-building are those which are operative in first language acquisition: the principles and parameters of Universal Grammar. This strategy requires us to collect observations from L2 performance data about patterns of syntactic development. These will be referred to as **descriptive generalizations**. An analysis is then undertaken which tries to show how the descriptive generalizations follow from learners establishing mental representations determined by principles and parameters.

By way of illustration, a possible grammar-building explanation of the acquisition of unstressed object pronouns in L2 French and L2 English was sketched in chapter 1. This involved a principle of Universal Grammar (phrase structure is projected from head categories), two parameters determining the linear order of heads, complements and specifiers, and a proposed movement operation: the movement of clitic pronouns to a preverbal position. From this chapter on I will be more systematic both in the collection of observations about development, and in my application of the principles and parameters approach to explaining those observations.

In this chapter evidence will be reviewed for a descriptive generalization which was uncovered in early empirical L2 studies, and which concerns the acquisition of **grammatical morphemes** in L2 English. Grammatical morphemes are forms like progressive *-ing* in *Tom is eating*, plural *-s* in *hot-dogs*, possessive *'s* in *Mary's brother*, and so on. We will see that, as far as morphemes relating to the verb are concerned, there is a scale of difficulty for second language learners of English which can be represented as follows, going from easiest (bare verb phrases) to most difficult (subject–verb agreement):

> bare verb phrases → copula *be* → aspect → tense → subject–verb agreement

The syntactic properties which underlie this generalization will be discussed, and a new category Infl (inflection) will be introduced and justified. We will then assess whether the scale of difficulty can be explained as the effect of learners establishing some syntactic representations before others in their mental grammars. The chapter begins by illustrating two concepts which will be important for understanding the discussion which follows: the contrast between **lexical** and **grammatical** forms, and the unit of syntactic analysis known as the **morpheme**.

2.2 Lexical and grammatical forms in language

> Section 2.2 explains and illustrates a contrast between **lexical forms** (like *money, arrange*) and **grammatical forms** (like *I/you/she, a, n't*).

The contrast between **lexical** forms and **grammatical** forms is an important one both for understanding the nature of sentence structure, and for understanding language acquisition, as we shall see. It is most clearly illustrated in 'telegraphic language'. In the days when people sent telegrams, and these were charged by the word, it was normal to omit items which receivers could reconstruct for themselves. An impecunious student miles from home might have sent her parents a message like:

  1 NO MONEY STOP ARRANGE TRANSFER FUNDS

In normal communication, the message would more likely have been:

  2 I haven't any MONEY. Could you ARRANGE for a TRANSFER of FUNDS?

Obviously, some of the forms present during normal communication are absent from the telegram message. But the choice of which forms can be omitted is not free. While (1) gets the gist of (2) across, (3) would be unlikely to elicit much help.

3   I HAVEN'T ANY STOP COULD YOU FOR A OF

Telegraphic language shows that some forms in sentences have greater **specific conceptual content** than others. *Money, arrange, transfer* and *funds* each refer to entities or events which in some sense have a fixed, definable meaning. These are **lexical** forms. The other forms, while nevertheless meaningful, have less specific conceptual content. For example, the meaning of *I* and *you* depend on who is talking, and who is being spoken to. The determiner *a* is a form which expresses indefiniteness, but needs to modify another form with specific conceptual content to do so: *a transfer*. In other words, the meaning of forms with less specific conceptual content is relational and variable, and is determined by other elements in the sentence, or beyond the sentence. These are **grammatical** forms.

2.3   What are morphemes?

> Section 2.3 explains what a **morpheme** is, illustrates the contrast between **lexical morphemes** (like *Jim, speak*) and **grammatical morphemes** (like *is, of, -s*), and describes the difference between **free** morphemes (like *Jim, is*) and **bound** morphemes (like *-s, -ly*).

The morphology of a language is the inventory of the smallest syntactically relevant items that sentences can be broken down into. For example, although the sentence in (4a) may consist of five words, it also consists of eight syntactically relevant items, as illustrated in (4b):

4a   Jim speaks six languages fluently.
  b   Jim speak -s six language -s fluent -ly.

The *-s* attached to *speak* is an agreement and tense/aspect marker. It indicates that the verb agrees with the subject, *Jim*, and gives the sentence a 'habitual' or 'non-specific tense/aspect' interpretation. The *-s* attached to *language* is a plural marker. The *-ly* attached to *fluent* changes the syntactic status of *fluent* from adjective to adverb. (4b) cannot be broken down into any smaller items which are syntactically relevant. Any further subdivision, e.g. *J -im, s -p -ea -k -s*, etc., might be relevant to sound structure but not to the syntactic structure of the sentence. The eight items of (4b) are therefore the minimal syntactically relevant items of that sentence. The minimal syntactically relevant items of a language are known as its **morphemes**. The distinction drawn in the previous section between lexical forms and grammatical forms can now be expressed as a distinction between **lexical morphemes** and **grammatical morphemes**. In (4), *Jim, speak, six, language* and *fluent* are lexical morphemes; *-s* (agreement/tense/aspect), *-s* (plural) and *-ly* are grammatical morphemes.

Some morphemes stand alone as words in their own right. Lexical morphemes like *Jim, speak, language*, etc., typically stand alone. Others, like *-s* (agreement), *-s* (plural), and *-ly* must attach to other morphemes to be grammatical. Morphemes that can stand alone are known as **free morphemes** or **free forms**. Morphemes that must attach to other morphemes are known as **bound morphemes, bound forms** or simply **affixes**. Grammatical morphemes can be either bound or free. The *is* of *Jim is eating*, or the *of* of *the side of the ship* are free grammatical morphemes.

Within the class of bound grammatical morphemes there is a further relevant distinction. Some morphemes, like the agreement morpheme *-s*, mark a relation between items occurring in the same sentence; in this case, agreement between the subject and the verb (as well as the tense/aspect of the verb). Such bound morphemes are known as **inflectional affixes**, or simply **inflections**. Other bound morphemes are more strictly relevant to particular lexical items. For example, the bound morpheme *-ly* converts the lexical category of adjective into a different lexical category: adverb. Such lexically relevant affixes are often called **derivational affixes**, because they typically derive one type of lexical category from another. The plural marker *-s* falls between the class of inflectional and derivational affixes. On the one hand it is more relevant to the lexical class of nouns than it is to the syntax of the sentence, turning one type of noun, singular nouns, into another type, plural nouns. On the other hand, it does not change the lexical category status of nouns, as the adverb-forming *-ly* does. One might describe it as a lexically relevant inflection.

Finally, it should be noted that although we have been describing the smallest syntactically relevant items that sentences can be broken down into as 'morphemes', in fact forms like *Jim, speak, -s*, and so on, are the spoken or written realizations of morphemes. Morphemes are really abstract entities which underlie spoken or written forms. Compare the following three sentences:

5a   Jim speak -s six languages
  b   Jim yell -s when he's angry
  c   Jim preach -es on Sundays

In each of (5a–c) the *-s/-es* inflections realize the same morpheme: 3rd person singular agreement, and habitual or non-specific tense/aspect. But in written English there are two distinct forms for this morpheme (*-s* and *-es*). In spoken English there are three phonetically distinct forms: in (5a) the *-s* is a voiceless fricative [s]; in (5b) it is a voiced fricative [z]; and in (5c) it is the syllabic [iz]. These differences are the effect of the preceding phonetic context: a voiceless [k] precedes in (5a), a voiced [l] in (5b) and an affricate [tch] in (5c). The phonetic environment conditions the form that the morpheme takes. Linguists refer to the spoken or written realizations of morphemes as **allomorphs**. It is important to be

aware that a morpheme is an abstract category which underlies surface realizations, but for the purposes of exposition we shall mostly be rather loose and use
'morpheme' to refer both to the abstract category and to its surface realizations.

2.4   Early studies of the L2 acquisition of grammatical morphemes

Section 2.4 describes some early L2 studies which looked at the acquisition of
grammatical morphemes (like -ing, be, the/a), and shows that the **accuracy profiles**
of L2 learners on these phenomena are broadly the same, even where learners speak
different first languages, learn English under different conditions, and start learning
at different ages.

2.4.1   L2 learners find the same morphemes difficult

The earliest empirical studies of second language development were studies of
the acquisition of grammatical morphemes, and they produced some surprising
results. Dulay and Burt (1973, 1974) used an elicitation procedure called the
Bilingual Syntax Measure to produce samples of speech from L2 speakers. This
consists of a series of cartoons, plus a question associated with each cartoon
requiring a second language speaker to produce a response (e.g. a picture of a fat
cartoon character, and the question 'Why is he so fat?'). The subjects in the 1973
study were three groups of five- to eight-year-old Spanish speakers in the United
States. One group consisted of 30 Puerto Rican children in New York City, who
had lived in the US for a year or less (the 'East Harlem' group). They were
exposed to English in school, where the curriculum was taught both through
Spanish and English, but they had no formal instruction in English. A second
group consisted of 95 children in Sacramento, California, most of whom were
born in the US. They were taught the school curriculum through the medium of
English, and also had English as a Second Language (ESL) classes. The third
group consisted of 26 Mexican children from Tijuana, who crossed the border to
attend an English medium school in Southern California every day, but returned
home every afternoon (the 'San Ysidro' group).

Dulay and Burt analysed the data they collected using the Bilingual Syntax
Measure for eight English grammatical morphemes (see figure 2.1). To do this
they determined what they called 'obligatory occasions': points in sentences where
grammatical morphemes are required in native speaker speech. They then scored
their subjects for whether they correctly supplied a morpheme on the obligatory
occasion. For example, in *He is eating a hot-dog*, the obligatory occasions for
grammatical morphemes are *he, is, -ing* and *a: (He) (is) eat(ing) (a) hot-dog*. If an

Figure 2.1   Acquisition of eight English functors by native Spanish-speaking children (from Dulay and Burt 1973: 255)

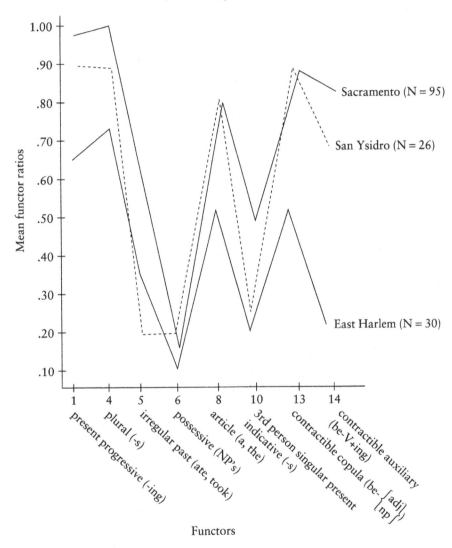

Functors

L2 speaker failed to realize all of the grammatical morphemes, then the sentence *eat hot-dog* would be the result.

By treating each obligatory occasion as a test item, and scoring their subjects 0 if they failed to supply an obligatory morpheme, 0.5 if they supplied a morpheme, but the wrong one (e.g. *He has eats a hot-dog*), and 1.0 if they supplied the correct morpheme, Dulay and Burt arrived at a score for each morpheme which was a proportion of the total possible number of obligatory occasions for that morpheme. By further adding together the scores for each subject in each group they produced a group score, and were able to compare accuracy on the eight morphemes tested across the three groups. Figure 2.1, which repesents the results in the form of a graph, is reproduced from Dulay and Burt's article (1973: 255 – 'functor' is their term for grammatical morpheme).

A striking finding was that within each group those morphemes on which subjects were most accurate, and those on which they were least accurate were consistently the same (although there were differences in the levels of accuracy between the three groups. The Sacramento group, with the longest exposure to English, tended to have the highest scores of the three groups overall). All three groups were most accurate in supplying the progressive -*ing* morpheme which attaches to verbs as in *eating*, plural -*s* as in *hot-dogs*, the contractible copula *be* as in *He's hungry*, and the articles *a/the*, as in *a hot-dog*. Subjects were least accurate on possessive *'s* (*John's book*) and 3rd person singular -*s* (*John eats hot-dogs*), with the other morphemes occupying an intermediate level of accuracy. Note that the -*ing* morpheme is treated separately from the auxiliary *be* which co-occurs with it in native English to describe an event in progress: *He is eating*. The subjects were less accurate in acquiring auxiliary *be*. This distinction will be important for our subsequent discussion.

An initial conclusion which might be drawn from this finding is that some grammatical morphemes in English are more difficult for child second language learners to acquire than others. Further, this relative difficulty is not affected by length of exposure: the Sacramento group had had greater exposure to English than the other two groups and, although globally more accurate, they showed more or less the same **accuracy profile**, as I will call it, as the other groups. Nor does relative difficulty seem to be affected by type of exposure: the Sacramento group had had exposure to English both as a medium of instruction and in ESL classes. The other two groups had had only exposure to English as a medium of instruction.

2.4.2   L1 influence on the difficulty of L2 morphemes

However, since all the subjects were L1 Spanish speakers, it is impossible to tell from the results what role the L1 might have played in determining the accuracy profile. To pursue the question further, Dulay and Burt (1974) repeated the study, but this time with two groups: 60 L1 Spanish ESL speakers who were 6–8 years old and 55 L1 Cantonese (Chinese) ESL speakers who were 6–8 years old. The elicitation and scoring methods were the same, although Dulay and Burt considered three further morphemes in their subjects' productions: the regular past tense marker -*ed* (*John cook-ed*), pronoun case (e.g. **He** *cooked* versus *I saw* **him**), and syllabic plural (e.g. *match-es* versus *book-s*). Although the Spanish

Figure 2.2 Comparison of the accuracy profiles of native Spanish- and Cantonese-speaking children on 11 English grammatical morphemes (from Dulay and Burt 1974: 49)

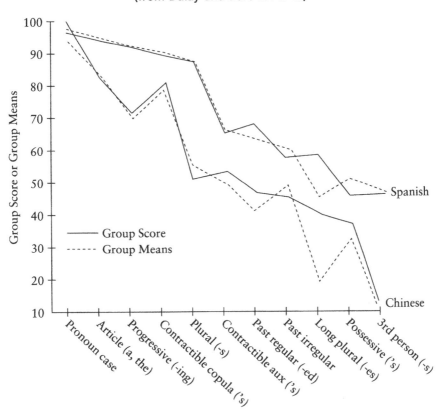

speakers achieved higher scores than the Cantonese speakers overall, the accuracy profiles for each group were very similar (see figure 2.2). The results suggest that some morphemes are comparatively more difficult than others for child L2 learners even where those learners speak typologically different L1s.

The subjects in both of Dulay and Burt's studies had been exposed to English in a context where a considerable amount of naturalistic input was available: the United States. A further question one might ask is whether the same accuracy profile occurs in L2 learners who have received predominantly formal (i.e. teacher-led and/or textbook-based) exposure to English. A study by Makino (1980) using an elicitation technique similar to the Bilingual Syntax Measure, but in a written form, examined the performance of 777 L1 Japanese adolescents distributed across 33 classrooms in Japan. Subjects were divided into two groups: those who had received two years of classroom instruction in English prior to testing

Table 2.1   Group accuracy scores (%) on nine English morphemes produced by 777 L1 Japanese adolescents in a written test

	8th graders (%)	9th graders (%)
prog -ing	84.4	88.4
article a/the	82.3	85.4
plural -s	75.8	81.0
possessive 's	67.3	68.7
copula be + adj/NP	66.6	72.8
regular past -ed	64.0	65.3
irregular past	62.3	63.9
auxiliary be (+ V-ing)	61.5	69.7
3rd person singular agreement marker -s	59.7	66.5

Source: Based on Makino 1980

(the 8th graders) and those who had received three years of classroom instruction prior to testing (the 9th graders). Makino found that while there were some differences in performance between Dulay and Burt's subjects and his, there were also strong similarities (which were statistically significant on a test known as the Spearman Rank-Order Correlation). The scores in table 2.1 are taken from Makino (1980: 124).[1]

Progressive -ing, as in *eating* (as distinct from the auxiliary *be* which accompanies progressive -ing in native English), and plural -s (*hot-dogs*) were among the most accurate morphemes in the accuracy profile of Makino's subjects, as they were in the case of Dulay and Burt's subjects. In contrast, Dulay and Burt's subjects were relatively more accurate than Makino's on copula *be*, while Makino's subjects were relatively more accurate on possessive 's (*John's book*). This might suggest some selective influence of the L1 (Japanese as opposed to Spanish) on the subjects' performance. We take this up in section 2.8, where other studies of Japanese learners of English are considered.

Interestingly, Makino evaluated the performance of his subjects against two independent factors: the order in which the morphemes were presented in the textbook series the students were using in class the year before he tested them, and whether the school they attended was in a rural or urban setting. He found a low correlation between the order in which grammatical morphemes were introduced in the textbooks and the accuracy profile of his subjects. Thus there appeared to be no primacy of input effect in producing the accuracy profile; i.e. subjects weren't necessarily most accurate on what they had been taught first. He also found that the school the subjects attended – rural versus urban – made no difference to their performance.

It seems, then, that a similar accuracy profile emerges for young children (five- to eight-year-olds) and adolescents in the domain of L2 English grammatical morphology. It is possible that this is independent of length of exposure, conditions of exposure and L1 background (with perhaps some selective influence of the L1 in a way as yet to be determined). However, we can only make these assumptions tentatively on the basis of the limited evidence we have considered so far.

2.4.3   Similarities between children and adults in the acquisition of L2 morphemes

Bailey et al. (1974) investigated whether a similar pattern would emerge in adult L2 learners. Using the Bilingual Syntax Measure, and the same scoring method as Dulay and Burt (1973), they tested 73 subjects aged from 17 to 55. Thirty-three of the subjects were L1 Spanish speakers, and 40 spoke a range of typologically different L1s. Some subjects were foreign students attending an ESL programme in preparation for study at American colleges; others were enrolled on a continuing education ESL programme. (Bailey et al. do not indicate the amount of prior exposure their subjects had to English.) The results of their study are given in figure 2.3 (taken from Bailey et al. 1974: 239).

Although there are differences in the accuracy profiles of the Spanish speakers and the non-Spanish speakers, there are also strong similarities. Progressive -*ing*, the contractible copula (*He's hungry*) and plural -*s* emerge again as relatively the most accurate, with possessive *'s* (*John's book*) and 3rd person singular -*s* (*John eats hot-dogs*) least accurate. The performance of the Spanish speakers on the articles (*a, the*) is more accurate than that of the non-Spanish speakers, while the Spanish speakers' performance on irregular past tense verb forms (*ate, took*) is relatively less accurate than that of the non-Spanish speakers.

2.4.4   Summary of section 2.4

The surprising conclusion from this cluster of early studies of grammatical morphology is that a number of factors have less influence in determining which morphemes in English are easy and which are difficult for L2 learners than one might intuitively have supposed at the outset. L2 speakers of different ages, from different L1 backgrounds, learning English under different conditions and with different kinds of input, have broadly similar accuracy profiles on tests like the Bilingual Syntax Measure (with some possible L1 influence).[2]

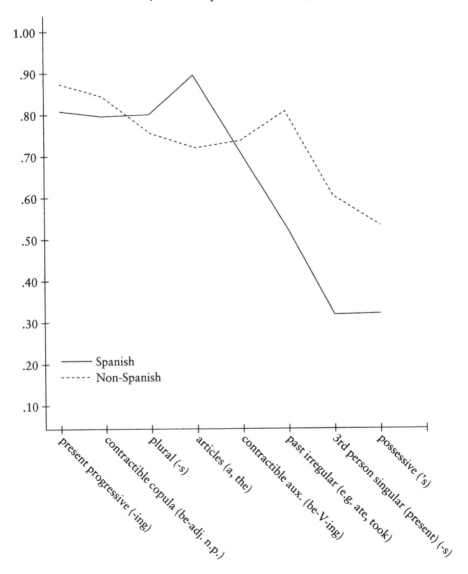

Figure 2.3 Comparison of Spanish-speaking and non-Spanish-speaking adults; relative accuracies for eight English grammatical morphemes (from Bailey et al. 1974: 239)

2.5 Linking L2 accuracy profiles on grammatical morphology to the building of a mental grammar

Section 2.5 discusses how the L2 accuracy profiles described in section 2.4 might be interpreted as evidence for L2 grammar-building, and presents a study by Andersen (1978) which suggests that the accuracy profiles of L2 learners on English grammatical morphemes reflect the acquisition of a number of specific underlying syntactic contrasts. It is suggested that this finding raises some interesting questions in need of explanation.

In section 1.9 a contrast was drawn between competence and performance (Chomsky 1965). Competence, in the context of an L2 learner, is the set of specifications which make up that learner's mental grammar at a given point of development. Performance is the use made of that set of specifications by the learner to produce and understand utterances in the spoken or written language in 'real time'. Our interest is in the properties and the development of the specifications of the syntactic component of L2 mental grammars; that is, we are interested in L2 syntactic competence. What the early morpheme studies provide us with is evidence of systematic patterns of accuracy on grammatical morphemes in performance. Therefore, we need to develop a theory of L2 competence on the basis of evidence from L2 performance. This is not, in fact, a straightforward task. There are at least three problems we need to be aware of in undertaking it.

Firstly, it is not necessarily the case that the observed accuracy profiles described in section 2.4 reflect the order of emergence of morphemes in development. Although the learners studied might be more accurate on the contractible copula (*He's hungry*) than on 3rd person -*s* (*He eats hot-dogs*), this does not necessarily mean that the syntactic property which underlies copula *be* emerges before the property which underlies 3rd person agreement in L2 development. Some researchers (for example, Grondin and White 1996; White 1996; Lardiere 1998a) argue that once a morpheme is used productively in performance, even if such productive use is confined to a small number of cases, it should be assumed that the syntactic property underlying that morpheme has emerged. In terms of the patterns we have just described, this view would imply that all the properties relating to aspect (progressive versus non-progressive), tense (present versus past), agreement (3rd person versus 1st/2nd person), definiteness (*the* versus *a*) have emerged in the mental grammars of the subjects studied because there is evidence of some productive use of the morphemes which realize them. On this view, differences in accuracy between morphemes would have to have a source other than representations in the learner's mental grammar, since all of the properties are in some sense 'present' in the mental grammar; for example, perhaps the differences in accuracy reflect a difficulty that learners have in realizing morphemes in performance. (For an early discussion of the difficulty of determining the emergence of a property in an L2 speaker's mental grammar from performance data see Meisel et al. (1981).)

Secondly, one has to be careful in interpreting the performance of groups of learners. The accuracy of a group of learners on a particular grammatical morpheme might result from different kinds of individual performance. Imagine a group of 40 subjects who, as a group, are 50% accurate in producing a target morpheme on an obligatory occasion. This could be the result of each member of the group being 50% accurate in using that morpheme, or it could be the result of 20 members of the group using the morpheme 100% accurately, and 20 members omitting the morpheme on every occasion. Each possibility might lead to radically different interpretations of the nature of the underlying mental grammars of these subjects. This suggests that while the performance of groups of L2 learners can indicate important, and sometimes surprising, tendencies in second language acquisition, it is also important to consider the performance of individual L2 learners (an issue I take up in section 2.8).

Thirdly, scoring L2 learners' suppliance of morphemes on obligatory occasions does not necessarily mean that the learner has assigned the same interpretation to the morpheme as native speakers of the target language. Suppose an L2 learner uses -ing correctly on every occasion where a native speaker would use -ing. This would produce an accuracy score of 100%. But suppose also that it turns out that this learner attaches -ing to every verb she uses, whether a progressive interpretation is appropriate or not. This could mean that the learner has a different interpretation for -ing from native speakers, or it could mean that she is simply marking the category 'verb' overtly, by using the inflection -ing. In either case, the degree to which an L2 learner is using a morpheme in a target-like way in performance will affect the kind of theory of L2 competence we construct. (This issue is also taken up in section 2.8.)

For the present we will make the assumption that the accuracy profiles in performance which were observed in the early morpheme studies do reflect the emergence of underlying syntactic properties in the mental grammars of L2 learners. That is, the higher degree of accuracy shown by subjects on progressive -ing than on, say, 3rd person singular -s does reflect a difference in the development of underlying competence where aspectual contrasts like progressive/non-progressive are represented earlier than agreement properties. Our reasons for making this assumption are not only that the patterns of accuracy are broadly consistent across groups of learners, but also, as we shall see, that such patterns of accuracy appear to correlate with longitudinal growth of accuracy in individuals. Nevertheless, we will review this assumption at various points as we proceed.

An early attempt to explain the accuracy profiles of L2 learners on grammatical morphemes as a direct reflection of the acquisition of underlying syntactic knowledge was a study by Andersen (1978). Adopting ideas already sketched in Krashen et al. (1975), and Krashen (1977), Andersen analysed data on the acquisition of English grammatical morphemes into two syntactic classes: verb-related morphemes and noun-related morphemes. As the basis for his study, he collected data from the written compositions of 89 Spanish-speaking ESL learners in their first year at the University of Puerto Rico. Subjects were 17–19 years of age, varied in proficiency level, and had had 12 years of compulsory ESL classes prior to testing. Andersen used the same 'obligatory occasion' method for collecting

Table 2.2 Implicational accuracy profile of 89 L1 Spanish speakers on verb-related and noun-related English morphemes

	Verb-related		
Copula *be*	→ Auxiliary *be* V-*ing*	→ Past Irregular Past Regular	→ 3rd person sing present
Example: John's hungry	Example: John is cook**ing**	Example: John **went** John walk**ed**	Example: John cook**s**

	Noun-related		
the		→ *a* plural -*s*	→ Poss *'s*
Example: **the** book		Example: **a** book book**s**	Example: John**'s** book

Source: Adapted from Andersen 1978

examples of morpheme use. However, his method of scoring was different. He used a technique known as **implicational scaling**. This is based on the idea that if a learner is accurate on a 'difficult' morpheme, she will also perform accurately on some 'easier' morpheme. There is an implicational relation between them: accuracy on difficult morpheme y implies accuracy on easier morpheme x. But the reverse is not necessarily the case. Another learner who is accurate on morpheme x may not be accurate on the more difficult morpheme y. Where a morpheme is difficult for second language learners in general, it should be the case that, taking any group of learners, subjects in that group who are accurate on the difficult morpheme y will always be accurate, by implication, on the easier morpheme x.

The results of Andersen's study are presented in table 2.2. (Three morphemes have been omitted which are not comparable with those in the Dulay and Burt studies: the perfective auxiliary *have* (as in *have taken*), the perfective participle V-*en* (the *taken* part of *have* **taken**), and zero article (in cases like *I go to φ school*).) The arrows indicate a statistically significant implicational relation between the morphemes. Subjects who were accurate on morphemes to the right of any arrow were highly likely to be accurate on every morpheme to the left of the arrow, on 80% or over of obligatory occasions – but not vice versa. For example, a subject who was accurate on past irregular and past regular verb forms was highly likely to be accurate on copula *be*, auxiliary *be* and V-*ing* as well. But a subject who was accurate on copula *be*, auxiliary *be* and V-*ing* was not necessarily accurate on past irregular and past regular verb forms.

The interesting result, as Andersen notes, is that by organizing subjects' performance on grammatical morphemes into verb-related and noun-related classes, it begins to appear that degree of difficulty may be a feature of the underlying syntactic properties which the morphemes realize, rather than the morphemes themselves. *Be* + V-*ing* realizes progressive aspect; for an L2 learner to use *be* + V-*ing* accurately in performance, the learner must have acquired an underlying aspectual contrast between progressive and non-progressive (*John is cooking* versus *John cooks*). Past irregular and past regular verb forms are the realization of a tense contrast; to use them accurately in performance an L2 learner must have acquired an underlying tense contrast between past and non-past (*John walked to work* versus *John walks to work*). In fact, the scale of difficulty of the verb-related morphemes can be characterized as involving the following syntactic properties (going from easiest to most difficult):

copula → aspect (±progressive) → tense (±past) → subject–verb agreement (±3rd person singular)

(We set aside the noun-related findings for the moment, returning to them in chapter 6.)

At the time Andersen was writing, observing that the accuracy profile of L2 learners on grammatical morphology appears to correlate with the acquisition of representations for specific syntactic properties was about as far as it was possible to take the account. But the results raise some interesting questions requiring explanation. Why should a copular construction (*John's hungry, She's the boss here*) become established in the mental grammar more accurately, apparently, than an aspectual one (*John is cooking*) or an aspectual construction become established before a representation for tense and agreement (*John walked; John walks*)? Why, despite the overall similarities across L2 learners from different L1 backgrounds, might there be some apparent L1-related differences on specific morphemes, as hinted by the results of the Bailey et al. (1974) and Makino (1980) studies? We would clearly like to be able to move towards answering such questions. To do so, however, we need to look in more detail at the syntactic structure of the phenomena in question.

Recent work in syntax has proposed a more articulated theory of clause structure than we have assumed up to now which offers the possibility of some interesting insights into these questions. In the next section we describe recent proposals for the structure of clauses. Following this we examine further the findings on L2 verb-related morphology in the context of these proposals.

2.6 The category Infl and phrase structure

Section 2.6 reviews arguments for proposing the syntactic category Infl, and its projection IP. The discussion in this section is by way of an introduction to the discussion in section 2.7, where the questions raised at the end of section 2.5 are reconsidered.

2.6.1 Infl

There is a generalization to be captured about the way that English marks subject–verb agreement and tense in simple sentences: it is always the first element in a sequence of verbs which carries the inflection. Compare the examples in (6)–(11) (we ignore orthographic adjustments which take place between the verb and the affix, e.g. *bake + -ed → baked, be + -s → is, have -ed → had*, etc.):

6a John **cook-s** couscous
 b His friends **bake-ϕ** a pie

7a John **cook-ed** couscous
 b His friends **bak-ed** a pie

8a John **is** cooking couscous
 b His friends **are** baking a pie

9a John **was** cooking couscous
 b His friends **were** baking a pie

10a John **has** cooked couscous
 b His friends **have** baked a pie

11a John **had** cooked couscous
 b His friends **had** baked a pie

(6a) contrasts with (6b) in that the verb carries the 3rd person singular inflection -s which agrees with the 3rd person singular subject *John*. (6b) has a null inflection -ϕ agreeing with the 3rd person plural subject *his friends*. The sentences of (6) contrast with those of (7) because the inflections carried by the verbs in (7) express past tense, while those in (6) express a non-specific tense which for the sake of exposition we will call 'present tense'. Comparing (8–9) with (6–7), we find the same contrasts of subject–verb agreement and past versus present tense, but now marked on *be*; *be* + V-*ing* is a progressive construction which expresses the fact that the event described by the verb is in progress. In (10–11) there is a perfective construction *have* + V-*ed*; the same contrasts are marked on *have*.

One way of capturing the generalization that it is always the first verbal element in a simple sentence which is inflected for agreement and tense is to propose that there is a grammatical category which is located between the subject of the sentence and the verb phrase. Chomsky (1981) called this category Infl (for 'inflection') or I for short, and this term has been widely used by linguists and L2 researchers ever since:

12 John [I(nfl) agreement/tense] $\left\{\begin{array}{l} \text{cook couscous} \\ \text{be cooking couscous} \\ \text{have cooked couscous} \end{array}\right\}$

2.6.2 Infl and phrase projection

In section 1.6.2 I described the **X'-theory** of phrase structure. X'-bar theory proposes that phrase structure is of the same basic type in all languages. A head category X optionally projects to an X' (X-bar) phrase consisting of the head and its complement, and the X' category optionally projects one further level to an XP (X phrase) consisting of X' and its specifier. I(nfl) is a head category, and so given X'-theory it too projects to I' and IP. We will assume, for now, that the complement of I is VP, and the specifier of I' is an NP subject as illustrated in (13):

13

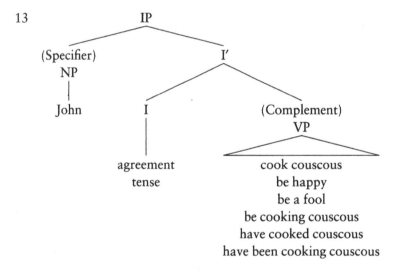

The difference between I and the other head categories discussed so far is that I can dominate bound morphemes in English, i.e. the inflectional affixes 3rd person singular -s and past tense -ed. The other categories we have looked at dominate free morphemes. Clearly some syntactic operation is needed to ensure that the bound morphemes are attached correctly to the first element in the VP. Otherwise nonsensical sentences like *John -ed cook couscous would result. One proposal which has been made in the linguistic literature (Emonds 1978; Pollock 1989; Chomsky 1995: chapter 2) is that the verbs *be* and *have* raise from the VP to I to 'pick up' the inflections. This is illustrated in (14); t (for **trace**) marks the position from which the verb has raised. We will return to discuss traces in due course:

14

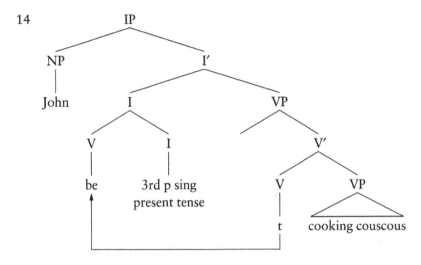

By contrast, when 'content' or **thematic** verbs (as they are usually called, and as I will call them from now on) like *cook* are the first element in VP, the inflections under I lower to VP; t (for trace) again marks the position from which the inflections have moved:

15

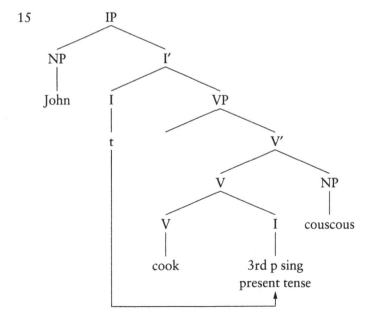

The reason for making this distinction between the raising of *be* and *have* to I, and the lowering of agreement and tense inflections to thematic verbs concerns the behaviour of these verbs with respect to other aspects of sentence structure. With the sentence negator *n't/not*, *be* and *have* occur to its left, whereas thematic verbs appear to its right, and a 'support' verb *do* has to be introduced:

16a   John isn't cooking
  b   John hasn't cooked
  c   *John cooks **not**
  d   John doesn't cook

This can be explained if, in the structure of the clause, the negator is located between I and VP, and *be* and *have* are raised to I, but *cook* isn't (see chapter 3 for discussion of how this works). Instead, when the negator and thematic verbs co-occur, the support verb *do* is inserted under I to 'carry' the inflections.

A related phenomenon is question formation. Question formation in English seems to be the result of moving the I category to the front of the sentence (in a way that will be explained in chapter 4). Where *be* and *have* have raised to I, they are carried along with I to the front of the sentence in questions. However, with thematic verbs again the support verb *do* appears:

17a   Is John cooking?
  b   Has John cooked?
  c   *Cooks John?
  d   Does John cook?

This is explicable if *be* and *have* raise to I, but thematic verbs do not. Inflections under I cannot both lower to V and move to the front of the sentence as well. The support verb *do* is inserted under I to carry the inflections, and moves to the front of the sentence with them.

Thirdly, when manner and frequency adverbs like *quickly* and *often* modify the verb phrase, *be* and *have* appear naturally to the left of them, but thematic verbs appear naturally to their right:

18a   John is **quickly** cooking some extra food for the unexpected
     guests
  b   John has **often** cooked for the whole family
  c   *John cooks **often** couscous
  d   John **often** cooks couscous

This is explicable if manner and frequency adverbs occupy a position between I and VP, say, the specifier of VP:

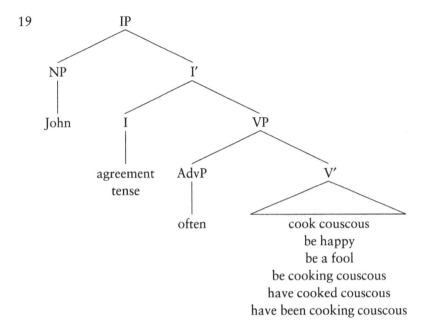

19

Be and *have* raise to I, so that they will appear to the left of the adverb in the surface sentence; the agreement and tense inflections of I lower to thematic verbs, so that thematic verbs will appear to the right of the adverb in the surface sentence. The details of verb movement are discussed more fully in chapter 3.[3]

2.6.3   Summary of section 2.6

In section 2.6 I outlined the rationale for the syntactic category I (Inflection). I is one of the syntactic categories that Universal Grammar makes available to language learners for grammar-building, along with categories like N, V, A, P. The principle of phrase projection (X'-theory) allows I to project, optionally, to I' and IP. When it projects to I' it selects VP as its complement; when I' projects to IP, the specifier is the subject of the clause. Unlike N, V, A and P, the category I in English can dominate bound morphemes like 3rd person singular -*s* and past tense -*ed*. Because bound morphemes must attach to other morphemes to be grammatical, the grammar is forced to incorporate a syntactic operation of movement: when *have* and *be* are selected in the VP they move up to I to pick up its bound morphemes; when thematic verbs alone are selected the bound morphemes of I move down to the VP, unless the clause is negated or turned into a question, when the 'support' verb *do* is inserted. We will see in chapter 3 that these movement operations appear to vary across languages, suggesting that movement is a parameter of variation allowed by Universal Grammar.

2.7   The role of VP and IP in the L2 acquisition of English verbal morphology: a first sketch

Section 2.7 is a first attempt to develop a grammar-building explanation for the relative accuracy of certain verb-related morphemes in the performance of L2 learners. A proposal that the operation moving free morphemes from V to I is easier for L2 learners than an operation moving bound morphemes from I to V is considered.

Having justified the presence of an I(nflection) category in the structure of clauses, we are now in a position to return to the questions raised at the end of section 2.5. They were: why should a copular construction, like *John's hungry*, become established in the mental grammar more quickly than an aspectual construction like *John is cooking*, which itself is apparently established before a representation for tense and agreement like *John walked, John walks*? Zobl and Liceras (1994) sketch the beginnings of an answer to these questions. Looking at the syntactic operations involved in generating the constructions in question, they observe that those on which learners are most accurate involve the movement of free morphemes from the VP to I, and those which are most difficult involve the movement of bound morphemes from I to VP. They then propose a simple grammar-building account: 'movement of lexical heads [i.e. *be*] is implemented early and independently of affix-movement' (Zobl and Liceras 1994: 175).

Recall that we are viewing syntactic development in second language acquisition as the consequence of learners building subconscious mental grammars on the basis of the principles and parameters made available by Universal Grammar. Zobl and Liceras's proposal is beginning to move us in that direction. However, the proposal is too coarse-grained to account for the full range of facts uncovered by Andersen. It fails to distinguish between copula *be* and the auxiliary *be* of *be* + V-*ing*, both of which are free forms and move from VP to I. But Andersen found that learners are more accurate on copula *be* than they are on auxiliary *be*. It also fails to distinguish between regular past tense and subject–verb agreement, both of which are bound forms which move from I to V, yet Andersen found that his L2 subjects were more accurate on tense than on agreement. We need a more fine-grained account of grammar-building to explain these observations. In order to develop that account, and bearing in mind the potential problems that group accuracy scores pose for interpretation (see the discussion in section 2.5) it is helpful to have data concerning the accuracy profiles of individual L2 learners, and to compare the profiles of individual learners with different L1 backgrounds. In the next section we review the findings of a study by Stauble (1984) who provides a detailed analysis of the frequency of accurate and inaccurate verbal morphology in the spontaneous productions of 12 L2 learners of English. Her study offers considerable insight into the empirical details, and has the bonus that six of the subjects are native speakers of Spanish and six are native speakers of Japanese, so that potential L1 influence can be considered.

2.8 Comparing the accuracy profiles of individual Spanish and Japanese learners of English

Section 2.8 describes a study which compares the target-like use of English verb morphology by Spanish and Japanese speakers at different proficiency levels. Strong similarities are found between the two groups, but performance in two areas suggests the influence of the L1.

Stauble (1984) is a quasi-longitudinal study which compares the accuracy profiles of six Spanish- and six Japanese-speaking individuals on verb-related morphemes in L2 English.[4] All of the subjects had lived for a considerable time in the United States, and were chosen so that within each group three different stages of L2 development were represented: low intermediate (two Spanish speakers and two Japanese speakers), intermediate (two Spanish speakers and two Japanese speakers) and advanced (two Spanish speakers and two Japanese speakers).[5] Making the assumption that the subjects are to some extent representative of Spanish and Japanese speakers more generally, this effectively enables us to compare the degree of difficulty that particular morphemes pose for these groups of learners over time.

All the subjects had lived in the United States for at least 10 years (the range was 10–63 years of residence in the United States). The Spanish speakers were between the ages of 19 and 30 when they first arrived, and the Japanese speakers were between the ages of 13 and 36. The subjects had either not studied English or had studied English for only a short time before arrival, and the amount of formal instruction they had received after arrival ranged from one month to one year. Exposure to English was therefore primarily naturalistic.

Because the subjects' backgrounds and experience of English were not homogeneous, Stauble determined the three proficiency levels on the basis of an independent linguistic measure: the stage of development reached by a subject in the acquisition of English negation. The particular defining characteristics she used are illustrated in table 2.3:

Table 2.3 Criteria for determining three levels of proficiency in L2 English

Stage	Criteria	Example
low intermediate	*no/not* + verb	She no saw him
		Not need shoes
	no/not + phrase	No too hard
intermediate	unanalysed *don't*	I don't saw him
	copula *be* + *not*	(= 'I didn't see him')
	auxiliary *be* + *not*	She isn't cleaning the house
	some modals + *not*	We can't eat anything
	decrease in *no/not* + *verb*	
advanced	analysed *don't/doesn't*	We didn't see nobody
	more modals + *not*	You mustn't say that
	elimination of *no/not* + verb	The glass will not break

Source: Based on Stauble 1984

I consider the acquisition of negation in chapter 3, and will comment on these stages there. Data were collected from the subjects in the form of two hours of spontaneous speech, and subjects' use of verbal morphology was recorded. There are two things which should be noted about the way that Stauble presents her results. Firstly, she regards the presence of at least ten contexts where the use of a particular morpheme would be obligatory for native speakers as optimal for assessing the level of accuracy of her subjects. Ten or more contexts allow a reasonable assessment of the productive use of a morpheme. Where fewer than ten such contexts occur for a particular subject, she indicates this in her results. (No cases of an item used in fewer than ten contexts are reported in the results we discuss below.)

Secondly, whereas the earlier morpheme studies described in section 2.4 based accuracy scores for subjects solely on morphemes supplied on obligatory occasions, Stauble used the more interesting idea of measuring target-like use. This involves determining not only the number of times a morpheme is used accurately in a context where it would be obligatory for a native speaker, but also the number of times it is used in contexts where a different morpheme is required (e.g. where an L2 speaker wrongly uses V-*ing* for a past tense, as in: *Joan cycling to town yesterday* instead of: *Joan cycled to town yesterday*).[6] This means that we can assess whether a subject really has acquired native-like use of a particular morpheme, or whether that morpheme has a quite different function in the subject's mental grammar. In the light of this, consider now table 2.4, which gives

Table 2.4 Scores (%) of target-like and non-target-like use of English verbal morphology by low-intermediate L2 speakers (2 Spanish, 2 Japanese)

Thematic V	Anita (Sp) %	Mona (Sp) %	Sumi (Jap) %	Tamiko (Jap) %
bare V	43 [48]	25 [58]	44 [54]	40 [57]
-ing	20 [76]	20 [77]	31 [15]	46 [50]
past irreg.	4 [9]	3 [1]	8 [1]	9 [1]
past reg -ed	0 [0]	0 [0]	0 [0]	3 [0]
3p sing -s	2 [0]	0 [0]	2 [0]	0 [0]

[ ] = % of non-target-like use
Source: Based on Stauble 1984

the results Stauble obtained for the four low-intermediate subjects' performance on verbal morphology with thematic verbs, and shows not only each subject's target-like use, but also, in square brackets, the proportion of each subject's non-target-like use of verb morphology.

The low-intermediate subjects use thematic verbs predominantly in two forms: bare verb forms (i.e. with no inflections): *I read*; and with the inflection *-ing*: *I reading*. But the high proportion of non-target-like use of these forms, together with the absence of any consistent tense or agreement inflections, strongly suggests that these subjects have not yet acquired any of the distinctions that English syntax makes. Forms like *read/reading* are used interchangeably as simple realizations of the lexical category verb; the marking *-ing* has little or no syntactic significance in the mental grammars of subjects at this stage. Contrast this with the scores of the advanced subjects on the same morphemes (table 2.5):

Table 2.5 Scores (%) of target-like and non-target-like use of English verbal morphology by advanced L2 speakers (2 Spanish, 2 Japanese)

Thematic V	Rosa (Sp) %	Paz (Sp) %	Mariko (Jap) %	Fuku (Jap) %
bare V	49 [50]	57 [42]	60 [39]	54 [43]
-ing	93 [3]	91 [9]	98 [2]	91 [9]
past irreg.	53 [1]	85 [3]	53 [1]	71 [2]
past reg -ed	4 [3]	24 [0]	22 [0]	18 [0]
3p sing -s	56 [6]	56 [5]	19 [6]	10 [9]

[ ] = % of non-target-like use
Source: Based on Stauble 1984

Note the high levels of target-like use of -*ing* and the low level of non-target-like use of that form by both the Spanish and Japanese subjects. This suggests that progressive aspect has been acquired.

The advanced subjects have made considerable progress over the low intermediates in acquiring past tense, but interestingly there appears to be a major difference in the difficulty of irregular past tense forms (like *sang, bought, wrote*) and regular past tense forms (like *talked, borrowed, painted*). Target-like use is greater on irregular past tense forms. This difference is equally strong both for the Spanish and the Japanese speakers. It is in conflict with Andersen's observation (table 2.2) that irregular and regular past tense forms are acquired simultaneously. Non-target-like use of past tense verbs of either kind is very low, suggesting that subjects know when they use a past tense verb form that it means past tense, but are having some difficulty in realizing it consistently.

Next consider the 3rd person singular present tense agreement marker -*s*. This inflection was effectively absent in the speech of the low intermediate subjects. In the advanced subjects an interesting divergence emerges between the Spanish and Japanese speakers. The Spanish speakers are more accurate in their target-like use of this morpheme than the Japanese speakers. Indeed, so much better that their performance is out of line with the predictions of Zobl and Liceras (see section 2.7): the subjects appear to be more accurate on the 3rd person agreement marker -*s* than on regular past -*ed* (Zobl and Liceras's proposal predicts that subjects should be equally accurate (or inaccurate) on -*s* and -*ed*). The Japanese speakers, on the other hand, conform to the prediction. This suggests that some L1 influence may be involved here. The non-target-like use of bare verb forms is still high, but this is because they are used as the **default** verb form in cases where subjects are not realizing regular past tense marking and agreement.

Consider now the accuracy of all 12 subjects in using copula *be* and auxiliary *be* (with V-*ing*):

We have now accumulated detailed empirical evidence about the acquisition of English verbal morphology by a group of Spanish speakers and a group of Japanese speakers. This has yielded a more differentiated account of the original descriptive generalization that L2 learners display similar accuracy profiles in this area. The next step is to try to explain the pattern uncovered in terms of learners building syntactic representations in their mental grammars. This requires the adoption of a more speculative mode of enquiry. It will be suggested that learners start building representations for the English clause with projections of thematic verbs, but without an IP projection. The appearance of IP is triggered by the acquisition of a morpheme which requires the barest of specifications: copula *be*. Copula *be* marks a local relation between its complement and its specifier, but little else. Learners refine this local relation subsequently to incorporate a specification for progressive aspect associated with auxiliary *be*. A present/past tense distinction is more difficult to acquire because it involves a non-local relation between I and a time reference specified outside IP. Subject–verb agreement (that is, person and number agreement between I and its specifier) is also more difficult to acquire, perhaps because specifier–head relations are inherently more difficult for L2 learners than head–complement relations. In section 2.11 we will consider how compatible these speculations are with several (equally speculative) more general theories about second language syntactic development which have been proposed recently in the L2 literature.

The low-intermediate subjects Stauble studied seem to have mental representations for the clause which involve VP and, possibly, a minimally specified IP, in the sense that the only element which could be claimed to be an instance of I in anything like target-like use is the copula *be*. These subjects are producing sentences like:

20a He cook (yesterday)/He cooking (yesterday)
  b She old/She's old
    (Examples invented for the purpose of exposition)

Even here, the Japanese speakers in Stauble's study produce a copula *be* in under a quarter of the contexts where native speakers would. Let us speculate that the earliest stage in the L2 acquisition of English verbal morphology is **a stage without IP**. L2 learners initially acquire thematic verbs, but not items associated with the category Infl. Suppose that they are guided by a universal principle of phrase projection (X'-theory); this allows structure to project, optionally, from head categories. So in the earliest stages, L2 learners acquire lexical items like *cook(ing)*, *he*, *she*, *old*, *fish*, and so on, and phrase projection enables them to construct phrases like:

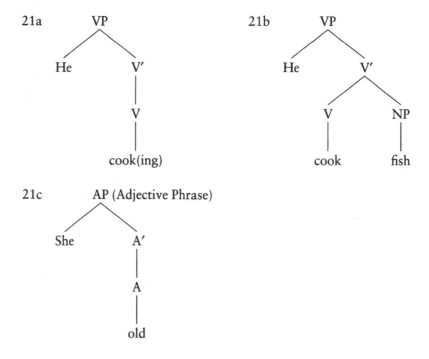

The acquisition of copula *be* by L2 learners could well be the trigger for establishing the category Infl and its projection IP. Recall that we are assuming that in native English copula *be* and auxiliary *be* are verbs which project to VP, but which also raise to I to pick up agreement and tense inflections. This assumption is based on the location of these verbs in relation to negation, in questions and with adverbs (see section 2.6). When copula *be* first appears in the productions of L2 learners, there are two possibilities for the underlying syntactic representation. Either *be* is treated like other verbs, and projects to VP, but does not raise to I because I is not yet available in the representation:

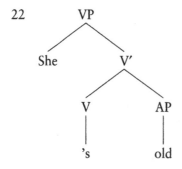

Or *be* projects to VP and is also raised to I, as in native English. This would mean that the acquisition of *be* triggers the establishment of the category I:

23

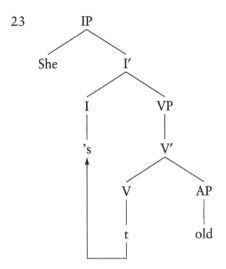

We cannot determine on the basis of the evidence we have seen so far which of these accounts, (22) or (23), is the more plausible: learner productions like *She's old* are compatible with either structure. However, in chapter 3 I will present evidence concerning negation which suggests that from early on L2 learners typically do not allow constructions like *She no is old*, preferring instead a null copula construction: *She no old*. When copula *be* does occur in negative contexts, it is typically in a pre-negator position: *She's not old/She isn't old*. This suggests that copula *be* does indeed move from VP to I early on in L2 learning, triggering the establishment of the category I and its projection. We will make that assumption.

Why should copula *be* act as the trigger for establishing I? Why should it be acquired before auxiliary *be* or before tense and agreement marking on thematic verbs? Copula *be* and auxiliary *be* share a property which distinguishes them from tense and agreement, and that is that they are free morphemes (as Zobl and Liceras (1994) observed). Both are also verbs which obligatorily select complements (**John is* – where *is* is a copula or auxiliary – is an ungrammatical sentence of English). But whereas copula *be* freely selects AP (Adjective Phrase), NP (Noun Phrase) or PP (Prepositional Phrase) complements, auxiliary *be* can only select VP complements in which the V has the *-ing* inflection:

24a She is [_{AP} very [_A fit [_{PP} for her age]]]
  b John is [_{NP} [_N a fool [_{PP} with his money]]]
  c They are [_{PP} in [_{NP} the garden]]

25a She is [_{VP} writ-ing [_{NP} a novel]]
  b *She is [_{VP} write [_{NP} a novel]]
  c *She is [_{VP} writt-en [_{NP} a novel]]

The ability of copula *be* to select complements fairly freely may well be related to the fact that it lacks specific conceptual content. It carries tense and agreement markings, but no meaning of its own, apparently. It is what has been called an **expletive verb** (Hyams 1996: 101); that is, it is a purely formal marker, like expletive *it* in sentences like *It seems that John is a fool*.

Suppose that, after an initial stage of acquiring thematic verbs, when L2 learners first begin to acquire grammatical morphemes they start with free morphemes which are minimally specified with respect to the kind of complement they require. Copula *be* is the least specified of the morphemes which can appear under the category I in English. Learners will only have to learn that it does not select a VP complement. Auxiliary *be*, by contrast, requires them to learn that it selects not only a VP, and no other type of complement, but a VP with a V-*ing* head describing an event in progress. Auxiliary *be* + V-*ing*, then, will appear early in learners' mental grammars because *be* is a free morpheme, but it will appear later than copula *be* because it has more complex selectional requirements.

Past tense marking on thematic verbs is more difficult for L2 learners than auxiliary *be*, though it is more consistently realized by irregular verb forms than by regular verb forms. For the subjects Stauble studied, the regular past tense forms were used correctly by the advanced subjects in less than a quarter of the required contexts (ranging from 4% to 24% for the four subjects – see table 2.5). There are two questions here. Why might tense emerge later than aspectual *be* + V-*ing*? And why might irregular past tense forms be easier than regular past tense forms?

Consider the first question. Copula *be* and auxiliary *be* are verbs which enter into a local selectional relation with their complements, and raise to I to pick up the affixes of I. Tense, by contrast, is a property of I which is determined by a time reference outside IP: either to indicate that the event is taking place simultaneously with the act of speaking, or that it occurred prior to speaking, or that it will occur at some point in the future. To account for the fact that the tense specification of I is not locally determined within IP, Guéron and Hoekstra (1995) have proposed that tense involves what is called a **binding relation**. Without going into the details of a rather complex proposal, the idea is that clauses are headed by a category called a Tense Operator which determines or 'binds' the interpretation the tense morpheme in I is given:

26   [T(ense) O(perator) [$_{IP}$ [$_I$ tense] [$_{VP}$ go [$_{PP}$ to town]]]]

When I is bound by this Tense Operator it receives a present tense interpretation (indicated by co-indexation in (27a)); when it is not bound by the Tense Operator, but by a tense reference outside the sentence, it has a non-present interpretation (indicated by contra-indexation in (27b)):

27a   [TO$_i$ [$_{IP}$ [$_I$ tense$_i$] [$_{VP}$ go [$_{PP}$ to town]]]]]
      'I'm going to town (at the moment)'
   b   [TO$_i$ [$_{IP}$ [$_I$ tense$_i$] [$_{VP}$ go [$_{PP}$ to town]]]]]
      'I was going to town (when I bumped into her)'

If this account is along the right lines, the task for the L2 learner is to match English tense morphemes to the appropriate binding relation. This is a less local relation than the complement selection properties required to establish representations for copula and auxiliary *be*. We might speculate that the non-localness of the relation is the reason why it is more difficult for L2 learners to acquire.

Turning to the second question, an interesting problem is posed by the considerably worse performance on regular past tense forms than on irregular past tense forms, by both the Spanish speakers and the Japanese speakers in Stauble's study. Firstly, the reason for this difference cannot be simply that bound morphemes are globally difficult for L2 learners. They clearly are difficult for the Japanese speakers who have very low accuracy scores both for tense and agreement inflections (see table 2.5). But the Spanish speakers perform better on the bound agreement morpheme 3rd person singular -s. Secondly, it is unlikely to be a problem of L1 influence. Both Spanish and Japanese have bound past tense morphemes, and if there were L1 influence it might be expected to be in the direction of making the acquisition of -ed in English easier, rather than harder.

It is known that first language learners of English go through three characteristic stages in acquiring past tense. In an early phase they acquire irregular past tense forms like *went, bought*; in a second phase they learn the regular pattern with -ed and overgeneralize it to irregular verbs, producing forms like *goed, buyed, wented*; in a third phase they learn to restrict the regular pattern to regular verbs, and the irregular forms are re-established in their grammars – this is the stage at which their performance on past tense morphology becomes native-like. By contrast, the second language learners under investigation seem to have difficulty establishing the regular pattern at all. Given the current stage of our knowledge, it is not clear how to explain this difficulty.[7]

Finally, in Stauble's study, the target-like use of the 3rd person singular present tense agreement marker -s was less difficult for the Spanish speakers than regular past tense -ed; the Spanish speakers also found it easier than the Japanese speakers. This is suggestive of L1 influence. Now, Spanish has a rich system of subject–verb agreement, while Japanese has nothing comparable (although one should qualify this by saying that it does have honorific pronouns which co-occur with some verbs but not others: Wakabayashi 1997). Subject–verb agreement relations involve heads and their specifiers, as illustrated in (28):

28a   [$_{IP}$ She$_i$ [$_I$ -s$_i$ [$_{VP}$ like jam doughnuts]]]
   b   [$_{IP}$ They$_i$ [$_I$ -ϕ_i [$_{VP}$ like jam doughnuts]]]

Suppose that specifier–head relations are inherently more difficult to establish for L2 learners than even the binding of I by a tense operator. This could perhaps be because they involve the matching of features for number (singular versus plural) and person (1st, 2nd, 3rd) across categories for a purely grammatical, but conceptually unnecessary, purpose: agreement. (The sentences would be perfectly interpretable whether there is agreement or not. In some languages there is no subject–verb agreement.) What we might say is that because Spanish has such a relation this facilitates the acquisition of a similar relation in the L2. Japanese does not have such a relation (except in the limited case of honorific pronouns), and so subject–verb agreement remains inherently difficult for them in English.

Recall that Andersen found no such facilitating effect on the performance of the 89 Spanish speakers he studied (table 2.2). But Andersen's subjects had had less exposure to English than Stauble's. One possibility is that L1 influence in L2 grammar-building only occurs at the point where the relevant representation in the grammar is being constructed. This is a view argued for by Zobl (1980), Wakabayashi (1997). One might claim that Andersen's subjects were not at a stage to even begin specifying I for agreement with the subject. Stauble's advanced subjects, by contrast, were at that stage, and because Spanish I is specified for agreement in number and person with the subject, this facilitated their acquisition of the -s/-φ contrast in English. Such a specification for I does not exist in Japanese, and so its acquisition remains very difficult even for the advanced Japanese speakers.

A similar interpretation might be given to the initial advantage that the low-intermediate Spanish speakers in Stauble's study had in acquiring the English copula. Spanish has a copular verb whose distribution is very similar to English *be*. Although Japanese does have a copular verb, its distribution is different. There are many adjectival constructions which do not occur with a copula:

29 niwa-ga   hiroi
    garden-Nominative spacious
    'The garden is spacious'

The absence of a copular verb in Japanese with a similar distribution to the copula in English may impede the early acquisition of *be* in English.

To conclude this section, we summarize the general properties of grammar-building which, it has been speculated, give rise to the observed development in the acquistion of English verbal morphology by L2 speakers. L2 speakers appear to start acquisition without any grammatical morphemes. They acquire thematic verbs (i.e. verbs with specific conceptual content) which, by X′-theory, project to V′ and VP. The establishment of a representation for VP is the first stage. In a second stage, IP becomes represented, initially via the minimally specified copula *be*. Learners then start to refine their representation for I: first they acquire auxiliary *be*, which requires a specific VP complement, one containing V-*ing*. This is a local head–complement relation. Then they acquire a non-local binding relation between I and the tense operator outside IP, which enables them to represent a present- to past-tense distinction. The past tense morpheme can be realized either through irregular forms like *went*, or through verbs with the regular inflection -*ed*: *walk-ed*. The latter is more difficult than the former for L2 learners. We had no explanation for this. Finally, the most difficult specification of I to acquire for L2 learners appears to be a specifier–head relation: agreement between I and the subject of the clause. The L1 appears to have a qualifying effect on this sequence, but crucially only at points where the relevant representation for a particular property becomes available in learners' mental grammars. Spanish speakers had an early advantage over the Japanese speakers in building IP because Spanish has a copular verb with a similar distribution to English *be*, and a late advantage in acquiring the subject–verb agreement relation because Spanish marks number and person distinctions in I, while Japanese does not.

2.11 Placing the account in the context of more general theories of L2 syntactic development

Section 2.11 assesses the extent to which the account of the L2 acquisition of English verb morphology developed in this chapter is compatible with several 1990s theories of general syntactic development in second languages. Although all are formulated within the framework of the principles and parameters approach to Universal Grammar, they embody different conceptions about the nature of second language syntax.

While the details of grammar-building in the acquisition of English verbal morphology by L2 speakers are interesting in their own right, SLA researchers are interested in a more ambitious goal: to give a general account of the developmental and logical problems in second language acquisition (see section 1.1). We might expect, then, that grammar-building in the domain of verb morphology reflects properties of grammar-building which are found more generally in the second language acquisition of syntax. We will consider the L2 acquisition of other areas of syntax in subsequent chapters, but it is useful at this point to measure the results outlined in this chapter against more general theories for the developmental and logical problems in SLA proposed by other researchers. During the 1990s, three types of theory emerged which assume that the logical problem can be addressed by hypothesizing a Universal Grammar of principles and parameters which constrains the nature of L2 grammar-building. They differ, however, in their assumptions about the developmental problem, and in particular about what is called the **initial state** in L2 acquisition: the point from which L2 learners start to build grammars. In this section we consider each in turn, and then come to the view that none is entirely consistent with the observations which have been made so far. A composite theory which draws on elements of each is proposed which will be referred to as **modulated structure building**. This will then form a 'working theory' which will be tested against other areas of L2 syntax as we encounter them.

2.11.1 'Minimal trees' (Vainikka and Young-Scholten 1994, 1996a, 1996b)

The 'minimal trees' account of second language syntactic development (Vainikka and Young-Scholten 1994, 1996a, 1996b) makes crucial use of the distinction between **lexical** categories (those like N, V, A, P to which lexical morphemes like *novel, write, fit, for* belong) and **functional** categories (like I, to which grammatical morphemes like 3rd person singular *-s*, past tense *-ed* belong). Recall that in section 2.2 it was observed that the contrast between lexical and grammatical morphemes is an important one for understanding language acqusition. Vainikka and Young-Scholten (1996a: 7) claim that 'only **lexical categories** are present at the earliest stage of . . . L2 acquisition, and that during acquisition **functional projections** develop in succession'. Their theory is formulated on the basis of the specific case of the acquisition of German as a second language by speakers of various L1s, but it is intended to be a general theory about development. (We consider details of their study of German in chapter 4.)

Further, they propose that there will be initial transfer from the L1 of the properties of lexical categories. So, for example, if the verb follows its complement in the VP in the L1, this will initially be transferred into the L2, even if the verb precedes its complement in the L2. With exposure to sufficient samples of the L2, these transferred lexical properties will be eliminated in favour of the L2 pattern. By contrast, there is no L1 influence on functional categories. These develop in the L2 mental grammar on the basis of learners encountering positive examples of their existence in the input. So, in the case of the acquisition of properties of the L2 clause, Vainikka and Young-Scholten (1996a: 15) propose that 'the learner transfers *only* his or her native language VP, and that no functional projections are transferred – neither initially, nor subsequently'.

Does this proposal explain the pattern of development observed in the acquisition of English verb morphology? We certainly seem to have found an early stage where a 'bare VP' predominates. Japanese is a head-final language, unlike English, so that verbs follow their complements:

> 30 Kodomo-ga terebi-o miru
> child-particle television-particle watches
> 'The child is watching television'

On Vainikka and Young-Scholten's account initial transfer of the head-final property of the VP by the Japanese speakers would be expected. There is no evidence of this in Stauble's data. However, the low intermediate subjects were not beginners, and it could be that Japanese speakers do transfer the head-final property of the VP into their L2 English at an earlier point of development.

Secondly, again on the basis of their study of the L2 acquisition of German, Vainikka and Young-Scholten (1994) propose that when the functional category I emerges, it is at first unspecified for tense and agreement. In their account it starts out as 'a position for verbs to raise to' (1996b: 144) (see chapter 3 for discussion of verb movement). In the data we have been considering, we have claimed that I first starts out as a position for copula *be* to move to, copula *be* being a meaningless or expletive element whose function is the purely grammatical one of selecting an AP, NP or PP complement. This is compatible with Vainikka and Young-Scholten's proposal. Finally, Vainikka and Young-Scholten's view about subsequent development is that it is incremental: learners proceed by adding more complex specifications to the functional structure dominating lexical projections. This is also compatible with the findings outlined in this chapter.

There is, however, one important area of incompatibilty between the 'minimal trees' account and the findings we have outlined. 'Minimal trees' allows L1 influence only in lexical projections: the transfer of the location of the head in the VP. We found two areas of apparent influence in the functional projection IP. The first was the considerable advantage the Spanish speakers at the low-intermediate level had over the Japanese speakers in acquiring copula *be* (although this advantage disappeared with proficiency). The second was the advantage that the Spanish speakers had at the advanced level on subject–verb agreement. If functional categories are not transferred from the L1 we would expect parallel development across L2 learners. It is difficult to explain this influence under the minimal trees hypothesis.

So while Vainikka and Young-Scholten's theory broadly makes the right predictions, which is a very interesting result given that it was formulated on the basis of different grammatical phenomena (word order) in a different second language (German), it seems that there is a residue (L1 influence on functional projections) which remains unexplained.

2.11.2 'Valueless features' (Eubank 1993/94, 1994a, 1996)

Eubank also makes crucial use of the lexical category/functional category distinction in his theory. In his early work (1993/94, 1994a) his idea was that all the categories instantiated in the L1 are initially transferred into the mental grammar for the L2, but that the particular specifications chosen for the functional categories by the L1 are neutralized: the features of, for example, I relating to the kind of agreement or tense distinctions which are made in the L1 become 'valueless'. This means that in the initial L2 grammar any functional categories present in the L1 will also be present, but they will simply mark structural positions, without any particular specification: 'lexical and functional projections transfer from the native language, and so do the headedness characteristics of those projections, but [the language specific] values under functional heads are not transferred' (1994a: 385).

The account is similar to Vainikka and Young-Scholten's in predicting that the language-specific properties of VP are transferred in the early stages: so Japanese-speaking learners of English would be expected to have verb-final VPs in early English. It differs in claiming that where a learner has a given functional category in the L1, this will be present from the earliest stages in the L2, albeit unspecified for any particular features.

In more recent work (Eubank 1996) he allows for the possibility that learners' grammars might initially have representations only for lexical projections, as Vainikka and Young-Scholten do. The transfer of functional categories from the L1 with valueless features still occurs, but only if there is positive evidence from the L2 for projecting the functional category in question. For example, where L2 learners of English have an IP category in their L1, on Eubank's view they will transfer this projection into their grammars for English only once they notice forms like copula *be* or 3rd person singular *-s* which are overt signals for such a projection.

One of the claimed advantages of this approach is that it allows for the possibility of **optionality** in L2 learners' syntactic representations. Optionality is not something we have focused on directly yet (and we will delay serious consideration of it until chapter 8). However, looking at tables 2.5 and 2.6 in section 2.8, it is clear that there is considerable optionality in the use of verb morphology by the individual L2 learners studied by Stauble. Take the case of the use of 3rd person singular *-s* by the advanced Spanish speakers: Rosa and Paz both produce this *-s* in 56% of cases where it would be required by a native speaker, and almost always use it correctly (they misuse it in only 6% and 5% of cases respectively). But this means that on 44% of occasions where they should use *-s* they fail to produce it, even though they appear to know the conditions under which it should be produced. Eubank claims that such optionality can be explained as the effect of learners' grammars preferring a syntactic representation which lacks agreement (as the direct result of projecting an IP with features for tense and agreement unspecified). At the same time, because they are presumably confronted with positive evidence from English for agreement in the form of *-s*, this leads learners to produce it on some appropriate occasions (see Eubank (1994b) for discussion of the English 3rd person singular *-s* case).

In relation to the specific phenomena we have discussed in this chapter, 'valueless features' appears less compatible with the observed patterns than 'minimal trees'. Assuming that both Spanish and Japanese have an IP projection (both languages have tense morphemes belonging to the category I), on the 'valueless features' account we would not expect there to be a difference between the Spanish and the Japanese speakers in the rate at which they acquire copula *be*, because whether or not they project IP from the very beginning, both sets of learners should establish an I with unspecified features on the basis of positive evidence. However, we saw that there was a considerable difference in rate of acquisition (see table 2.6), with the Spanish speakers having an advantage over the Japanese speakers. Similarly, if I has no transferred features, we would not expect the advanced Spanish speakers to have an advantage in acquiring the 3rd person singular agreement marker *-s*, but they appear to have such an advantage (see table 2.5).

More generally, if the initial L2 grammars of Spanish and Japanese speakers contain a transferred but unspecified functional category I, it is not entirely clear how the theory would go about explaining the order of development of verb-related morphemes that we observed: copula *be* → auxiliary *be* → past tense → subject–verb agreement. It would need some additional proposal along the lines of Vainikka and Young-Scholten's that the acquisition of functional categories proceeds incrementally. On the basis of the evidence we have accumulated so far, it appears that Vainikka and Young-Scholten's proposal deals more elegantly with the observations than the 'valueless features' theory (but bearing in mind the 'residue' of L1 influence on the development of I which remains unexplained).

2.11.3 'Full access' theories (Schwartz and Sprouse 1994, 1996; Epstein et al. 1996; Grondin and White 1996)

A number of L2 researchers hold the view that second language learners potentially have full access from their first encounter with an L2 to all the lexical and functional categories relevant to the construction of a mental grammar for that language. The only limitation on such access is a practical one: the learner has had insufficient time to experience enough samples of L2 data to establish the relevant categories. And it is this which gives rise to the transfer of syntactic properties from the L1. In the absence of relevant experience of the L2, the learner relies on the syntax of the L1 to construct sentences. The 'full transfer/full access' theory of Schwartz and Sprouse (1994, 1996) is a good example of this position. Schwartz and Sprouse propose that in SLA all the syntactic properties of the L1 are initially transferred into the L2 grammar. Hence the initial state for the L2 learner is the set of grammatical representations determined by the L1. It should be noted, however, that this excludes the surface phonological realizations of morphemes, i.e. forms like *-s, -ed*. So an English speaker learning French would not, say, produce sentences like *Je mang-ed la pomme*, 'I ate the apple' (for the native French *J'ai mang-é la pomme*). Rather, an English speaker would transfer a representation for I into her L2 grammar for French which carries an abstract feature for 'past tense'.

'Full transfer/full access' then contends that learners restructure this initial-state grammar on the basis of the L2 input they hear (or read). There will be aspects of the L2 input which cannot be generated by the initial-state grammar, because the properties in question do not exist in the L1, and this will lead learners to build new syntactic representations. There will also be properties transferred from the L1 into the initial-state L2 grammar for which there is no evidence in the L2 input – this may or may not lead learners to restructure their L2 grammars (see chapter 8 for discussion of whether learners can retreat from transferred grammatical properties for which there is no evidence in the L2 input). An important aspect of restructuring of the initial-state L2 grammar is that it may be fast or slow: 'In some cases, this restructuring may occur quite rapidly; in others, much more time may be needed' (Schwartz and Sprouse 1996: 41). The restructuring of syntactic representations, Schwartz and Sprouse propose, draws on all the options made available by Universal Grammar, hence the idea that L2 learners have 'full access' to the language faculty: in this respect L2 and L1 learners are alike. They differ, however, in development because of their poten-tially radically different starting points: in the case of L2 learners the starting point is their L1 syntax; and in the case of L1 learners the starting point is the open parameter values made available by Universal Grammar.

One of the interesting aspects of the proposal, in relation to the data that we have considered in this chapter, is that it offers some account of the apparent advantage that Spanish speakers have over Japanese speakers, early on in the acquisition of copula *be*, and later in the acquisition of subject–verb agreement. If learners transfer the syntactic properties of their L1s, Spanish speakers may be primed to notice copula *be* and 3rd person singular *-s* precisely because the abstract features underlying these morphemes are already present in their L2 grammars. By contrast, the lack of these features in the initial-state L2 grammars of the Japanese speakers might explain why it takes them longer to acquire the morphemes in question. The problem for the 'full transfer/full access' theory in relation to the same data is to explain, if our analysis is correct, why there is an early phase of acquisition without IP for both Spanish and Japanese speakers, followed by a stage where I is represented, but minimally specified. This is un-expected if learners' initial-state grammars contain all the syntactic features of the L1: both Spanish and Japanese have specified IPs, and it might be expected that they would have no more difficulty mapping English morphemes onto I than they do in mapping English morphemes onto V and N.

However, as observed in section 2.5, some researchers have argued that the use of overt morphemes by L2 speakers may not be a good guide to the extent to which they have acquired underlying syntactic representations. For example, Epstein et al. suggest that it is simply not clear whether there is a correlation between any percentage of correct usage of a particular aspect of grammar and knowledge of that aspect. Thus it is conceivable that a learner may in fact know the target language . . . but the learner never uses certain structures, or uses them incorrectly, for performance reasons. (1996: 692)

On this view, the analysis we have proposed here is possibly mistaken, and IP is in fact present from the earliest stages of the L2 acquisition of English by Spanish and Japanese speakers, although without consistent realization by overt morphemes in samples of their speech. If this is correct, the problem is one of explaining why they display the particular accuracy profile observed in performance. We will not pursue this particular line of enquiry here, but return to reconsider it in chapter 8.

2.11.4 A composite 'working theory' of L2 syntactic development: modulated structure building

It appears that elements both from the 'minimal trees' and the 'full transfer/full access' theories predict the observations we have made in this chapter about the L2 development of English verb-related morphology, but neither theory is fully compatible with those observations. ('Valueless features' appears to have less to say in this domain, although we will reconsider its predictions about optionality in L2 learners' grammars in section 8.4.2.) I will therefore propose a provisional 'working theory' which combines insights from both to account for what we have observed. I call this **modulated structure building**, and will carry it forward as a 'working theory' into subsequent chapters, where the extent to which it is predictive of other areas of L2 syntactic development will be assessed.

Modulated structure building is this: learners' initial L2 grammars consist, in principle, of lexical projections like VP, NP, AP, PP, and these have the structural properties of their L1 grammars, again in principle (i.e. the position of the head, complement and specifier are initially determined by the L1). This is the first part of Vainikka and Young-Scholten's 'minimal trees' proposal. We say that initial L2 grammars consist of lexical projections 'in principle', and that their structural properties are determined 'in principle' by the L1, because restructuring towards the L2 may be very rapid, depending on the evidence available to the learner and the nature of the transferred property in question, so that it may be difficult to detect initial transfer empirically: this is an idea contained in the 'full transfer/full access' theory. For example, head–complement order in lexical projections, where it differs between the L1 and L2, appears to be restructured very rapidly by L2 learners, and it is not always easy to find evidence for it in learners' productions. Thus although Japanese is an SOV (Subject-Object-Verb) language, the low-intermediate Japanese speakers in Stauble's study showed no evidence of OV order in their VPs. However, other researchers have found evidence of L1 orders in lexical projections in the very earliest stages of L2 acquisition (see section 4.6).

Functional projections are established later than lexical projections (as proposed by 'minimal trees'), but again this is 'in principle' for the same reason: the rapidity with which they are established depends on the evidence available to the L2 learner. In the case of the establishment of English I and its projection IP there appears to be a prior VP-only stage. We will see in section 3.6, however, that certain kinds of evidence in other languages lead learners to establish I apparently from the very earliest stages of acquisition and simultaneously with lexical projections.

The idea that learners start their L2 mental grammars with lexical projections and add functional categories on the basis of positive evidence from the L2 is the 'structure building' part of the theory, and is identical to 'minimal trees' in this respect. It is only once functional categories are established in the L2 grammar that the influence of L1 functional categories becomes evident, and even then only at the relevant points of development. Thus when Spanish and Japanese speakers initially establish a minimally specified I in their L2 English grammars, the influence of the L1 on the property of subject–verb agreement (Spanish has such agreement, but Japanese does not) is not yet relevant, because learners are not at the point of development where they need to have a representation for specifier–head agreement. This means that initially both sets of learners produce equally low proportions of 3rd person singular -s (see table 2.4). By the time learners are at an advanced stage of development, however, and are acquiring non-local grammatical dependencies, the abstract feature requiring agreement between I and its specifier transferred from Spanish does become relevant, and gives the Spanish speakers a considerable advantage over the Japanese speakers (see table 2.5). This is the 'modulated' part of structure building: structure building is influenced by properties of the L1 at the relevant point in the construction of a grammar, and not before. This is an important point of divergence from the 'full transfer/full access' proposal – L1 transfer is relevant, but only once syntactic representations have been sufficiently elaborated to instantiate the property in question. These ideas will be tested and developed as we proceed in our consideration of other areas of L2 syntactic development.

2.12   Summary of chapter 2

The main points made in chapter 2 are the following:

• The development of accuracy in the use of English grammatical morphemes like copula *be*, auxiliary *be*, past tense, 3rd person singular -s, the articles *a, the*, plural -s, and so on, in unplanned, spontaneous production appears to be very similar across L2 learners who speak different first languages, vary in age and learn English under different conditions. Some morphemes appear easy to acquire, others are more difficult and take longer. In some cases, if the L1 marks a grammatical distinction corresponding to an English grammatical morpheme, this appears to facilitate the acquisition of that morpheme (sections 2.1–2.4).

- By assuming that observed patterns of accuracy reflect the underlying building of syntactic representations in learners' mental grammars, it was noted that development of knowledge of English verbal morphology consists in learners constructing representations in the following sequence (section 2.5):

  copula → aspect (±progressive) → tense (±past) → subject–verb agreement (±3rd person singular)

- It was argued that L2 learners of English start grammar-building with lexical projections of thematic verbs, but without IP. The establishment of the functional category I is triggered by the acquisition of a morpheme with the barest of specifications: copula *be* (an expletive verb). Thereafter, learners refine their representation for I in a systematic sequence. First, learners acquire morphemes belonging to I which mark a local head–complement relation (auxiliary *be*); then learners acquire morphemes which mark non-local tense binding relations (past versus present tense); finally, learners acquire purely formal specifier–head agreement relations (subject–verb agreement). L1 influence on rate of development occurs only at the point in the sequence where the particular property becomes relevant; for example, the fact that Spanish marks subject–verb agreement only speeds up the acquisition of subject–verb agreement in English by Spanish speakers in advanced stages of acquisition (sections 2.6–2.10).

- Placing the analysis in the context of several proposed more general theories of L2 syntactic development – 'minimal trees', 'valueless features', and 'full access' theories – it was argued that none fully predicted the observations made, and a modulated structure-building theory was proposed (section 2.11) whose assumptions are that

  (a) the L2 initial state consists in principle of lexical projections with the structural properties of the L1 (as in 'minimal trees');

  (b) functional projections like I are triggered by positive evidence in the L2 (again like 'minimal trees');

  (c) development proceeds incrementally from local head–complement relations to non-local binding relations to purely formal specifier–head agreement relations;

  (d) syntactic properties of the L1 transfer into the L2 grammar (as in 'full transfer/full access'), but only at points of development where the relevant property emerges as part of the general sequence of development.

2.13 Exercises

(a)   Divide sentences (1)–(3) into their constituent morphemes:

Example: She wanted to buy a new hair-dryer
She | want | ed | to | buy | a | new | hair | dry | er

1. Tony liked listening to Erica's disks.
2. The gardener repaired the lawn-mower.
3. The shoe fitted Cinderella like a glove.

(b)   Which of the morphemes in sentences (1)–(3) would you class as grammatical? Which of these are inflectional and which derivational?

(c)   How does the 'past tense' morpheme, as it appears in these examples, illustrate the concept of 'allomorph'?

(d)   Now try to divide the following sentences into their constituent morphemes. How do examples like these lead one to propose that morphemes are abstract units of syntactic analysis?

4. Tony caught two fish.
5. The postmen went on strike.
6. The children outgrew their jeans.

Below is an instruction leaflet which accompanied a child's clockwork money bank. There are a number of places where the English diverges from that of native speakers of standard British or American English. Indicate where these differences occur, and try to determine whether they are lexical or grammatical differences.

YOU MUST NOTICE

BEFORE WINDING!

THIS BANK HAVE BEEN FULLY PRE-WOUND AT
FACTORY. TO AVOID OVERWINDING, BE SURE
TO PRESS BUTTON FOR REPEAT ACTION UNTIL
IT HAS BEEN FULLY UNWINDED. ALWAYS WIND
THE KEY AS THE ARROWHEAD DIRECTION. IF
WINDING AGAINST OPPOSITE DIRECTION, THE
GEAR BOX WILL BE SMASHED.
IN CASE YOU FIND THE SELF-ADHESIVE.
PLEASE TEAR OFF BEFORE PLAYING.

DO NOT OVERWIND!

PRINTED IN HONG KONG

Exercise 3: Assessing the effectiveness of counting morphemes used on 'obligatory occasions' (section 2.4)

One kind of criticism directed at the early morpheme studies was that their method for scoring accuracy in the use of morphemes by L2 speakers did not reflect the extent to which learners had acquired target-like use of those forms. Read again the description in section 2.4.1 of how Dulay and Burt (1973, 1974) scored data collected via the Bilingual Syntax Measure, and then explain why L2 data like the following show that scoring morphemes by suppliance on 'obligatory occasions' may be misleading about how target-like an L2 learner's grammar is:

Yesterday, I walking to town to meeting my friend, Carlos. He staying in a flats with her mother. He having a sisters an' two brother. He living here three year more than me. He speaking better English than me.

Exercise 4: Practice in analysing the constituent structure of
simple sentences (section 2.6)

Draw tree diagrams for the initial syntactic structure of the following sentences,
and show how the inflections of Infl are associated with a verb in each sentence:

1. John often cooked the supper.
2. John has sometimes missed classes.
3. Sally has secretly been seeing Gerald.

Exercise 5: Analysing the syntactic representations underlying
L2 utterances I (section 2.10)

Consider the following native forms of French verbs with their English translations:

> *aller*, 'to go' (infinitive); *je vais*, 'I am going'; *ils vont*, 'they are going'
> *mettre*, 'to put' (infinitive); *elle met*, 'she is putting'
> *mordre*, 'to bite' (infinitive); *il mord*, 'he is biting'

Now consider the examples below produced by English-speaking seven-year-olds
after two years in a Canadian French-immersion programme (reported by Selinker
et al. 1975):

1. Mon maman et mon papa *aller* à Glendon.
    'My mother and my father go to Glendon.'
2. L' autre fois je *aller* camping.
    'The other time I went camping.'
3. Je *aller* le français camp.
    'I'm going to French camp.'
4. La fille *mettre* du confiture sur le pain.
    'The girl is putting some jam on the bread.'
5. Le chat toujours *mordre*.
    'The cat always bites.'

In the light of the discussion in section 2.10, what kind of syntactic representation might underlie examples like these?

Exercise 6: Analysing the syntactic representations underlying
L2 utterances II (section 2.10)

In the table below are examples of object pronoun use in the L2 Spanish of a 12-
year-old native speaker of English, Anthony, collected by Andersen (1984: 84–5)

in the course of an oral interview. Anthony was acquiring Spanish in Puerto Rico through daily interaction with his peers. Compare Anthony's productions (in the left-hand column) with their native equivalents (in the right-hand column). On the basis of your reading of chapters 1 and 2, what would you say about the nature of Anthony's grammar for object pronouns in Spanish?

Object pronouns produced by Anthony		Native equivalents
ayúdame	*to help me*	ayúdarme
dame	*help me!*	ayúdame
y compre a mi un camisa	*and she bought me a shirt*	y me compró una camisa
ven y busco nosotros	*came and looked for us*	vino y nos buscó
nada puede pasó pa mi	*nothing can happen to me*	nada me puede pasar
la policía quiere él	*the police want him*	la policía lo quiere

Note that Spanish has two sets of forms for object pronouns: a set used in unstressed contexts and a set used in stressed contexts:

Unstressed		Stressed
me 'me'		mí
te 'you'		tí
lo 'him'		él
nos 'us'		nosotros

Exercise 7: Problematic data for the account of development given in section 2.10 (sections 2.10, 2.11)

Hakuta (1976) studied a 5-year-old Japanese-speaking girl called Uguisu, acquiring English naturalistically in the United States over a period of 13 months. By recording her spontaneous productions for two hours every week, Hakuta collected 30 samples of data from her. Although during this period Uguisu came to use the following forms productively:

am, are, is, was
do, did
don't, didn't

she did not use any forms of the past tense with thematic verbs (either irregular like *bought, came* or regular like *walk-ed, arrive-d*) or the 3rd person singular present tense morpheme (*buy-s, walk-s*). In these cases she used bare verb forms, as in: *She like something; she love a money; she live with her.* What problems might these data pose for the account of the development of L2 syntactic knowledge outlined in section 2.10? Is it possible to find a way of reconciling these data with that account?

Exercise 8: Extending the analysis to new data (section 2.10)

In section 2.5 we presented Andersen's (1978) implicational accuracy profile of Spanish speakers on English grammatical morphology. In addition to the verb-related morphemes described in table 2.2, Andersen found that his subjects were even less accurate on the pairing *have* + past participle, e.g. *I **have broken** the vase, He **has missed** his train*. In view of the fact that the structurally similar pairing *be* + present participle (e.g. *I **am breaking** the vase*) is among the most accurate morphemes, what account would you give of *have* + past participle? (Hint: Think about the kind of meaning that *have* + past participle expresses. Does it involve a local modification of the verb phrase only, or is tense-binding (i.e. a non-local relation – see section 2.10) involved?).

2.14 Further reading

For an overview of the objectives and methods of the early morpheme studies see Dulay, H., Burt, M. and Krashen, S. 1982: *Language Two*. Oxford: Oxford University Press. Many critical reviews of the early morpheme studies have been published; two balanced accounts can be found in chapter 4 of Larsen-Freeman, D. and Long, M. 1991: *An Introduction to Second Language Acquisition Research*. London: Longman, and in chapter 3 of Ellis, R. 1994: *The Study of Second Language Acquisition*. Oxford: Oxford University Press.

For an account of the category Infl and the nature of phrase structure see chapter 2 of Haegeman, L. 1994: *Introduction to Government and Binding Theory* (2nd edition). Oxford: Blackwell, and chapter 1 of Roberts, I. 1997: *Comparative Syntax*. London: Arnold.

A discussion of the importance of having a detailed theory of syntax at the heart of an account of second language development can be found in Gregg, K. 1996: The logical and developmental problems of second language acquisition. In W. Ritchie and T. Bhatia (eds), 1996: *Handbook of Second Language Acquisition*, San Diego: Academic Press.

Notes

1 The scoring procedure used by Makino differed slightly from that of Dulay and Burt. He scored 1.0 for a correct morpheme supplied on an obligatory occasion, and 0 both if a subject failed to supply a morpheme and if a subject supplied an inappropriate morpheme. Recall that Dulay and Burt scored inappropriate morphemes as 0.5.

2 One qualification should be borne in mind at this point. The descriptive generalization concerns L2 speaker productions in unplanned, fairly spontaneous language use. As noted in section 1.7, where tests used to elicit responses from subjects are more 'academic', for example in grammar tests which require subjects to produce properties of the L2 which they might have learned, different accuracy profiles may emerge. In section 1.7 we described a study by Larsen-Freeman (1975), which found different accuracy profiles on tasks where planned responses were possible.

3 In chapter 8 we will reconsider the lowering of inflections from I to V and the location of adverbs like *quickly, often* in the light of recent proposals in syntactic theory.

4 A quasi-longitudinal study is one which compares cross-sectional data from speakers of the same first language at different proficiency levels. On the assumption that such subjects are representative of speakers of their first language more generally, this is often a more practical way of tracking syntactic development over time than collecting data from the same subjects over several years.

5 Stauble did not use the terms low intermediate, intermediate and advanced herself, but rather labels drawn from sociolinguistic work on pidgin/creole languages: 'basilang', 'mesolang' and 'acrolang'. Since the import of these labels is not relevant here, we have preferred the more transparent terms.

6 Stauble's (1984: 329) method for calculating target-like use is as follows: firstly, subjects are scored for the number of morphemes they correctly supply on obligatory occasions; for example, if there are 10 occasions on which a native speaker would use V-*ing*, and a subject supplies -*ing* on 6 occasions, the subject scores 6/10. Then, the number of occasions a subject uses -*ing* in other (non-target-like) contexts is counted, and this number is added to the denominator of the first score. So if the subject in the example used -*ing* on 5 other occasions, this would produce a target-like use score of 6/15, or 40%.

7 Beck (1997) provides evidence from a test requiring L2 learners of English to produce past tense verb forms from verb stems in isolation (e.g. presented with *walk, go,* they are expected to produce the forms *walked, went*) which shows that they are not significantly different from native speakers in their ability to produce the regular forms. This might suggest that the difficulty lies in the use of regular past tense forms in sentences. But nothing is currently known beyond this.

3 The Second Language Acquisition of Negation and Verb Movement

3.1 Introduction

In chapter 2 we began to explore the idea that syntactic development in second language acquisition is a consequence of learners building representations in their mental grammars. In particular, it was proposed that the accuracy profiles displayed by L2 learners in using English verb morphology imply that they begin with a mental representation for the verb phrase (VP), add the inflection phrase (IP), initially as a minimally specified structural position, and then add specifications to I for progressive aspect, tense and agreement. Looking more generally at second language syntactic development, we asked whether this pattern of grammar-building was compatible with one of three types of theory which have recently been proposed in the literature: a structure-building theory known as 'minimal trees' (Vainikka and Young-Scholten 1994, 1996a, 1996b), the 'value-less features' theory of Eubank (1993/94, 1994a, 1996), or 'full access' theories like those of Schwartz and Sprouse (1994, 1996), Epstein et al. (1996), Grondin and White (1996). It seemed that there was no neat fit between the findings and any one of the theories. While the initial VP phase that learners were claimed to go through was predicted by minimal trees, L1 influence also appeared to be involved in the specification of IP: Spanish speakers acquired copula *be* earlier than Japanese speakers, and were more accurate on subject–verb agreement than on regular past tense marking, while the Japanese speakers found subject–verb agreement and past tense marking equally difficult. This led us to adopt a composite 'working theory' of L2 syntactic development which we called **modulated** structure building. This proposes that the initial state of L2 grammars consists in principle of lexical projections with the structural properties of the L1; functional categories are triggered by positive evidence from the L2; development is incremental, proceeding apparently from local syntactic dependencies to less local ones; and syntactic properties of the L1 are transferred into the L2 grammar, but only at relevant points in the developmental sequence.

In this chapter we look for descriptive generalizations in other areas of L2 syntactic development in order to see to what extent 'modulated structure building' makes the right predictions. The topics we will cover are negation and verb movement. The two are closely related, as we shall see. Additionally, verb movement interacts with other aspects of sentence structure such as the location of adverbs and quantifiers, and we will examine evidence about how L2 learners develop knowledge of such properties.

3.2 Negation in English and a second language descriptive generalization

Section 3.2 illustrates three types of negation in English, and discusses a descriptive generalization which has emerged from studies of the second language acquisition of sentential negation.

Three kinds of syntactically expressed negation in English have been discussed in the SLA literature. The first is **sentential negation**. This is illustrated in (1):

   1   Sally didn't buy a dress on Saturday

Here the negative force of *n't* (the unstressed form of *not*) can range over the whole sentence, so that the interpretation is 'It wasn't the case that Sally bought a dress on Saturday'; it can also range over just the constituent *a dress*, so that the interpretation is 'It wasn't a dress that Sally bought on Saturday (she bought something else)'. The range of a negator is normally referred to as its **scope**. *Not* can be positioned so that its scope is restricted to a single constituent. **Constituent negation** is illustrated in (2), where *not* has scope over the constituent *on Saturday*:

   2   Sally bought a dress, but not on Saturday

English also has another form, *no*, which can be used as a negative determiner, as in *Sally has no money*, or as a negative response to questions. The latter use is sometimes called **anaphoric negation**:

   3   – Will she buy that dress?
         – No.

Table 3.1   Stages of development in the acquisition of English negation by
Spanish speakers

Stage	Type of negation		Example
1	*no*	+ verb	You no tell your mother
			But no is mine, is my brother
			I no can see
2	*no*	+ verb	He no like it
	don't	+ verb	He don't like it
	(unanalysed)		I don't can explain
3	copula/	+ *no/not*	It's not danger
	auxiliary		No, he's not skinny
			Somebody is not coming in
			He can't see
4	*don't*	+ verb	He doesn't laugh like us
	(analysed)		I didn't even know
	(*no* + verb disappears)		

NB: 'Unanalysed' *don't* is an item with no internal structure – i.e. there are no
contrasts *don't/doesn't/didn't*. A speaker in stage 2 of Cancino et al. would produce
utterances like *I no can explain, I don't can explain* with the same intended meaning.
Source: Based on Cancino et al. 1978: 210–11

We will be interested here primarily in the syntax of sentential negation as illustrated in (1), and how second language learners acquire it.

It has been known for some time that second language learners of English
acquire sentential negation systematically. Cancino et al. (1978), on the basis of
longitudinal data collected from six Spanish-speaking learners of L2 English,
formulated an early proposal for a descriptive generalization. They suggested
that there are four stages in development, illustrated in table 3.1.

One can immediately see some possible connections here between stages in the
development of sentential negation and the findings in chapter 2 about how IP
emerges. The fact that the form *no* is used preverbally in the early stages may be
linked to the absence or underspecification of I at this point of development in
learners' mental grammars. The fact that when *not* emerges, following the early
use of *no* as a sentential negator, it follows a copula or auxiliary verb and may be
linked to the establishment of I in the mental grammar. However, the analysis of
Cancino et al. does not draw sufficiently fine syntactic distinctions to enable us to
make those connections. They do not distinguish between 'thematic' verbs and
copula *be*; they do not distinguish tense and agreement when *don't* becomes an

analysed form. These distinctions turned out to be crucial in chapter 2 in understanding how IP is acquired. (This is not a criticism of their study, but a statement of fact. At the time they were writing little was known either about descriptive generalizations in second language development or about the structure of clauses. Their study was, in fact, a major contribution to establishing that a descriptive generalization is involved.) As we now know that L2 learners of English become accurate on copula *be* before they become accurate on the auxiliary *be* involved in marking progressive aspect, and accuracy in the marking of aspect on thematic verbs precedes accuracy in the marking of tense and agreement, we need information about how these finer syntactic distinctions interact with the development of sentential negation.

Consider first a study by Shapira (1976, reported in Schumann 1978). Shapira studied the development of English negation in a 22-year-old Spanish speaker from Guatemala living in the United States. She collected three samples of spontaneous speech, the first shortly after the subject's arrival, the second 6 months later, and the third 11 months after that. Shapira found the pattern of development illustrated in table 3.2. Here each type of sentential negation used by the subject is shown as a proportion of the total number of negative sentences produced at each of the three data collection points:

Table 3.2 Development of English negation in a Spanish speaker

Sentence type	Example	Data collection time					
		I		II		III	
		%	n	%	n	%	n
copula be							
no + ϕ	(she) no old	40	$2/5$	67	$12/18$	54	$8/13$
no + be	(it) no is too little	20	$1/5$	5	$1/18$	0	
be + no	The water is no good	40	$2/5$	28	$5/18$	38	$5/13$
thematic verb							
no + V	I no call anymore	100	$15/15$	100	$19/19$	73	$50/69$
don't + V	I don't think so	0		0		27	$19/69$

n = number of tokens of a particular type of negation out of the total number of negative sentences produced by the subject
NB: The expression *I don't know* appeared in data collected at times I and II, but it was used as an unanalysed routine. It was only at time III that a productive contrast emerged where *don't* was used with other verbs. At time III *don't* means the same thing as, and alternates with, *no*.
Source: Based on Shapira 1976, cited in Schumann 1978

There are two things to note particularly about these results. Firstly, the subject appears to remain at an elementary level of development even at the third sampling. This is reflected in the predominant use of *no* as the sentential negator throughout, and the appearance of *don't* only at the third sampling – features of the first two stages of development of Cancino et al. The sentential negator in Spanish is also the form *no*, so there could be an L1 effect here. We return to this below. Secondly, Spanish has a copula verb similar to English in adjective constructions: *El agua no es buena*, 'The water isn't good'. The almost total absence, though, of the pattern *no + be* in this speaker's English (only 1 example out of 5 possible contexts at time I, 1 out of 18 at time II, and 0 out of 13 at time III) suggests that while the L1 may be influential in determining the phonological form of the negator in L2 English, it has little influence on the construction of IP in English at this early stage. The Spanish IP appears not to be transferred into L2 English. This is compatible with the speculation made in chapter 2 that in the early stages of L2 development IP is absent from L1 learners' mental grammars, so that a representation for a sentence like *she no old* would not have an IP: [$_{NegP}$ she [$_{NEG}$ no [$_{AP}$ old]]].

In section 2.10 we also speculated that the acquisition of copula *be* is the trigger for learners to establish an IP projection; that is, when copula *be* is acquired, so is movement of *be* from VP to I. But at that point there was insufficient evidence to decide between an analysis with or without movement of *be* from VP. Data from negation offer the possibility of deciding between the two analyses. If copula *be* moves from VP to I, the negator will appear to its right (as in native English): [$_{IP}$ The water [$_{I}$ is no [$_{VP}$ t good]]]. (Recall that t = trace: the position from which *be* has moved.) If copula *be* remains in VP, L2 learners would produce sentences where the negator is to the left of *be*: *The water no is good*. Shapira's subject, once *be* begins to appear in her productions, shows a predominance of *be + no* constructions, suggesting that *be* moves from VP to I. However, this is only one subject, and more evidence is required to strengthen the speculation.

To gain a clearer picture of what is going on here we need information about the later stages of the development of negation in Spanish speakers, and comparative data from speakers of typologically different languages. The study by Stauble (1984) described in section 2.8 provides a perspective on both of these. Stauble collected cross-sectional data of the L2 English of six Spanish speakers and six Japanese speakers at three proficiency levels: low intermediate, intermediate and advanced (see section 2.8 for details of the study and the subjects' background). Results are presented in table 3.3. In each group there are two Spanish speakers and two Japanese speakers:

Table 3.3 Proportions (%) of types of negation used by three groups of L2 speakers at different levels of proficiency

	Low intermediate				Intermediate				Advanced			
	An	Mo	Su	Ta	Jo	Je	Ke	Ku	Ro	Pa	Ma	Fu
copula be	%				%				%			
no + ø	86	58	–	78	9	–	–	–	–	–	–	–
not + ø	–	–	–	–	–	18	79	50	–	5	3	25
no + be	14	25	–	–	64	–	–	–	–	–	–	–
not + be	–	–	–	–	–	–	–	–	–	–	3	–
be + no	–	17	–	11	–	9	7	–	–	–	–	–
be + not	–	–	–	11	18	73	14	50	100	95	94	75
thematic V	%				%				%			
no + V	87	94	64	79	40	14	–	5	–	–	–	–
not + V	–	–	11	–	–	–	10	13	–	–	2	–
Unanalysed: don't	13	6	24	21	60	81	90	26	15	13	12	7
Analysed:												
don't	–	–	–	–	–	–	–	33	24	46	45	56
didn't	–	–	–	–	–	–	–	13	42	35	29	17
doesn't	–	–	–	–	–	–	–	–	17	3	11	16

Spanish subjects: An = Anita   Mo = Mona
                    Jo = Joe   Je = Josie
                    Ro = Rosa   Pa = Paz
Japanese subjects: Su = Sumi   Ta = Tamiko
                    Ke = Keiko   Ku = Kumi
                    Ma = Mariko   Fu = Fuku

NB: The low intermediate subject Sumi produced no contexts for negation + copula *be*.
Source: Based on Stauble 1984

The data show that at the low intermediate level the Spanish speakers are quite comparable with Shapira's subject. They display a predominant use of *no + ø* in copula constructions, considerable use of *no* + thematic verb, with some use of unanalysed *don't*. They do, however, make some use of *no + be* constructions (we return to this in section 3.4).

More surprisingly, the Japanese speakers use *no* as a sentential negator as much as the Spanish speakers, both with thematic verbs and (in the case of the subject Tamiko) in copula *be* contexts. It is unlikely that this is the effect of L1 influence, because negation in Japanese is very different from both English and Spanish. Japanese is a head final language in which the verb follows its complement; the sentential negator is a form which follows, and attaches to, the verb, with adjustments in the phonological shape of the verb, as illustrated in (4):

4a Kodomo-ga   terebi-o   miru
    child-particle television-particle watches
    'The child is watching television'

 b Kodomo-ga   terebi-o   mi-nai
    child-particle television-particle watch-not
    'The child isn't watching television'

Since both the Japanese and the Spanish speakers use *no* as the predominant negator at the low intermediate level, this casts doubt on the initial supposition that the L1 influences the choice of this form.

At the intermediate level, there seems to be an important correlation in the performance of three of the subjects: Josie, Keiko and Kumi. Growth of the pattern copula *be* + negator has been accompanied by growth in the use of *n't/not* as the negator, replacing *no*. There is also a big increase in the use of unanalysed *don't* (and even analysed *don't* for the subject Kumi) in comparison with the low intermediate subjects. (Stauble notes that although the subject Joe displays characteristics of her intermediate stage – a low proportion of *no* + φ in copular contexts, and a high proportion of unanalysed *don't* – he is nevertheless less advanced than the other three subjects at this level.)

At the advanced level subjects appear nearly to have acquired the target properties of negation. The *do* of *don't* is specified for tense and agreement, and the occurrence of unanalysed *don't* is minimal. The use of the copula *be* + *not* pattern is almost target-like.

I will use the empirical insights provided by the studies of Cancino et al. (1978), Shapira (1976) and Stauble (1984) to argue that, in the initial stages of the acquisition of negation, IP is absent, and will speculate that a negator generalized from anaphoric negation in English (recall that anaphoric negation is the use of *no* to respond to questions) selects the VP as its complement. Subsequently, IP is established when learners acquire copula *be*, which moves from VP to I. This is accompanied by the introduction of the target sentential negator *not*. We will suggest that the acquisition of I facilitates the acquisition of *not*, and also triggers growth in the use of unanalysed *don't*. To argue the case, we need to consider the syntax of sentential negation, and examine what kind of syntactic knowledge L2 learners acquire when they acquire negation.

3.3 The category Neg in English, Spanish and French

Section 3.3 describes the distributional differences between sentential negation in English, Spanish and French, and discusses what kind of syntactic representation might give rise to such differences. The differences are linked to different parameter settings in the three languages.

3.3.1 Distributional properties

Consider the location of the sentential negator *n't/not* in relation to the kinds of verbs which were under discussion in chapter 2: copula *be*, auxiliary *be*, modal verbs like *can, will, must*, etc., and thematic verbs like *walk, dance, sing*. *N't/not* follows copula *be*, auxiliary *be* and modal verbs. But it precedes thematic verbs, and has to be 'supported' by the introduction of the meaningless verb *do*:

5a Joanna isn't happy (copula *be*)
  b Joanna isn't dancing (auxiliary *be*)
  c Joanna can't open the window (modal)

6a *Joanna speaks **not/n't** Greek
  b *Joanna **not** speaks Greek
  c Joanna doesn't speak Greek

In Spanish the sentential negator is the form *no*, which always precedes the agreement- and tense-marked verb:

7a Juana **no** es feliz (copula)
   Juana no is happy

  b Juana **no** puede abrir la ventana (modal)
   Juana no can open the window

  c Juana **no** habla griego (thematic verb)
   Juana no speaks Greek

French has a form of sentential negation which superficially incorporates elements of both Spanish- and English-type negation. There is a preverbal element *ne* (often omitted in spoken French) and a postverbal element *pas*. Unlike English *n't/not*, however, *pas* follows all agreement- and tense-marked verbs, including thematic verbs:

8a Jeanne **n'** est **pas** contente (copula)
   Jeanne neg is not happy

  b Jeanne **ne** peut **pas** ouvrir la fenêtre (modal)
   Jeanne neg can not open the window

  c Jeanne **ne** parle **pas** grec (thematic verb)
   Jeanne neg speaks not Greek

3.3.2   The category Neg

Since the function of sentential negation is the same in all three languages, we might try to capture this fact by proposing that there is a single category in each language – Neg (for negation) – which appears in the same place in phrase structure. By X'-theory (see sections 1.6.2 and 2.6.2) Neg projects to Neg' and NegP. Suppose that NegP is the complement of I, and that Neg selects VP as its own complement, as illustrated in (9). Suppose further that Spanish *no* and French *ne* are morphemes which are head categories, while French *pas* and English *n't/ not* are negative adverbs located in the specifier position of NegP:

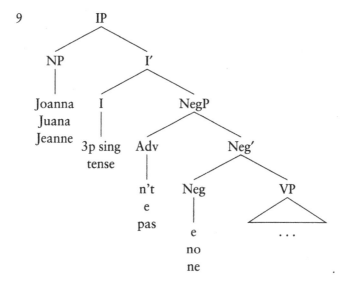

9

In (9), e stands for 'empty'. So the head of NegP in English is empty (but the specifier is filled), while the specifier of NegP in Spanish is empty (but the head is filled). In French both head and specifier of NegP are filled (although, as noted above, in spoken French *ne* tends to be absent, i.e. the head is empty in spoken French).

In section 2.6.2 I described a proposal that *be* and *have* move from VP to I to 'pick up' the agreement and tense inflections under I (following Emonds 1978; Pollock 1989; Chomsky 1995, chapter 2). This analysis also extends to Spanish and French. Suppose we assume that when negation is present *be* and *have*, and their equivalents in Spanish (*ser* and *haber*) and French (*être* and *avoir*), move in steps. This would be compatible with a proposed principle of Universal Grammar known as the 'Head Movement Constraint' which requires that when a head moves it must always move to the nearest head (Travis 1984; Chomsky 1995: chapter 2). So *be, have, ser, haber, être, avoir* first raise to Neg, the head of NegP, and then to I. In Spanish, in a sentence like *Juana no es feliz, ser* raises from VP to Neg, where it picks up *no* as a prefix, and then moves on up to I, where it picks up agreement and tense. This two-step movement is illustrated in (10) (remember, t = trace: the position from which a constituent has moved):

10a   Step 1

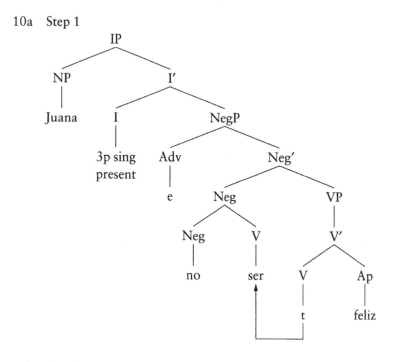

b   Step 2

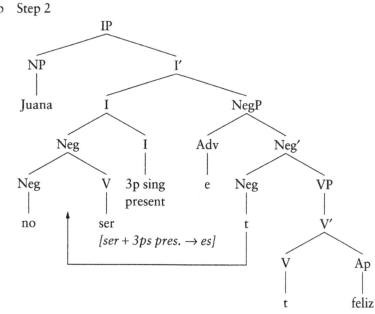

A similar movement takes place in the case of French and English.[1] In French the verb picks up the *ne* on its way up to I. But because *pas* and *n't* are in the specifier of NegP, and the verb moves from head to head (from V to Neg, and from Neg to I) *pas* and *n't* are left behind:

11a   Step 1

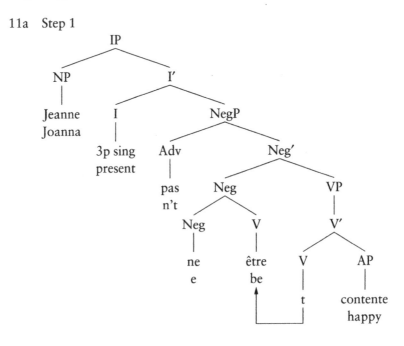

b   Step 2

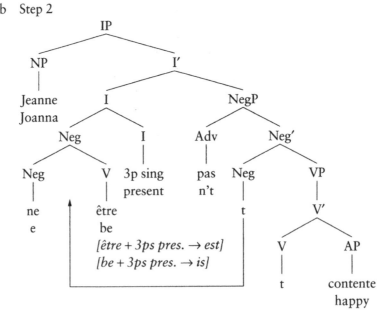

The verb-movement analysis, coupled with the proposal that NegP is located between IP and VP in the phrase structure of the clause, produces just the right result for sentential negation with verbs like copula *be* and *have* (also *can, will, must,* and other modal verbs) in English and their equivalents in Spanish and French.

3.3.3 Strong and weak inflections in I

There is, however, a major difference between Spanish and French on the one hand, and English on the other, when it comes to thematic verbs. Recall that it was suggested in section 2.6.2 that affix lowering occurs with thematic verbs in English, rather than verb raising:

12

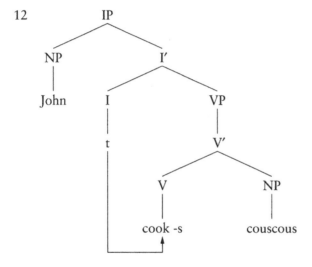

The reasons given there for this were the absence of verb raising with negation and in question formation (where the support verb *do* is required), and with manner and frequency adverbs (like *carefully, often*), which it was suggested are located in the specifier of the VP:

13a John [$_I$ do-es] n't [$_{VP}$ cook couscous]]

  b Does [$_{IP}$ John t [$_{VP}$ cook couscous]]?

  c John [$_I$ t] [$_{VP}$ often cook-s couscous]]

In Spanish and French, by contrast, thematic verbs as well as copulas, auxiliaries and modals move to I, as we can tell from the position of thematic verbs with negation in French:

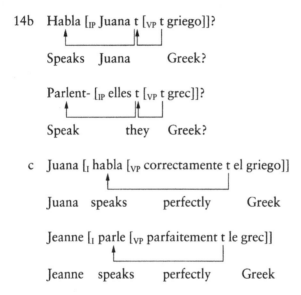

14a   Jeanne [₁ ne parle [_NegP pas t [_VP t grec]]]

Jeanne   neg speaks   not   Greek

Also from the position of thematic verbs in questions and with manner and frequency adverbs in Spanish and French:

14b   Habla [_IP Juana t [_VP t griego]]?

Speaks   Juana   Greek?

Parlent- [_IP elles t [_VP t grec]]?

Speak   they   Greek?

c   Juana [₁ habla [_VP correctamente t el griego]]

Juana   speaks   perfectly   Greek

Jeanne [₁ parle [_VP parfaitement t le grec]]

Jeanne   speaks   perfectly   Greek

So it seems that verb movement affects all verbs in Spanish and French **including thematic verbs**. In English, verb movement affects verbs other than thematic verbs (i.e. copula *be*, auxiliary *be*, auxiliary *have*). Let's say for the moment (following Pollock 1989; Chomsky 1995: chapter 2) that this is a difference between 'strong' inflections in I in Spanish and French and 'weak' inflections in I in English. 'Strong' inflections can support all kinds of verbs including thematic verbs. 'Weak' inflections can only support semantically 'light' verbs (those with little specific conceptual content) like copula *be*, auxiliary *be*, the support verb *do*, etc. I will assume these notions here, and have more to say about them in section 3.6.

3.3.4   Principles and parameters in relation to negation

Consider now how the distributional properties of negation just described might follow from principles and parameters of Universal Grammar. All languages have a syntactic mechanism for expressing sentential negation. It might be claimed, then, that Neg is one of the categories which Universal Grammar makes available, along with N, V, A, P, I. By X′-theory, a principle of Universal Grammar, Neg can project to Neg′ and NegP. There are clearly language-particular differences, however, in the form and position of elements within NegP. Some languages, like French, realize both the head and specifier of NegP overtly (with *ne . . . pas*). Languages like English and Spanish have overt morphemes either in the head position (the *no* of Spanish) or the specifier position (the *n't/not* of English). This is a parameter of variation. A strong hypothesis would be that the location of NegP in the phrase structure of the clause is fixed universally; i.e. NegP, although an optional element of the clause, when present, is always selected as a complement by I, as in (15):

15

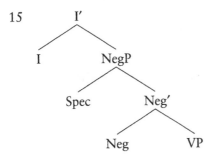

We will adopt this hypothesis.[2] This means that superficial differences in the location of negation in the clause in particular languages must be the effect of other parameters of variation. One such parameter of variation concerns the strength of inflections under I. We have seen that in some languages the inflections are 'strong' and support the raising of all verbs, including thematic verbs. In other languages they are weak and do not support the raising of thematic verbs. This is a parametric difference between languages: inflections under I can be either strong or weak. Since verbs which raise move from VP through Neg to I, the parametric difference in the strength of inflections in I will have an effect on the superficial location of negation. In French, for example, thematic verbs will appear superficially to the left of the negator *pas*; in English thematic verbs will appear superficially to the right of the negator *n't/not*.

3.3.5 Summary of the syntactic properties associated with negation

The syntactic account which I have given of sentential negation in section 3.3 can be summarized as follows:

- Neg projects to Neg′, Neg′ projects to NegP (by X′-theory, a principle of Universal Grammar).
- I (optionally) selects NegP as its complement (a universal selectional property of the category I, we are claiming).
- Spanish *no* and French *ne* are heads, while French *pas* and English *n't/not* are specifiers of NegP (language-specific properties).
- Inflections belonging to the category I can be either 'strong' or 'weak' (a parameter of variation between languages).
- Semantically 'light' verbs (like *be* and *have*) raise to pick up both strong and weak inflections in I.
- Thematic verbs can only raise to pick up strong inflections in I. Weak inflections cannot support thematic verbs. In English negative clauses, the semantically 'light' verb *do* is inserted to carry the weak inflections.
- In Spanish and French the heads of NegP (*no* and *ne* respectively) are carried along by the verb when it moves from VP to I.

3.4   The L2 acquisition of sentential negation as the acquisition of NegP and IP

In section 3.4 it is argued that negation involving *no* in the early English of Spanish and Japanese speakers is a lexical projection, and that when IP is established this opens the way for the acquisition of *n't/not* and the dropping of *no* as the sentential negator. It is also suggested that the establishment of IP gives rise to an increased use of *don't* with thematic verbs. The idea that the word order '*no* + thematic verb' in the early English of Spanish speakers is the effect of the influence of the L1 is discussed and rejected.

Recall that our working assumption is that descriptive generalizations about L2 syntax are indicative of the acquisition of underlying syntactic representations in learners' mental grammars. In the studies by Shapira (1976) and Stauble (1984) it was found that beginner and low intermediate learners of L2 English, both Spanish and Japanese speakers, use a high proportion of *no* + zero copula constructions in contexts where English has an overt copula (*she **no** old*) and a high proportion of *no* + thematic verb constructions (*I **no** call anymore*). This is surprising on two counts: (a) we might expect that because Spanish, like English, has a copula verb in negative contexts this would influence the acquisition of English negation – but it appears not to; (b) although negation in Japanese appears to be realized in a very different way from English and Spanish, the use of negation by Japanese speakers in early L2 English is very like that of Spanish speakers, including use of the form *no* as the sentential negator.

In chapter 2 I speculated that in early L2 English the category I is absent, and that learners only have VP projections in their mental grammars. The data on the

early/low intermediate acquisition of negation is suggestive that sentential negation is acquired before I becomes active. Let's speculate that the reason why *no* is
acquired first is because it is a frequent and salient form in its use in anaphoric
negation (i.e. as a negative response to questions). Once it is in the L2 learner's
lexicon and specified as belonging to the category Neg, if universal principles are
available to L2 learners, by X'-theory it will project to Neg' and NegP. This will
allow learners to construct negative sentences like (16) in the absence of the
category I, where *no* is the head of a NegP, and VP is its complement:

16a [$_{NegP}$ I [$_{Neg}$ no [$_{VP}$ call anymore]]]

  b [$_{NegP}$ She [$_{Neg}$ no [$_{AP}$ old]]]

The interaction between learning a language-particular negative morpheme and
innate knowledge about phrase structure allows L2 learners to construct negative
sentences which are different in structure both from their L1 and from the L2.

Note that at this stage *no* must be the head of NegP. This is incorrect for
target English if *n't/not* is the specifier of NegP, as we have been assuming. Note
further that where cases of *no* and an overt copula appear in learners' productions – *no is too little* – these could not be cases of the copula being in I, given
this analysis. One possibility is that for Spanish speakers who use *no is* it has the
status of an unanalysed form, just as *don't* is treated as an unanalysed form by
many L2 speakers when it is first acquired (see below for discussion of *don't*). As
unanalysed forms, *no is* and *don't* are alternatives to *no*; they all mean 'negator'.
The difference would be that whereas *don't* is acquired on the basis of English
input, *no is* is an unanalysed form directly attributable to the Spanish negative
copular construction *no es (feliz)*, and which selects AP, PP or NP complements.
If *no is* functions as an unanalysed alternative to *no* in copular constructions in
the English of (some) Spanish speakers, we might expect two things: not to find
no is in the grammars of speakers of other languages, and to find considerable
variation between individual speakers of Spanish in the use of *no is*, because it
is an idiosyncratic lexical phenomenon rather than a regular syntactic one. If
we look again at table 3.3, it is significant that none of the low-intermediate
or intermediate Japanese speakers use *no is*. And it seems that there is some
variability between the Spanish speakers in the use of *no is*. Both Anita and
Mona use *no is* in a low number of copular constructions (preferring *no* + ϕ), Joe
uses *no is* in a high proportion of cases, and Josie does not use *no is* at all. These
findings are compatible with the idea that *no is* is a 'chunk' in the early grammars
of some Spanish speakers.

The second stage in the development of L2 English clause structure hypothesized
in chapter 2 was that the acquisition of copula *be* triggered the establishment of
I and its projection IP. The data provided by Stauble's study (table 3.3) seem to

indicate that appearance of copula *be* with negation coincides with the appearance of *n't/not* as sentential negators. For the low-intermediate subjects the majority of negative copular constructions do not involve *be*, and the form *n't/not* is only used by one subject, Tamiko, in a small number of cases. By the intermediate stage there is a much greater use of *be* in negative copular constructions, the use of *n't/not* has risen considerably, and there has been a decrease in the use of *no* (except in the case of Joe).

It is possible that the establishment of IP in learners' mental grammars is directly responsible for the acquisition of *n't/not*. We can explain this in the following way. On the assumption that Universal Grammar is involved in the construction of L2 mental grammars, learners will have access to the universal selectional properties of I, which optionally selects NegP as its complement (see section 3.3.5). This means that when a copular construction is negated, *be* will move from the VP first to Neg, and then to I:

17

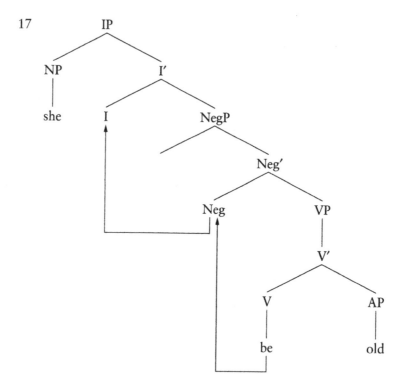

I have suggested that in the pre-IP stage learners treat *no* as the head of NegP. If *no* continues to be treated as the head of NegP when IP becomes established, copula *be* will pick it up on the way up to I, producing ungrammatical negative sentences in English like **She no is old*. Because learners do not encounter such cases in the native English input they receive, they must restrict their use of *no*. A simple solution is to drop *no* as the head of NegP, and to assign *n't/not*, a form for which there will be considerable evidence in the input, to the specifier position of NegP. The specifier position of NegP, which before the establishment of IP was filled by the subject of the sentence, has become newly available because the subject of the sentence is now in the specifier of IP. With *n't/not* in the specifier of NegP, when *be* moves from VP to Neg to I, *n't/not* is left where it is. Hence there is a restructuring in learners' representations for negation as the direct result of the establishment of IP, which is triggered by the acquisition of copula *be*:

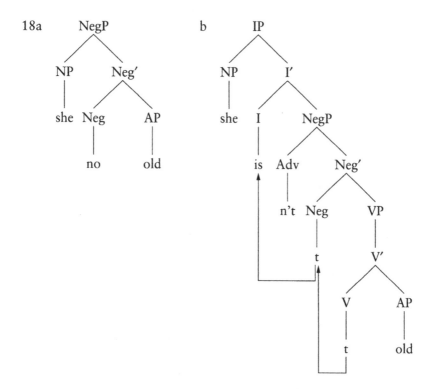

The appearance of *n't/not* also coincides in Stauble's data with a rise in the use of unanalysed *don't* with thematic verbs. At the low-intermediate level only one speaker – Tamiko – uses *be + not* (and only in 11% of cases); *don't* is used by all four speakers, but as a low proportion of the total number of negative contexts (13%, 6%, 24% and 21%). At the intermediate level, increase in the use of *n't/ not* is accompanied by increase in the use of *don't* (Josie 81%, Keiko 90%, Kumi 26% (who also uses analysed forms of *do + not* in a further 46% of cases)).[3] One possible explanation for this increase is that the establishment of the category I, which is triggered by the acquisition of the copula *be*, provides a structural position into which *do* can be inserted:

19

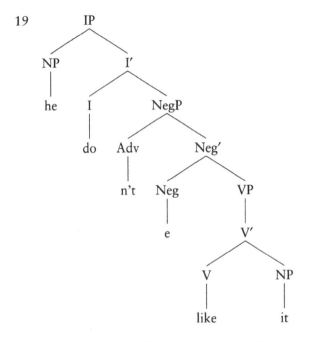

If this is correct, the use of the term 'unanalysed' for *don't* at this intermediate stage is misleading: while *do* is as yet mostly unspecified for tense and agreement, so in that sense is unanalysed (although note that Kumi seems to have analysed *do* for tense), *don't* nevertheless consists of two constituents, [₁ do] and [NegP n't [Neg e]], and so has been 'analysed' by informants.

It is noteworthy that Stauble's Spanish subjects use the support verb *do* with sentential negation involving thematic verbs, rather than raising the thematic verb to I, as they would in their native Spanish. More generally, errors like *I like not it* are almost never found in the L2 English of Spanish speakers (Schumann 1978). It might be argued that this is not so surprising since in Spanish the negator *no* always precedes thematic verbs – *Juana no habla griego*, 'Juana does not speak Greek.' Spanish speakers may simply be transferring a surface property of Spanish into L2 English. However, the use of *do*-support and the non-movement of thematic verbs over negation appears also to be true of French speakers. In French, unlike Spanish, the negator *pas* follows thematic verbs: *Jeanne (ne) parle pas grec*, 'Jeanne does not speak Greek.' We have claimed that, like English *n't*, *pas* is in the specifier of NegP. Unlike English, however, thematic verbs in French raise through Neg to I. If transfer is involved in the case of Spanish speakers, it might also be expected to apply in the case of French speakers. But it turns out that French speakers almost never make such errors. White (1992a) conducted various tests with 97 French-speaking children in intensive ESL programmes in Canada. They were 10- to 12-year-olds and had received no more than two hours per week of instruction in English in the year or two prior to testing, although at the time of testing they were in the middle of an intensive language programme involving approximately five hours per day of communicatively based classroom instruction. White found that on a grammaticality preference task (where subjects are presented with pairs of sentences like *The boys like not the girls/The boys do not like the girls* which they have to compare for grammaticality) subjects correctly rejected thematic verb movement over *n't/not* in over 80% of cases. Moreover, on an oral production task White found that of 1171 English questions produced by the subjects, only 0.17% incorrectly involved thematic verb movement (although thematic verb movement is possible in questions in French: *Aiment-elles les garçons?*, literally, 'Like they the boys?'). These findings suggest that French speakers know from very early on that thematic verbs do not move from the VP to Neg to I in English. We look more closely at why the L1 appears not to influence L2 development in these cases in section 3.6.

3.5 Placing the account in the context of the 'modulated structure building' theory of L2 syntactic development

Section 3.5 summarizes the main elements of the account of sentential negation proposed in this chapter, and assesses the account against the modulated structure building view of general L2 syntactic development introduced in section 2.11.4.

The main elements of our analysis of the L2 development of sentential negation can be summarized as follows:

- L2 learners initially acquire *no* as a lexical item belonging to the category Neg, and we speculated that the reason why *no*, rather than *not*, is acquired initially is because of its frequency and salience in anaphoric negation (i.e. as an answer to a question).

- A principle of Universal Grammar – X'-theory – allows Neg to project, optionally, so that it can take VP, AP, NP complements, and NP specifiers. This allows learners to produce sentences like: $[_{NegP}$ (she) $[_{Neg'}$ no $[_{AP}$ old]]], $[_{NegP}$ (I) $[_{Neg'}$ no $[_{VP}$ like]]]. At this stage, *no* is the head of NegP.

- When copula *be* is acquired, it triggers the establishment of IP, and this forces restructuring of NegP; *no* can no longer head NegP, otherwise it would be carried along when *be* moves through Neg to I, producing ungrammatical strings like: *She no is old.* Restructuring facilitates the acquisition of *n't/not* which is located in the specifier position of NegP, and the form *no* as a sentential negator gradually disappears from learners' mental grammars.[4]

- The establishment of I also creates a position into which *do* can be inserted when negation occurs with thematic verbs, and so increase in the appearance of *be* + *not* coincides with increase in the use of *don't*.

Do these observations follow from the modulated structure building theory of L2 syntactic development which was proposed in section 2.11.4, and which drew ideas from two other theories: 'minimal trees' (Vainikka and Young-Scholten 1994, 1996a, 1996b) and 'full transfer/full access' (Schwartz and Sprouse 1994, 1996)? Recall that in modulated structure building the L2 initial-state grammar consists, in principle, of lexical projections with the structural properties of a learner's L1 grammar, but no functional projections. Functional projections like IP are triggered by positive evidence from the L2 input. Specification of the properties of L2 functional categories proceeds incrementally from local head–complement relations to non-local and specifier–head relations, and properties transferred from the L1 influence the L2 grammar only at points in the develop-mental sequence where the property in question is emergent. We said that the initial-state consists of lexical projections with the structural properties of the L1 'in principle' because restructuring of the initial-state grammar to accommodate L2 input may be very rapid. Thus it may be difficult to detect empirically a pre-functional stage of L1-influenced development. In section 2.11.4 we speculated that the rapidity with which development proceeds depends on the evidence available to the learner and the nature of the transferred properties in question. For example, where head–complement order in lexical projections differs between the L1 and L2, reordering appears to take place very rapidly. Thus, low-intermediate Japanese learners of English studied by Stauble (1984) had apparently already acquired VO order in the English VP, even though Japanese has OV order.

Our analysis of the L2 acquisition of English sentential negation suggests that there is an early lexical stage without IP for both Spanish and Japanese speakers (assuming Neg to be a lexical, rather than a functional, category[5]). Only sub-sequently is IP activated when copula *be* is acquired. This is compatible with modulated structure building. Furthermore, there is little apparent evidence of L1 influence in this development. Spanish (and also French) speakers do not move thematic verbs above NegP to I once I is established, even though in their L1 grammars thematic verb movement to I is obligatory. On the contrary, the establishment of I in their L2 grammars appears to facilitate the acquisition of the English expletive verb *do*, which is a consequence of the failure to move thematic verbs. This apparent lack of L1 influence is surprising in view of the fact that we found empirical evidence in chapter 2 for L1 influence in the develop-ment of other features of I: Spanish speakers initially acquire copula *be* faster than Japanese speakers, and have an advantage in acquiring subject–verb agree-ment in later development. Modulated structure building predicts, following the 'full transfer/full access' account, that there will be L1 influence in principle at the point where the relevant property of the functional category is emergent. This appears not to be the case for the Spanish speakers acquiring English sentential negation. Why might transfer affect the acquisition of copula *be* and specifier–head agreement, but not thematic verb movement from V to I? Perhaps this is another area where there is L1 influence in principle, but the nature of the evidence available to the L2 learner overrides that influence. In considering this possibility it is interesting to compare the results of speakers of languages with thematic verb movement (Spanish, French) learning a language without thematic verb movement (English) with the opposite situation: speakers of a language without thematic verb movement (English) learning a language with thematic verb movement (French). In the next section we consider the results from a study of the early stages of English speakers learning French. It will be found that in this case there is little evidence for an initial lexical phase, and the implications of this finding for modulated structure building will be assessed.

More Advanced Discussion

3.6   Considering verb movement in more detail

Section 3.6 describes evidence that English speakers learning French rapidly establish the category I in conjunction with sentential negation. This contrasts with the claimed lexical phase L2 learners go through in acquiring sentential negation in English. The suggestion is made that the complement selectional properties of Neg, and of heads more generally, are particularly salient for L2 learners in early grammar-building, and this explains the rapid establishment of I with sentential negation in L2 French. The implications of this finding for the modulated structure building theory of L2 development are considered.

So far, the evidence we have considered from the L2 acquisition of English sentential negation has pointed in the direction of an initial lexical phase of grammar-building without IP. If this is a general property of early second language acquisition we would expect that English speakers acquiring French sentential negation would also show an early lexical phase. English has weak inflections in I and lacks thematic verb movement with negation. French has strong inflections in I and thematic verb movement. If English speakers construct mental grammars for French which initially consist only of lexical projections it would be expected that they would go through a stage where they do not raise thematic verbs over negation, just as they would not in English.

Devitt (1992) studied five children acquiring French in a naturalistic environment in France from almost their first contact with the language. His two (Irish) English subjects are of interest here: Marie, aged 11-and-a-half at the time of

Table 3.4 Number of negative sentences by type produced by Marie and Ann over time involving thematic verbs and copula *être*

Sample		1	2	3	4	5	6	7	8	9	10	11
Thematic V												
ne V pas	M	1	10	1	1	9	2	6	5	7	2	10
	A		1	1		1		1	4	1	3	
V pas	M	0	0	0	1	1	0	1	0	4	0	12
	A		0			0		2	5	4	7	
*ne V	M	0	6	0	1	1	0	0	0	0	0	0
	A		0	1		0		0	0	0	0	
*pas V	M				no examples							
	A				no examples							
Copula												
n'est pas	M	0	0	0	0	1	0	0	0	2	0	1
	A		0	0		0		0	0	0	0	
est pas	M	0	0	0	0	0	0	1	0	0	0	1
	A		0	0		0		0	0	0	1	
*n'est					no examples							
*pas est					no examples							

M = Marie; A = Ann
* = ungrammatical for native speakers
NB: Sampling of Ann's development was at less frequent intervals than for Marie
Source: Based on Devitt 1992

arrival in France, and Ann aged 8. Neither had studied French at school prior to arrival, and had visited France before for only a few weeks' holiday. Both attended normal French schools on arrival. Devitt made a number of recordings of their naturalistic productions as they interacted with French-speaking peers over the first few months of development. His results for their use of sentential negation with thematic verbs are given in table 3.4. Recall that sentential negation in French consists of two particles *ne ... pas*; tense-marked thematic, copula, auxiliary and modal verbs all move through Neg to I, so that they are to the left of *pas* on the surface; *ne*, though, is often omitted in spoken French:

> 20a Elle (n') aime pas le film   'She doesn't like the film'
>   b Elle (n') est pas contente   'She isn't happy'
>   c Elle (n') a pas vu le film   'She didn't see the film'
>   d Elle (ne) peut pas venir   'She can't come'

If the subjects go through an early phase of non-verb movement, they should produce constructions like *(Elle) n'aime le film, (Elle) pas aime le film* (both ungrammatical for native speakers). For purposes of comparison, Marie and Ann's use of negation with copula *être* is also given.

As can be seen from the results, while there are a small number of cases of *ne V* in the earliest productions of Marie, which might suggest non-movement of thematic verbs over negation, at the very earliest stages Marie also produces *ne V pas* constructions where there is thematic verb movement. Ann produces only one example of *ne V*, and by sample 9 her predominant pattern for sentential negation with thematic verbs is *V pas*. There are no examples from either subject of the **pas V* pattern.

These English speakers, then, appear to establish I in their mental grammars almost immediately to host a moved thematic verb when the clause is negated. (Recall that we are assuming that, universally, Neg selects VP as its complement, and I selects NegP. If thematic verbs appear to the left of negation, they must have moved to I – see section 3.3.2.) Either the modulated structure building claim that L2 learners start acquisition with lexical projections is wrong, or there is something about the nature of French sentential negation which allows learners to move beyond the lexical phase of grammar-building immediately. This is where the notion that L2 learners start with lexical projections 'in principle' is relevant: although their initial-state grammars consist of lexical projections 'in principle', specific factors in the L2 input may allow them to establish functional projections in practice very early on. Let us pursue this second line of argument.

In section 3.3.3 it was said that thematic verb movement in native French and Spanish is the effect of strong inflections belonging to the category I, while inflections belonging to the category I in English are weak and there is no thematic verb movement. Does this mean that from the outset English speakers can establish that the inflections in French I are strong? Not necessarily, apparently. Although English speakers acquiring L2 French appear to acquire thematic verb movement with sentential negation very quickly, they have more difficulty acquiring the fact that thematic verbs move in other contexts, for example over manner and frequency adverbs, or over floated quantifiers, as illustrated in (21):

21a Il décroche vite le récepteur
   He lifts quickly the receiver
   'He quickly lifts the receiver'
   (*vite* = manner adverb)
 b Les journalistes aiment tous une vedette
   The reporters love all a star
   'Reporters all love a star'
   (*tous* = floated quantifier)

A study by Hawkins et al. (1993) compared the performance on a grammaticality judgement task of two groups of adult English-speaking learners of L2 French. One group consisted of 75 intermediate-level learners, the other of 29 advanced learners. The grammaticality judgement task was a set of French sentences involving both the grammatical and ungrammatical placement of the negative particle, an adverb and a floated subject quantifier, as well as other types of sentences. While it was found that both the intermediate and advanced learners were accurate at locating thematic verbs with negation (as expected if Devitt's findings are generalizable to English speakers learning French),[6] it was also found that a significant proportion of the intermediate subjects (40%) allowed both the French and the English location of thematic verbs with manner/frequency adverbs (while the advanced group behaved like native speakers), and an even greater proportion (60%) allowed the English location of thematic verbs with floated quantifiers (a tendency shared by 36.2% of the advanced subjects). This suggests that it may not be the 'strong inflections' of French I which English-speaking learners acquire when they initially acquire thematic verb movement with negation.

Similar results have been obtained by White and Trahey in a series of studies (White 1990/91, 1991, 1992a; Trahey and White 1993; Trahey 1996) with French-speaking learners of L2 English. The subjects were, like those described earlier in section 3.4, 10- to 12-year-olds in grades 5 and 6 in Quebec schools who, following one or two years of normal instruction in English (2 hours per week), were participating in an intensive programme (5 hours per day) of communicatively based English instruction over a 5-month period. One of the things White and Trahey were interested in was the development of the non-movement of thematic verbs in English with manner/frequency adverbs. As we have seen, French and English contrast in this respect:

22a Normand lit souvent des romans
   b *Normand souvent lit des romans

23a *Norman reads often novels
   b Norman often reads novels

After three months of the intensive programme, subjects underwent a two-week period of 'specialized' exposure to English. For one group this was form-focused instruction on question formation, for another it was form-focused instruction on adverb placement (White 1990/91, 1991, 1992a – form-focused instruction consists of explaining the particular property in question, and then giving learners follow-up activities). For yet another group it was exposure to naturalistic materials which contained a 'flood' of examples of appropriate adverb placement (Trahey and White 1993; Trahey 1996).[7] In each case the effect of the 'specialized' exposure was tested via a number of different types of task: oral production, a grammaticality preference task (where subjects rate pairs of sentences for their relative grammaticality), a grammaticality judgement task, sentence manipulation (where subjects are presented with one type of sentence and have to form another). Subjects were given these tests before they received the 'specialized' exposure (pre-testing), immediately after the instruction (immediate post-testing) and then a year later (delayed post-testing).

The results of the tests as they relate to the location of thematic verbs with adverbs can be summarized as follows: On the pre-tests subjects had a strong preference for the French location; i.e. for sentences like *Norman reads often novels*. On the immediate post-tests there was an interesting difference between the group which had been instructed on adverbs and the group which had been given the 'flood' input. The instructed group showed a strong preference for the English location; i.e. for sentences like *Norman often reads novels*. The 'flood' group allowed both the French location and the English location. On the delayed post-tests a year later, however, both instructed and flood groups were allowing both locations. For example, the scores, after a year, on the grammaticality preference task were (Trahey 1996: 125 and 131):

Instructed group: French location 68.2%   English location 67.3%
Flood group: French location 73.3%   English location 79.1%

These results show that although French speakers are quick to eliminate thematic verb movement with negation from their L2 grammars for English (see section 3.4), they are not quick to do so with manner/frequency adverbs. At the pretest, the French property of thematic verb movement still seems to be operative. After 'specialized' exposure learners come to allow the non-movement of thematic verbs, but this appears to be optional for them. The instructed group show only a temporary elimination of verb movement with adverbs. The implication would seem to be that learners have not acquired the 'weak inflections' of English I, even though they establish early on that thematic verbs do not move to I with negation. If they had acquired this property, they would disallow verb movement under any circumstances. This finding confirms the similar finding with English-speaking learners of French that acquisition of thematic verb movement to I with negation does not imply acquisition of the 'strong inflections' of French I.

We are beginning to see that there is something particular about sentential negation, rather than the movement or non-movement of thematic verbs per se, which allows L2 learners of English and French to acquire its properties very early on in acquisition. In the case of English speakers learning French, negation allows them to establish an IP projection quickly for thematic verbs to move to, and in the case of Spanish and French speakers, English negation prevents them from transferring thematic verb movement from their L1 grammars into their L2 grammars. However, this knowledge does not generalize to other aspects of thematic verb movement. English speakers continue not to move thematic verbs over adverbs and floated quantifiers into intermediate and advanced stages of acquisition. French speakers continue to move thematic verbs over adverbs into intermediate stages of acquisition. How are we to account for this?

White (1992a) accounts for her French subjects' development by drawing on a proposal by Pollock (1989) to split IP into two separate projections: an Agreement category which projects to AgrP, and a Tense category which projects to TP. Pollock's rationale for splitting IP in this way is, among other things, a difference in the movement of thematic verbs with negation and adverbs in finite and non-finite clauses in native French. While thematic verbs cross both negation and adverbs in finite clauses in native French, in non-finite clauses they move optionally over adverbs, but do not cross negation:

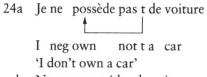

24a   Je ne possède pas t de voiture

        I   neg own   not t a car
        'I don't own a car'

  b   Ne pas posséder de voiture en banlieue rend   la vie difficile
        Neg not to-own   a car   in suburbs makes the life difficult
        'Not to own a car in the suburbs makes life difficult'

  c   *Ne posséder pas t de voiture en banlieue rend la vie difficile

25a   Elle paraît souvent t triste aujourd'hui

        She seems often   t sad   nowadays
        'She often seems sad nowadays'

  b   Souvent paraître triste, c'est rare
        Often   to-seem sad   it is rare
        'Often to seem sad is rare'

  c   Paraître souvent t triste, c'est rare

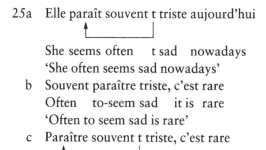

Pollock suggests that the structure underlying these sentences is as follows (omitting irrelevant details):

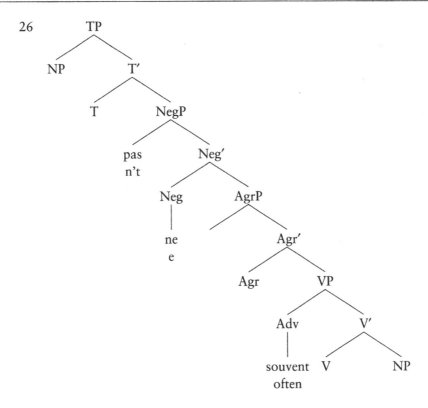

In French, where Tense is finite its inflection is strong, and so is the inflection in Agr. This causes thematic verbs to move to Agr to Neg to T to pick up the inflections. Where Tense is non-finite, its inflection is weak, although the inflection in Agr remains strong. Hence in French non-finite clauses thematic verbs cannot move to T and so do not cross negation. They can, however, move to strong Agr and cross adverbs (optionally, for reasons which need not concern us here). In English the inflection in Agr is weak, whether tense is finite or not, and this prevents thematic verbs from moving either in finite or non-finite clauses.

White's (1992a) account of the behaviour of the French speakers learning English that she studied is that they discover early on that the English inflections in T are weak, but fail to discover, at least initially, that the inflections in Agr are also weak. Hence in their L2 English they do not move verbs over negation, but they do move them (optionally) over adverbs to Agr, just as they would in non-finite clauses in French. In other words the influence of what White calls the 'short movement' property of French on their mental grammars for English is persistent, while the influence of 'long movement' is minimal.

While an ingenious solution for the French L1-to-English L2 case, this account does not, unfortunately, work in the other direction: English L1-to-French L2. The fact that English speakers acquire thematic verb movement with negation in

French finite clauses very rapidly means, on the above account, that they have acquired 'long movement'. The implication would necessarily be that they have also acquired 'short movement' (i.e. movement over manner/frequency adverbs and floated quantifiers), since when heads move, they move in steps from one head to another, and by hypothesis cannot 'skip' intervening head positions (see section 3.3.2). But as we saw above, acquisition of thematic verb movement with negation does not imply that learners have also acquired thematic verb movement with adverbs and quantifiers.

It seems rather that in some sense both English and French speakers acquire the **position** of thematic verbs **relative to Neg and its projection** very early on. This is unconnected, however, with the acquisition of the strength of the inflections in I, at least initially (or the strength of the inflections in T and Agr, given Pollock's split-I proposal). Suppose we continue, following modulated structure building, to assume that early grammar-building is concerned in principle with lexical projections. But suppose further that L2 learners are sensitive, also from very early on, to the **complement selectional properties of heads**. That is, they notice the kinds of complements which can follow particular heads. I already speculated in section 2.10 that the reason why copula *be* and auxiliary *be* appear early on in the elaboration of English I is because they enter into local selectional relations with their complements. When L2 learners of English acquire a negative morpheme, like *no*, X'-theory allows them to project this morpheme, optionally, to Neg' and NegP. Thus *no* will be able to take complements such as [$_{VP}$ like the film], [$_{AP}$ too old], [$_{NP}$ my brother] in their grammars:

27a no [$_{VP}$ like the film]
  b no [$_{AP}$ too old]
  c no [$_{NP}$ my brother]

By the same token, when L2 learners of French acquire the negative morpheme *pas*, X'-theory will allow them, in principle, to project this to Neg' and NegP, and *pas* should be able to take complements equivalent to English like [$_{VP}$ aime le film], [$_{AP}$ trop vieux], [$_{NP}$ mon frère]:

28a pas [$_{VP}$ aime le film]
  b pas [$_{AP}$ trop vieux]
  c pas [$_{NP}$ mon frère]

However, the possibilities made available in principle by X'-theory are tempered by the sensitivity of the learners to the complement selectional properties of Neg in the input they receive. In the case of VP complements containing thematic verbs, L2 learners of English will encounter input which appears to confirm their 'lexical projection' analysis for sentential negation. That is, encountering examples like *(I) don't like the film* reinforces their representations for lexical projections where thematic verbs follow Neg. By contrast, L2 learners of French will encounter examples in the input like *(Je n') aime pas le film* which conflict with their lexical representation for sentential negation. Here the thematic verb precedes Neg, rather than following it. If they are sensitive to the complement selectional properties of heads early on, they will recognize the conflict: in French finite clauses Neg does not select a VP complement with a filled head: *[NegP pas [VP aime le film].

The question then is what effect this recognition has on learners' mental grammars. If grammar-building is guided by Universal Grammar, as we have been assuming, learners will expect that NegP is selected as a complement by I (see section 3.3.4 where it was proposed that NegP is always selected as a complement by I). If L2 learners of French notice that Neg does not select a VP complement with a filled head, and that the thematic verb is located to the left of NegP, Universal Grammar will force them to project I above NegP as the position to which thematic verbs can move to satisfy Neg's complement selectional requirements.

Notice that because the thematic verb is forced to move specifically by the complement selectional requirements of Neg, there is no implication that the thematic verb need move in the context of other categories. Manner/frequency adverbs and quantifiers have been assumed so far to be located in the specifier position of VP (but we will review this assumption in chapter 8). Because they are in a specifier position, there is no head–complement selectional relation between them and the thematic verb.

The thrust of this speculation is that the strength of inflections in I in French (which is what is assumed to drive thematic verb movement for native speakers) is not what causes thematic verbs to move above NegP to I in the early grammars of English learners of French. If the selectional requirements of Neg are what is involved, then there is one case where this difference between native speakers and L2 learners might possibly show up: the location of thematic verbs with respect to negation in non-finite clauses. Recall that in native French thematic verbs do not move above NegP in non-finite clauses (see example (24c)). This is because, it was proposed, non-finite tense inflections are weak. If L2 learners of French in early stages of acquisition move thematic verbs in response to the complement selectional properties of Neg, rather than because of the strength of inflections in I, they may overgeneralize this possibility to constructions like (24c). In the study already cited by Hawkins et al. (1993), four sentences were included in the grammaticality judgement task which involved non-finite thematic verbs with sentential negation: two grammatical and two ungrammatical sentences. Hawkins et al. found that their intermediate subjects accepted ungrammatical *ne V pas in 39.3% of cases. This compared with an acceptance rate of only 8.6% by the advanced group of learners and 4.1% by the native-speaker control group. These results are compatible with the view that learners might initially be guided by the head–complement selectional requirements of Neg. Clearly the advanced subjects have acquired the fact that thematic verbs do not move across NegP in non-finite clauses in French. It may also be that the intermediate subjects are already on their way to acquiring this knowledge, given that they accept the moved verb in under 40% of cases.

If this account is along the right lines, in the acquisition of L2 French the complement selectional property of Neg (the requirement that it not be followed by a VP with a filled head) triggers the early establishment of I. In the acquisition of L2 English, Neg does not have this triggering function because its complement selectional requirements are compatible with the early lexical projections which constitute the initial state of mental grammar-building. Learners encounter examples of native English which conform with their lexical projections. Rather, in English, it is copula *be* which seems to be the trigger for the establishment of I, following an early stage of lexical projections, as I argued in chapter 2. These proposals are beginning, then, to give some content to the idea that while the initial stages of L2 grammar-building consist of L1-influenced lexical projections 'in principle', input may lead to rapid restructuring of specific properties. Evidence in the input for head–complement selectional relations appears to be salient, in some sense, for L2 learners and can potentially trigger movement from the complement of a lexical head to a higher functional head.

Once I is established, it appears that it is subject to L1 influence. Evidence for L1 influence on I was already found in chapter 2, where we saw that Spanish speakers have two advantages over Japanese speakers: they are quicker to acquire copula *be* in the early stages, and they are quicker to establish subject–verb agreement in later stages. We attributed this advantage to the presence of these phenomena in Spanish and their absence in Japanese. In the case of French speakers learning English, once I is established it appears as if the 'strength' associated with inflections in the French I is transferred to learners' representations for English I; while French speakers do not allow the thematic verb to move to I in English in the presence of negation (because English *n't/not* selects a VP with a filled V head), they do allow the verb to move in the absence of negation, because the I category has the feature 'strong', transferred from French. In other words, it may be that 'strong' is the default setting for I in the L2 English grammars of French speakers. This means that they will allow movement over manner/frequency adverbs and floated quantifiers. We would have to claim, then, that optionality in these cases results because learners 'become aware' from exposure to examples like *Norman often reads novels, Reporters all love a star,* etc., that English allows cases where the thematic verb does not raise; but this would be idiosyncratic knowledge, not encoded in the feature specification for I. With continued exposure to English this knowledge may be generalized, perhaps even leading to the acquisition of the appropriate strength of the inflections belonging to English I.

Similarly, in the case of English speakers learning French, once I is established it appears as if the 'strength' associated with inflections in the English I is transferred to learners' representations for French I. Thus, while English speakers move thematic verbs over Neg to I very early in development, they continue not to move the verb in other contexts. 'Weak' I may then be the default setting in their L2 grammars. Again, with continued exposure to French they come to recognize that French finite thematic verbs also move to I over manner/frequency adverbs, and this may lead to their acquiring the appropriate strength of the inflections of English I.

3.7   Summary of chapter 3

The main points made in chapter 3 are the following:

- Spanish and Japanese learners of English appear to go through an early phase in the acquisition of sentential negation during which their grammatical representation consists of a lexical projection of the category Neg. Neg is typically instantiated by the morpheme *no* at this stage, a salient and frequent item in the input learners get, we presumed. They only establish a representation for I in English when they acquire copula *be*. Once I is established, it appears to pave the way for the acquisition of *n't/not* as sentential negators, and for the acquisition of so-called 'unanalysed' *don't*, although it was suggested that the term is misleading: while *do* is unanalysed in the sense that it is unspecified for tense and agreement, *don't* appears to consist of two constituents: [I do] and [NegP n't [Neg e]] (sections 3.2–3.4).
- A rather surprising lack of L1 influence was found in the development of these speakers' knowledge of sentential negation in English. This was surprising because such influence had been found in the acquisition of verb morphology (chapter 2), and our 'working theory' of L2 syntactic development predicts that there will be L1 influence in principle, although such influence can in practice be overridden by the availability of certain kinds of data in the input to the L2 learner. To investigate this possibility we compared Spanish and French speakers learning English with English speakers learning French. We found that whereas L2 learners of English establish a lexical projection for sentential negation initially, English-speaking learners of French appear to establish I in their mental grammars for French sentential negation almost immediately (sections 3.5–3.6).
- It was argued that the rapidity with which English speakers establish I, and move thematic verbs over negation to I, in L2 French was not because they had acquired the knowledge that inflections belonging to French I are strong

(the presumed reason for verb movement in native French). Rather, learners are sensitive to the complement selectional properties of heads. This means that early on English speakers notice that Neg selects an empty-headed VP complement, and Universal Grammar then forces them to establish an I category above NegP to host the moved thematic verb (since we are assuming that I universally selects NegP as its complement, when NegP is present). Once I is established, it is subject to L1 influence in cases other than sentential negation. Thus the mental grammars of French speakers continue to allow thematic verbs to move above manner/frequency adverbs and floated quantifiers, and the mental grammars of English speakers continue to allow thematic verbs not to move above manner/frequency adverbs and floated quantifiers. With exposure to the L2, learners come to recognize whether verb movement is possible in these other contexts too, and this is possibly the result of their acquiring the appropriate strength of the inflections belonging to the category I (section 3.6).

3.8   Exercises

Exercise 1: Determining the categorial status of modal verbs (section 3.3)

We have not discussed in the text the categorial status of modals like *can, must, may, will*, but this is important for determining their distribution with sentential negation. There seem to be three possibilities to consider:

(a)   They belong to the category 'verb', are located in the VP, and like thematic verbs they do not move to I to pick up tense and agreement inflections.
(b)   They belong to the category 'verb', are located in the VP, and like *be* and *have* they raise to I to pick up tense and agreement inflections.
(c)   They are like neither thematic verbs nor *be* and *have*. Modals belong to the category I and are inserted directly under I in clause structure.

Which of the above proposals do you think is most consistent with the following set of data?

1a   She must have left early
     They must have left early

b   *She has must left early
    *They have must left early

2a   The computer has been sold
     The computers have been sold

 b   *The computer mays have been sold
     The computers may have been sold

3a   To be able to solve these problems is remarkable
     To have left early would have been boring

 b   *To can solve these problems is remarkable
     *To will leave early would be boring

Exercise 2: Evaluating the account of the development of L2 sentential negation against new data (sections 3.4, 3.5)

(Material used in this exercise is reprinted with the permission of Cambridge University Press)
The following data were collected by Robison (1990) during an interview with a Spanish speaker from El Salvador, given the pseudonym 'Rogelio', who had been living in the United States for several years. The table compares Rogelio's production of utterances involving sentential negation with the forms native speakers would have used had they produced those utterances. Are these data consistent with the account given of the development of sentential negation in L2 English in sections 3.4–3.5 of this chapter? Can you say anything about the use by Rogelio of the modal verb *can* with sentential negation? (Try to relate this use of *can* to the proposal you opted for in your answer to Exercise 1.)

Forms of English sentential negation produced by a native speaker of Spanish (R), compared with the forms a native speaker (NS) would have produced in the same contexts. Number of tokens used by R are given in brackets (based on Robison 1990: 321)

Copula *be*					
NS *form*	*is not*				
R's forms	is not (x3)				
	is no (x1)				

Aux/modal					
NS *form*	*can't*	*isn't*	*wasn't*	*weren't*	*haven't*
R's forms	can't (x6)	don't (x1)	don't (x1)	no (x1)	don't (x3)

Thematic verbs					
NS *form*	*don't*	*doesn't*	*didn't*		
R's forms	don't (x44)	don't (x6)	don't (x11)		
	no (x2)		no (x1)		

Exercise 3: predicting likely L2 development (section 3.6)

(a) *Never*, like *n't/not*, is a negative morpheme which can have scope over the whole clause: *Sally has never done her shopping on Saturdays* (= 'It has never been the case that Sally does her shopping on Saturdays'). The syntactic distribution of *never*, however, is different from that of *n't/not*. On the basis of examples like the following, where would you locate *never* in a tree diagram of the clause?

> 1 Tim never works on Friday evenings
> Tim has never worked on Friday evenings
> Tim is never going to pass his exams

> 2 Tim doesn't ever work on Friday evenings
> Tim hasn't ever worked on Friday evenings

> 3 Tim $\begin{Bmatrix} \text{seldom} \\ \text{often} \end{Bmatrix}$ works on Friday evenings
> Tim has $\begin{Bmatrix} \text{seldom} \\ \text{often} \end{Bmatrix}$ worked on Friday evenings

(b) To my knowledge, no study has investigated the acquisition of *never* as a sentential negator in L2 English. In French, the equivalent negator (*jamais*) behaves just like the French negator *pas*, and unlike *never*. (The preverbal *ne* is often absent in informal spoken French – ignore it for the purposes of this exercise):

> 4a Tim (ne) travaille $\begin{Bmatrix} \text{jamais le} \\ \text{pas} \end{Bmatrix}$ vendredi soir
> Tim Neg works $\begin{Bmatrix} \text{never} \\ \text{not} \end{Bmatrix}$ the Friday evening
> 'Tim $\begin{Bmatrix} \text{never works} \\ \text{doesn't work} \end{Bmatrix}$ on Friday evenings'

> b Tim (n') a $\begin{Bmatrix} \text{jamais} \\ \text{pas} \end{Bmatrix}$ travaillé le vendredi soir
> Tim Neg has $\begin{Bmatrix} \text{never} \\ \text{not} \end{Bmatrix}$ worked the Friday evening
> 'Tim $\begin{Bmatrix} \text{has never worked} \\ \text{hasn't worked} \end{Bmatrix}$ on Friday evenings'

On the basis of your answer to the first part of this exercise, and your reading of section 3.6 in this chapter, what predictions would you make about how French speakers might develop mental representations for the use of *never* as a sentential negator in English?

Exercise 4: Evaluating research design (section 3.6)

In section 3.6 it was argued that the complement selectional properties of the category Neg are salient for L2 learners and override the effects of their transferring the 'strength' of inflections in Infl from their L1 into their L2. Thus English speakers appear to acquire movement of thematic verbs above negation in L2 French very early on, even though in English there is no verb movement, and transfer of the strength of the inflections in English Infl would dictate no verb movement. Similarly, French speakers learning L2 English do not allow English thematic verbs to move above Neg (correctly), even though transfer of the strength of inflections belonging to Infl in French would dictate that they should. The comparison groups of learners we used to provide evidence for this claim were:

- 10- to 12-year-old French speakers who were tested on their English after one to two years of normal classroom instruction and after three months of an intensive programme of exposure which included two weeks of 'specialized exposure' (studied by White and Trahey – see section 3.6 for details);
- 18- to 22-year-old English-speaking intermediate to advanced university learners of French, with at least seven years of classroom instruction in French (studied by Hawkins et al. – also see section 3.6 for details).

Do you see any problems with the choice of comparator groups which may undermine the validity of the evidence? (Think about age and length of exposure to the L2.) Could you design a better study to provide clearer evidence bearing on the claim that the complement selectional properties of heads like Neg trigger the early acquisition of syntactic structure in second languages? What would be an ideal pair of comparator groups to test this claim (in terms of age, type and length of exposure to the L2)?

Exercise 5: Evaluating the account of the development of L2 sentential negation against more new data I (sections 3.4, 3.5, 3.6)

Recall that in Spanish the sentential negator *no* appears to the left of both auxiliary and thematic verbs: *Juana no es feliz*, 'Juana isn't happy'; *Juana no habla griego*, 'Juana doesn't speak Greek'. In French there are two morphemes involved in sentential negation which appear on either side of the tense-inflected verb (although the first of these is optional and often absent in spoken French): *Jeanne (n') est pas contente*, 'Jeanne isn't happy'; *Jeanne (ne) parle pas grec*, 'Jeanne doesn't speak Greek'. Trévise and Noyau (1984) collected data on the use of sentential negation in L2 French by a group of native speakers of Spanish (from Latin America) living in France. The box below presents brief biographical information about five of the subjects, three women (F1–F3) and two men (M1–M2), followed by details of their use of three different ways of realizing sentential negation (expressed as %) during an interview where they were asked to talk about themselves. Two of the ways of expressing sentential negation are grammatical in native French: __ *pas* (i.e. *Jeanne parle pas grec* – found in informal spoken styles); *ne* __ *pas* (i.e. *Jeanne ne parle pas grec* – used in formal spoken and most written styles). The third is not possible in native French: *ne* __ (i.e. **Jeanne ne parle grec*).

How compatible are the data from these Spanish speakers with the account given in section 3.6 of how English speakers acquire French negation? Given the biographical information, do you think that the kind of contact a speaker has with French might have some bearing on how the data should be interpreted?

Biographical and linguistic data from five Spanish-speaking learners of French (based on Trévise and Noyau 1984)

Subject	Length of residence	Age	Occupation	Level of education
F1	3 years	30	University teacher	Taking a Master's degree in France
F2	3½ years	32	Spanish teacher	BA degree + 9-month course in French
F3	3 years	40	Print office worker	Primary school
M1	3½ years	49	Print office worker	Primary school + 3-month course in French
M2	3 years	41	Print office worker	Primary school + 3-month course in French

Type of sentential negation used (%)

	__ *pas* %	*ne* __ *pas* %	*ne* __ %
F1	33	66	1
F2	34	64	2
F3	35	45	20
M1	1	67	32
M2	51	38	11

Exercise 6: Evaluating the account of the development
of L2 sentential negation against more new data II
(sections 3.4, 3.5, 3.6)

(Material used in this exercise is reprinted with the permission of Camilla Bardel)
Bardel (1997) investigated the development of verb morphology and sentential
negation in L2 Italian by native speakers of Swedish. In main clauses in Swedish
the negator *inte* 'n't/not' follows the tensed verb, just like the negator *pas* in
French (all examples from Bardel):

   1a Maria läser inte boken
       Maria reads n't book-the
    b Maria har inte läst boken
       Maria has n't read book-the

In Italian, by contrast, the sentential negator *non* appears in main clauses in
front of any tensed verb, just like Spanish:

   2a Maria non legge il libro
       Maria n't reads the book
    b Maria non ha letto il libro
       Maria n't has read the book

Data were collected from six Swedish-speaking adults who live in Italy. All had
some knowledge of Italian before arrival, and all were taking Italian lessons in
Italy. Bardel collected data from mostly spontaneous dialogues at intervals over
one year. Compare her findings for two of the informants, Stina and Karl, collected at five sampling sessions separated each by three months, in terms of the
development of verb morphology and the use of different kinds of sentential
negation; Bardel considered a verbal morpheme to be present (+) if it was not a
repeated form and was used appropriately at least once.

Use of verb morphology and types of sentential negation (with number of tokens) in the L2 Italian of two native speakers of Swedish, sampled at three-monthly intervals (based on Bardel 1997)					
Informant: Stina	Sample				
	1	2	3	4	5
Verb morphology					
present tense	+	+	+	+	+
past participle	−	−	+	+	+
aux + past participle	−	−	+	+	+
imperfect	−	−	−	+	+

Informant: Stina (*cont.*)	Sample				
	1	2	3	4	5
Negation					
neg + thematic verb	3	8	8	17	22
neg + modal	0	0	0	1	0
neg + aux	0	0	0	0	2
neg + copula	0	0	0	0	0
thematic verb + neg	0	0	1	0	1
modal + neg	0	0	0	0	0
aux + neg	0	0	1	0	0
copula + neg	0	0	3	1	11

Informant: Karl	Sample				
	1	2	3	4	5
Verb morphology					
present tense	+	+	+	+	+
past participle	+	−	−	+	+
aux + past participle	−	−	+	+	+
imperfect	−	−	−	−	+
Negation					
neg + thematic verb	0	9	4	6	16
neg + modal	0	0	0	0	0
neg + aux	0	0	0	0	0
neg + copula	0	0	0	1	0
thematic verb + neg	0	0	1	1	3
modal + neg	0	0	0	0	0
aux + neg	0	0	0	0	0
copula + neg	0	1	4	1	9

Assuming that use in production by these speakers reflects development of their underlying competence, what conclusions would you draw from these data about

(a)   the presence of the functional category IP in their grammars;
(b)   the influence of the L1 on the development of their knowledge;
(c)   the representation that these informants have for the Italian copula and Italian thematic verbs?

Exercise 7: Assessing whether L2 learner performance reflects underlying grammatical knowledge (section 3.6)

(Material used in this exercise is reprinted with the permission of Arnold Publishers)
In English, while manner adverbs cannot occur between thematic verbs and their

direct objects (1a), they can occur between some thematic verbs and their prepositional complements (1b):

    1a   *Mary drank quickly her coffee
     b   Mary ran quickly to school

The account we gave of (1a) is that thematic verbs do not raise to Infl because
inflections in English are weak. One analysis of (1b) assumes equally that the
thematic verb has not raised (as is clear in sentences like *Mary didn't run quickly
to school*), that *quickly* is initially located in a VP-final position and that the
prepositional complement has undergone optional movement to the right: *Mary
[ran to school quickly]* → *Mary [[ran t_i quickly] to school$_i$]*.

    White (1991) conducted an experiment to look at the effects of explicit instruc-
tion about adverb position in English on the competence of low-intermediate
L2 learners (L1 French-speaking adolescents). One group (of 82 students) was
given two weeks' instruction on adverb placement in sentences like (1a), but not
on sentences like (1b) (the Adverb group); another group (of 56 students) was
instructed on an entirely different property: English question formation (the Question group). Informants' knowledge of adverb placement was tested before
instruction and five weeks after instruction. Consider the choices they made on a
preference task where it was necessary to decide if, in pairs of sentences like

    2a   Harry quickly runs to his house
     b   Harry runs quickly to his house

both are right, both are wrong, or only one is right. There were 28 pairs relating
to adverb placement in the test. The box below gives the results, in percentages,
including the performance of a control group of monolingual native speakers of
English of the same age:

Preference task – manner adverbs: SAdvVPP versus SVAdvPP in percentages (based on White 1991: 149)					
Choices from pairs like (2)	Native Controls (n = 26)	Adv Group (n = 82) pre-test post-test		Q Group (n = 56) pre-test post-test	
	%	%	%	%	%
Only (2a)	5.77	10.19	76.62	11.21	18.52
Only (2b)	7.69	63.69	5.19	42.06	24.07
Both	86.54	18.47	11.04	28.97	50.93
Neither	0	4.46	5.84	11.21	4.63
Don't know	0	3.18	1.3	6.54	1.85

Observe that, prior to instruction, the Adverb Group mostly accepted sentences like (2b), but after instruction they mostly accepted (2a). Do you think that instruction about the impossibility of manner adverbs in sentences like (1a) has allowed the Adverb Group to establish that inflections under English Infl are weak? (For discussion of the issue by L2 researchers themselves, see Schwartz and Gubala-Ryzak (1992), and the response by White (1992b).)

Exercise 8: Discussion topic

Why is it important to determine the function of grammatical forms in an L2 learner's mental grammar independently of the way they function in the grammars of native speakers of the target language?

3.9   Further reading

For recent discussion of the significance of negation in establishing whether functional categories are present early on in L2 acquisition or not see Tomaselli, A. and Schwartz, B. 1990: Analysing the acquisition stages of negation in L2 German: support for UG in adult SLA. *Second Language Research* 6, 1–38; Eubank, L. 1996: Negation in early German-English interlanguage: more 'valueless features' in the L2 initial state. *Second Language Research* 12, 73–106; Prévost, P. and White, L. 2000: Missing surface inflection or impairment in second language acquisition? Evidence from tense and agreement. *Second Language Research* 16, 103–33. For a counter view that functional categories are not involved in the acquisition of negation in French and German, see Meisel, J. 1997: The acquisition of the syntax of negation in French and German: contrasting first and second language development. *Second Language Research* 13, 227–63.

The acquisition of thematic verb movement, or lack of it, continues to be a topic of considerable interest to L2 researchers. The classic studies are: White, L. 1990/91: The verb-movement parameter in second language acquisition. *Language Acquisition* 1, 337–60; White, L. 1992a: Long and short verb movement in second language acquisition. *Canadian Journal of Linguistics* 37, 273–86; Schwartz, B. and Gubala-Ryzak, M. 1992: Learnability and grammar reorganisation in L2A: against negative evidence causing the unlearning of verb movement. *Second Language Research* 8, 1–38; White, L. 1992b: On triggering data in L2 acquisition: a reply to Schwartz and Gubala-Ryzak. *Second Language Research* 8, 120–37.

Recent discussion of the topic can be found in Lardiere, D. 1998b: Dissociating syntax from morphology in a divergent L2 end-state grammar. *Second Lan-*

guage Research 14, 359–75; Beck, M.-L. 1998a: L2 acquisition and obligatory head movement: English-speaking learners of German and the local impairment hypothesis. *Studies in Second Language Acquisition* 20, 311–48; the introduction and Part I of Flynn, S., Martohardjono, G. and O'Neil, W. (eds) 1998: *The Generative Study of Second Language Acquisition.* Mahwah, NJ: Lawrence Erlbaum Associates.

Notes

1   Notice that when a category x moves and adjoins to another category y, the phrase created is still a category of type y: when V moves to Neg, the category created is still a Neg, when Neg moves to I, the category created is still an I:

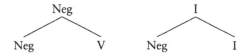

2   The 'universally fixed location' view is argued for in Zanuttini (1996), but from a slightly different perspective. There appears to be no consensus in the literature, however, about how negation should be represented. For discussion of the issues see Haegeman (1995), Zanuttini (1997).

3   The data from the Spanish speaker Joe are again out of line with the other intermediate subjects. Although Joe is using *don't* with 60% of thematic verbs, he uses *no* in the other 40% of cases, and *not* only appears in 18% of the cases involving copula *be*.

4   This means that for a time, L2 speakers are alternating between forms like *She no old/ She isn't old*. Optionality of this sort, and the causes of optionality in L2 speakers' mental grammars, have become the focus of considerable interest in recent work on SLA. We will discuss this along with other issues of current debate in SLA research in chapter 8.

5   That Neg is a lexical rather than a functional category is not self-evident. It is often treated as a functional category because it displays some of the typical properties of functional categories: the morphemes belonging to Neg are a 'closed class' (it is normal to create new nouns or verbs in English, but not new negators, tense markers, agreement markers and so on); *not* has an unstressed variant *n't*, and phonological 'weakness' is a characteristic of functional categories; although Neg has a meaning, it is not the same kind of specific conceptual content associated with nouns, verbs, adjectives and other lexical categories. Note, though, that our proposal is that there is a shift in L2 development from the use of *no* to the use of *n't/not*. This could be construed as a shift in learners' mental grammars from treating negation lexically to treating it functionally, once the functional category I emerges.

6   Julia Herschensohn (personal communication) has data from English-speaking tutored learners of French (first year college students in the United States) which indicates that they also place thematic verbs consistently to the left of *pas* very early on.

7   One of the aims of these studies was to investigate the effects of different kinds of input on L2 syntactic development.

4 The Second Language Acquisition of Word Order

4.1 Introduction

At the end of chapter 3 we arrived at the view that there is a difference for second language learners, at least in the early phases of acquisition, between the basic geometry of structural representations, and the more detailed specification of functional categories. For example, while English learners of French apparently project an IP above NegP quite early on in order to provide a position to host thematic verb movement, and L2 learners of English acquire early on the fact that an IP must project above VP to provide a position to host a copula verb, the more detailed specification of I (for properties like the strength of inflections, tense and subject–verb agreement) takes longer to establish, and is subject to influence from the first language.

In this chapter we will look more closely at word order in languages and its acquisition by L2 learners. Word order is the result of the interplay between the projection of structure from particular categories, as determined by X′-theory, and the feature specifications of particular functional heads like I, and so it is a fruitful area in which to consider grammar-building. An assumption made by some linguists is that each language has its own basic word order from which other orders in the language are derived. For example, the basic word order of transitive clauses in native French is one where the verb is adjacent to and followed by its complement, as illustrated in (1a). The order which surfaces when the verb is finite, however, is one where the verb has moved to I because I hosts strong inflections (section 3.3.3). And where the complement is an unstressed pronoun, this is an inflection-like element which moves and attaches to V (section 1.6):

1a   Jeanne [$_I$ agrmt, tense] [$_{NegP}$ pas ne [$_{VP}$ souvent mang- [$_{NP}$ des huîtres]]]
      Jeanne   not neg   often   eat   oysters

 b   Jeanne [$_I$ [$_{Neg}$ ne [$_V$ mange$_i$]]] [$_{NegP}$ pas t$_i$ [$_{VP}$ souvent t$_i$ [$_{NP}$ des huîtres]]]
      Jeanne   neg eats   not   often   oysters
      'Jeanne doesn't often eat oysters'

 c   Jeanne [$_I$ [$_{Neg}$ ne [$_V$ les$_j$ mange$_i$]]] [$_{NegP}$ pas t$_i$ [$_{VP}$ souvent t$_i$ t$_j$]]]
      Jeanne   neg them eats   not   often
      'Jeanne doesn't often eat them'

(We will encounter a semantic rationale for basic word orders in chapter 5.) Other linguists even go so far as to claim that all languages have the *same* basic word order, and that the surface differences between them are the result of different feature specifications in functional categories like I which force constituents to move in some languages but not others, or allow some categories to delete in some languages but not others (Kayne 1994; Zwart 1997). If this view is correct, then Universal Grammar provides a universal basic order of constituents, and surface differences between languages are the result of parametric variation in the feature specification of categories like I.

We will look in this chapter at how L2 learners acquire these properties; whether development can be characterized as the effect of modulated structure building, and what influence the L1 has on that development. We start with some well-known studies of the acquisition of German word order. In section 1.7 we briefly described a number of studies of L2 German which found that speakers of Romance languages (Italian, Spanish and Portuguese) and English appear to acquire word order in German clauses in the same way. We start by considering this case in more detail, firstly recalling the main features of the location of verbs in German clauses.

4.2   Location of verbs in German

Section 4.2 describes informally some basic properties of word order in tensed main and embedded clauses in German.

In declarative main clauses in German, where the verb is in a simple tense form, word order is similar to English Subject-Verb-Object (SVO), although adverbs can appear between thematic verbs and their objects, suggesting that verb raising is involved:

2   Johann kaufte heute ein Buch
    John   bought today a   book
    'John bought a book today'

But if the verb is in a compound form (is in an auxiliary + past participle construction, is accompanied by a modal verb, or is a verb with a particle), the nonfinite part of the compound must appear at the end of the clause:

3a   Johann **hat** heute ein Buch **gekauft** (auxiliary + past participle)
     John   has today a   book bought
     'John bought a book today'

 b   Johann **wird** heute ein Buch **kaufen** (modal + infinitive)
     John   will today a   book buy
     'John will buy a book today'

 c   Johann **nahm** heute ein Buch **auf** (verb + particle: 'aufnehmen')
     John   picked today a   book up
     'John picked up a book today'

If, for the purposes of emphasis or other stylistic effect, a constituent other than the subject is moved to the front of the clause, the finite part of the verb must move into second position in the clause, pushing the subject into third position. This phenomenon is known by linguists as the **verb second** or **V2** effect. Note that in English when *today* is moved to the front there is no effect on the word order of the rest of the clause:

4a   Heute **hat** Johann ein Buch **gekauft**
     Today has John   a   book bought
     'Today John has bought a book'

 b   Heute **wird** Johann ein Buch **kaufen**
     Today will John   a   book buy
     'Today John will buy a book'

 c   Heute **nahm** Johann ein Buch **auf**
     Today picked John   a   book up
     'Today John picked up a book'

In embedded (i.e. subordinate) clauses the picture changes again. Here simple and compound verb forms must appear at the end, with the finite part of the verb the final element:

    5a Sie weisst, dass [Johann heute ein Buch **gekauft hat**]
        She knows that John   today a   book bought has
        'She knows that John has bought a book today'

     b Sie weisst, dass [Johann heute ein Buch **kaufen wird**]
        She knows that John   today a   book buy   will
        'She knows that John will buy a book today'

     c Sie weisst, dass [Johann heute ein Buch **aufnahm**]
        She knows that John   today a   book up-picked
        'She knows that John picked up a book today'

To summarize, a number of the features of the clause interact to determine the location of verbs in German:

- Whether the verb is finite (tense-bearing) or non-finite.
- Whether the clause is a main clause or an embedded clause.
- The precedence relations between constituents (whatever comes first in a main clause, the finite verb must come second).

4.3   The second language acquisition of verb location in German

Section 4.3 describes four stages which L2 learners of German appear to go through in acquiring the appropriate location of verbs in tensed clauses.

Several studies of the acquisition of German as a second language have found that L2 learners go through stages in acquiring the location of verbal elements. Clahsen and Muysken (1986) describe a series of stages which a group of (adult) speakers of L1 Italian, Spanish, Portuguese and Turkish go through. The data on which their analysis is based were drawn from a number of sources: in a study by Klein and Dittmar (1979) there were 48 Italian and Spanish foreign workers from whom data were collected via a single interview; in another study (Clahsen et al. 1983) the productions of 45 adult Italian, Spanish and Portuguese foreign workers were studied both cross-sectionally and longitudinally; in a third study (Clahsen and Muysken 1986: 109), data were collected from interviews with 10 L1 Turkish subjects, aged 14–16.

Italian, Spanish and Portuguese are like English in having basic Subject-Verb-Object (SVO) word order both in main and embedded clauses. In these languages there is typically no V2 effect in a main clause when an adverb or other non-subject noun phrase is moved to the front (although specific fronted adverbs may allow V2, just as they do in English: *Before her stood a policeman; Never had they seen anything like it*). Turkish, by contrast, is a rigid Subject-Object-Verb (SOV) language, which means that the finite verb is always in clause-final position, both in main and embedded clauses.[1]

With some idealization of the data, Clahsen and Muysken propose that the subjects studied proceed through the following stages in acquiring German word order:

I An SVO stage

Subjects initially produce main clauses like:

> 6 Ich studieren in Porto
> 'I study in Porto'
> (Example from Clahsen and Muysken (1986) – the inflection on the verb is non-native; in native German the form would be *studiere*)

They also show no evidence either of putting non-finite parts of verbs at the end of the clause, or of the V2 effect when they use adverbs in clause-initial position. Rather, they produce sentences like:

> 7 Vielleicht andere Kollege sagen . . .
> 'Perhaps other colleague say . . .'
> (Example from Clahsen and Muysken 1986)

II A finite verb/non-finite verb separation stage

In a second phase, the subjects begin to locate non-finite parts of verbs at the end of the main clause, but there is no evidence yet for V2:

> 8 Wir haben drei Feuer gesehen
> We have   three fires   seen
> 'We saw three fires'
> (Example from DuPlessis et al. 1987)

At this stage they are still producing examples like (7).

III   A verb second stage

In a third phase, subjects begin to place the finite verb in second position when constituents other than the subject appear in first position in main clauses:

9   Vielleicht wissen viele Leute nicht
    Perhaps   know many people not
    'Perhaps many people don't know'
    (Example from DuPlessis et al.)

IV   A verb-final-in-embedded-clauses stage

Throughout stages I–III learners appear to continue with SVO order in embedded clauses, producing sentences like:

10   Wann wir **fahren** hier in Deutschland, drei Feuer gesehen
     When we   drive   here in Germany,   three fires   seen
     'When we came back to Germany, we saw three fires'
     (Example from Clahsen and Muysken)

Native speakers of German would put the finite verb in the first (embedded) clause in clause-final position: *Als wir nach Deutschland fuhren* . . . In a final stage, subjects distinguish between main and embedded clauses, and place finite verb forms at the end of embedded clauses, as in the target pattern.

As noted in section 1.7, similar patterns of development have been observed by other researchers studying other learners (Pienemann 1989; Ellis 1989). We have, therefore, a descriptive generalization: the location of finite and non-finite verb forms in tensed clauses in German is acquired in systematic stages, at least by speakers of Romance languages, Turkish and English. (We consider whether there is L1 influence on acquisition in section 4.6.) The pattern of development goes from an early stage of SVO not involving verb separation, to verb separation, to verb second, to verb final in embedded clauses. One can imagine other orders. For example, a pattern where verb second is acquired before verb separation, or where verb final is the initial hypothesis rather than SVO. There clearly is some underlying rationale to the pattern which requires explanation. The earliest attempt to provide such an explanation by linking the descriptive facts to the idea that L2 learners build a mental grammar for the L2 using the constructs provided by Universal Grammar is a study by DuPlessis et al. (1987). To understand their account we need to extend the Inflection Phrase (IP) analysis of clauses which we have been developing in chapters 2 and 3.

4.4 The category Complementizer, its projection CP and the structure of German clauses

Section 4.4 justifies the postulation of a category C, and its projection CP, and illustrates how this constituent is involved in producing the verb separation, verb second and verb final effects in German.

There are good reasons to assume that embedded clauses are not just IPs (Inflection Phrases), but are C(omplementizer) P(hrase)s. Consider the following examples:

11a   They wonder [if [John will cook couscous]]
   b   They knew [that [Anthea liked to party]]
   c   They were keen [for [her to finish the book by Christmas]]

The embedded clauses in each case are introduced by an item which serves to link the verb in the main clause to its clausal complement. Linguists have proposed that the structure of the bracketed embedded phrases in (11) is as follows:

12

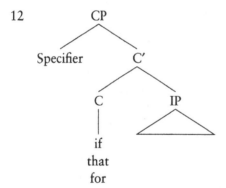

Notice that the structure of CP is similar to the structure of the other phrases we have considered (NP, VP, PP, AP, IP, NegP). It consists of a head (the complementizer C) which projects to C' (C-bar: a phrase consisting of the head C and an IP complement) which then projects to a CP (consisting of a C' and a specifier – the specifier of CP in the examples of (11) is empty).

4.4.1 The basic word order of German

Many current proposals for accounting for German word order extend the CP analysis to main clauses. (See Travis 1984, for an early account. Because the

DuPlessis et al. (1987) study assumes Travis's account, we initially present that analysis here, although it will be modified subsequently.[2] For a review of studies of word order in the Germanic languages see Schwartz and Vikner, 1996.) These proposals suggest that the basic or initial position of the verb in the VP is not to the left of its complement, as it is in English, but to the right. The initial structure which underlies a sentence like (2) *Johann kaufte heute ein Buch* is that in (13):

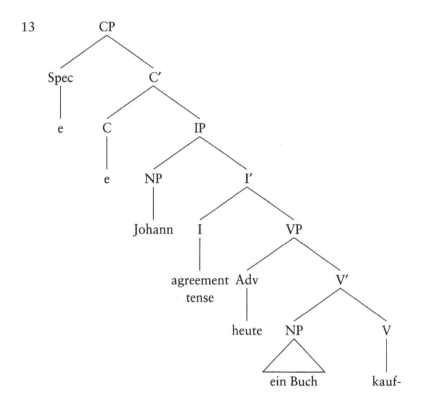

But if left like this, of course, the sentence would be ungrammatical. To produce the right *surface* sentence *kauf-* has to be associated with the agreement/ tense morphemes of I. This requires that the verb move to I so that it ends up in the right position in the surface sentence. Movement of agreement and tense down to *kauf-* would give the wrong result: *Johann heute ein Buch kaufte*. Hence, assuming that what gives rise to thematic verb movement is the fact that inflections in I are strong (see section 3.3.3), German has strong inflections. Movement of the verb in (13) produces the derived structure in (14) (where t stands for 'trace'):

14

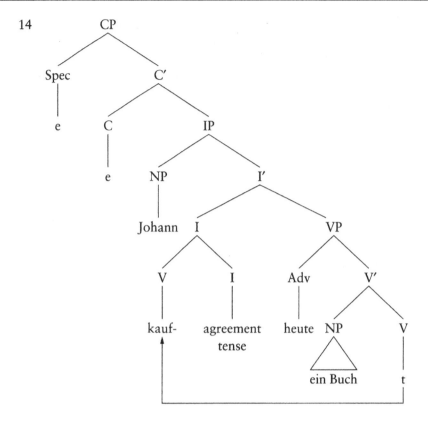

4.4.2 'Verb second' in main clauses

Now consider what happens if *heute* 'today' is moved to the front of the sentence
for stylistic reasons. Recall that whatever comes first in a German main clause,
the verb must come second: *Heute kaufte Johann ein Buch*. To derive this sentence, the proposal goes, the initial structure is again (13). But this time *heute*
moves to the specifier position of CP, an empty position in the tree. Unlike *kauf-*,
which **adjoined** to a position already filled by the agreement and tense morphemes,
the movement of *heute* to the specifier of CP is a **substitution** operation; C is
empty, and the adverb *heute* substitutes for it. The verb *kauf-* again moves to I,
but it moves a second time as well to the head of CP. Again, because C is empty,
this second movement involves substitution, rather than adjunction. Both *heute*
and *kauf-* leave traces behind in the positions they have moved from. The initial
structure (13) therefore gives rise to the derived structure (15), through these
movement operations. To distinguish the trace left by *heute* and the traces left by
kauf-, we add subscript letters showing which trace belongs to which moved
constituent. These are called **indices**:

15

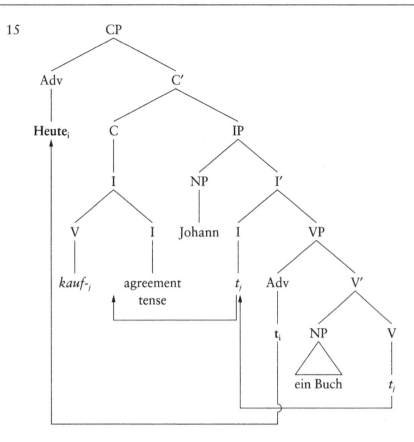

4.4.3   The 'verb separation' effect

The above analysis also produces the correct results when non-finite parts of verbs are present. Take a sentence like:

16   Heute **hat** Johann ein Buch **gekauft**
     Today has John   a   book bought
     'Today John bought a book'

Assuming that [gekauft hab-] is, like English [hav- bought], a verb with a verbal complement – [$_V$ [$_{VP}$ ein Buch gekauft] hab-], [$_V$ hav- [$_{VP}$ bought a book]] – and assuming the same underlying initial verb-final structure, *heute* moves to the specifier of CP, *hab-* moves first to I, and then the [V + I] constituent created moves to C, producing the 'verb separation' effect:

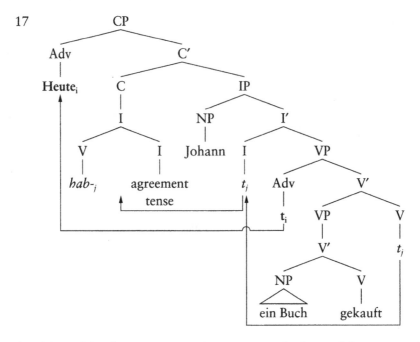

Even the object of the clause may sometimes move to the front of the sentence for stylistic reasons. This also produces the 'V2 effect', and is equally describable within this framework:

18a   Ein Buch hat Johann heute gekauft

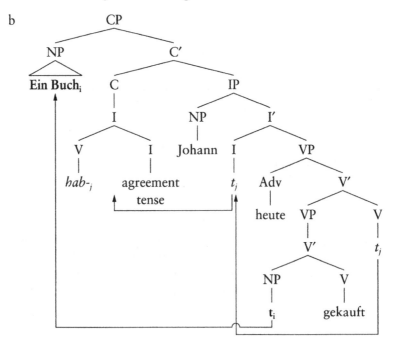

4.4.4 Embedded clauses

Now consider embedded clauses. In embedded clauses, the tensed verb appears in clause-final position, and an overt complementizer fills the C position. The basic structure of a sentence like (19a) would be as in (19b) (where the structure of the upper IP is simplified for illustrative purposes):

19a Sie weisst [dass [Johann heute ein Buch kaufte]]
     She knows that John   today a   book bought
     'She knows that John bought a book today'

19b

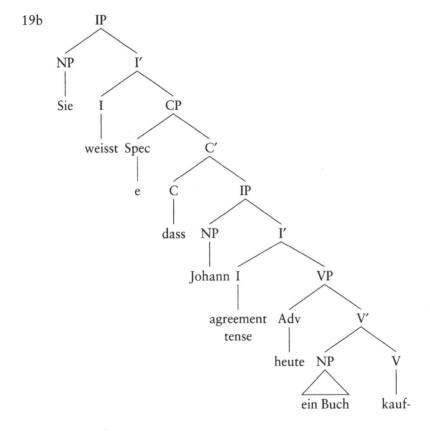

Because *dass* already fills the C position, and I-to-C movement is a substitution operation (rather than adjunction) I cannot move to C in this case. But why does the verb remain in the VP, rather than moving to I as it does in main clauses? The spirit of the answer that Travis (1984) and DuPlessis et al. (1987) give is that *dass* is in a position to govern I, effectively cancelling the strength of the inflections in I, and allowing the verb to remain in its basic word order position. The agreement/tense inflection then lowers to V.[3]

4.5 Explaining the second language acquisition of German word order as grammar-building

Section 4.5 describes an analysis of the L2 development of German word order where learners' early representations consist of head-initial IP and VP, to which a CP layer of structure is subsequently added.

Now we know the main word order properties of German clauses, we are in a position to consider the proposals of DuPlessis et al. (1987) about how the acquisition of these properties by L2 learners gives rise to the stages of development described in section 4.3. DuPlessis et al. propose that in early stages of learning German, where L2 speakers are producing sentences like (20a), they have underlying representations for these sentences like (20b):

20a　*Heute Johann hat gekauft ein Buch
　　　Today John　has bought a　book
　　　(where * means 'non-native German')

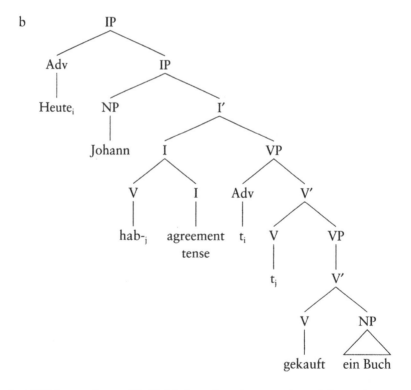

Note that (20b) contains an IP. If this is truly representative of the earliest stages of acquisition, it would be incompatible with the claim made in chapter 2 that L2 learners of English start out with lexical projections without IP. Three possibilities appear to arise: (a) the claim in chapter 2 is wrong, and early L2 grammars can include functional categories; (b) an IP projection in early L2 German is triggered by positive evidence from the L2 (e.g. by evidence for the selectional requirements of a head category, as I argued in section 3.6 that the selectional requirements of Neg in French trigger the early L2 acquisition of thematic verb movement to I); (c) the first stage of Clahsen and Muysken's account does not represent the earliest stage in the L2 acquisition of German. These issues are discussed in section 4.6.

DuPlessis et al. observe that there are some striking differences between the configuration in (20b) and the proposed structure of similar clauses in native German (see example (17) in section 4.4.3). The adverb *heute* is **adjoined** to IP, whereas in native German it **substitutes for** the specifier of CP. In fact, no CP is present in the configuration in (20b). The verbal complex [v hat [vp gekauft . . .]] precedes its complement, *ein Buch*, whereas in native German the verb/verbal complex follows its complement. A possible reason for these differences could be transfer of the word order properties of the L1 into the L2 grammar for German. Romance languages, including Italian, Spanish and Portuguese, are Subject-Verb-Object languages, like English, rather than Subject-Object-Verb languages like German, and they also allow adverbs to adjoin to IP to produce Adv-S-V-O, unlike German, (although this would not explain why speakers of Turkish, an SOV language, also apparently go through this SVO stage). We will return to these matters in section 4.6.

In the second stage of development learners begin to separate finite from non-finite parts of verbs and locate the non-finite parts at the end of the sentence. DuPlessis et al. suggest that this results directly from learners reordering V and its object complement. The effect on the configuration in (20b) is minimal: (20b) becomes (21):

21

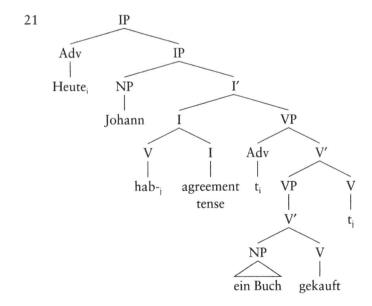

The verb *hab-* still moves to I to pick up the agreement and tense inflections, but this time from a VP-final position. The non-finite *gekauft* is left in a VP-final position. Thus a change in the ordering of constituents in L2 learners' mental representations for VP gives rise to the 'verb separation' effect in their productions.

In the third stage of development learners begin to place the finite verb in second position in the clause when a constituent other than the subject is in first position. DuPlessis et al. propose that this stage is the result of learners activating a CP projection above IP. They move non-subject constituents to the specifier position of CP, and the verb in I moves to C[4]:

22

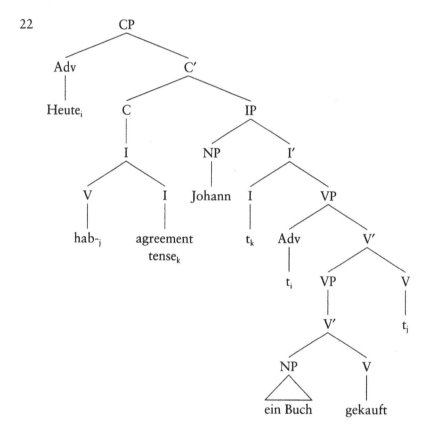

Up to the third stage of development the structural properties underlying verb separation and verb second are apparently overgeneralized to embedded clauses. This is incorrect in native German where all parts of the verb appear in clause-final position in embedded clauses. DuPlessis et al. explain this as the failure of learners up to this point to build into their grammars the fact that a filled C (e.g. filled by the complementizer *dass* 'that' or other overt complementizers) governs I, effectively cancelling the strength of the inflections in I (see section 4.4.4), and allowing the verb to remain in its clause-final position. The fourth stage occurs when learners recognize this possibility.

4.6 Refining the account of grammar-building in the acquisition of German word order

Section 4.6 considers some questions raised by DuPlessis et al.'s account of the development of German word order. It discusses evidence presented by Vainikka and Young-Scholten (1994, 1996a, 1996b) to suggest that early representations are in fact lexical, rather than functional, and that IP and CP develop subsequently. Also considered is the extent to which properties of the L1 determine development, and the extent to which properties of the input, like the complement selectional requirements of heads, might facilitate development.

Let us summarize at this point the grammar-building account of the L2 acquisition of German word order proposed by DuPlessis et al.:

- Speakers of Romance languages (Italian, Spanish, Portuguese) and Turkish start with a representation of the clause which can be characterized as SIVO (Subject-Infl-Verb-Object).
- In a second phase SIVO is restructured to SIOV, and this produces the verb separation effect.
- In a third phase a CP layer of structure is added to SIOV: CSIOV. In the case where a non-subject constituent (e.g. an adverb or the object) is fronted, it moves to the specifier of CP, and the verb, which has already moved to I to pick up the agreement/tense inflection, moves on to the head C.
- In a final stage, where CSIOV is an embedded clause, L2 learners acquire the fact that C is able to govern I, cancelling the strength of its inflections. This allows the verb to remain in clause-final position.

On a descriptive level this is a perfectly adequate account of the developmental behaviour of Romance- and Turkish-speaking L2 learners of German described in section 4.3, and is formulated within the spirit of a grammar-building approach to the explanation of L2 development. However, it poses a theoretical problem and leaves some questions about the observed L2 developmental pattern unanswered. The theoretical problem is why embedded C in German should have the ability to govern I, neutralizing its strong inflections. Proposing this property certainly helps to explain why L2 learners might overgeneralize SIVO word order to embedded clauses, but it is not clear whether it has any role to play within Universal Grammar other than explaining this case. Schwartz and Tomaselli (1990), following a proposal made for German by a number of linguists, starting with den Besten (1983), have suggested a simple modification to the account which is equally adequate descriptively, and which eliminates the need for C to govern I in this way. If, in native German, both VP and IP are head final, as illustrated in (23), then at the fourth stage L2 learners can be said to reorder I and its VP complement in their mental grammars, changing SIOV to SOVI:

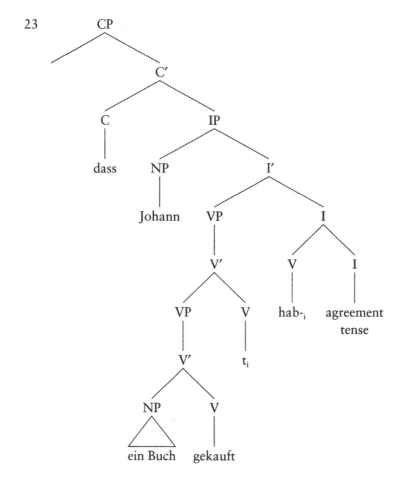

The possibility that I may follow, rather than precede its complement, is allowed within Universal Grammar in a general way by X'-bar theory. This means that no special mechanism is required to account for the final stage of L2 grammar-building as it is in the account of DuPlessis et al. Note that this change means that in main clauses every sentence of native German must be a case of verb second, with I moving to C even where the subject comes first in the sentence, as illustrated in (24). If I did not move to C, the tensed verb would end up in clause-final position in main clauses, which is not the case:

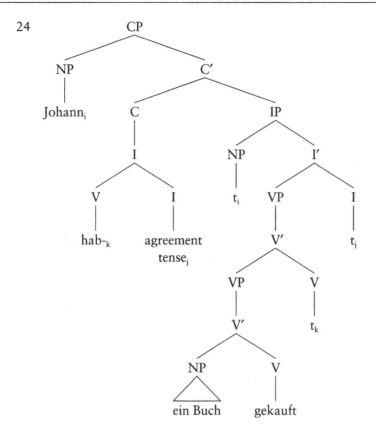

The unanswered questions about word-order development in L2 German are these:

- Is I really present from the earliest stages, especially since it was argued in chapter 2 that I is initially absent in the acquisition of L2 English?
- What is the role of the L1 in development?
- Why does verb separation emerge before verb second?
- Why does restructuring from I–VP order to VP–I order appear last in the sequence of development?

To address some of these questions Vainikka and Young-Scholten (1994, 1996a, 1996b) studied rather more closely the development of L2 German in speakers of SOV L1s – in particular speakers of Turkish and Korean – and compared that development with the development of L1 speakers of Italian and Spanish. Turkish and Korean have head-final VP and IP both in main and embedded clauses, as German does, but I does not move to C in main clauses, unlike German. So the tensed verb appears in final position in every clause, including main clauses (examples from Vainikka and Young-Scholten 1994):

Turkish

25a Helmut [_{VP} simdi Istanbul-da Türkçe ögren-iyor]
   Helmut   now Istanbul-part Turkish learn-part
   'Helmut is now learning Turkish in Istanbul'

Korean

b Helmut-ka [_{VP} Peter-eke chaek-ul   chu-oss-ta]
   Helmut-part   Peter-part book-part give-part-part
   'Helmut gave the book to Peter'
   (part = particles of various kinds irrelevant to the discussion)

Vainikka and Young-Scholten examined data collected from 11 Turkish and 6 Korean adult learners of German during a 45- to 90-minute test session. During the session a range of elicitation tasks were used (cartoon-strip description, picture description, description of an action, a grammaticality judgement test). Subjects ranged in age from 28 to 60, had had little or no formal instruction, had arrived in Germany after the age of 20, and had been resident in Germany for between one-and-a-half and 24 years. These data were compared with cross-sectional and longitudinal data from Spanish and Italian speakers. Since a number of the subjects who were studied cross-sectionally had spent a considerable period of residence in Germany, Vainikka and Young-Scholten used implicational scaling on four syntactic properties in order to determine the stage of development which each subject had reached in the acquisition of German. (See section 2.5 for discussion of implicational scaling.)

On this basis there were three Korean/Turkish speakers and four Italian/Spanish speakers deemed to be at the earliest stage of L2 development. Vainikka and Young-Scholten observed the following in the data from these informants:

(i)   Where utterances involved a verb and an object, for the Korean/Turkish speakers 98% of these displayed OV order, while only 19% of the Italian/Spanish speakers' utterances displayed OV order.

(ii) There was little overt evidence for an IP projection: informants used almost no auxiliary verbs; inflections marking tense, person and number were typically absent; where time adverbs and negation were present, finite thematic verbs typically appeared to the right of them, whereas in native German finite thematic verbs appear to the left, as illustrated in (26) (examples from Vainikka and Young-Scholten 1996a: 18):

26a Für mei Junge **immer** vo   mir schimpfe (Antonio – Spanish)
   for my boy   always from me scold
   'My boy always scolds me'
   Mein Junge schimpft_i immer mit mir t_i   (Native German)

b   Nein en matina   nix essen   (Bongiovanni – Italian)
    no   in morning not eat
    'I don't eat in the morning'
    Nein, morgens esse$_i$ ich nicht(s) t$_i$ (Native German)

These observations led Vainikka and Young-Scholten to conclude that one question raised by the work of DuPlessis et al. (is I present from the earliest stages of the acquisition of L2 German?) receives a negative answer. They argue that learners start with bare lexical projections for VP and NegP, just as I argued in the case of the early acquisition of English clauses. It may be that the informants investigated by DuPlessis et al. (essentially those of Clahsen and Muysken's (1986) study) had already progressed beyond the early lexical stage.

Interestingly, there were four slightly more advanced Romance speakers in their sample who, while showing no evidence of an IP, changed the word order in the VP from VO to OV, producing verb-final matrix clauses in 64% of their utterances. If this is representative of L2 learners of German whose L1s have SVO order, it means that early on they notice that German is a verb-final language, and integrate this knowledge into their early (lexical) mental grammars. This would not only be compatible with the claim we made in connection with French that L2 learners are sensitive to the complement selectional requirements of heads, but would set the scene for verb separation to be the first target-like word order property to emerge. If, following a stage where clauses are VPs with OV word order, I is triggered to the left of the VP, this would produce the verb-separation effect.

This is exactly what Vainikka and Young-Scholten (1996a: 20) propose. They suggest, though, that at first this I does not have the full specification required by target German: 'learners project an underspecified IP-level functional projection . . . providing a position for a raised verb, as well as a position for modals and auxiliaries' (1996a: 20). The evidence to support this claim is that when L2 speakers start to use I-related morphemes (auxiliaries and modal verbs) they do so in a position preceding the VP; and when there are no auxiliaries, thematic verbs move to the left of an object complement, an adverb or Neg, suggesting that an I is present. But at the same time there is little evidence of tense or person/number agreement inflections on the verbs under I, suggesting that I is underspecified.

The second claim that Vainikka and Young-Scholten make about the development of the functional projection IP is that there is **no L1 influence** on that development. According to them, the L1 only influences the structural properties of early lexical projections. Once functional projections like IP develop, that development is identical across L2 learners. This does not accord, however, with our earlier finding (section 2.10) that Spanish speakers acquire copula *be* and subject–verb agreement at a faster rate than Japanese speakers, and this appears to be connected with the absence of the relevant properties in Japanese. To support their claim, Vainikka and Young-Scholten firstly note that when I develops in the L2 grammars of their subjects, it is invariably to the left of its VP complement, and not to the right as it is in Korean/Turkish. Secondly, in their six most advanced Korean/Turkish speakers 'agreement is correct over 90% of the time' (1996a: 23), even though in Korean there is no subject–verb agreement. If this is correct, then it poses a serious problem for the 'modulated structure-building theory' of L2 development, which suggests that there will be L1 influence *in principle* at all points of L2 grammar-building in both lexical and functional projections. However, it is the influence *in principle* which is important. I have claimed that other factors may override such influence (the nature of the input that learners receive, and the nature of the syntactic property in question). The I–VP relation is one where an I head selects a VP complement, and I have already argued (section 3.6) that head–complement selectional relations are highly salient in early L2 acquisition. It may be, then, that the L1 VP–I order of Korean/Turkish speakers' grammars is quickly overridden by evidence from German main clauses, which superficially appear to have I–VP order. In the case of the advanced Korean learners of German, who use subject–verb agreement as accurately as the Turkish speakers, it is not clear whether they went through an earlier stage where the Turkish speakers acquired agreement more quickly. Recall that 'modulated structure building' proposes that L1 influence becomes evident at the point where the relevant property develops in the L2 grammar. Turkish speakers may have had an early advantage in this area which disappeared over time. The evidence reported in Vainikka and Young-Scholten's studies does not enable us to address this question. In the absence of relevant evidence, though, we must note that this is a potential problem for our 'working theory'.

Given this account, the third and fourth questions raised earlier (why does verb separation emerge before verb second, and why is restructuring from I–VP order to VP–I order last to develop) receive one kind of answer. Since verb second involves the movement of I to C, an I category (to which finite verbs move, creating the 'verb separation' effect) must be in place before movement to the higher C category is possible. And since the verb-final property of embedded clauses is the effect of a filled C blocking such I-to-C movement, I must already be moving to C for such movement to be blocked.

4.7   Summary of the grammar-building account of the acquisition of German word order

Section 4.7 summarizes the main features of development in the L2 acquisition of German word order, and relates that development to the 'modulated structure building' theory of general second language syntactic development which was proposed in chapter 2.11.4.

The work of DuPlessis et al. (1987), Schwartz and Tomaselli (1990) and Vainikka and Young-Scholten (1994, 1996a, 1996b) seems to lead to the following analysis of the development of word order in the L2 German grammars of native speakers of SVO and SOV languages:

- In the earliest stage of acquisition representations consist of lexical projections (VP, NP, NegP, and so on). The location of the verbal head of VP in relation to its object complement appears to be influenced by the native language of the L2 learner. Initially, speakers of Romance languages adopt a predominantly VO order for German, while speakers of Korean/Turkish adopt a predominantly OV order. Romance speakers quickly restructure their representations for VP to OV order, however, presumably on the basis of salient examples of OV order in the German input they receive. Hence we have more evidence that initially L2 grammars consist in principle of lexical projections, and that learners are sensitive early on to head–complement relations.
- In a second stage, learners establish I and its projection IP. From the start I is to the left of its VP complement for all subjects, even though I follows its VP complement in Korean/Turkish. Vainikka and Young-Scholten claim that this is because the L1 does not influence functional projections. However, it could equally be that because I–VP is a head–complement relation, learners are sensitive to the predominant surface order of German main clauses when they begin to establish I in their grammars. I is initially underspecified in the sense that it does not have features for tense or person/number agreement with the subject. Rather, it acts as a position to host moved thematic verbs, and some auxiliary and modal verbs. Verb movement from a head-final VP in L2 German to a head-initial IP creates the 'verb separation' effect. It is unclear whether the L1 of learners influences the development of the specification for I; in particular, whether Italian/Spanish/Turkish speakers have an advantage over Korean speakers in acquiring subject–verb agreement.
- In a third stage learners establish a CP layer to host fronted non-subject constituents and a verb moved from I. This produces the 'verb second' effect. The reason why learners acquire 'verb second' later than 'verb separation' is, then, a direct effect of grammar-building. An IP layer, which determines verb separation, needs to be established before the CP layer, which determines verb second, can come into being.
- Finally, learners restructure the order I–VP to VP–I in order to produce the 'verb final' effect in embedded clauses, where all parts of the verb occur at the end of the clause. Such restructuring is dependent on learners having built a CP layer. Once they have done so, they become aware that when C is filled by an overt complementizer like *dass* 'that', I follows, rather than precedes, the VP.

These findings are compatible with the 'modulated structure building' account of L2 grammar-building which we have been developing. Initial grammars consist of lexical projections with the structural properties of the L1 in principle – but evidence in the input for different head-complement orders in those projections may lead to rapid restructuring. Functional projections like IP and CP are established later than lexical projections, again in principle, but the rapidity with which they are established depends on the property of I or C in question, and the evidence available in the input the learner gets. Vainikka and Young-Scholten claim that there is no L1 influence on the way that the functional category I develops in L2 German. However, given that 'modulated structure building' proposes that L1 influence only becomes relevant at appropriate points in the specification of functional categories, it could be that Vainikka and Young-Scholten's subjects are either too elementary or too advanced in their development to show such effects.

In the next section we will consider the role that CP plays in the structure of English questions, and examine whether L2 learners of English acquire English question formation by building the appropriate representation for CP in their mental grammars.

More Advanced Discussion

4.8   The second language acquisition of English questions

Section 4.8 illustrates the difference between yes/no and *wh*-questions, and outlines a descriptive generalization about the L2 development of questions. The role that CP plays in question formation is then discussed, and a proposed parametric difference between languages is described. Finally, we ask whether the L2 descriptive generalization can be explained as the result of learners building a grammatical representation for CP.

There are two main types of question in English. Firstly, yes/no questions to which one can answer simply 'yes' or 'no'; these are formed by moving copula *be*, auxiliary *be*, *have*, a modal verb (like *can, must, may*) or expletive *do* (when a thematic verb is the main verb) to the front of the sentence, as illustrated in (27a); or by using a 'tag' formula at the end of the sentence, as in (27b). Secondly, there are information or *wh*-questions, which are introduced by phrases which go generally under the name of *wh*-phrases like *who? what? which book? why? how?* In *wh*-questions a finite copula, auxiliary, modal or expletive *do* moves to second position in the clause, as illustrated in (27c); i.e. the contruction is just like the more general 'verb second' construction in German:

27a Is she happy?
      Can I have some?
      Does she know you?
    b She's happy, isn't she?
      I can have some, can't I?
      She knows you, doesn't she?
    c Why is she happy?
      What can I have?
      Which book did you buy?
      How do you do that?

There is also a syntactic difference between questions in main clauses, and questions in embedded clauses (indirect questions). In embedded clauses, the finite copula, auxiliary, modal or expletive *do* do not move to first or second position in the sentence, but remain in the position they would occupy in ordinary declarative clauses (*do* does not appear as an expletive in embedded clauses):

28a I wonder if she **is** happy/*I wonder if is she happy
    b I'll ask what I **can** have/*I'll ask what can I have
    c They know which book you **bought**/*They know which book did you buy

As in the case of negation, discussed in section 3.2, it has been known for some time that L2 learners of English go through systematic stages of development in acquiring questions. Lightbown and Spada (1993) have proposed the stages illustrated in table 4.1.

Stage 3 requires a brief comment. It appears that at this stage learners mark questions by placing a question word of some kind in front of declarative clauses. This can be either a *wh*-word or phrase to produce an information question, or a verb-like element (*do, is*), which appears to be used more like a question marker than a verb because it is often accompanied by the use of another verb in its normal declarative position: *Is he is happy? Do you can go?* (Cancino et al. 1978).

4.8.1 The role of CP in question formation, and a parametric difference between languages

Do all languages form yes/no and *wh* questions in the way that English does? The answer to this is no, but the range of ways in which the world's languages form questions is in fact quite limited. Two of the principal types of question

Table 4.1 Proposed stages in the L2 development of English questions

Stage	Description	Example
1	Rising intonation on words/formulae	Four children?
2	Rising intonation on clauses	The boys throw the shoes?
3	A question word is placed at the front of the clause, but often without a copula, auxiliary, etc., moving	Is the picture has two planets on top? Where the little children are?
4	Copula *be* moves to the front in yes/no questions, and to second position in *wh*-questions	Is there fish in the water? Where is the sun?
5	Auxiliaries, modals and *do* move to the front or to second position	Can you tell me? What is the boy doing? How do you say 'proche'?
6	*Non-movement of the copula, auxiliaries, etc., in embedded questions is acquired	Can you tell me what the date is today?
	Question tags are acquired	It's better, isn't it?

*Up to this point L2 learners produce embedded questions with moved copula, auxiliaries, modals, etc.: *I wonder what can I have; She asked how do you do that.*
Source: Based on Lightbown and Spada 1993: 63 (their examples)

formation are illustrated by English and Chinese. In English, as we have seen, copula *be*, auxiliary *be/have*, modal verbs and expletive *do* move to the front of the sentence in yes/no questions. In *wh*-questions additionally a *wh*-phrase moves to the front. In Chinese, by contrast, yes/no questions are formed by the introduction into a clause-final position of an overt question marker, *ma*, as in example (29a). And *wh*-questions are formed by inserting a *wh*-phrase into the position where an ordinary constituent would occur in a declarative clause, as in example (29b) (examples from Aoun and Li 1993)[5]:

    29a Ta lai   ma?
           He come Q?
           'Is he coming?'

      b Zhangsan kandao shenme?
         Zhangsan saw   what?
         'What did Zhangsan see?'

It has been standardly assumed by linguists (e.g. Huang 1982) that question sentences in the two languages have the same basic underlying structure, but that their surface differences are the result of a parametric difference in the way the underlying structure is realized. Without going into the detail of specific proposals, the spirit of this account is that universally questions are signalled by the presence of a question morpheme, often represented by Q, belonging to the category C. In some languages Q is a free morpheme. This is the case of Chinese. CP in Chinese is head-final (Y. Li 1990), so that Chinese C follows its complement IP, in contrast to English where C precedes its complement IP. In Chinese yes/no questions, Q is realized as the free-form question marker *ma*:

30a

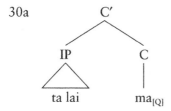

In Chinese *wh*-questions, Q is usually null, although the morpheme *ne* can optionally appear in some contexts (see note 5), and additionally a specific constituent in the clause is replaced by a *wh*-phrase: *shenme*, 'what'; *shei*, 'who'; and so on. This suggests that Q is still a free morpheme which has different variants depending on the context: *ma*, ϕ, *ne*. A question like (29b) therefore has the underlying structure (30b):

30b

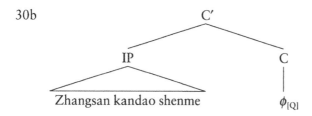

In other languages Q is a bound morpheme (an inflection). This is the case of English, although in English the bound morpheme which realizes Q is always null. Because Q is an inflection in English, that inflection must be associated with another head to be grammatical. The head in question is I. Since I moves to Q for this association to occur, given our assumptions about strong and weak inflections (see section 3.3.3), the null inflection realizing Q must be strong. So we get surface structures like:

31a [$_C$ is + $\phi_{[Q]}$ [$_{IP}$ he t [$_{VP}$ t coming]]]?

In the case of *wh*-questions not only is a specific constituent in the clause replaced by a *wh*-phrase, but it also moves to the specifier of CP, unlike Chinese:

b $[_{CP}$ what$_j$ $[_C$ is + $\phi_{[Q]}$ $[_{IP}$ he t$_i$ $[_{VP}$ t$_i$ eating t$_j$]]]]?

The requirement that a *wh*-phrase move to the specifier of CP is usually assumed to be the effect of an agreement relation: *wh*-phrases in English must appear in a local specifier–head relation in surface structure with a head which is specified for (Rizzi 1996). Rizzi, in fact, proposes that there is a principle of Universal Grammar applicable to all languages that *wh*-phrases appear in a local specifier–head agreement relation with a head specified for Q at some point in the derivation of sentences. In English this requirement holds of surface syntax. In Chinese it holds at a level of interpretation known as **Logical Form** (Huang 1982, 1995 – we will not be concerned with issues of logical form in SLA in this book). It is this agreement requirement which forces *wh*-phrases to move to the specifier of CP.

Note that in English, free forms located in the category I are the ones which move to C to pick up the question inflection, rather than a verb located in the VP. This means that when the main verb is a thematic verb, which does not raise to I because the inflections of I are weak in English, the expletive verb *do* surfaces in I, and it is this form which moves to C:

32a $[_{IP}$ He -s $[_{VP}$ speak Chinese]] $\rightarrow$ $[_{IP}$ He t $[_{VP}$ speaks Chinese]]

b $[_C$ -$\phi_{[Q]}$ $[_{IP}$ He -s $[_{VP}$ speak Chinese]]] $\rightarrow$
$[_C$ Does-$\phi_{[Q]}$ $[_{IP}$ he t $[_{VP}$ speak Chinese]]]

Thus expletive *do* surfaces both with sentential negation and with question formation in English:

33a   He **doesn't** speak Chinese

b   **Does** he speak Chinese?

Consider now the case of embedded questions in English. In embedded questions I does not move to C, although *wh*-phrases still move to the specifier of CP:

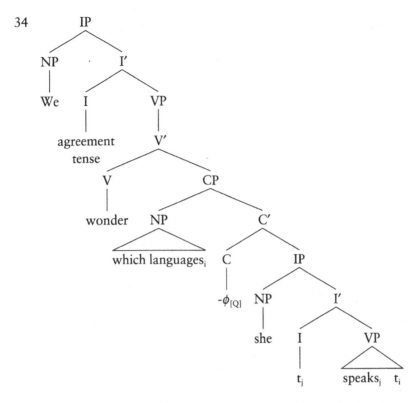

There are various possible explanations. The one we will tentatively adopt is the following. When verbs like *wonder* select CP complements, they require that those complements are specified for Q. Compare:

35a   I wonder [$_{CP}$ which languages she speaks]
   b   I wonder [$_{CP}$ whether/if she speaks three languages]
   c   *I wonder [$_{CP}$ she speaks three languages]

We will say that through this requirement verbs like *wonder* identify the embedded clause as a question, and it is unnecessary to introduce a Q inflection. Thus, although Q is still present, it is now realized as a free morpheme in the form of *if* (in embedded yes/no questions) or ϕ (in embedded yes/no questions where *whether* is in the specifier of CP, and in all embedded *wh*-questions).

4.8.2   The L2 acquisition of English questions as the acquisition of CP

Given the 'modulated structure building' perspective I have adopted on L2 development (stages of development are the result of learners building grammatical

representations for the L2) how might we relate the stages of development proposed by Lightbown and Spada (1993) to the acquisition of CP? One possibility
is that the first two stages, where learners use rising intonation, are stages without a CP projection. Recall that in the case of the acquisition of English declarative clauses it was argued that learners initially start with lexical projections but
without IP (see chapter 2). Perhaps the acquisition of questions begins as a stage
without CP, where learners simply add rising intonation to lexical projections
like VP, NegP, and then later IP. This is, of course, speculative, and it is not clear
whether there is currently any evidence which would confirm or disconfirm the
proposal. It would require making the claim that L2 learners are sensitive to the
intonational properties of English questions before they are sensitive to their
structural properties. On the other hand, initial absence of the CP in questions
is compatible with the analysis of German word order discussed in this chapter:
L2 learners of German appear to start grammar-building without a CP layer of
structure.

   If CP is initially absent, the trigger for its establishment in questions might be
the recognition by learners that in the English input they receive, questions are
marked by a question word located in front of IP: a form like *is*, *do* or a *wh*-
phrase. If, by Universal Grammar, C always selects IP as its complement, and
if L2 learners have access to Universal Grammar, then recognition of question
markers appearing in front of IP will lead them automatically to locate these
markers under C, or somewhere in its projection CP. In the case of yes/no questions, it seems initially that learners treat forms like *is*, *do* as if they were like the
question marker *ma* of Chinese; that is, *is*, *do* are free Q morphemes, and there is
no movement of I to C to pick up a bound Q morpheme. Thus at Lightbown and
Spada's stage 3, *is*, *do* duplicate an auxiliary verb in I:

36

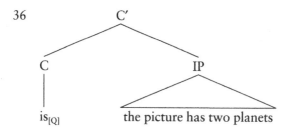

   In the case of *wh*-phrases, if learners know from Universal Grammar that *wh*-
phrases must appear in a local specifier–head agreement relation with a head
with the specification Q at some point in the derivation of sentences, then once
they recognize that *wh*-phrases are located in front of IP in English, by Universal
Grammar they will automatically project a CP, and place the *wh*-phrase in its
specifier position:

37

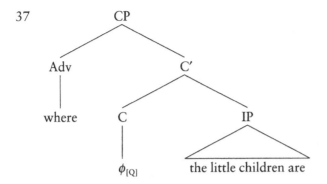

The fact that Q is realized at this stage in L2 English as a free morpheme might explain why *wh*-questions are not accompanied by movement of I to C. Movement of I to C in native English, it was argued in section 4.8.1, is the effect of Q being realized as a strong bound morpheme. If L2 learners are realizing Q at this stage as a free morpheme, there is no reason to move I to C. And it may be that there is some kind of principle of economy of representation operating in development which requires that features like Q be marked only by one overt morpheme. This would require a form to appear under C in yes/no questions, but since a *wh*-phrase appears in the specifier of CP in *wh*-questions, the head C can remain silent.

If this is the appropriate characterization of Lightbown and Spada's stage 3, we might ask why learners initially assume that the question morphemes in C are free forms rather than inflections. This might follow if, as we have been proposing up to now, functional projections like CP are initially minimally specified; a free question morpheme realizing C and selecting an IP complement requires less grammatical machinery than moving I to C. Note that this account is compatible with 'modulated structure building'. Here a CP layer of structure is built once IP is established, and initially it is an underspecified position which simply hosts overt markers to signal that the sentence is a question.

In stages 4 and 5 learners acquire the fact that verbs in I move to C (including the movement of expletive *do*, inserted under I when thematic verbs are involved). This would follow if at this point they start to refine their analysis for C, acquiring the inflectional status of the morpheme realizing Q, the fact that it is null and the fact that it is a 'strong' morpheme. We would then expect that forms like *is*, *do* cease to copy a verb already in I, and at the same time that *wh*-phrases start occurring with copula *be*, auxiliaries, modals and *do* in second position. The overgeneralization of the movement of I to C in embedded questions might then be explained as the overgeneralization of the inflectional status of Q to all CP contexts. It appears that it takes learners longer to acquire the fact that verbs like *wonder* cancel the inflectional status of the Q of CPs which they select as complements.

More Advanced Discussion

4.9   The second language acquisition of relative clauses

Section 4.9 first describes and illustrates the structure of relative clauses in English, and then goes on to propose that the difference between relative clause formation in English-type languages and Chinese-type languages is the effect of a parameter of Universal Grammar: whether the category C is specified for the feature [wh] or not. Studies of the L2 acquisition of relative clauses are then considered and it is argued that learners initially establish a minimally specified C (without the feature [wh]). When, subsequently, they start to acquire the appropriate specification for C, development is subject to L1 influence.

As a final example in this chapter of the second language acquisition of word order, we consider the case of relative clauses, and to what extent observed patterns of L2 development of knowledge of relative clauses are compatible with 'modulated structure building'. We will see that a similar kind of difference exists between languages in their realization of relative clause structure as existed in the way that they realize questions.

4.9.1   The structure of relative clauses in English

Relative clauses are clauses which are complements to nouns, for example:

38a   The boy **who came**
   b   The melons **which they bought**
   c   John, **who works in a bank**, is an Oxford graduate

They fall into two major types: non-restrictive relative clauses like the one illustrated in (38c), where a pause separates the clausal complement from the noun, and restrictive relative clauses where there is no pause. We will be concerned here only with restrictive relative clauses.[6]

The structure of English restrictive relative clauses (henceforth RRCs) is fairly complex. Firstly, the main noun to which the clause is a complement – the so-called **head** of the relative clause – is co-referential with (i.e. refers to the same conceptual entity as) a noun in the complement clause, although this noun is null in English. These null nouns can be in subject position, direct object position, object of a preposition position, they can be the object of a comparison or they can be part of a possessive construction, as indicated by the gaps in (39):

39a The boy [who ___ came] is ill   Subject
  b The melons [which he bought   Direct Object
     ___] are ripe
  c The woman [who he gave the   Object of a preposition
     book to ___] is old
  d The runner [who John is faster   Object of a comparison
     than ___] won
  e The girl [whose brother ___ is a   Possessive construction
     sailor] phoned
  f The girl [whose brother I know   Possessive construction
     ___] phoned

Secondly, the morpheme which 'links' the head noun and its complement clause can, for many speakers, in most contexts, alternate between a *wh*-word, as illustrated in (39), *that* as illustrated in (40) and ϕ as illustrated in (41):

40a The boy [that ___ came] is ill
  b The melons [that he bought ___] are ripe
  c The woman [that he gave the book to ___] is old
  d The runner [that John is faster than ___] won

41a The melons [___ he bought ___] are ripe
  b The woman [___ he gave the book to ___] is old
  c The runner [___ John is faster than ___] won

Thirdly, in the case where the head noun is co-referential with the object of a preposition in the complement clause, the preposition may be stranded, as illustrated in (42a), or carried along with the *wh*-word, an operation known as 'pied-piping' (Ross 1967), as illustrated in (42b):

42a The woman [{ who / that / ___ } he gave the book to ___]

  b The woman [to whom he gave the book ___]

A standard account of the structure of English RRCs is that they are CPs which are complements to the head noun. In those cases where the head noun is linked to the relative clause by a *wh*-word, as in (39), this *wh*-word is moved from a position in the clause to the specifier position of CP and the morpheme realizing C is null, as illustrated in the case of a direct object relative clause in (43):

43a   The melons [CP which_i ɸ [IP he bought t_i]] are ripe

b

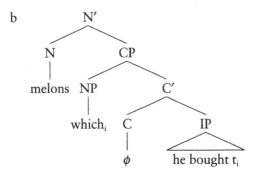

In those cases where the head noun is linked to the relative clause by *that*, this is the head of CP and a null operator, usually referred to as Op, is moved from a position in the clause to the specifier of CP:

44a   The melons [CP Op_i that [IP he bought t_i]] are ripe

b

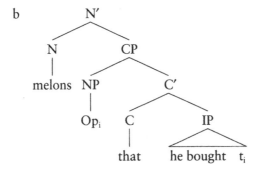

In those cases where there is no overt form linking the head noun and the relative clause, the morpheme realizing C is null, and a null operator has moved from a position in the relative clause to the specifier of CP:

45a   The melons [CP Op_i ɸ [IP he bought t_i]] are ripe

b

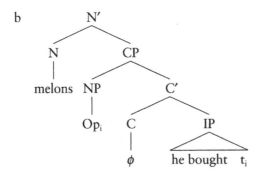

Finally, in the case of preposition stranding versus pied-piping, movement is either of a *wh*-word alone (46a) or of a prepositional phrase (PP) containing a *wh*-word (46b):

46a   The woman [$_{CP}$ who$_i$ ϕ [$_{IP}$ he gave the book [$_{PP}$ to t$_i$]]]
  b   The woman [$_{CP}$ [$_{PP}$ to whom$_i$] ϕ [$_{IP}$ he gave the book t$_i$]]

4.9.2   A parametric difference between languages in the construction of relative clauses

English relative clauses, then, have two potential 'relativizers' – *wh*-words and Op – and two potential complementizer heads in RRCs: *that* and ϕ. But they are not freely interchangeable. While Op can co-occur both with *that* and ϕ, only ϕ can freely occur with *wh*-words and Op. The combination *[*wh*-word *that*] is not possible in modern standard English, as illustrated in (47):

47a   The melons [$_{CP}$ which ϕ [$_{IP}$ he bought t]]
  b   The melons [$_{CP}$ Op ϕ [$_{IP}$ he bought t]]
  c   The melons [$_{CP}$ Op that [$_{IP}$ he bought t]]
  d   *The melons [$_{CP}$ which that [$_{IP}$ he bought t]]

One proposal for explaining this distributional restriction links it to the movement of *wh*-words and Op. Recall that in questions *wh*-phrases must appear in a local specifier–head relation with a head specified for Q at some point in the derivation of a sentence (see section 4.8.1). Suppose that a similar sort of requirement holds of *wh*-words in relative clauses. This would imply that at some level question CPs and relative clause CPs are similar. A proposal by Rizzi (1990: 67) tries to formalize this similarity. He proposes that, in English, morphemes belonging to C are specified for two binary features: [±predicative] which distinguishes between those clauses which are 'predicated' of nouns (i.e. relative clauses), and are [+predicative], and those which are free-standing or embedded clauses but not predicated of nouns ([−predicative]). The other binary feature is [±wh]. Under Rizzi's analysis this is a way of capturing the similarity between the Q morpheme of questions and the complementizer in RRCs. [±wh] distinguishes between those complementizers which can agree with *wh*-phrases in the specifier of CP [+wh], and those which cannot [−wh]. Rizzi suggests that different combinations of these features uniquely define specific morphemes belonging to the category C. For example, *that* used in relative clauses has the features [−wh, +predicative] in contrast to the null morpheme ϕ which has the features [+wh, +predicative]. If it is assumed that overt *wh*-words in relative clauses have the feature [+wh], while null operators have a [wh] feature, but with an unspecified value, then the CPs of (47) have the feature combinations illustrated in (48):

48a   The melons [$_{CP}$ which$_{i[+wh]}$ $\phi_{[+wh, +pred]}$ [$_{IP}$ he bought t$_i$]]
  b   The melons [$_{CP}$ Op$_{i[wh]}$ $\phi_{[+wh, +pred]}$ [$_{IP}$ he bought t$_i$]]
  c   The melons [$_{CP}$ Op$_{i[wh]}$ that$_{[-wh, +pred]}$ [$_{IP}$ he bought t$_i$]]
  d   *The melons [$_{CP}$ which$_{i[+wh]}$ that$_{[-wh, +pred]}$ [$_{IP}$ he bought t$_i$]]

It can now be said that *wh*-words and the null operator in relative clauses fall under the same requirement as *wh*-phrases in questions: because they have the feature [wh], they must occur in a local specifier–head agreement relation with a head with the feature [wh] at some point in the derivation, and this forces them to move to the specifier of CP. In addition, the values of the features must agree. The one case where they clash is (48d), where the [+wh] of *which* clashes with the [–wh] of *that*, and the clause is ungrammatical.

It seems that there is a major parametric difference between English-type languages, where *wh*-phrases and null operators move to the specifier of CP in relative clauses, and Chinese-type languages, where in relative clauses a pronoun – known as a **resumptive pronoun** – often appears in the position from which a *wh*-word or operator has moved in English. Consider the following examples from Mandarin Chinese. Note that the head of the RRC in Chinese normally follows its relative clause (examples from Hawkins and Chan 1997):

49a   [$_{CP}$ [$_{IP}$ Wo sung liwu   gei ta $_{IP}$] de $_{CP}$] neige nuhai
            I   gave present to   her   'that' the   girl
            'The girl that I gave a present to'
  b   [$_{CP}$ [$_{IP}$ Wo jiao **ta**   lai $_{IP}$]   de $_{CP}$] neige nuhai
            I   ask   her to-come 'that' the   girl
            'The girl who I asked to come'
  c   [$_{CP}$ [$_{IP}$ Wo xihuan **ta** $_{IP}$] de $_{CP}$] neige nuhai
            I   like   her 'that' the   girl
            'The girl who I like'

While *de* appears to be a complementizer in these examples, like English 'that', there is no gap in the relative clause from which a *wh*-word might have moved; instead there is a resumptive pronoun.[7] One interpretation of these data is that English and Chinese differ in the presence or absence of the [wh] feature on predicative C. In English the feature is present in the form [±wh], and this requires the presence of *wh*-words or operators with the feature [wh] which move to the specifier of CP. In Chinese the feature [wh] is simply absent from predicative C; Chinese *de* realizes a minimally specified C which marks 'predication', but the relation between the head of the RRC and a position within the relative clause is just like any other antecedent–pronoun relation. If Universal Grammar makes available the [wh] feature, but languages have the option of whether they specify particular categories for that feature or not, then the contrast between

English-type relative clause formation and Chinese-type relative clause formation can be viewed as a difference in the setting of this particular parameter of variation.

4.9.3 The second language acquisition of restrictive relative clauses and the 'modulated structure building' theory of syntactic development

There have been many studies of the L2 acquisition of the various properties associated with relative clauses in English and other languages: the acquisition of the range of relativizable positions (subject, direct object, object of a preposition, and so on); the acquisition of the appropriate form that *wh*-words and predicative complementizers take; the acquisition of preposition stranding. These studies have been undertaken from a number of different theoretical perspectives. (For a concise overview see Ellis 1994: 417–26; for more detailed consideration from specific perspectives see Tarallo and Myhill 1983; Pavesi 1986; Doughty 1991; Wolfe-Quintero 1992; Hamilton 1995.) The one property we shall consider here is the acquisition of movement of *wh*-words/operators to the specifier of CP. The reason I focus on this is because it requires learners to develop a CP layer of structure in their mental grammars where C is realized by morphemes which force non-local syntactic movement to the specifier position of CP. If modulated structure building is correct, we should find that when learners initially establish predicative C it will not allow movement, because initially functional categories are minimally specified for head–complement relations only. That is, learners should treat RRCs in languages like English as if they had the structure of RRCs in Chinese. Once learners begin to refine the specification for C, we might expect to see L1 influence, because according to modulated structure building, the L1 influences development at relevant points in L2 grammar-building, speakers of languages with *wh*-word/operator movement in relative clauses might acquire movement in the L2 more quickly than speakers of languages without movement.

Hyltenstam (1984) investigated the L2 acquisition of Swedish by speakers of four different native languages: Spanish, Finnish, Greek and Persian. Swedish, like English, is a language which has gaps in relative clauses, and it is usually assumed that this is the result of an operator moving to the specifier of CP (example from Hyltenstam):

50   Pojken [$_{CP}$ Op$_i$ som [$_{IP}$ jag gav bollen till t$_i$]]
     boy-the   that   I   gave ball-the to
     'The boy that I gave the ball to'

Although Swedish has relative *wh*-words (*vilken/-t/-a*, 'which'), according to Hyltenstam they are hardly used in spoken Swedish, so that movement of a null operator to the specifier of CP with *som* realizing C is the norm.

The subjects were speakers of Spanish and Finnish, languages also with gaps in all relative clauses, apparently the result of operator movement, and Greek and Persian, which are like Chinese in having resumptive pronouns in many types of relative clauses, for example:

> 51a   O fititis   pou **tu**   edhoses to vivlio   (Greek)
>   The student that to-him gave-you the book
>   'The student that you gave the book to'
>   b   Maerd-i   ke to ketab-o   be-es dadi (Persian)
>   the-man-part that you book-part to-him gave
>   'The man that you gave the book to'
>   (part = particle)

Using the same logic used above in discussing Chinese, the [wh] feature is absent from C in these cases, and there is no movement of a *wh*-word or operator.[8]

There were 12 subjects representing each of the languages Spanish, Greek and Persian in Hyltenstam's study, and 9 speakers of Finnish. All subjects were over 20 years of age, had been resident in Sweden for under 2 years, and had had between 350 and 600 hours of instruction on Swedish at the time of testing. Hyltenstam classed them as 'advanced' learners. The test took the form of a one-to-one interview with a researcher, in which subjects had to describe a series of pictures. Each picture was drawn to represent eight simple actions which could be described by using relative clauses, and a number was attached to each of the actions. Subjects were asked questions like 'who is number x?', where their expected response would be something like 'the man who sings'.

The results of the study show that all the subjects produce resumptive pronouns in relative clauses, even those who speak Spanish and Finnish, languages without resumptive pronouns. However, the total numbers of resumptive pronouns produced by each group of speakers varies quite considerably, as illustrated in table 4.2:

Table 4.2 Number of resumptive pronouns (RPs) used in Swedish RRCs by L2 speakers

Language	Total no. of RPs	No. of subjects	Mean per subject
Finnish	27	9	3
Spanish	144	12	12
Greek	205	12	17.1
Persian	240	12	20

Source: Based on Hyltenstam 1984

Furthermore, the proportions of resumptive pronouns were distributed differently across relative clause types. While no resumptive pronouns were used by any speakers in subject relative clauses (i.e. *the man who sings* type clauses), over half of the Persian speakers used resumptive pronouns in all other contexts, and over half of the Greek speakers used resumptive pronouns in all other contexts except direct object relatives (i.e. *the melons that I bought* type clauses – here 5 out of the 12 Greek speakers used RPs). By contrast, resumptive pronouns were used by more than half of the Finnish speakers only in possessive constructions (i.e. *the girl whose brother I know* type clauses), and by more than half of the Spanish speakers only in possessive and object-of-comparison relatives (i.e. *the man who he is taller than* type clauses).

These results are compatible with two of the hypotheses of modulated structure building. The first is that when learners initially establish representations for functional categories these will be minimally specified. In the case of relative clauses, a minimally specified predicative C would not incorporate the feature [wh] and there would not be *wh*-word or operator movement. The results suggest that learners to some extent do treat predicative C in Swedish as if it were unspecified for the feature [wh], and use resumptive pronouns even where their L1 does not have resumptive pronouns (Spanish, Finnish) and even though there is no evidence in the input that Swedish allows resumptive pronouns. Secondly, because not all the subjects use resumptive pronouns everywhere, it appears that at the time of testing some subjects have already begun to refine the specification for predicative C to allow for the feature [wh]. But at this point there seems to be influence of the learner's first language. Speakers of Persian and Greek, languages with resumptive pronouns which we have suggested indicate lack of the feature [wh], appear to be considerably slower in eliminating resumptive pronouns from relative clauses than Spanish or Finnish speakers, languages where predicative C has the feature [wh]. This difference is consistent with the idea that once learners start to refine the specification for predicative C, similar features in the L1 facilitate acquisition.

A similar kind of result is reported in a study by Hawkins and Chan (1997) which compares the performance of Chinese speakers and French speakers in judging and correcting ungrammatical resumptive pronouns in English RRCs. Chinese, we have assumed, does not have *wh*-word/operator movement. Given this assumption, this means that the feature [wh] is absent from Chinese predicative C. French, by contrast, is like English in having movement of *wh*-words/operators from all relativizable positions (except the object of a comparison, which is not a relativizable position in French), hence predicative C in French has the feature [wh]. Hawkins and Chan matched Chinese- and French-speaking learners of English at three proficiency levels – elementary, intermediate, advanced – on the basis of an independent general test of proficiency (the Oxford Placement Test – Allan 1992) and then compared them with a group of native speakers on a grammaticality judgement and correction test. The results are presented in table 4.3:

Table 4.3   Correct judgements (%) about ungrammatical resumptive pronouns
in a range of relativized positions, and accuracy of corrections (%)

Groups (N = number of subjects)	Judgement scores %	Correction scores %
Chinese elementary (N = 47)	38	27
Chinese intermediate (N = 46)	55	41
Chinese advanced (N = 54)	90	70
French elementary (N = 33)	81	65
French intermediate (N = 40)	90	82
French advanced (N = 40)	96	87
English controls (N = 32)	98	97

Source: Based on Hawkins and Chan 1997

Assuming that at the elementary level of proficiency learners have already
begun to specify their representations for English predicative C, the elementary
French speakers appear to be well in advance of the elementary Chinese speakers
in recognizing that resumptive pronouns do not occur in English RRCs, and in
correcting them in a grammaticality judgement test. On the assumptions being
made, the ability to recognize the ungrammaticality of resumptive pronouns in
English RRCs is the result of having specified predicative C for the feature [wh],
which forces operator movement to the specifier of CP. Since French predicative
C also has such a feature, while Chinese predicative C does not, the results
here are consistent with the claim that the L1 is influencing development. Note,
however, that with exposure to English the Chinese speakers 'catch up' to a
considerable extent, so that by the advanced proficiency stage the Chinese
subjects are responding more like the advanced French subjects and the native
English-speaking controls (although on a statistical test known as an 'Analysis of
Variance', the Chinese subjects were still significantly less accurate than either
the French subjects or the English controls).

4.10   Summary of chapter 4

The main points made in chapter 4 are the following:

• In the second language acquisition of word order in German clauses, Vainikka
  and Young-Scholten (1994, 1996a, 1996b) have argued that there is evidence

that learners start initially with lexical projections like VP, but without the functional projections IP and CP. The representation for VP is influenced by the learner's L1, so that Turkish/Korean speakers initially have a predominantly head-final VP, while Italian/Spanish speakers initially have a predominantly head-initial VP. The rapidity with which the Italian/Spanish speakers switched to OV in the VP led to the suggestion that they were sensitive to head-complement selectional properties. When IP is established it is at first head-initial for all subjects. It is the combination of the establishment of early OV order with the emergence of head-initial I which causes the verb-separation effect to appear early in development. I is initially acquired as an unspecified position to host auxiliaries, modals and moved thematic verbs. CP was established only once IP was established, and this aspect of grammar-building explained why 'verb second' emerged later than 'verb separation'. The correct word order in embedded clauses was only established when learners realized that the sentence internal location of I was inappropriate to embedded clauses, and switched the ordering I–VP to VP–I (sections 4.2–4.7).

- In the acquisition of English question formation learners' early syntactic representations lack a CP layer of structure. When C is established it is initially minimally specified as a position which signals that the clause is a question. The morpheme Q is first instantiated as a free form, but subsequently learners refine this specification so that Q is realized as a strong inflection which forces I to move to C (section 4.8).

- In acquiring relative clauses L2 learners appear to treat C initially as a minimally specified position indicating that the clause is predicated of a head noun. This syntactic representation gives rise to resumptive pronouns in the embedded clause even where neither an L2 learner's native language nor the L2 provide evidence for resumptive pronouns. For L2s which require *wh*-word or null operator movement (like English) learners must refine the specification of C to incorporate the feature [wh], which is what forces movement. Such further specification appears to be subject to L1 influence, because native speakers of languages which also have the feature [wh] (like French) develop knowledge of *wh*-word/null operator movement more quickly than speakers of languages which do not (like Chinese). These findings are consistent with modulated structure building which proposes that L2 learners first establish representations for local relations like head-complement selection, and only subsequently for non-local relations like *wh*-word/operator movement, and that L1 influence occurs at points of development where the cognate property in the L2 emerges.

4.11   Exercises

In the sentences of (1) and (2), move the italicized constituents to the front of the sentence:

> *Example*:   Lou *carefully* unwrapped the present → *Carefully*, Lou unwrapped the present

What effect does this have on word order in the sentences of (1)? What syntactic properties do you think distinguish the italicized constituents of (1) from those of (2)? Can you suggest an explanation for the contrast between (1) and (2) by exploiting the CP analysis of clauses described in this chapter?

1a   I had *never* run so fast before
  b   They *seldom* leave the village these days
  c   He would travel by air *under no circumstances*
  d   Such a talented group of writers can *rarely* have been brought together in the same place
  e   She found a warmer welcome *nowhere else*

2a   I had *amazingly* run faster than the current champion
  b   They *often* leave the village to go into town
  c   He loves to take the aeroplane *under normal circumstances*
  d   A group of well-known writers gathers at the King's Head *every month*
  e   People were dancing in the streets *everywhere*

(Material used in this exercise is reprinted with the permission of Arnold Publishers)
Hulk (1991) tested the intuitions of native speakers of Dutch (a language with similar word order properties to German) learning French (an SVO language) primarily in the classroom.

There were four groups of informants in the study: adolescents who had just started French at school (first graders), students in the following two years at school (second and third graders) and first-year university students majoring in French. The test was a 40-sentence grammaticality judgement task balanced between grammatical and ungrammatical French sentences, where some of the ungrammatical word orders would be grammatical in equivalent Dutch sentences, and some ungrammatical in both languages.

Some of the sentence types used in the test, and the percentage of informants who accepted each type as grammatical, are given in the box below. We follow Hulk in using the same basic sentences to illustrate the results, although the vocabulary in the test was varied: *(Hier) Jean mangeait les fraises* (imperfect tense), *(Hier) Jean a mangé les fraises* (perfect tense), both meaning '(Yesterday) Jean ate the strawberries.'

Percentage of subjects who *accepted* different sentence types in French (based on Hulk 1991)				
Word order type	Groups			
	1st grade n = 26 % accept	2nd grade n = 21 % accept	3rd grade n = 25 % accept	Univ. students n = 16 % accept
1. *Jean a les fraises mangé (grammatical in Dutch)	73	40	2	0
2. Jean a mangé les fraises (ungrammatical in Dutch)	42	86	100	100
3. *Hier mangeait Jean les fraises (grammatical in Dutch)	92	50	32	10
4. *Hier a Jean les fraises mangé (grammatical in Dutch)	92	38	0	0
5. *Hier a Jean mangé les fraises (ungrammatical in both French and Dutch)	38	64	8	6
6. Hier Jean mangeait les fraises (ungrammatical in Dutch)	38	80	100	100
7. Hier Jean a mangé les fraises (ungrammatical in Dutch)	19	85	100	100

Given that main clauses in Dutch have verb-separation and verb-second properties, like German, but French word order is like English in the relevant respects:

(a)   What might these results suggest about the properties of French word order appearing most quickly in informants' grammars?

(b)   What might the results suggest about the development of knowledge over time (consider particularly the responses to sentence 5)?

(c)   Do the results pose any problems for the view that learners' grammars consist initially of lexical projections, with functional projections appearing later?

Exercise 3: Effects of headedness on L2 knowledge of other properties of grammar (section 4.6)

(Material used in this exercise is reprinted with the permission of Josien Lalleman)
When two clauses are coordinated in English by *and* (or *but*), and a portion of the second clause containing the verb is identical to a portion of the first clause, it can optionally delete:

> 1a   Jerry *wants to buy* a house, and Tom *wants to buy* a car
> b   Jerry *wants to buy* a house, and Tom ___ a car

This is known as **gapping**. Gapping only works in English if the 'gapped' portion follows the retained portion in surface structure:

> c   *Jerry ___ a house, and Tom wants to buy a car

This appears to be related to the headedness of the verb in relation to its complement. If the complement follows the verb, as in English, the 'gap' must be in the second clause. In languages where the verb normally follows its complement, like Japanese, the 'gap' must precede the retained portion (all following examples from Lalleman 1999):

> 2a   Kyou-ha sakano-o ___ ashita-ha niku-o tabetai
>   today-part fish-Acc tomorrow-part meat-Acc eat-want
>   'Today ___ fish, (and) tomorrow I want to eat meat'
>   (part = particle; Acc = accusative)
> b   *Kyou-ha sakano-o tabetai ashita-ha niku-o ___

In both Dutch and German, verbs precede their complements in surface structure in main clauses, but follow them in embedded clauses. In main clauses in these languages 'gaps' must follow the retained portion, but in embedded clauses they may follow or precede. The following are from Dutch:

> 3a   Sarah drinkt wijn en Robert ___ bier
>   'Sarah drinks wine and Robert beer'
> b   *Sarah ___ wijn en Robert drinkt bier

4a   Ik zie dat Sarah wijn drinkt en Robert bier ___
    'I see that Sarah wine drinks and Robert beer'
  b   Ik zie dat Sarah wijn ___ en Robert bier trinkt

While examples like these suggest a link between headedness and gapping, it is not entirely clear what the link is, and whether it relates to the verb, or Infl, or both in relation to their complements.

Lalleman (1999) tested L2 learners of Dutch on their knowledge of gapping possibilities. In her sample there were 16 native speakers of languages where the verb always precedes its complement (like English), 6 native speakers of Japanese, and 6 native speakers of German. Informants were all elementary learners who had recently arrived in the Netherlands. They 'knew the 1200 most frequent words of Dutch' but had had little instruction. She gave them a judgement task with a balanced number of sentences involving both gap possibilities in main clauses (where only a following gap is grammatical) and both gap possibilities in embedded clauses (where both are grammatical). Informants had to indicate the correctness of each type of sentence. The accuracy of subjects' responses (i.e. proportion of native-like responses) is shown in percentages in the box below:

Accuracy in judging the correctness of 'gapped' constructions: (a) all preceding gaps, (b) all following gaps, (c) gaps in main clauses, (d) gaps in embedded clauses (based on Lalleman 1999)				
Subjects	(a) Accuracy on preceding gaps %	(b) Accuracy on following gaps %	(c) Accuracy on main clause gaps %	(d) Accuracy on embedded clause gaps %
L1: (Infl)VO	59.2	78.3	81.7	55.8
L1: Japanese	72.5	68.3	75	65
L1: German	83.3	95.8	95.8	83.3

What might we infer from these results about the nature of the mental grammars for Dutch of these speakers:

(a)   if gapping were determined by the headedness of the verb?
(b)   if gapping were determined by the headedness of Infl?

What interpretation would you give to L1 influence on each of these scenarios?

Exercise 4: Evaluating whether Infl is underspecified in early L2 grammars (section 4.6)

In chapters 2 to 4 it has been argued that functional categories are established in L2 grammars on the basis of overt evidence in the input for such categories. Initially L2 learners appear to detect evidence which requires the minimum specification for a functional category; so it was argued that copula *be* triggers the establishment of Infl in L2 English because it is an expletive verb simply marking a position in the clause, and without further specification.

However, in native English *be* is not just a place-holder, but also inflects for agreement (*I am, you are, she is*) and tense (*I am, I was*). Below are data from Stauble's (1984) study on the use of agreement- and tense-inflected forms of copula *be* by her 12 informants (see section 2.8 for details of the informants and their proficiency levels). Are these data consistent with the claim that the copula in the grammars of L2 speakers of English is initially a realization of an underspecified Infl, and that specification of Infl occurs incrementally over the course of development?

Proportion (%) of target-like use of inflected forms of the copula *be* in the spontaneous English of 12 non-native speakers (based on Stauble 1984)					
Low intermediate	% is	% am	% are	% was	% were
Anita	78 [13]	(20) [(0)]	0 [0]	0	0
Mona	61 [36]	14 [0]	17 [0]	0	0
Sumi	63 [5]	(50) [(0)]	(40) [(0)]	0	0
Tamiko	9 [12]	48 [24]	0 [0]	0	0
Intermediate	is	am	are	was	were
Joe	87 [10]	65 [29]	23 [5]	19 [2]	(0) [(0)]
Josie	92 [4]	92 [0]	83 [6]	74 [0]	(33) [(0)]
Kuko	45 [9]	40 [55]	20 [10]	0 [0]	0 [0]
Kumi	76 [17]	45 [45]	0 [8]	2 [0]	0 [0]
Advanced	is	am	are	was	were
Rosa	97 [1]	94 [5]	73 [4]	88 [3]	(38) [0]
Paz	96 [2]	100 [0]	86 [0]	91 [2]	92 [0]
Mariko	90 [5]	100 [0]	50 [0]	79 [7]	(14) [(0)]
Fuku	92 [3]	78 [11]	0 [0]	79 [5]	(33) [(0)]
[ ] = percentage of non-target-like use of the form in a copula context (e.g. *is* when *am* or *was* is required) ( ) = fewer than 10 occasions for the use of the copula					

(Material used in this exercise is reprinted with the permission of Cambridge University Press)

Exercise 5: Evaluating the early development of question formation in L2 French (section 4.8)

Myles et al. (1999) recorded the development of interrogatives in the L2 French of 16 English-speaking adolescents over the first two years of their exposure to French in a classroom setting. These students were initially drilled in using pre-fabricated expressions ('chunks') like:

Quel âge as-tu?   'How old are you?'
What age have-you

Comment tu t'appelles?   'What's your name?'
How you self-call

Qu'est qu'il aime faire?   'What does he like doing?'
What is that he like do

Où habites-tu?   'Where do you live?'
Where live-you

As-tu des frères ou des soeurs?   'Do you have brothers or sisters?'
Have-you some brothers or
some sisters

One of the things Myles et al. were interested in was how learners developed from repeating chunks to using novel questions in French. To collect data for this they asked their informants to engage in 'semi-spontaneous' dialogues in pairs; the stimuli for discussion were information-gap tasks and family photographs. Participants were recorded at six sampling points over two years. Myles et al. present the results in terms of three types of question produced by the informants:

(a)   Questions formed from the chunks they had been drilled on.

(b)   Novel question constructions lacking verbs, e.g.

Où la piscine?   'Where the swimming pool?'
Où la plage?   'Where the beach?'
Jaune?   'Yellow?'
La dame à la stade?   'The lady at the stadium?'

(c)   Novel question constructions with verbs (which they suggest are mostly infinitive forms), e.g.

Je manger douze heures?	'I eat 12 o'clock?'
Tu et moi visiter le cinéma?	'You and I visit the cinema?'
J'aller au musée . . . samedi	'I go to the museum . . . Saturday
. . . dimanche?	. . . Sunday?'

The number of tokens of each of these question types used by the 16 informants at each of the sampling points is given in the box below:

Proportion of French question types used by 16 informants at 6 sampling points over two years (based on Myles et al. 1999: 69)						
Question type	Sample					
	1	2	3	4	5	6
Chunk	143/186 77%	264/418 63%	47/111 42%	214/483 44%	261/622 42%	40/264 15%
V-less	41/186 22%	129/418 31%	53/111 48%	235/483 49%	287/622 46%	182/264 69%
with V	2/186 1%	25/418 6%	11/111 10%	34/483 7%	74/622 12%	42/264 16%

Assuming that the questions produced by these speakers reflect their underlying competence, what conclusions would you draw about the nature of their grammars: (a) at sample 1; (b) at sample 6? How would you interpret the observation made by Myles et al. that questions involving verbs are 'initially (and mostly) untensed, with a few learners managing sentences with a finite verb' (1999: 69)?

Exercise 6: Choosing elicitation tasks for investigating L2 learners' knowledge of the properties of Infl and C in English (sections 4.6, 4.8)

Imagine that you want to investigate whether a group of intermediate-level L2 speakers of English know the features of Infl and C which determine the distributional properties of copula be, auxiliary be, modals, thematic verbs and the feature [±past], as illustrated in (1) and (2):

1a John isn't happy/John wasn't happy
  b Mary isn't working now/Mary wasn't working then
  c Sue can't swim yet/Sue couldn't swim then
  d Harry doesn't go to the cinema/Harry didn't go to the cinema

2a   Is John happy?/Was John happy?
  b   Is Mary working now?/Was Mary working then?
  c   Does Harry go to the cinema often?/Did Harry go to the cinema often?
  d   What does Joe eat?/Who did Mary marry?

What kind of elicitation task or tasks would be appropriate, in terms of practicality, efficiency and naturalness, for obtaining the information you need? (Consider tasks like grammaticality judgement, gap-filling, sentence changing, picture description, an oral interview, story retelling, or any others that seem appropriate.) Would the same kind of elicitation procedure be appropriate for eliciting information about both (1) and (2)? What kinds of control would you introduce to ensure that any data obtained were not entirely an effect of the test itself?

Exercise 7: Discussion topic (section 4.9)

'The development of second language grammatical knowledge can be attributed entirely to the frequency with which particular forms occur in the input.' Discuss why this is an unlikely characterization of how L2 speakers acquire relative clauses.

4.12   Further reading

For discussion of recent analyses of the structure of clauses, including a good discussion of the role of CP in clauses, see Haegeman, L. and Guéron, J. 1999: *English Grammar: A Generative Perspective*. Oxford: Blackwell (chapter 3).

Discussion of the acquisition of German word order which argues against an initial lexical projection phase, and in favour of the presence of IP and CP, can be found in the papers in part I of Flynn, S., Martohardjono, G. and O'Neil, W. (eds) 1998: *The Generative Study of Second Language Acquisition*. Mahwah, NJ: Lawrence Erlbaum Associates. For a slightly different proposal from 'minimal trees' which also argues for an early VP stage in L2 German see Beck, M.-L. 1998a: L2 acquisition and obligatory head movement: English-speaking learners of German and the local impairment hypothesis. *Studies in Second Language Acquisition* 20, 311–48.

Evidence against an early lexical projection phase in L2 English is presented in Gavruseva, L. and Lardiere, D. 1996: The emergence of extended phrase structure in child L2 acquisition. In A. Stringfellow, D. Cahana-Amitay, E. Hughes and A. Zukowski (eds), *Proceedings of the 20th Annual Boston University Conference on Language Development*, Somerville, Mass.: Cascadilla Press, 225–36.

Notes

1 The acquisition of German by Turkish speakers seems to be somewhat different from the acquisition of German by Romance speakers. We consider this in more detail in section 4.6.
2 In particular, Travis claims that Infl precedes its complement VP (i.e. is head-initial, as in English). There are good reasons, however, discussed in section 4.6, for thinking that IP is head-final in German.
3 The details of Travis's account are slightly different, and are not unproblematic (see Schwartz and Vikner (1996) for discussion). We will not consider these problems here because, as we shall see below, an alternative proposal by den Besten (1983) taken up by Schwartz and Tomaselli (1990) offers a more elegant solution.
4 DuPlessis et al. do not distinguish between thematic verbs and auxiliary verbs like *haben* in their account. It appears, though, from the examples cited by them (and also from the examples cited by Clahsen and Muysken 1986) that the verb-second stage involves the movement of both thematic and auxiliary verbs from I to C.
5 A question particle may also optionally appear in *wh*-questions in Chinese in some contexts, as in:

> Shei lai (ne)?
> Who comes (Q)?
> 'Who is coming?'

6 For a discussion of the differences between the two types of relative clause, see Fabb (1990).
7 It should be noted that some relative clause types in Chinese do not have overt resumptive pronouns. This is always the case when the RRC is a subject relative, and optionally the case when it is an object relative:

> φ/*ta gongzuo qinglao de   neige nuhai
> she   work   hard   'that' the   girl
> 'The girl who works hard'

> Wo xihuan φ/ta de   neige nuhai
> I   like   her 'that' the   girl
> 'The girl who I like'

Since Chinese is a language which more generally allows null subjects and objects, Hawkins and Chan (1997) have proposed that in these cases too there are resumptive pronouns, but they are null.
8 The situation is complicated, though, by the fact that Greek and Persian normally allow gaps in subject and direct object relative clauses. Whether these gaps are to be treated like the gaps in Chinese (i.e. as null resumptive pronouns) or differently is not clear. For different points of view on the status of gaps like these in different languages see Shlonsky (1992), Tsimpli (1997). We will assume, for the purpose of the argument here, that at least in some cases in Greek and Persian the predicative complementizer is not specified for [wh], and hence there is no operator movement.

5 The Second Language Acquisition of Subjects, Objects and Other Participants in Clauses

5.1 Introduction

From the evidence we have looked at so far, a consistent pattern seems to be emerging in the way that second language learners build syntactic representations in their mental grammars. In principle it would appear that they start by learning morphemes belonging to lexical categories like N, V, A, P, Neg, which by X′-theory then project, optionally, into phrases consisting of the head and a complement (N′, V′, A′, etc.) and phrases consisting of N′, V′, A′, etc., and a specfier (NP, VP, AP, etc.). Functional categories like I and C (and their projections I′, C′ and IP, CP) emerge as learners encounter evidence in the input which cannot be accommodated within the lexical projections they have established, and forces them to create new structural positions. For example, when English speakers encounter negative finite clauses in French where a thematic verb is to the left of the NegP, I have speculated that the complement selectional requirements of Neg force learners to establish an I above NegP, as a position to which the thematic verb can move (section 3.6). When L2 learners of English begin to notice question words at the beginning of question clauses (forms like *is, can, do* and *wh*-words) this triggers the establishment of C. That learners should project specifically an I in the case of negatives and a C in the case of interrogatives, rather than some other category to host the relevant morphemes, follows from the assumption that I universally selects NegP as its complement, when NegP is present, and C universally selects IP as its complement.

L2 learners start grammar-building with lexical projections in principle, but in practice the speed with which functional categories are established appears to depend on the nature and salience of the triggering data in the input. Thus English speakers learning French appear to acquire the fact that thematic verbs move through Neg to I almost immediately. My speculation is that this is because the complement selectional requirements of Neg are highly salient, and this is what forces the thematic verb to move every time. The salience of complement selectional requirements is also what I have claimed leads L2 learners of English to acquire copula *be* and auxiliary *be* + V-*ing* before tense or agreement (section 2.10). This much is consistent with the 'minimal trees' theory of early development in second language acquisition that was discussed in section 2.11.1 (Vainikka and Young-Scholten 1994, 1996a, 1996b).

When functional categories like I and C are initially established in L2 grammars, they appear to be minimally specified. They are basically positions set up to host other items which move to those positions (copula *be*, thematic verbs with negation in French, *is, can, do* and *wh*-words in English questions). However, once they are established, learners begin to distinguish morphemes belonging to I and C, and when they do the L1 appears to influence how that knowledge develops. Some features of I and C in the L1 are transferred into the L2 grammar. For example, if the L1 has morphemes belonging to I which mark subject–verb agreement, this appears to facilitate the acquisition of subject–verb agreement in the L2 (section 2.10). If the inflections in I are strong in the L1, this appears to be transferred as the default case to the L2, so that French speakers continue to accept the raising of thematic verbs across manner/frequency adverbs to I (but not across negation or in questions). If the inflections in I in the L1 are weak, this also appears to be transferred to the L2 as the default case, so that English speakers continue to allow non-raising of thematic verbs to I, again across manner/frequency adverbs. This led me to propose a modified version of the 'minimal trees' account of early L2 development which I have called 'modulated structure building'. 'Minimal trees', and therefore 'modulated structure building', is just one of a number of competing theories of early L2 development. As we have already seen there is also the 'valueless features' theory of Eubank (1993/94, 1994a, 1996), and 'full access to UG' theories such as those of Schwartz and Sprouse (1994, 1996), Epstein et al. (1996) and Grondin and White (1996).

The focus of attention up to now has been primarily on the **initial state** of L2 learners' mental grammars, and the subsequent **transitional states** they pass through in the course of development. In this chapter we will do two things. Firstly, investigate further whether the kinds of developmental properties we have observed in initial and transitional states of grammar-building emerge in other areas of syntactic knowledge. Secondly, begin to consider what sort of characteristics the **final state** mental grammars of L2 learners might have; that is, where they appear to be approaching native-speaker-like proficiency in the target language. The theories we have considered so far all assume ultimate potential full access to UG (differing in how they view the way that UG interacts with L2 input in the early stages). Is the assumption that L2 learners will ultimately establish native-like grammars, given enough time and the right kind of input, correct?

The area of investigation in this chapter is how humans appear universally to conceptualize events for the purposes of linguistic expression, how this is converted into language-specific syntactic structures, and how L2 learners acquire those language-specific syntactic structures. The underlying assumption is that Universal Grammar defines a set of participant roles in events; these are roles like the person or thing initiating the event, the person or thing affected by the event, the location where the event occurred, etc. Participant roles are a finite (and small) set from which all languages draw. At the same time they can be realized syntactically in a limited number of different ways. That is, there are parameters of variation in the syntactic realization of participant roles.

5.2   Some cross-linguistic differences in the syntactic realization of event structure

Section 5.2 illustrates how two types of event – activities and benefactives – can vary in their syntactic realization in different languages.

Verbs, and the NPs which accompany them, describe events (states of affairs, activities, achievements, etc.). But different languages can have different ways of realizing the same event syntactically. For example, in English we can turn a simple activity of 'melting' into a caused activity simply by making an intransitive verb a transitive one:

   1a   The snow is melting   (intransitive)
     b   The sun is melting the snow   (transitive)

In French and Chinese, however, an additional 'causative' verb has to be introduced:

   2a   La neige fond
          The snow is melting
     b   Le soleil **fait** fondre la neige
          The sun makes to-melt the snow

3a   Xue hua le
     Snow melt Aspect marker
 b   Taiyang **shi** xue (rong)hua le
     Sun make snow melt Aspect marker
     (Chinese example from Juffs 1996: 90)

Whereas verbs describing activities like *telephone* and *go* occur with the auxiliary *have* in the present perfect in English, in French and Italian the equivalent of *telephone* occurs with *have*, but the equivalent of *go* occurs with *be*:

4a   John **has** telephoned
 b   Jean **a** téléphoné
 c   Gianni **ha** telefonato

5a   John **has** gone home
 b   Jean **est** rentré chez lui
 c   Gianni **è** andato a casa

In English, some verbs describing events which benefit one of the participants ('benefactives') can alternate between an [___ NP PP] complement and an [___ NP NP] complement (this is known as the 'dative alternation'):

6a   Jane gave the book to Tom
 b   Jane gave Tom the book

French, by contrast, realizes dative verbs only with [___ NP PP] complements:

7a   Jeanne a donné le livre à Tom
 b   *Jeanne a donné Tom le livre

The main observation about examples like these is that languages have different ways of expressing syntactically what is essentially the same event. This being the case, we can ask if there are any systematic ways in which lexical structure is converted into syntactic structure. Are any universal principles involved? What are the limits of variation between languages?

In the next section I explain the notion of **argument structure**, which means the number and type of participants involved in the events described by verbs, adjectives or nouns, and outline a standard account of how argument structure is linked to syntactic representations. In subsequent sections I describe some of the L2 studies which have looked at how successful L2 learners are in acquiring the syntactic correlates of argument structure.

5.3 Argument structure and thematic roles

Section 5.3 explains what arguments and adjuncts are, and shows that some arguments can be null. The idea that arguments play specific roles in events – called 'theta-roles' – is discussed, and a proposal for how theta-roles are assigned to positions in syntactic configurations is described. The notion that noun phrases must be Case-marked is introduced, and it is shown how theta-roles and Case interact.

5.3.1 Arguments and adjuncts

Verbs, and some types of adjectives and nouns, describe events in which there is at least one participant doing something, being affected by the event, being the recipient of some action, and so on, as illustrated in the following:

8a   Tony laughed
     (*Tony* is the doer)

  b   The paper boat sank
     (*The paper boat* is affected by the event in question)

  c   Tom showed the painting to his mother
     (*His mother* is the recipient, in some sense, of Tom's action)

Every verb (from now on we will focus on verbs, although the same properties can apply to some adjectives and nouns) is accompanied by a number of obligatory participants, usually from one to three, which express the core meaning of the event. Some of these participants must always be overt; others can be null, but they remain active in the interpretation of the event in some abstract sense. For example, the participants affected by the actions described by the verbs in (9) cannot be null:

9a   Eric buttered the toast
     *Eric buttered
  b   Tom showed the painting to his colleagues
     *Tom showed to his colleagues
  c   Hilary put the revolver in the drawer
     *Hilary put in the drawer

By contrast, the participants affected by the actions in the following can be null, but they are understood to be present in the interpretation of the event:

10a   John drinks vodka
      John drinks
      (understood as 'John is a drinker of alcohol')

   b Tom showed the painting to his colleagues
      Tom showed the painting in London
      (understood as 'John showed the painting to an unspecified
      audience')

The obligatory participants in the event described by a verb should be distinguished from other, non-obligatory, participants and descriptions of the time,
place, manner, etc., in which the event occurred:

11a   Eric buttered the toast *with a fish-knife*
   b Jim showed the painting to his colleagues *for Emily*
   c Hilary put the revolver in the drawer *the day before yesterday*

The italicized constituents in (11) add meaning to the events, but they are not
core elements in those events. In an act of 'buttering' someone or something
necessarily does the buttering, and something is necessarily buttered. But the
instrument employed in the buttering is not a core part of the event. Participants
which are core elements in the meaning of an event are known as **arguments**.
Other constituents which are optional are known as **adjuncts**.

5.3.2 Argument structure

It will have become obvious already that different verbs can have different
numbers of arguments. One line of research in linguistics has developed the idea
that there are a fixed number of participant roles made available by Universal
Grammar which arguments can assume. These are known as **thematic roles** or
theta-roles (θ-roles). They are roles like:

12   AGENT: the instigator of an event (*Jim* in *Jim melted the ice*)
     THEME: a participant affected by an event (*ice* in *Jim melted
     the ice*)
     EXPERIENCER: a human participant who undergoes some
     change in mental state as the result of an event (*John* in *John
     fears dogs*)
     GOAL: The target of an event (*Eric* in *Brian sold Eric a watch*)

Others have also been proposed (see Larson (1988) and Parsons (1995)) for
some discussion of θ-roles.

There appear to be important generalizations to be captured about the connections between the number of arguments a verb has, the θ-roles assigned to those arguments, and the positions the arguments occupy in syntactic structure. For a start, there cannot be more NPs in a clause than are allowed by a verb's argument structure, because they will just not receive an interpretation:

13a   *Tony laughed Alice
   b   *Harry sank the paper boat the river
   c   *The breakfast Eric buttered the toast

Secondly, there cannot be fewer NPs in a clause than is required by the verb's argument structure (unless they are null and understood in some abstract sense, as described above):

14a   *Eric buttered
   b   *Jane filled with water
   c   *Hilary put in the drawer

Facts like these led Chomsky (1981) to propose a principle of Univeral Grammar known as the θ-criterion:

The θ-criterion
Each θ-role is assigned to exactly one argument, and each argument receives exactly one θ-role.

The θ-criterion ensures that the NP constituents which appear with a verb receive an interpretation in the event described by the verb, and that any extraneous NP is uninterpretable (unless it is an adjunct).

The θ-criterion does not tell us, however, which syntactic positions arguments with specific thematic roles occupy. There appear to be generalizations to be captured in this area, and one line of research has attempted to do so (Larson 1988; Hale and Keyser 1993; Levin and Rappaport Hovav 1995). For example, AGENTs always surface as subjects in English:

15a   *James* hit Bill
   b   *Harry* sank the boat
   c   *Ellen* passed the package to Tom

When no AGENT argument is present, but a THEME argument is, that tends to surface as the subject:

16a   *The boat* sank
   b   *The package* passed to Tom

On the basis of evidence like this, one early proposal (Jackendoff 1972; Larson 1988) was for a Thematic Hierarchy which determined the order in which arguments are assigned to syntactic positions:

Thematic Hierarchy
AGENT > THEME > SOURCE > GOAL > OBLIQUES (manner, location, time . . .).

The idea here is that the argument with the highest role on the hierarchy is mapped to subject position, the next highest to direct object position, the next highest to indirect object position, and so on down the hierarchy. So, in

> 17   John gave his pocket-money to his little sister

the AGENT *John* is mapped to subject position, the THEME *his pocket-money* is mapped to direct object position, and the GOAL *his little sister* is mapped to indirect object position. If no AGENT is present, the THEME is mapped to subject position, as in (18):

> 18   The pocket-money passed from John to his little sister

There is, however, a fairly basic empirical problem with the Thematic Hierarchy. While AGENTs always seem to map to subject position, THEME, SOURCE and GOAL can appear in different positions, as in (19):

> 19a   John gave his pocket-money (THEME) to his little sister (GOAL)
>   b   John gave his little sister (GOAL) his pocket-money (THEME)
>   c   The message (THEME) passed from Tom (SOURCE) to Alice (GOAL)
>   d   Alice (GOAL) received the message (THEME) from Tom (SOURCE)

One proposal for dealing with this problem is Baker's (1988: 47) Uniformity of Theta Assignment Hypothesis (UTAH):

Uniformity of Theta Assignment Hypothesis
Identical thematic relationships between items are represented by identical structural relationships between those items at D-structure.

By 'D-structure' is meant a clause's initial syntactic structure, before any operations like movement apply. To illustrate, compare the pair of sentences in (20):

20a Jim (AGENT) sank the boat (THEME)
   b The boat (THEME) sank

Given UTAH, although *sink* has a THEME argument which surfaces in two different syntactic positions (direct object in (20a), subject in (20b)), in the clause's initial structure the THEME argument should be mapped onto the same syntactic position. By virtue of the fact that AGENTs are always mapped onto subject position, the underlying position for the THEME in (20) would be direct object position:

21a [$_{IP}$ Jim past [$_{VP}$ sink the boat]]
   b [$_{IP}$ e past [$_{VP}$ sink the boat]]

In (21b) the specifier of IP, the subject position, is empty, and *the boat* moves to this position giving:

21c [$_{IP}$ The boat$_i$ past [$_{VP}$ sink t$_i$]]

5.3.3 Case assignment and the Case Filter

What forces *the boat* to move to the subject position in (21c)? Why can't we, in English, say *Sank the boat* with the meaning 'The boat sank'? The standard answer is because of **Case** requirements. Grammatical Case (with a capital 'C' to distinguish it from the ordinary use of the word 'case') is a property which is associated with certain syntactic positions. Case in modern English is only visible in a few forms, like pronouns. For example, the *they* form of the third person plural pronoun can only appear in subject position, while the *them* form appears in all non-subject positions:

22a The boats/They/*Them sank
   b Harry sank the boats/*they/them
   c Jim told Julie about the boats/*they/them

Using terms from traditional grammatical theory, it can be said that *they* is a **nominative** form of the pronoun and *them* is an **accusative** form. A number of English pronouns have nominative and accusative forms (nominative: *I, he, she, we, they*; accusative: *me, him, her, us, them*). Although the effects of grammatical Case are only visible in a small number of cases in English, many languages have more widespread visible effects. In German, for instance, Case is visible in the determiner system of nouns:

23a   **Der** Mann ist gekommen
The man has come

b   Ich habe **den** Mann gesehen
I have the man seen
'I saw the man'

Standard accounts of Case propose that the category Infl assigns nominative Case to its specifier position (the subject of the clause). Where verbs have two arguments, the verb assigns accusative Case to the argument that is its complement (*I saw him/*he*). However, when the verb has only one argument, it does not assign accusative Case – the argument gets its Case from Infl (*He/*Him laughed; They/*Them arrived*). Prepositions in English assign a Case, which is sometimes called 'oblique', to their complements, although its visible form is indistinguishable from accusative Case (*I bought the tickets for **them**; I have nothing against **him***). In nominal possessive constructions a genitive Case appears to be assigned to an NP in a specifier-like relation to another NP: *Jeremy's uncle*. (We return to the genitive Case in chapter 6.) Thus Case is always assigned to subjects, to objects of verbs, to objects of prepositions, and to the specifiers of NPs even if it is not always visible. This is regarded by linguists as the effect of another principle of Universal Grammar frequently referred to as the **Case Filter** (Vergnaud 1985):

Case Filter
*NP, if NP does not have Case

The Case Filter says that any NP must receive a Case to be grammatical. So to be interpretable and grammatical in sentences, NPs must have both theta-roles (by the θ-criterion) and Case (to satisfy the Case Filter).

5.3.4   The interaction of Case assignment and argument structure: unaccusative and unergative verbs

Returning now to (21b)–(21c) and the issue of what forces *the boat* to move from object to subject position. If verbs with only one argument do not assign accusative Case, *sink* cannot assign Case to its complement *the boat*. And since, by the Case Filter, NPs must have Case to be grammatical, *the boat* is forced to move to the specifier position of IP, because that is the only position in the clause to which Case is assigned. We see here, then, the interaction of two principles of Universal Grammar. The first, the principle of Uniformity of Theta Assignment, requires *sink* to assign the THEME role to an argument in object position. But because in (21b) *sink* is a one-argument verb which does not assign Case, the Case Filter forces the THEME argument to move in order to be Case-marked.

Sink is a verb which alternates between a simple 'activity with an endpoint' interpretation (*the boat sank*) and a 'caused activity with an endpoint' interpretation (*Harry sank the boat*). There is also a class of verbs which allow only the first kind of interpretation, where a single participant is the THEME: *John arrived; Harry left; Susie died*. These verbs, too, have initial syntactic structures where the THEME argument is generated in the object position, necessarily by UTAH. Because they are one-argument verbs, the THEME argument does not receive accusative Case from the verb, and the argument must move to subject position in order to satisfy the Case Filter:

24a $[_{IP}$ e past $[_{VP}$ arrive John]]
  b $[_{IP}$ John$_i$ past $[_{VP}$ arrive t$_i$]]

These are known as **unaccusative** verbs. As a rough semantic guide, unaccusative verbs typically describe events over which the participant does not have 'volitional control' (Perlmutter 1978). They contrast with another class of one-argument verbs whose participants do have volitional control, and are not THEMEs but AGENTs: *John laughed; Harry telephoned; Jane spoke*. In these cases, the AGENT argument is generated directly in subject position, and does not have to move to receive Case:

25 $[_{IP}$ John past $[_{VP}$ laugh]]

These are known as **unergative** verbs.

Interestingly, a number of syntactic properties correlate with the contrast between unaccusative and unergative verbs. I shall describe them when the L2 studies are discussed. To give one example by way of illustration, only unaccusatives can appear in a construction in English with *there* as the subject:

26a There arrived three men
  b There came a stranger
  c *There laughed three men
  d *There telephoned a stranger[1]

This behaviour would be explicable if the arguments of unaccusative verbs are generated in complement position, while the arguments of unergative verbs are generated in a specifier position. In the case of unaccusatives, two possibilities are then available in English. Either the argument moves to the specifier position of IP, or the **expletive pronoun** *there* is inserted in the specifier position of IP. (An expletive pronoun can now be defined technically as a pronoun without a theta-role.)[2]

5.3.5   Summary of section 5.3

We have seen, then, the effects of the interaction of three principles of Universal Grammar on the structure of clauses: the Uniformity of Theta Assignment Hypothesis (UTAH), which requires that specific theta-roles be linked to particular positions in initial syntactic structure (before any operations like movement have applied); the θ-criterion, which requires that every NP have a theta-role, and that every theta-role which is required by a verb's meaning be assigned to an NP; and the Case Filter, which requires that all NPs have abstract Case. While UTAH and the θ-criterion appear to be invariant in their application across languages – they seem to be constants in the design of human language – satisfaction of the Case Filter is subject to some variation. English requires that the THEME argument of unaccusative verbs move to the specifier of IP in order to receive nominative Case; in other languages nominative Case may be assigned to the THEME in the VP so that it does not have to move (see section 5.4.1). The movement operation itself may be accompanied by language-specific consequences: although in English unaccusatives co-occur with the auxiliary *have*, as unergatives do, in Italian unaccusative verbs co-occur with the equivalent of *be* as an auxiliary (*essere*), while unergatives co-occur with the equivalent of *have* (*avere*).

We have, then, the kind of situation with regard to the argument structure of verbs, and how that structure is linked to syntactic representations, where it is possible to investigate whether L2 learners build mental grammars which are constrained by the principles of Universal Grammar, what role the L1 might play in grammar-building, and the extent to which the salience of head–complement relations affects development. Work in this area of SLA is relatively new. Some of the findings are discussed in the following sections.

5.4   The second language acquisition of unaccusative verb constructions

Section 5.4 describes a number of studies which have found that L2 learners are aware of the argument structure distinction between unaccusative and other types of verbs, with this guiding the way they construct mental grammars for the L2. It is shown, though, that learners have difficulty determining the range of appropriate syntactic realizations of the distinction in question, and that this can persist into near-native levels of proficiency.

5.4.1   Evidence that awareness of the unaccusative/unergative distinction guides grammar building

Zobl (1989) noticed, in a corpus of the written English of a group of students from various L1 backgrounds attending universities in Canada and the United

States, that some speakers were producing ungrammatical verb–subject orders with unaccusative verbs as in (27), and were overgeneralizing passive verb morphology to unaccusative verbs as in (28) (examples from Zobl 1989: 204):

27a I was just patient until dried my clothes
  b Sometimes comes a good regular wave

28a My mother was died when I was just a baby
  b The most incredible experience of my life was happened 15 years ago

In (27) the speakers seem to have failed to move the THEME argument to the specifier of IP in order to get nominative Case. In (28) they have moved the THEME argument into the subject position, but have added passive morphology, unnecessarily and ungrammatically. Passive morphology in English – that is, the *be + past participle* construction which turns transitive clauses like *He wrote the song (in an afternoon)* into *The song **was written** (in an afternoon)* – appears to have the effect of deleting the AGENT θ-role from the verb's argument structure, making it a one-argument verb and hence unable to assign accusative Case:

29 $[_{IP}$ e past $[_{VP}$ be written the song]]

By the Case Filter, therefore, the argument of *write* must move to the specifier of IP to receive nominative Case. In (28) the speakers have assumed that passive morphology is required even though no AGENT role was initially present.

Zobl examined the corpus in greater detail to see whether these non-native-like forms correlated with unaccusative verbs more generally, or whether they were just random overgeneralizations. The corpus was drawn from the coursework of 114 L2 speakers, all university-age students in ESL programmes, who were advanced enough to be marking tense distinctions, and whom Zobl classified as ranging in proficiency from low to high intermediate. Ninety were native speakers of Japanese, and the other 24 were distributed across Arabic, Spanish, Chinese, Turkish, Thai and Indonesian. Zobl found that there were 13 cases of verb–subject order with 80 unaccusative verb tokens, but no cases of verb–subject word order with any other type of verb. Moreover, 10 of the sentences with verb–subject order were produced by native speakers of Japanese.

Although the number of cases is small, this is a striking result. Japanese is a language with verb-final word order; the tensed verb must normally appear at the end of a clause, whether it is a matrix or embedded clause. Thus one could not attribute the source of verb–subject order to Japanese. Furthermore, in English there is no overt marking which distinguishes unaccusatives from other types of verb; with both unaccusatives and unergatives the one argument that the verb requires surfaces in the specifier of IP. So there is no evidence from English to lead Japanese speakers to produce verb–subject word order. The conclusion one is drawn to is that these Japanese-speaking learners of English have unconscious knowledge of a distinction between unaccusative and other types of verb in English, even though there is no evidence on the surface for such a distinction, and this influences the representation they construct for clauses with unaccusative verbs.[3]

The reason why Japanese speakers in particular might produce English sentences with verb–subject order may be related to Case assignment. There is some evidence that the arguments of unaccusative verbs in Japanese receive Case within the VP, and do not move out of the VP (see below for discussion). The interaction between this transferred property from the L1 (that the arguments of unaccusative verbs remain within the VP) coupled with the acquisition of the fact that verbs precede their complements in English, would give rise to the possibility of verb–subject order.

As far as the use of passive morphology is concerned, the situation is not so straightforward. Zobl found cases of the ungrammatical use of the passive both with unaccusative verbs (as in (28)), and with unergative (*She was smiled) and ordinary transitive verbs (*I was studied English). But the ratio of use was different. Whereas there were 25 unaccusative passives out of a total of 110 unaccusative verbs (a ratio of roughly 1 to 4.5), there were 11 passives with unergatives/ transitives out of a total of 173 tokens (a ratio of roughly 1 to 16). So, although there is overgeneralization of the passive construction, it is more likely to occur with unaccusatives, suggesting that 'unaccusative' again forms a representational category in the grammars of these L2 speakers.

In a related study, Balcom (1997) investigated the judgements of 38 L1 Chinese speakers of the ungrammaticality of unaccusative passives in English like the following:

30a *This soup was tasted good after the cook added some salt
  b *The door was closed smoothly because Mary had remembered to oil the hinges
  c *This dress was only cost $40, because Janet bought it on sale

Informants were students enrolled at an English-speaking university and were of roughly high intermediate to advanced proficiency level. The task was a grammaticality judgement task consisting of 20 grammatical and 15 ungrammatical sentences. Balcom shows that passive morphology was accepted by her subjects significantly more often with unaccusatives than with other types of verb.

Such sensitivity to the unaccusative–unergative distinction can also be found where the L2 is not English. Hirakawa (2000) investigated whether L1 English and L1 Chinese speakers were aware of certain interpretive differences in L2 Japanese. Japanese is a language that allows both subjects and objects to be null under some circumstances, for example (all examples from Hirakawa):

31   Takusan   yon-da
        e_subj a-lot   e_obj read-past
        'He/she/they/we etc. read a lot (of things)'

Here e_{subj} (e = 'empty') is a null subject which can have the same interpretation as one of the referential pronouns *he, she, they, we,* etc., of English, and e_{obj} is a null object with the same meaning as referential *it, them* or generic *things* (see section 5.7 for more discussion of null subjects and objects). The form *takusan* 'a lot' is a kind of adverbial or numeral quantifier, like English 'a lot, much, many'. In (31) *takusan* modifies the null object. An interesting difference arises when *takusan* co-occurs with unaccusative verbs and with unergative verbs. With unaccusatives it can be interpreted as modifying the THEME argument:

32a   Takusan tui-ta   (unaccusative)
      a-lot   e arrive-past
      'A lot (of people) arrived'

But with unergatives it can only be interpreted as an adverbial modifying the verb, not as modifying the AGENT:

32b   Takusan oyoi-da   (unergative)
      e a-lot   swim-past
      'We/they/he etc. swam a lot'
      ['*A lot (of people) swam']

To account for this, Hirakawa followed Kageyama (1993) in assuming that the THEME argument of unaccusative verbs remains in the VP (and is assigned Case in the VP). It is not moved out of the VP in order to get Case as the THEME arguments of English unaccusatives are. Assuming that *takusan* is a VP-internal adverbial/numeral quantifier, the interpretations in (32) can be explained, because only a THEME argument is potentially within the scope of *takusan*; AGENT arguments are outside the VP.

Hirakawa tested two groups of L2 learners of Japanese on their ability to detect these differences of interpretation determined by whether null subjects are inside the VP (unaccusatives) or outside the VP (unergatives): 13 native speakers of English, and 13 native speakers of Chinese. To do this she used a picture-sentence matching design. Subjects were presented with, for example, a cartoon where it is suggested that one person has done a lot of swimming, and another where there are a lot of people swimming. Informants then have to judge whether a sentence like (32b) is a 'true' interpretation of the first picture, the second picture or both. (Only the first picture showing a person who has done a lot of swimming corresponds to (32b).) Other pictures were drawn to show, for example,

Table 5.1 Mean acceptance (out of 5) of sentences which are a 'true' or 'false' interpretation of a series of cartoons

Subjects	Unerg. (true)	Unerg. (false)	Unacc. (true)
English (n = 13)	3.54	2.38	4.23
Chinese (n = 13)	3.77	2.38	4.31

Source: Adapted from Hirakawa 2000

a lot of people arriving, and informants similarly had to judge whether sentence (32a) is a 'true' interpretation of the picture. The full test included five unergative sentences which were 'true' interpretations of five cartoons, five unergative sentences which were 'false' interpretations of five cartoons, and five unaccusative sentences which were 'true' interpretations of another five cartoons. The results are given in table 5.1, where the scores indicate the mean of each group's acceptance of sentences as appropriate interpretations for the cartoons.

The results show that both L1 English and L1 Chinese speakers of L2 Japanese are less likely to accept the 'A lot of people swam' interpretation of *Takusan oyoida* than they are the 'They/she/we swam a lot' interpretation. At the same time, they accept the 'A lot of people arrived' interpretation of *Takusan tuita*. This shows that the L2 speakers make a distinction between unaccusative and unergative verbs, and that they have correctly realized that THEME arguments remain within the VP in Japanese when unaccusative verbs are involved. Given that in *Takusan tuita/Takusan oyoida* there is nothing on the surface to indicate which is an unaccusative and which an unergative, this suggests that learners' knowledge of Japanese is underdetermined by the input.

All of the L2 speakers in the studies we have just looked at appear to be at intermediate to advanced levels of proficiency, and are able to use tense marking, passive morphology and assign Case to some degree. This suggests that IP is already established in their mental grammars. In the case of the L2 learners of English, however, their knowledge is not completely like that of native speakers. Some subjects allow nominative Case to be assigned to a THEME argument in the VP (Zobl's subjects), and some assume that when a THEME moves from the VP to the specifier of IP, overt morphology (passive morphology) is required to mark the movement, even where unaccusative verbs are involved (Zobl's and Balcom's subjects). This shows that informants are aware (subconsciously) of the argument structure properties of verbs and use these properties to guide the construction of syntactic representations for an L2 in ways which could not have been inferred from the input – an example of the principles of UG operating in L2 mental grammars. At the same time it shows that the language-specific ways in which Case-assignment is realized are not yet fully established.

5.4.2 Persistent difficulty in establishing the syntactic realization of argument structure

An interesting question is how persistent the difficulties of establishing the language-specific realization of argument structure distinctions might be for L2 learners. Sorace (1993) provides some interesting evidence about the nature of such knowledge in the near-native L2 Italian of speakers of L1 French and L1 English. The evidence concerns language-specific differences in the choice of verbs that can serve as auxiliaries in compound tenses.

Sorace first observes that there are a number of subclasses of verb within the category 'unaccusative'. Of relevance to her L2 study is a distinction between unaccusatives which express some notion of movement and change of location (*Jim arrived*), those which express a state (*The paintwork has lasted*) and those which have a causative alternant (*The boat sank/Harry sank the boat*). In Italian, the auxiliary *essere*, 'be' co-occurs with all three, whereas in French *être* co-occurs only with unaccusative verbs which denote a change of location. The others co-occur with *avoir*, 'have', like English (compare: *Jim est/*a arrivé*, 'Jim arrived'; *Les peintures ont/*sont duré*, 'The paintwork has lasted').

In addition, modal verbs in Italian, which normally co-occur with the auxiliary *avere* 'have', can optionally co-occur with *essere* when they take unaccusative verbs as complements (examples from Sorace 1993: 26–7):

33   Mario ha/è dovuto andare a casa
      Mario has had   to-go   home

Italian also allows, optionally in such constructions, what is known as **clitic climbing**: the raising of unstressed preverbal object pronouns. In this case, when the clitic climbs, the auxiliary co-occurring with *dovere* is obligatorily *essere*:

34a   (A casa), Mario ha/è dovuto andar-ci
      (Home), Mario has had   to-go-there

  b   (A casa), Mario ci è/*ha dovuto andare
      (Home), Mario there has had   to-go

In French, clitic climbing is not possible, and in neither of the above contexts does *être* occur:

35a   Mario a/*est dû aller chez lui
      Mario has   had to-go home

  b   Mario a/*est dû y   aller
      Mario has   had there to-go

  c   *Mario y   a/est dû aller
      Mario there has had to-go

In English, of course, the only auxiliary possible in any of these constructions is *have* and not *be*.

Sorace compared knowledge of the properties of Italian auxiliary choice in two groups of very advanced near-native L2 speakers: 24 with English as their L1, and 20 with French as their L1. They were aged between 23 and 46, and had all started learning Italian after the age of 15. All subjects had received some formal instruction, but most reported having acquired Italian by being in Italy for long periods, or through being in contact with Italians. A control group of 36 native speakers also took the test.

The test was a grammaticality judgement task involving 48 sentences which included unaccusative verbs of different types, modal verb constructions, and clitic climbing constructions, some where *essere* was the auxiliary, and some where *avere* was the auxiliary. To obtain judgements from informants, Sorace used a technique called Magnitude Estimation. This requires an informant to assign an acceptability rating to an initial sentence in the form of a random number, and then to rate the acceptability of subsequent sentences in relation to the first by assigning higher or lower numbers. Sorace then converted the scores of individuals into ten-point scales for comparison. The results for auxiliary choice are presented in table 5.2. The scores are the group means on the converted ten-point scale. The higher the number, the more acceptable the subjects find the sentence:

Table 5.2 Mean acceptability judgements of auxiliary choice in Italian with different types of unaccusative verbs

Type of verb		L1: Italian		L1: French		L1: English	
			Aux in L1		Aux in L1		Aux in L1
Change of	E	9.509	*essere*	9.927	*être*	9.248	*have*
location	A	1.653		1.875		2.224	
(*arrive*-type)							
Describes	E	9.203	*essere*	8.930	*avoir*	8.088	*have*
a state	A	2.922		4.375		3.930	
(*last*-type)							
Has a	E	9.340	*essere*	9.825	*avoir*	9.170	*have*
causative	A	3.562		6.629		5.353	
alternant							
(*sink*-type)							

E = test sentences where the auxiliary was *essere* (grammatical in Italian)
A = test sentences where the auxiliary was *avere* (ungrammatical in Italian)
Source: Adapted from Sorace 1993: 37

The results broadly suggest that both non-native speaker groups are sensitive to the fact that *essere* is the normal auxiliary co-occurring with unaccusative verbs in Italian. However, statistical analysis by Sorace (using a repeated measures analysis of variance) found that the native language has a significant effect on the extent to which the groups reject the sentences involving *avere*. The French and the English subjects were more likely to accept *avere* with unaccusatives describing a state than were the Italian native speakers.

The results of subjects' judgements about the choice of *essere/avere* in modal constructions with and without clitic climbing are presented in table 5.3:

Table 5.3 Mean acceptability judgements of auxiliary choice in Italian with modal verbs

Sentence type		L1: Italian	L1: French	L1: English
(a) Optional aux	E	9.260	3.824	7.231
è/ha dovuto andare	A	9.749	9.420	6.977
(b) Clitic: no movnt.	E	8.159	4.065	6.784
è/ha dovuto andarci	A	8.779	7.841	6.211
(c) Clitic: climbing	E	8.587	8.525	6.286
*ci è/*ha dovuto andare*	A	3.143	4.285	6.623

E = test sentences where the auxiliary was *essere*
A = test sentences where the auxiliary was *avere*. (In context (c) where there is clitic climbing, *avere* is ungrammatical.)
Source: Adapted from Sorace 1993: 39

On type (a) sentences there is a statistically significant difference for the French subjects between their use of *essere* and *avere*. There is no such difference for the Italian or English speakers. The French speakers have failed to acquire to any significant degree the fact that these constructions allow the *essere* auxiliary. The English speakers, while less accurate than the Italians, appear to allow both correctly. A similar pattern emerges on type (b) sentences. On the type (c) sentences, however, the judgements of the French speakers are similar to the Italians; i.e. they accept (correctly) *essere* significantly more often than *avere*. The English speakers, however, do not distinguish the two. In fact their responses are very similar to their responses on the other two types of construction.

Sorace (1993: 42) interprets these results as showing that English speakers have **indeterminate** mental representations for these constructions, while French speakers have acquired **divergent** mental representations from those of native speakers of Italian. The English speakers accept both *essere* and *avere* in all the contexts to more or less the same degree. It is almost as if they cannot sort out when to use one or the other verb. By contrast, the French correctly select *essere* with clitic climbing (note: this is not possible in French), but they behave in a French-like way on non-clitic-climbing constructions, preferring *avere* to *essere*. They have clearer intuitions, but their intuitions are different from those of native speakers of Italian.

How might we explain this difference in the nature of the L2 mental grammars of English and French speakers? We assumed in our discussion of auxiliary *be* and *have* in English that these are verbs which select VP complements (see section 2.6.2), for example:

36

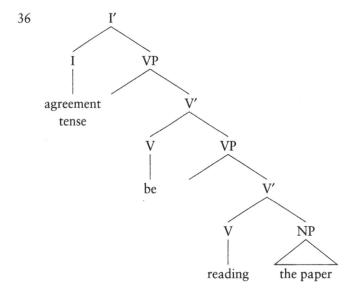

Specifically, *be* is an auxiliary which selects a VP complement with a V + *ing* head. An extension of this idea to auxiliary verbs in Italian and French may be to say that *essere* and *être* select VP complements with past participle heads which have particular properties. In Italian *essere* selects any unaccusative participle which denotes a change of location or a state; in French *être* selects any unaccusative participle which denotes a change of location:

37

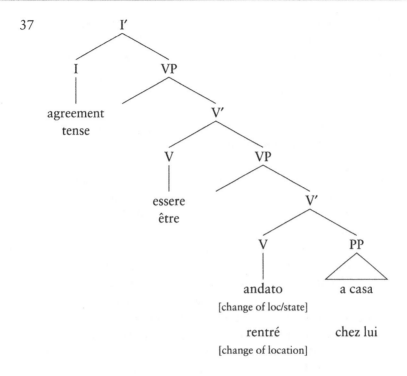

If the choice between the appearance of *avere* and *essere* with past participles in Italian is a matter of the complement selectional requirements of the auxiliary in question, given that we have claimed that head–complement selectional properties are salient for L2 learners, we would expect both French and English learners of Italian to acquire the appropriate use of *essere* and *avere* with unaccusative participles in simple clauses. And this prediction appears to be borne out by the data presented in table 5.2. Both French and English speakers perform very like the native Italian group in accepting the use of *essere* with unaccusative verbs of all classes.

What appears to be more difficult for the French and English speakers is eliminating the possibility of *also* allowing *avere* to select the unaccusative past participles describing states, and to a greater extent those with causative alternants, since both groups are significantly more likely to accept *avere* in these cases than the Italian speakers. This would seem to suggest that although the L2 learners acquire the complement selectional properties of *essere*, there may be residual L1 influence of *avoir* and *have* on their acquisition of *avere*.

How the behaviour of the L2 learners on the choice of auxiliary with modal verbs is interpreted depends on the syntactic analysis one gives to such constructions. Since Italian allows modals to occur optionally with *essere* when the verb in the subordinate clause is unaccusative, but requires *essere* obligatorily when a clitic pronoun has climbed up to the clause containing the modal, it may be suggested that the modal can 'incorporate' the lower verb, and in doing so inherits its features. When there is no clitic climbing such incorporation is optional (a bit like the optionality of the operation involved in the English alternation *She let the rope go/She let go the rope*, where *let* seems optionally to incorporate *go*) and modals may occur either with *avere* or *essere*:

38a Mario [$_V$ ha [$_{VP}$ [$_V$ dovuto [$_{VP}$ andare$_{[unaccusative]}$ a casa]]]]
  b Mario [$_V$ è [$_{VP}$ [$_V$ dovuto andare$_{[unaccusative]}$] a casa]]]

When there is clitic climbing, incorporation of the lower verb into the modal is obligatory. One may turn this around and say that it is precisely because there is incorporation of one verb into another, creating a kind of single compound verb, that clitic climbing is possible.

On the basis of an analysis of this kind, we may be able to explain the French speakers' intuitions about the use of *essere* with modals. Where there is no clitic climbing they prefer *avere* to a significantly greater degree than *essere*. This suggests that they have not acquired the fact that Italian modals allow incorporation whether a clitic is present or not. But when a clitic which has climbed is present, they know that the modal has incorporated the lower verb (otherwise the clitic could not have climbed). And since, with incorporation, the modal necessarily inherits the features of the unaccusative verb, they know that *essere* is required.

By contrast, the English speakers have a kind of 'middle of the road' set of intuitions about the properties of Italian modals, whether clitics have climbed or not. Sorace describes this state of affairs as 'indeterminate', and this could well be right. What seems to be clear is that clitic climbing does not have the same significance in the L2 mental grammars for Italian of the English speakers as it does in the L2 mental grammars for Italian of the French speakers. Since French has object clitic pronouns, but English does not, one may conclude that it is this difference between the L1s which gives rise to distinct outcomes.

The findings of Sorace's study are consistent with the claim that L2 learners are aware of 'unaccusative' as an argument structure subtype because they are more likely to select *essere* than *avere* as the auxiliary with the class of unaccusative verbs. At the same time they have difficulty realizing the range of syntactic contexts in which *essere* may appear in Italian. The English speakers allow both *essere/avere* in a range of modal contexts, even though in one case (clitic climbing) *avere* is impossible. The French speakers are aware that *essere* should be the auxiliary with modals when clitics have climbed, but disallow *essere* in other modal contexts. If 'verb incorporation' is what determines these contexts, both groups of speakers appear not to have acquired the range of its operation, and this is a persistent problem, even for these near-native speakers. But there is obviously also persistent L1 influence, since the English and French speakers differ in the ways that their grammars are dissimilar to those of native speakers of Italian.

5.4.3 Summary of section 5.4

In section 5.4 we have considered a number of L2 studies which provide evidence about how two invariant principles of Universal Grammar, one parametrized principle and certain language-specific properties of lexical selection relating to argument structure are involved in the development of L2 mental grammars:

- The two invariant principles are the Uniformity of Theta Assignment Hypo-thesis (UTAH) and the θ-criterion. These are constants in the design of natural language grammars in that, by hypothesis, they operate in the same way across languages.
- Satisfaction of the Case Filter may have different syntactic manifestations in specific languages, for example:

  (a) in the case of unaccusative verbs, THEMES in English move to the specifier of IP to receive nominative Case (except when expletive *there* is present – see example (26)), while in Japanese they receive nominative Case in the VP;

  (b) passive morphology in English has the effect of turning a transitive verb into an unaccusative where the THEME again moves to the specifier of IP to receive nominative Case, but is ungrammatical with intrinsically unaccusative verbs;

  (c) the choice of verbs which can serve as auxiliaries is a language-specific property, but nevertheless is sensitive to argument structure distinctions: in Italian *essere*, 'be', co-occurs with the class of unaccusative verbs, or with verbs which have incorporated unaccusatives (modals); in French *être*, 'be', occurs only with a subset of unaccusatives; in English *have* is the auxiliary which co-occurs with all verbs, whether unaccusative or not.

- Results from studies of L2 learners with 'transitional state' L2 grammars (i.e. intermediate and advanced learners) which have focused on unaccusative verbs suggest that learners are sensitive to UTAH and the θ-criterion. In particular, Japanese speakers studied by Zobl (1989) produce non-target-like unaccusatives like *I was just patient until dried my clothes* even though there is no evidence for such constructions either in the L1 or the L2. English and Chinese speakers of L2 Japanese studied by Hirakawa (2000) are aware of different interpretations of *takusan*, 'a lot', with unaccusative and unergative verbs, even though again there is no surface evidence for such a difference. Such underdetermination of knowledge argues that learners have built mental grammars which are constrained by UTAH and the θ-criterion.
- Results from the studies considered also suggest that learners with 'transitional state' and even 'final state' grammars may have difficulty determining the

range of parameter settings in the L2, or the range of language-specific lexical properties associated with principles of UG. Speakers of L1 Japanese do not always move THEMEs to the specifier of IP in L2 English in order to satisfy the Case Filter (Zobl 1989). Japanese and Chinese speakers of L2 English overgeneralize passive morphology to unaccusative verbs (Zobl 1989; Balcom 1997). English and French speakers of Italian correctly allow auxiliary *essere* to select unaccusative verbs, but do not disallow *avere*.

Some of the results are consistent with two characteristics of L2 development we have encountered before: the salience of head–complement relations and the selective influence of the L1 on grammar building. The English- and French-speaking learners of L2 Italian are most target-like in choosing *essere* in simple clauses where the unaccusative verb is the direct complement of the auxiliary. The fact that French has a *be*-type auxiliary, but English does not, does not influence the development of L2 knowledge. But where clitic climbing with modals is involved, the French speakers have a clear advantage over the English speakers; the fact that French has clitic pronouns seems to facilitate their acquisition of *essere* in clitic climbing constructions in Italian.

These cases suggest that 'transitional-state' and 'final-state' L2 mental grammars display similar characteristics to those we have found in 'initial state' L2 grammars: principles of UG appear to be centrally involved in grammar building, head–complement relations are particularly 'acquirable' and there is apparent L1 influence on some (but not all) aspects of grammatical knowledge. At the same time, we have found some evidence that even at advanced levels of proficiency there is divergence between L2 speakers and native speakers of the target language on some properties. As noted in section 5.1, the theories of L2 development we have been considering so far assume potential full access to UG. Evidence of persistent divergence suggests that we need to consider how such cases may be dealt with. In the following sections we discuss further studies of phenomena related to argument structure, and encounter a proposal to account for why L2 mental grammars might diverge from those of native speakers, even into advanced stages of proficiency.

5.5 Null subjects in Greek, Italian and Spanish and second language acquisition

Section 5.5 describes a contrast between languages in whether they require the argument in subject position to be phonetically realized or whether they allow null subjects, and discusses a standard account which explains this contrast as a difference in the inflectional properties of Infl. The claim that null subjects cluster together with two other syntactic properties to form the 'pro-drop' parameter is discussed. Several L2 studies of the pro-drop parameter are then considered, and a proposal is outlined to account for why L2 mental grammars may continue to differ from those of native speakers of the target language, even into advanced stages of proficiency.

5.5.1   The licensing and identification of null subjects

Up to this point we have been assuming that the specifier of IP in tensed clauses – the position occupied by the subject – is either filled directly by an AGENT-like argument or expletive pronoun (as in (39a–d)), or through the movement of an argument from a postverbal position into the specifier, as in (39e):

39a John phoned
  b He phoned
  c There arrived some men
  d It is possible that John phoned
  e Some men$_i$ arrived t$_i$

Sentences like (40), where the specifier of IP is not realized overtly, are usually ungrammatical in English:

40a *Phoned
  b *Arrived some men
  c *Is possible John phoned

There are some restricted registers in which the specifier of a tensed IP can be null, but these are not the norm. For example, Haegeman (1990) has observed that in 'diary contexts' subjects can be dropped:

41 Got up, had a shower and went to the office

But such null subjects are not possible in embedded clauses or more generally when there is an overt CP heading the clause (as in questions), nor when the subject is second person:

42a *Dreamed that got up (versus Dreamed that I got up)
  b *After got up, had a shower
  c *Where did go after breakfast?
  d *Got up, had a shower and went to the office (where the intended reference is: 'You got up, you had a shower . . .')

In contrast to English, however, Greek, Italian and Spanish regularly have null subjects in cases where English has unstressed pronouns. Compare the English and Spanish examples below:

43a I live in Madrid
    ϕ Vivo en Madrid
  b Have **you** received any letters from your family?
    ¿Has ϕ recibido cartas de ta familia?
  c I believe that **she** speaks English
    ϕ creo que ϕ habla inglés

These languages do have pronouns, but they are stressed pronouns, and are used in contexts where English would use contrastive stress:

44 HE might do that, but SHE wouldn't

What allows null subjects to exist more freely in Greek, Italian and Spanish? Since the work of Taraldsen (1981), Rizzi (1982) and Chomsky (1982) it has generally been assumed that the possibility of null subjects in these languages is connected with the range of subject–verb agreement inflections which they realize. All three distinguish six different agreement inflections on thematic verbs in the simple present: first, second and third person, singular and plural. Consider the Spanish verb *hablar*, 'to speak':

45 hablo   I speak   hablamos   we speak
    hablas   you speak   habláis   you speak (plural)
    habla   he/she speaks   hablan   they speak

The idea has been that because these inflections uniquely define the person and number of the subject, that subject need not be overt. There is still a subject, because the range of interpretations assigned to the argument in subject position is just the same as if it were an overt pronoun (AGENT, THEME, etc.). To capture this idea, Rizzi (1982, 1986, 1990) has proposed that the null subject be referred to as *pro* ('small pro') a null pronoun which is **licensed** (i.e. allowed to exist) by Infl, and **identified** by the particular agreement inflection under Infl which attaches to the verb. Both conditions – licensing by Infl and identification by the agreement morphology on the verb – are necessary for *pro* to appear.

The difference between English on the one hand, then, and Greek, Italian and Spanish on the other can be interpreted as a difference in the setting of a parameter associated with a principle of Universal Grammar. The principle is that all clauses have subjects (usually known as the **Extended Projection Principle**, Chomsky 1986b). The parameter (known as the **pro-drop** or **null subject parameter**) is that whereas English Infl requires that its specifier (the subject) be realized overtly (even in cases where that specifier has no theta role, and an expletive pronoun must fill the specifier slot), the differentiated person and number agreement inflections of Greek, Italian and Spanish permit null subjects.[4]

5.5.2   The pro-drop parameter

One of the interests of the claim that principles of UG allow (limited) parameters of variation between languages is that a difference in a single parameter can give rise to a number of surface syntactic consequences. We came across this idea in connection with strong and weak inflections in Infl (section 3.3.3); whether a language has selected one or the other value of the parameter determines different surface locations for thematic verbs with sentential negation, interrogatives, VP adverbs and quantifiers. Similar sorts of consequences have also been claimed to be associated with the pro-drop parameter.

Rizzi (1982, 1990), for example, has proposed that two other syntactic properties cluster together with null/overt subjects. The first is that languages like Greek, Italian and Spanish allow the possibility in ordinary declarative clauses of verb–subject order. The following are equally possible in all three languages (Greek examples from Alexiadou and Anagnostopoulou 1998):

> 46a   Gianni ha telefonato   (Italian)
>   John has telephoned
>   Ha telefonato Gianni
>
>   b   ¡El médico viene!   (Spanish)
>   The doctor is-coming!
>   ¡Viene el médico!
>
>   c   O Petros pandreftike tin Ilektra   (Greek)
>   the Peter married the Ilektra
>   'Peter married Ilektra'
>   Pandreftike o Petros tin Ilektra

Rizzi argues that this is the direct result of these languages allowing null subjects, because in the VS examples null subject *pro* is present, with the overt subjects adjoined to VP:

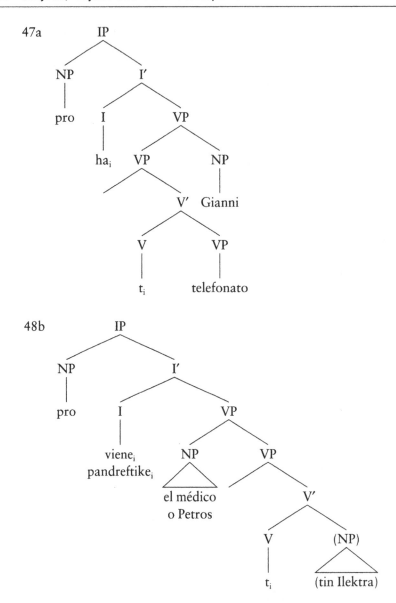

47a

48b

The postverbal subject does not receive Case in this position, but shares Case with *pro* (just as *there* shares Case with the postverbal subject in unaccusative constructions like *There arrived three men* – see section 5.3.4. Cardinaletti (1997) discusses issues to do with Case assignment in constructions involving *pro*). Such inversion is not possible in English precisely because English does not allow null subjects, so there is no mechanism by which postverbal subjects can receive Case.

The second syntactic property which clusters with null subjects is the possibility of extracting an embedded subject across an overt complementizer, for example in question formation. This possibility does not exist in English (examples from Rizzi 1997):

    49a   Chi credi [che [___ telefonerà]]?
           Who you-think [that [___ will telephone]]?
      b   *Who do you think [that [___ will telephone]]?

The problem with the English case is the presence of the complementizer *that*. If the complementizer is null, the sentence becomes grammatical:

    50   Who do you think [ɸ [___ will telephone]]?

The reason why extraction is not possible in English when the complementizer is overt is that the gap in (49b) is a trace left behind by the movement of *who*, and traces are universally ungrammatical unless they are governed by certain kinds of category. This is known as the **Empty Category Principle** (Chomsky 1981, 1986a). For Rizzi, government means governed by the head of the projection in which the trace is a complement:

51

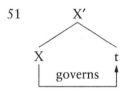

Rizzi suggests that the kinds of head which are potential governors in the configuration in (51) are lexical categories (V, N, P, A) and categories with agreement or tense features. The overt complementizer *that* in English is not a potential governor, and so the subject trace in (49b) is unlicensed and hence ungrammatical. Contrast this with a sentence where an object is extracted, as in (52):

    52   Who do you think [that [Bill will phone t]]?

Here the trace of *who* is governed by the verb *phone*, a lexical head, and so it is licensed and grammatical. The reason why (50) is grammatical is that the null complementizer, ɸ, has the feature [agreement], which licenses the following trace.[5]

    The Empty Category Principle is a proposed invariant universal; a constant in the design of human language, like the θ-criterion and UTAH (see section 5.3.2). How, then, is it possible to move a subject across an overt complementizer in Italian as in (49a) (and equivalent cases in Greek and Spanish)? Rizzi proposes that the Empty Category Principle holds for these languages too, but because they allow postverbal subjects, which are in fact complements to Infl, a trace left behind by movement will be properly head-governed and therefore licensed (because Infl is a head which has both tense and agreement features).

So, on this account three surface-syntactic differences cluster together as the result of the parametric difference in the licensing/identificational properties of Infl: null versus overt subjects, the availability of VS word order in declaratives, and the possibility of extracting subjects across overt complementizers.

5.5.3   Resetting the pro-drop parameter in SLA

White (1985, 1986) was one of the first to investigate the L2 acquisition of the cluster of properties associated with pro-drop. In the 1986 study she compared the performance of two groups of speakers: one group formed the 'null subject L1' group and consisted of 32 native speakers of (Latin American) Spanish and 2 Italian speakers; a second group formed an 'overt subject L1' group and consisted of 37 native speakers of (Quebec) French. French is essentially like English with respect to the pro-drop parameter. If learners have difficulty changing a parameter value of their L1 to a different setting in the L2, then it would be expected that the null subject L1 group would perform differently from the overt subject L1 group.

The informants were all adults attending intensive day courses in ESL, and were classed as low to high intermediate learners. Almost all the subjects reported little exposure to English in secondary school. There were two tests in the study: a grammaticality judgement test consisting of 28 English sentences presented in written and aural form simultaneously, and to which informants had to respond by choosing one of three responses – 'correct', 'incorrect', 'not sure' – and to indicate where a sentence was ungrammatical if they responded 'incorrect'. Twelve of these were grammatical and 16 ungrammatical, the ungrammatical sentences illustrating all three properties associated with the pro-drop parameter.

In addition to the grammaticality judgement test there was a question formation task consisting of 12 sentences where a phrase was highlighted and informants were asked to question that phrase. For example:

> 53   Mary believes that Fred will call *his mother*.
> [Expected response: Who does Mary believe that Fred will call?]

Three of these sentences involved questioning an embedded subject following the overt complementizer *that* (which would produce an ungrammatical sentence if an informant mechanically moved the questioned phrase to the front of the sentence). The purpose of this test was to ensure that informants who were scored for their ability to recognize *that*-trace violations in English were sufficiently advanced to produce grammatical questions involving embedded clauses. In fact only 22 of the informants belonging to the null subject L1 group and 30 of the

Table 5.4   Grammaticality judgement: Group responses to sentences with overt and missing subject pronouns, and SV versus VS word order

	Accept	*Reject*	*Not sure*
Overt pronoun subjects			
Nsub	122/136 (90%)		
Fr	143/148 (97%)		
Missing subjects			
Nsub	84/238 (35%)	145/238 (61%)	9/238 (4%)
Fr	22/259 (8%)	230/259 (89%)	7/259 (3%)
SV order			
Nsub	111/136 (81%)		
Fr	126/148 (85%)		
VS order			
Nsub		155/170 (91%)	
Fr		178/185 (96%)	

Nsub = Null subject L1 group (n = 34)
Fr = L1 French group (n = 37)
Source: Based on White 1986 (information not available for some cells)

Table 5.5   Question formation: Types of question formed from embedded subjects in the presence of overt *that*

	that-*trace*	φ *complementizer*	*Other errors*
Nsub	47/66 (71%)	11/66 (17%)	8/66 (12%)
Fr	38/90 (42%)	18/90 (20%)	34/66 (38%)

Nsub = Null subject L1 group (n = 22)
Fr = L1 French group (n = 30)
Source: Based on White 1986

French-speaking subjects met this criterion, and so only they were included in the results of the question formation task.

The results of informants' performance on subjects and SV/VS word order in the judgement task are given in table 5.4, and on *that*-trace in the question formation task in table 5.5.

The results in table 5.4 show that the null subject L1 group are less accurate than the French speakers in rejecting null subjects in English (and this was statistically significant). There is no significant difference, however, in acceptance of sentences with overt subject pronouns. This is a pattern reminiscent of White's (1991) and Trahey and White's (1993) studies of French speakers' performance on adverb placement with thematic verbs in English (section 3.6), where they optionally allowed thematic verb raising. In the same way at least some of the null subject L1 group are apparently allowing both overt and null subjects, where null subjects would be the normal case in their L1s. By contrast, both groups of speakers are extremely accurate in rejecting VS order. This is not surprising in the case of the French speakers, but it is in the case of the Spanish/Italian speakers given that some of them are optionally allowing null subjects.

On the third property, the French speakers do produce some questions involving a *that*-trace sequence, but not as many as the null subject L1 group; and the types of 'other errors' that the French speakers produce could be construed as attempts to avoid producing *that*-trace violations. (The category of 'other errors' covers all cases of attempts to produce questions which were neither the expected response – replacement of *that* by the ϕ complementizer – nor sequences of *that*-trace; for example, the use of resumptive pronouns or dislocations of the sentence.)[6]

Broadly, these results suggest that there is L1 influence on the acquisition of the English value of the pro-drop parameter by intermediate-level L2 learners. Speakers of Spanish/Italian appear to transfer the feature specification of Infl in their native language to some extent, allowing both null subjects and extractions which leave *that*-trace sequences to a significantly greater degree than speakers of French. Before going on to discuss a possible explanation for these observations, consider some further evidence about how speakers of null subject L1s acquire obligatory subjects in English.

In her 1985 study, using a grammaticality judgement task with a similar design to the one in the 1986 study, White compared 54 Spanish-speaking and 19 French-speaking learners of English by level of proficiency: beginner, intermediate and advanced. Table 5.6 presents the results of informants' responses of 'correct' to ungrammatical sentences with null subjects:

Table 5.6 Group responses of 'correct' to ungrammatical null subject sentences

Level		Score	%
Beginner	Sp (n = 17)	66/102	64.7
	Fr (n = 5)	10/30	33.3
Intermediate	Sp (n = 8)	20/48	41.7
	Fr (n = 8)	7/48	14.6
Advanced	Sp (n = 29)	53/174	30.5
	Fr (n = 6)	3/36	8.3

Source: Based on White 1985

Although Spanish speakers appear to accept a significant proportion of null subjects when they start learning an overt subject language like English, with proficiency that tendency decreases, although it remains greater than in the case of speakers of an overt subject L1 like French.

Phinney (1987) has found that Spanish speakers make a distinction between types of pronoun in development: expletive pronouns (*it, there*) are more likely to be absent in more advanced speakers than referential pronouns (*I, you, he, she,* etc.). Taking samples from the free compositions in English of two groups of students at the University of Puerto Rico with 12 years of tutored instruction in English, she found that while referential pronouns were omitted by each group in only 13% and 6% of contexts where a pronoun would have been required by a native speaker, expletive pronouns were omitted in 56% and 76% of contexts. Since neither Spanish nor English marks expletive pronouns out as distinct from unstressed referential pronouns – in Spanish they are all null, in English they are all overt – this particular pattern is suggestive of the involvement of UG in development. UG defines expletives as pronouns lacking theta-roles (see section 5.3.4). If UG were not involved, it would be difficult to explain why exactly expletives appear to be developmentally delayed.

Tsimpli and Roussou (1991) found a similar pattern in the acquisition of English by speakers of Greek. Their study involved six intermediate speakers (with one year of intensive training in English) and seven post-intermediate speakers (with two years of intensive training). There were two tasks: a grammaticality judgement test of 30 sentences involving grammatical and ungrammatical cases of the three properties associated with the pro-drop parameter, and 10 sentences in Greek for translation into English. The Greek sentences were all grammatical, but involved null subjects, VS word order and one sentence involving an extraction across an overt complementizer (*oti,* 'that').

Tsimpli and Roussou found that while all their informants rejected null referential subject pronouns in the judgement task, and correctly translated null subjects in Greek by referential pronouns in English, nearly 80% of their responses allowed null expletive subjects. This distinction between referential and expletive pronouns is similar to Phinney's finding with Spanish speakers. All the subjects rejected VS word order, and translated VS word order in the Greek sentences into SV orders in English. Over 95% of the responses allowed *that*-trace constructions both in the judgement and the translation tasks. But it was clear that subjects were aware of the optionality of *that* in English, because 95% of responses were acceptances of null complementizer sentences like *Who do you think ate ϕ the strawberries?* (complementizers are obligatory in Greek). It is not possible therefore to attribute their poor performance in rejecting *that*-trace sequences to the fact that they don't allow complementizer deletion.

As in the case of the responses of Spanish speakers in White's (1985, 1986) studies, we see that in development not all properties associated with the pro-drop parameter appear to be acquired at the same time. Again the VS order of the L1 seems to have been eliminated very early in development; overt referential pronouns are used more accurately than overt expletives, and the impossibility of extracting a subject across *that* in English has not been recognized.

What can be concluded from the fact that the cluster of properties assumed to be linked to the pro-drop parameter does not emerge as a cluster in development? Are learners unable to reset the parameter? One response would be that nothing can be concluded about parameter resetting from these data. The L2 speakers in question all have 'transitional state' grammars, and differences in their performance on each property in the cluster while their knowledge is developing does not necessarily mean that they will not eventually reset the parameter. They may, for example, not yet have sufficient control over embedded clauses to make the right judgements about *that*-trace effects. Or the test instruments employed may not be reflecting speakers' underlying competence accurately – given more appropriate tasks, learners might be more successful on *that*-trace and expletive pronouns. Another approach might suggest that it was a wrong theoretical move in the first place to link VS word order and *that*-trace with null subjects (White 1989: 90).

A different response can be found in Tsimpli and Roussou (1991). They have argued that the results do in fact reflect a difficulty that L2 speakers have with parameters of UG. They claim that beyond a certain age, L2 learners cannot reset parameters associated with functional categories whose values differ between the L1 and the L2. In the case at hand, Greek speakers (and by implication speakers of other similar pro-drop languages) do not reset the pro-drop parameter to its English value. The apparent success they have results from misanalysing English syntactic and morphological properties to make them compatible with the properties of the Greek setting of the pro-drop parameter. When IP is initially established in their L2 grammars, Greek speakers treat English subject pronouns as agreement markers, so that they have representations like the following (with the thematic verb having raised from VP to I, because Greek has strong inflections in I):

54

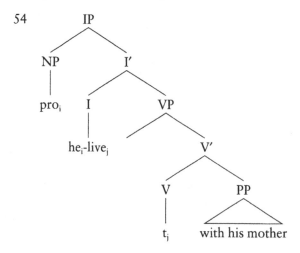

Here the pronoun *he*, as an agreement prefix, identifies the null subject, just as an agreement suffix does in Greek. Interestingly, this makes two predictions about how Greek speakers will treat expletives and VS word order. Since expletives do not have theta roles – they are pure Case receivers – they do not need to be identified. On this analysis we might expect Greek speakers to have problems with expletives *it/there* because they are not necessary for the purposes of identification. Secondly, where referential pronouns are absent, *pro* cannot be identified. This would make it impossible to have VS word order. An NP would have to appear in the specifier of IP. The performance of Tsimpli and Roussou's Greek informants is consistent with these predictions.

Tsimpli and Roussou also note that their intermediate subjects accept dislocated constructions like *John, he broke the plates* in 90% of cases, although these are quite unnatural in native English. This would be expected if *he* is being treated as an agreement prefix. *John* is simply an overt subject agreeing with *he*. However, the post-intermediates do not accept such dislocated constructions, and this leads Tsimpli and Roussou to propose that their informants come to realize that pronouns are not agreement inflections in English. But still they do not reset the parameter. Rather, they move pronouns into a topic position, perhaps the specifier of CP (see section 5.7.1). Greek Infl continues to license the null subject, but now it is identified from this topic position:

55

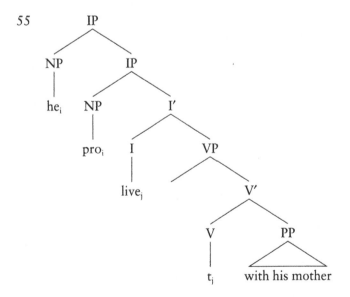

Given that this account assumes that *pro* continues to be licensed in the L2 English grammars of these speakers, extraction from a postverbal subject position is still allowed, producing the cases of subject extraction across *that*. In this case, the extracted *wh*-phrase will identify the embedded subject *pro*.

More Advanced Discussion

5.6 Difficulties with parameter resetting as a potential source of divergence between L2 and native mental grammars

If Tsimpli and Roussou's claim is correct that beyond a certain age L2 learners cannot reset the L1 values of parameters associated with functional categories, cases where the L1 and L2 differ on such values would lead to permanent differences between the mental grammars of L2 speakers and native speakers of the target language. However, since learners can nevertheless often appear on the surface to perform in a native-like way (through 'misanalysis' of surface properties of the L2) it is important to be clear about the implications of this account.

Firstly, the proposal still assumes that L2 learners build L2 mental grammars which are constrained by principles of Universal Grammar. For example, observe that awareness of the identificational requirement on null subjects (a principle of UG) is what forces speakers of Greek (and other pro-drop languages) not to allow VS word order in English right from the start – the absence of an overt agreement marker within the $[_{IP}$ pro Infl ... $]$ construction means that pro is not identified. Secondly, the proposal makes no direct claims about initial-state L2 grammars. It is potentially compatible with the view that learners initially construct grammars involving only lexical projections ('minimal trees'), or with the view that functional categories are initially transferred from the L1 with their L1 properties ('full transfer') or with unspecified features ('valueless features'). The reason for this is that the proposal concerns what happens to the development of grammatical knowledge about the properties of functional categories in transitional and final-state grammars. Thirdly, the proposal makes a number of interesting predictions:

(i) If learners cannot reset the values of parameters associated with functional categories, we wouldn't necessarily expect there to be a connection between the acquisition of morphology and the acquisition of syntactic constructions. The acquisition of, say, agreement and tense inflections in English and German by speakers of pro-drop languages would not 'trigger' the acquisition of obligatory subjects because triggering means resetting the licensing and identificational property of these inflections.

(ii) We might find unexpected UG-driven distinctions arising in learners' grammars as the result of misanalysis of the L2 data. For example, the identificational requirement on pro forces speakers of pro-drop languages to acquire English referential pronouns in order to maintain an underlying pro-drop representation; but since expletives do not need to be identified, there is no grammatical impetus to acquire them. Hence they appear later.

(iii) Finally, the proposal predicts that where superficial similarities between languages conceal different parameter settings at a deeper level, native speakers of those languages may construct very different grammars for a specific target L2, and have different kinds of persistent difficulty.

The last prediction appears to be consistent with an intriguing difference which has been observed in the acquisition of obligatory subjects in English by speakers of Greek, Italian and Spanish, and speakers of a different type of null subject language: Chinese, Japanese and Korean. We consider this case in the next section.

More Advanced Discussion

5.7 Null subjects and objects in Chinese, Japanese and Korean and second language acquisition

Section 5.7 describes how null subjects and objects in languages like Chinese, Japanese and Korean are identified by topics rather than by agreement inflections in Infl, and considers how this is determined by specific parameter settings. A number of studies of how speakers of Chinese-type languages acquire obligatory subjects and objects in English are discussed. It is argued that the pattern of development observed, being different from that observed in speakers of Greek-type languages, suggests L1 influence on the acquisition of functional categories in the L2, and persistence of L1 parameter settings even at advanced levels of L2 proficiency.

Greek, Italian and Spanish are null subject languages with rich verbal inflections. As we have seen, linguists have argued that Infl in these languages licenses (i.e. allows) a subject *pro*, and the differentiated person and number marking on the verb identifies who or what *pro* refers to. Chinese, Japanese and Korean are also languages which license null subjects, but in these languages verbs have no person and number inflections. For example, the following sentence of Mandarin Chinese has a null subject (represented for the moment by *e*, 'empty', until we have discussed its status) which can mean any of *I, you, he, she, we, they* without any change to the verb:

56   e xihuan pingguo
     e like   apple
     'I/you/she/etc. like(s) apples'

5.7.1   Null subjects and topicalization in Chinese-type languages

An early attempt to provide a unified account of the null subject property in Greek-type and Chinese-type languages focused on the fact that in one case the verb is always inflected, and in the other it is never inflected. The proposal, by Jaeggli and Safir (1989), was that if Infl in a language required every verb form to be inflected or required every verb form to be uninflected, then it would license null constituents in its specifier (i.e. the subject position). This was known as the **morphological uniformity condition** and was formulated as follows (Jaeggli and Safir 1989: 29):

> 57   Null subjects are permitted in all and only languages with morphologically uniform inflectional paradigms

However, a number of empirical problems arise in trying to extend this account to null/overt subject languages generally (Roberts 1997: 151–7) which make its descriptive adequacy questionable.

Alternative accounts have proposed that the syntactic mechanism that licenses/identifies null subjects in Chinese-type languages is different from Greek-type languages. One reason for thinking that this approach might be correct is that the cluster of syntactic phenomena which accompany null subjects in Chinese-type languages is different. Firstly, not only do Chinese-type languages allow null subjects, but they also freely allow null objects in cases like the following (from Xu 1986: 75):

> 58   Speaker A: Ni du guo zheben shu ma?
>   You read ASP this book Q?
>   'Have you read this book?'
>   Speaker B: e du guo e
>   e read ASP
>   'I have read it'

Here both subject and object in the second sentence are null. The possibility of null objects appears to be quite frequent in the ordinary use of Chinese-type languages. In a study of a group of Mandarin speakers in adult-to-adult informal conversation, Wang et al. (1992) found that null objects represented 40% of all objects used. By contrast, null objects are not the norm in Greek-type languages, which typically behave like English in this respect (although for some limited differences see Rizzi 1986).

Secondly, Chinese-type languages characteristically make greater use of topic constructions than Greek-type languages (or indeed English). Topic constructions involve the highlighting or foregrounding of a particular constituent which is already known from the discourse or context of utterance, and then using the rest of the sentence to say something about it. Topic constructions are certainly possible in English or Greek-type languages in sentences like the following, where the topic is coreferential with an empty position in the sentence:

59   Those mussels$_i$, I wouldn't touch e$_i$ with a barge pole!

But in Chinese-type languages not only is topicalization used in cases like these, but also in several ways which would be unnatural in English or Greek-type languages:

(a)   Topics do not need to have a coreferential empty constituent in the sentence:

60   Neihui da huo xingkui xiaofangdui dao   de   zao
     that   big fire luckily brigade   arrive Prep early
     'As for that big fire, it was lucky the fire-brigade arrived early'

In English the fronted constituent in such constructions needs to be the complement of an adjunct-forming expression like *as for . . .* as the translation in (60) shows.

(b)   Topic constructions are used in a number of cases where English or Greek-type languages would use passives. Passives exist in Chinese-type languages, but they are apparently only used 'where the subject is "adversely affected" by the action' (Yip 1995: 80). This means that English passives like *S/he is liked by many people* are quite unnatural, and a topic construction is used instead (Mandarin example from Yip):

61   Ta$_i$, hendou ren xihuan e$_i$
     S/he many people like e

(c)   Chinese-type languages allow what have been called 'topic chains' (Tsao 1977; Huang 1984). As well as subjects and objects, topics themselves can be null, providing that there is an antecedent somewhere in the discourse or context of utterance which can identify the topic. Consider the following short dialogue:

62   A: Shei kanjian-le Zhangsan$_i$?
         Who see-ASP Zhangsan
         'Who saw Zhangsan?'
     B: [$_{top}$ ϕ_i [Li Ming shuo Lisi kanjian-le e$_i$]]
               Li Ming say   Lisi see-ASP e
         'Li Ming says that Lisi saw him'

Here the topic of speaker B's sentence, *Zhangsan*, can be identified from what A has just said, and so it is not necessary for it to be overt. *Zhangsan$_i$* and $[_{top}\ \phi_i]$ therefore form a 'topic chain'.

(d) Chinese-type languages allow multiple topic constructions (with the topics unordered), which are at best marginal in English or Greek-type languages:

> 63   Li xiansheng$_i$, zheijian shi$_j$, wo gaosu guo e$_i$ e$_j$
>   Li Mr,   this event,   I tell-about ASP e e
>   Zheijian shi$_j$, Li xiansheng$_i$, wo gaosu guo e$_i$ e$_j$
>   This event,   Li Mr,   I tell-about ASP e e
>   '??This event, Mr Li, I've told about'

The widespread presence of topic constructions like these in Chinese-type languages has led some linguists to argue that they are directly connected with the possibility of null subjects and objects in these languages. Huang (1984), for example, argues that topicalization in Chinese is an obligatory property of every sentence (whereas in English and Greek-type languages topicalization is optional). This means that even apparently simple SVO sentences like (64) are in fact topic constructions in Chinese:

> 64a   Zhangsan renshi Lisi
>   Zhangsan know Lisi
>   'Zhangsan knows Lisi'
>   b $[_{[topic]}$ Zhangsan$_i$ [e$_i$ renshi Lisi]]

If every sentence involves topicalization, and topic chains (where the topic itself is null under identity with a discourse or context antecedent) are a possibility, then null subjects and null objects arise where a topic is co-referential with an empty constituent in its own sentence, and is itself null as part of a topic chain:

> 65a   Speaker A: Zhangsan renshi shei?
>   Zhangsan know who?
>   'Who does Zhangsan know?'
>   Speaker B: e renshi Lisi
> $[_{top}\ \phi_i$ [e$_i$ know Lisi]]
>   'He knows Lisi'
>   b Speaker A: Ni du guo zheben shu ma?
>   You read ASP this book Q?
>   'Have you read this book?'

Speaker B: e du guo e
$[_{top} \; \phi_i \; \phi_j \; [e_i \; read \; ASP \; e_j]]$
'I have read it'

So while null subjects in Chinese-type languages might look like null subjects in Greek-type languages, their origin is quite different.

If we recall the two criteria which Rizzi (1982, 1986, 1990) proposed as necessary to allow null subjects to exist in Greek type languages (section 5.5.1) – they must be both licensed and identified – the identificational requirement is met for null subjects (and objects) in Chinese-type languages by the presence of the obligatory topic (whereas is Greek-type languages it is met by the rich agreement inflections under Infl). Most linguists are agreed on this. More controversial is the mechanism which licenses null subjects (and objects). Huang (1984) proposes that the empty categories, *e*, in examples like (64) and (65) are traces which are the result of the topic having moved to the front of the sentence. As such they are comparable to the traces left behind by *wh*-movement in questions in English (*Who_i does Lisi know t_i?*).[7] This would make the licensing mechanism for null subjects (and objects) also very different from Greek-type languages.

A variation on Huang's analysis, which is assumed by Yuan (1997) and will be of importance in considering an L2 study undertaken by him, introduces a third parametric difference between Chinese-type languages and English and Greek-type languages: absence of agreement inflections in Infl (as in Chinese-type languages) licenses *pro* in the specifier of IP, rather than a trace. (Note that this is reminiscent of Jaeggli and Safir's (1989) 'morphological uniformity condition'.) Thus Chinese- and Greek-type languages would both allow subject *pro* on this account, but for different reasons, and contrast with English which does not. This proposal also means that the status of null subjects and null objects is different in Chinese: subjects are *pro*, objects are traces.

The structural representation of topicalized constructions is also controversial, but consideration of this would take us too far afield. We will assume that topics, universally, are located in the specifier position of a functional category which is either a specific topic projection (Puskas 1997) or CP, where the head C has the feature [topic]. In either case, the head of this projection requires a constituent to appear in its specifier position by virtue of a specifier–head agreement relation analogous to the relation that forces a *wh*-phrase to move to the specifier of a C specified for Q in English (see section 4.8.1). The difference between Chinese-type languages and English/Greek-type languages is that [topic] is an obligatory component of every matrix clause in the former, but is optional in the latter. Let's assume, for the purpose of exposition, that the functional category in question is a CP:

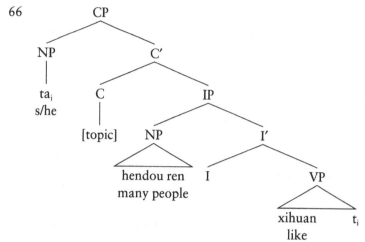

'As for her, many people like her'

To summarize: from the proposals discussed in this section, two (or possibly three) parameters distinguish Chinese-type languages from both English and Greek-type languages. The first is the obligatory presence of a [topic] feature in C which requires a constituent to appear in the specifier of CP. By contrast, in English and Greek-type languages this feature is optional. The second is that Chinese C licenses a null specifier that is identified by the discourse or context of utterance. (The possible third parameter, assumed by Yuan, is that the empty category in subject position is *pro* and not trace, and is licensed by the lack of inflections in Chinese Infl.) If this account is along the right lines, whereas speakers of Greek-type languages acquiring English have to reset a parametric difference relating to features of Infl, speakers of Chinese-type languages have to reset a parametric difference associated with features of C (as well as resetting a difference in Infl, if Yuan is correct).

5.7.2 Differences between speakers of Chinese-type languages and Greek-type languages in the acquisition of English

There have been a number of studies of the acquisition of obligatory subject English by speakers of Chinese, Japanese and Korean. One of the most striking contrasts with the studies of speakers of Greek-type languages is that speakers of Chinese-type languages appear to realize that English requires overt subjects from the earliest stages of acquisition. Zobl (1990) examined a 40,000-word written corpus of compositions/journal entries in English produced by 72 speakers of L1 Japanese. Informants were drawn from six proficiency levels (high beginner to advanced) of students attending an eight-week intensive ESL programme in Hawaii. The results for the total number of null subjects produced by the

Table 5.7   Total number of null subjects produced per proficiency level

Level	1	2	3	4	5	6
Score	4/202	8/655	4/248	14/683	9/868	1/300
	1.9%	1.2%	1.6%	2%	1%	0.3%

Source: Zobl 1990: 52

Table 5.8   Number of null expletives produced compared with Phinney's Spanish-speaking subjects

Level	1	2	3	4	5	6
Score	0/8	3/24	1/28	5/28	4/48	13/169
	0%	12.5%	3.6%	17.8%	8.3%	7.7%
Phinney	56%		76%			

Source: Based on Zobl 1990: 54

informants are given in table 5.7. Recall that the acquisition of overt expletives took some time in the case of speakers of Greek-type languages. Table 5.8 presents the proportion of ungrammatical null expletives produced by Zobl's informants compared with those of Phinney's (1987) Spanish-speaking informants. Zobl estimates that the proficiency of Phinney's subjects corresponds roughly to levels 1 to 3 or 4 of his Japanese speakers.

The important observation here is the high accuracy of informants in the production of overt subjects even at the lowest proficiency levels, and particularly in the use of overt expletive pronouns by comparison with Phinney's Spanish-speaking subjects. Furthermore, and interestingly, Zobl found that his subjects tended to overgeneralize expletive *it* to constructions where it is unnatural in English, for example:

> 67a   I think it continue of today condition forever (= 'I think today's conditions will continue forever')
>
> b   It is so changing everything now (= 'Everything is changing so much nowadays')
>
> c   It's the best way to talk in Japanese for us (= 'The best way for us is to speak Japanese')

Such findings are not isolated. Wakabayashi (1997) compared the results of Phinney's study with his own study of 39 high school students in Japan, using a similar free composition design. Wakabayashi's informants were native speakers of Japanese with only four years of classroom English, and little exposure to native English. From a sample of 407 sentences where a null subject would have been possible, he found only one example. Chaudron and Parker (1990) used free and guided picture description tasks with three groups of Japanese speakers learning English in the US. There were 11 low proficiency, 10 middle proficiency and 9 high proficiency informants who had been exposed to classroom English for between 1 to 15 years and who had been resident in the US for between 1 to 15 months. They found no cases of null subjects. Lakshmanan (1991), in a review of longitudinal data collected by Hakuta (1976) from a child Japanese speaker (called Uguisu) learning English in the US, found a similar pattern. Hakuta observed Uguisu over 60 weeks, starting when she was 5 years 4 months old and had been living in the US for 5 months. She received peer input from children in her neighbourhood and at kindergarten/elementary school. Lakshmanan found almost no null subjects, and examples of the presence of expletive *it* from the first sample. Fuller and Gundel (1987) collected data from 25 students in low-intermediate level ESL classes at the University of Minnesota. The task was the retelling of a silent film with a native speaker. Eleven of the subjects were speakers of Chinese/Japanese/Korean. Fuller and Gundel found few null pronouns, but those they did find were in *object* and not subject position in the productions of the Chinese, Japanese and Korean speakers.

The findings of these studies seem to suggest that speakers of Chinese-type languages realize that English is an obligatory subject language much faster than speakers of Greek-type languages. At the same time, there is a hint in the Fuller and Gundel findings that they may continue to allow null objects.

Yuan (1997) set out to investigate systematically the intuitions about null subjects and objects in the L2 English of 159 native speakers of Mandarin Chinese, with a view to understanding why they might acquire obligatory subjects faster. His informants consisted of 73 middle school students, 65 students majoring in English at university, and 21 university teachers of English, all living in China, together with a control group of 16 native speakers of English. On the basis of a proficiency test, he divided the informants into seven proficiency groups (1 = most elementary, 7 = most advanced). The most advanced group's performance on the proficiency test was not significantly different statistically from the performance of the native speaker control group.

The experimental test consisted of a grammaticality judgement task of 54 sentences. Half were ungrammatical, involving either a null subject or a null object. These were equally distributed across matrix (main) clauses and embedded clauses; and Yuan distinguished animate, inanimate and expletive contexts. The other half of the sentences were structurally parallel, but included grammatical overt subjects and objects. For example:

68a I once met John's girlfriend. (She) was very beautiful (animate matrix subject)

b Mary lost her bike last week, but John says the police have found (it) for her (inanimate embedded object)

c (It) seems that Peter is ill (expletive matrix subject)

etc.

Yuan found that all the experimental groups, with the exception of 1 and 3, were not significantly different statistically from the native speaker controls in preferring overt subjects over null subjects in English. This suggests that Chinese speakers, like Japanese speakers, realize very early on that English requires obligatory subjects. Particularly noticeable was that there were no significant differences between any of the experimental groups and the native speakers on expletives. However, all of the groups, including the most advanced group who had performed like native speakers on the general proficiency test, were significantly worse at rejecting null objects than the native speaker control group. This is consistent with their mental grammars for English continuing to allow null objects.

Yuan accounts for these findings in the following way. He assumes that Chinese speakers transfer the obligatory [topic] feature of C into their L2 grammars for English. This means that potentially their English grammars could allow null topics identifying null subjects and objects. However, he claims that noticing that English has verbal inflections leads Chinese speakers to realize early on that English Infl cannot license subject *pro*. The kind of evidence in question, according to Yuan (1997: 489), 'includes the verbal inflections for tense and agreement, use of copulas and auxiliaries, *do*-support'. Because subject *pro* is not licensed, UG forces speakers to use overt subjects, and this includes expletive subjects. At the same time, because learners have transferred the obligatory [topic] feature of C into their English grammars, they will continue to allow null objects. The reason for this is that there is no specific evidence in English to tell speakers that null objects are not possible.

There are, however, a number of problems with this account. Firstly, it is not obvious that Chinese speakers are aware of the inflectional properties of English Infl at the earliest stages of acquisition. It is known, in fact, that they have long-term difficulty with verbal inflections (Lardiere 1998a, 1998b). To counter this Yuan distinguishes Chinese speakers' production of inflectional forms from their underlying knowledge of such forms. He suggests (1997: 491) that 'their encounter with the informative data in their input should be sufficient . . . It is true that Chinese learners generally have problems with the English inflectional paradigm; even learners at an advanced level often fail to use appropriate verb forms in English. This, however, does not rule out the possibility that learners know that English has distinctive features for [agreement] . . .' This would not, however, explain the findings of a study undertaken by Davies (1996). Davies conducted a grammaticality judgement task with 45 ESL learners of whom 41 were speakers of Chinese/Japanese/Korean. For a sizeable number of this group (13) there was little correlation between recognition of S–V agreement errors and recognition of null subject errors. If learners 'know that English has distinctive features for [agreement]', it is surprising that in a recognition task they fail to detect inflectional errors.

Secondly, it is not entirely clear why speakers of Chinese notice the impoverished nature of English verbal morphology early on, while speakers of Greek-type languages do not. It may be possible to counter this by suggesting that it is easier to notice the presence of inflections in an L2 when your L1 has none, than to notice that an L2 has fewer inflections than your L1. However, this kind of 'noticing' would require some independent justification before it could be considered seriously.

Thirdly, it has been observed that early-stage Chinese-speaking learners of English can detect the ungrammaticality of null subjects well when they are clause-initial, but their performance declines considerably when some other constituent is in clause-initial position. Xiao (1998) gave two 20-item grammaticality judgement tests to six low- to intermediate-level adult Chinese speakers who had been in Hawaii no longer than six months at the time of testing. She found that whereas all the subjects rejected sentences like (69a) and accepted sentences like (69b), they were highly likely to accept sentences like (70):

		No of acceptances
69a	Is raining	0/6
b	It is raining	6/6
70a	Every day eat breakfast	5/6
b	Beijing snows a lot	6/6
c	Chicago happened a big fire	6/6
d	Here cannot swim	6/6

She found a similar pattern in embedded clauses. While informants rejected null subjects where they headed the embedded clause, they were less likely to do so if the clause was headed by another constituent:

71a	Feng Yi says failed the test	1/6
b	The teacher says that tomorrow must come early	6/6

A similar finding emerged in a study by Yip (1995) of 20 Mandarin-speaking graduate students taking courses in the US. Ten were in intermediate-level classes and ten in advanced classes. She gave her subjects a grammaticality judgement task involving ten ungrammatical sentences like (72a) where there is a sentence-initial topic and a null subject, and randomly mixed them up with grammatical subject-initial sentences like (72b):

72a   This film must see as soon as possible
   b   The teacher has made the announcement

She found that each of her intermediate-level group accepted at least 3/10 of the ungrammatical sentences. If early-stage Chinese-speaking learners of English are successful in recognizing the ungrammaticality of null subjects only when they occur clause-initially, this casts some doubt on the idea that it is knowledge that English has verbal inflections which causes Infl to cease licensing subject *pro*. We would expect no effect of constituents occurring to the left of the subject if this account were correct.

An alternative possibility is to follow the logic of Tsimpli and Roussou's (1991) idea that L2 learners do not reset parameters but misanalyse L2 data to make them compatible with transferred properties from the L1. Recall that Huang's account proposes that in Chinese null subjects and objects are traces bound by topics which may themselves be null as part of a topic chain. Suppose that when Chinese speakers encounter English, they notice that declarative clauses never begin with verbal constituents, and convert this observation into the hypothesis that at least one topic must be overt (i.e. that English makes more restricted use of topic chains than Chinese). For example, in the English equivalent of example (65b), repeated here as (73), they would allow Speaker B to produce options (a) and (b), but disallow the Chinese option (c):

73   Speaker A: 'Have you read this book?'
     Speaker B: (a) $[\phi_j \, I_i \, [t_i \text{ have read } t_j]]$
                  (b) $[\text{This book}_j \, \phi_i \, [\, t_i \text{ have read } t_j]]$
                  (c) $*[\phi_j \, \phi_i \, [\, t_i \text{ have read } t_j]]$

Such a hypothesis would not require Chinese speakers to reset the obligatory [topic] feature in C to 'optional'; it would simply require them to restrict the possibilities for topic chains, which are optional in Chinese anyway. While this is speculation, it is consistent with the observed early-stage behaviour of Chinese learners of English: their ability to recognize the ungrammaticality of null subjects except when some other constituent is clause-initial, their accuracy in using expletive subjects (to ensure that the topic position is overt), and the fact that they have difficulty detecting the ungrammaticality of null objects (because their 'misanalysis' of English only bears on the topic position, not on argument positions).

Clearly, though, Chinese speakers' recognition of the ungrammaticality of null subjects improves with time. Yuan (1997) found that his more proficient groups were indistinguishable from native speakers. Yip (1995) found that her more advanced group did not accept sentences like (72a). At the same time, Yuan found that even his most advanced group, who were indistinguishable from the native speaker controls on a general test of proficiency and on rejecting null subjects, were significantly worse at rejecting null objects. Can this be accounted for within a no-parameter-resetting view? Speculating again: suppose that Chinese speakers come to assume that their 'one overt topic' hypothesis must be restricted further in English to 'at least one topic must be overt and it must bind the closest available trace'. This would restrict overt topics to binding subjects. Speakers would then reject both sentences (73b–c), but continue to allow sentences like (73a). Whether this is an appropriate interpretation of the facts remains to be seen.

5.8 Summary of chapter 5

In this chapter we have considered a number of studies bearing on how second language learners develop knowledge about the syntactic realization of argument structure. It was assumed that the θ-criterion (which requires that each argument in a verb's argument structure be assigned a θ-role), the Extended Projection Principle (requiring that all clauses have subjects), UTAH and the Case Filter (requiring that all NPs be assigned a Case) are constants in the design of human language; they are principles of UG. If L2 learners construct mental grammars in a UG-determined way, we would expect them to show evidence that these principles are involved. It was also assumed, however, that the way that the Case Filter is satisfied, and the way that argument structure is encoded in syntax, can vary from language to language along a number of parameters of variation.

Several cases of what appear to be underdetermination of syntactic knowledge were discussed which are consistent with the principles being involved in L2 grammar building. Japanese speakers produce VS word order in English with unaccusative verbs (*I was just patient until dried my clothes*) but not with other types of verb (Zobl 1989), a possibility that exists neither in Japanese nor in English. L1 English and L1 Chinese speakers of L2 Japanese are aware of an interpretive difference in the use of *takusan*, 'a lot', with unaccusative and unergative verbs, although there is nothing on the surface in Japanese to indicate this. It was argued that the treatment of VS word order in English as ungrammatical by speakers of Greek-type languages followed from the absence of a mechanism for identifying null subject *pro* in such cases. All of this is evidence compatible with the claim that grammatical knowledge develops in ways which are constrained by UG.

First language influence also appears to play a role in the way that knowledge develops. The L1 French and L1 English informants in Sorace's (1993) study of near-native L2 speakers of Italian differed in their knowledge of the distribution of auxiliary verbs *essere* and *avere* with modal verbs in clitic-climbing constructions. When clitic climbing had occurred, the French speakers chose *essere* like native speakers; but in the absence of clitic climbing they did not. The English speakers chose *essere* to the same degree in both contexts, and in both contexts were unlike the native speakers. The availability of clitics in French (although not clitic climbing), but not in English appears to give rise to this difference.

The findings of these studies are compatible with findings reported in earlier chapters in that they show evidence of the involvement of UG in grammar building, and the influence of the L1 on the development of L2 syntactic knowledge. However, whereas in previous chapters we have been concerned with learners with initial-state and transitional-state grammars, in this chapter we also encountered evidence from speakers in more advanced stages of development, perhaps even with final-state grammars. In these cases we found some areas where L2 speakers show persistent differences from native speakers: non-native-like auxiliary verb selection in the case of Sorace's study, willingness to accept null objects in the case of Yuan's advanced Chinese speakers of English. We encountered one possible account of this: the proposal of Tsimpli and Roussou (1991) that L2 learners are unable to reset parameter values associated with functional categories which have been fixed in their L1s, this being, perhaps, the result of a critical period beyond which the range of parametric options offered by UG becomes inaccessible. Where learners have some success in acquiring syntactic properties in the L2 which are different from their L1, this is the result of 'misanalysing' the input. The grammars they construct are still constrained by principles of UG, and this is detectable in the kind of underdetermined knowledge described at the beginning of this section; but their L2 grammars still essentially contain the parameter settings of the L1. It was argued that this led to a number of interesting predictions about the L2 English grammars of speakers of Greek-type and Chinese-type null subject L1s.

It should be noted here that the no-parameter-resetting proposal is controversial. Much current research is directed at trying to understand the reasons why adult L2 speakers with final-state grammars might diverge from native speakers of the target language. An alternative view is that divergence is not located in syntactic knowledge per se, where L2 learners can acquire full target-like competence, but in performance: L2 speakers have difficulty using their knowledge in real time, or have trouble accessing appropriate lexical items in real time (Epstein et al. 1996; Lardiere 1998a, 1998b; Prévost and White 2000). Issues concerning the final-state grammars of L2 learners will come more to the fore in the next two chapters. In chapter 8 we will return to discuss this controversy in more detail.

5.9   Exercises

Compare the following pairs of sentences:

> 1a   Keith poured whisky into the glass
> b   *Keith poured the glass with whisky

> 2a   *Keith filled whisky into the glass
> b   Keith filled the glass with whisky

> 3a   Keith sprayed paint onto the wall
> b   Keith sprayed the wall with paint

Assuming the theta roles involved here are AGENT, THEME and LOCATION, describe the differences between each of these verbs in the way that their thematic structure is realized syntactically in English.

Spanish has verbs equivalent to *pour* and *fill* whose theta roles are realized syntactically in a similar way to the examples (1) and (2) of exercise 1. However, the equivalents of verbs like *spray* only allow a construction similar to (3b):

> 4a   *Pablo roció pintura sobre la pared
>   Pablo sprayed paint onto the wall
> b   Pablo roció el muro de/con pintura
>   Pablo sprayed the wall with paint

Párraga (1998) tested knowledge of the syntactic realization of theta roles with verbs of these three types in English in a group of adult native speakers of Spanish – 7 classed as intermediate learners and 6 as advanced – compared with an age-matched group of 13 native speakers of English.

   The test was a grammaticality preference task where informants were given a context like *Before they set off, they loaded* ___, and four phrases to choose from to complete the sentence like (a) *the van with medical supplies,* (b) *medical supplies into the van,* (c) *the van under medical supplies,* and so on. Some of the phrases gave rise to grammatical sentences, others to ungrammatical sentences, and yet others were grammatical but involved different theta roles. The verbs used in the test had the same syntactic realization possibilities as *pour* (*shake, paste, tip, drip*), or *fill* (*flood, pollute, plug, cover*) or *spray* (*load, pile, spalsh, cram*). Results are given below:

Number of each construction type, grammatical and ungrammatical, accepted by informants (based on Párraga 1998)						
	Verb type					
Subjects	pour		fill		spray	
	into	*with	*into	with	into	with
Intermediate	16/35	24/35	10/35	29/35	18/35	27/35
	45.7%	*68.6%*	*28.6%*	*82.9%*	*51.4%*	*77.1%*
Advanced	29/30	7/30	8/30	27/30	28/30	25/30
	96.7%	*23.3%*	*26.7%*	*90.0%*	*93.3%*	*83.3%*
Native speaker	65/65	6/65	16/65	63/65	59/65	59/65
	100%	*9.2%*	*24.6%*	*96.9%*	*90.8%*	*90.8%*

What do you infer from these results about the influence of the syntactic realization of argument structure in the L1 on the development of the L2 grammar? How would you explain the apparent retreat from overgeneralization on *pour*-type verbs shown by the advanced group in comparison with the intermediate informants (i.e. the decrease in acceptance of sentences like *Keith poured the glass with whisky*)?

Exercise 3: Assessing whether L2 speakers can acquire the syntactic realization of argument structure in an L2 which differs from the L1 II (section 5.4)

Some verbs in English which have direct object and prepositional object complements also allow an alternative 'double object' complement. The preposition involved in these cases is sometimes *to* and sometimes *for*:

1a   Tom sent the package to Mary
  b   Tom sent Mary the package

2a Tom built a kennel for his dog
 b Tom built his dog a kennel

In cases like (1) the verb seems to assign a GOAL theta role to the constituent introduced by *to* and in (2) a BENEFACTIVE theta role to the constituent introduced by *for* (the participant 'benefits' from the event described by the verb).

Not all verbs with these argument structures allow the alternation seen in (1) and (2), however:

3a Tom despatched the package to Mary
 b *Tom despatched Mary the package

4a Tom constructed a kennel for his dog
 b *Tom constructed his dog a kennel

As we saw in section 1.4, one of the factors determining that a verb allows a double object construction is that it must be monosyllabic (or stressed on the first or second vowels). French, in contrast to English, does not allow double object constructions at all; only prepositional objects are grammatical in equivalent constructions.

R. Hawkins (1987) investigated the intuitions of ten intermediate to advanced L2 speakers of English, all native speakers of French, about the grammaticality of cases like (1)–(4). The test was a grammaticality judgement task. While the informants accepted over 90% of the constructions involving a prepositional phrase, the *acceptance* of grammatical [___ NP NP] constructions and the *rejection* of ungrammatical *[___ NP NP] differed as shown below:

Proportion of acceptances of grammatical [___ NP NP] constructions and rejection of ungrammatical *[___ NP NP] constructions by ten French-speaking learners of English		
	Construction type	
	Acceptance of grammatical [___ NP NP], e.g. *sent Mary the package*	Rejection of ungrammatical *[___ NP NP], e.g. *despatched Mary the package*
GOAL argument (preposition = *to*)	120/190 (63.2%)	32.5/50 (65%)
BENEFACTIVE argument (preposition = *for*)	24/80 (30%)	3/40 (7.5%)

Given that French does not allow double object constructions in these cases, what might these results suggest about the role that knowledge of argument structure plays in the construction of an L2 grammar for English by a French speaker?

French speakers are known to have persistent difficulty restricting double object constructions in English, once acquired, to the appropriate classes of verbs, and continue to overgeneralize to sentences like *She explained me the problem*. In the light of the discussion of Sorace's (1993) findings in section 5.4.2, how would you interpret this persistent difficulty? How might this case be different from the case of the Spanish speakers described in exercise 2, where overgeneralization on *pour*-type verbs declined with proficiency?

Exercise 4: Evaluating the role that knowledge of unaccusativity plays in the development of an L2 grammar for Spanish (sections 5.4, 5.5)

(Material used in this exercise is reprinted with the permission of Tammy Jandrey Hertel and Ana Pérez-Leroux)
In Spanish, a null subject language, declarative sentences can have both SV and VS word order. Hertel and Pérez-Leroux (1998) suggest, though, that where intransitive verbs are involved, there is a difference between unaccusative verbs (i.e. those whose subjects start out initially as complements to the verb – see section 5.3.2) and unergative verbs. With unaccusative verbs the VS surface order is the normal or 'neutral' word order, while SV focuses special attention on the subject:

1a Llegó Susana, 'Susana arrived'
 b Susana llegó, 'It was Susana who arrived'

By contrast, with unergative verbs SV is the neutral order, and VS focuses special attention on the subject:

2a Jorge telefonéo, 'Jorge telephoned'
 b Telefonéo Jorge, 'It was Jorge who telephoned'

Hertel and Pérez-Leroux asked three groups of Spanish speakers to judge the grammaticality of 18 sentences like these with VS and SV order on a 5-point scale (1 = ungrammatical, 5 = grammatical). There was a group of 16 L1 English undergraduates in a third-semester Spanish course in the United States ('beginners'), a group of 5 L1 English students doing graduate work in Spanish ('advanced'), and 5 native speakers of Spanish. The results are as follows:

Mean acceptance (out of 5) of SV and VS word order by type of verb (figures approximate – based on Hertel and Pérez-Leroux 1998)				
Subjects	SV order		VS order	
	Unaccusative	Unergative	Unaccusative	Unergative
Beginners	3.80	4.3	3.0	2.25
Advanced	4.7	4.8	4.8	4.2
Native	4.9	5.0	4.7	3.6

What conclusions do you draw from these results about informants' preferences for inversion? How might these data illustrate the idea that L2 learners' grammars are underdetermined by input?

Exercise 5: Speculating about the status of subjects in the L2 English grammar of a native speaker of Chinese (section 5.7)

Yip (1995: 86–7) notes that indefinite NPs, including NPs quantified by expressions like *one, some, several*, cannot appear in clause-initial position in Chinese (examples from Yip):

> 1a   *Yige/yixie/jige ren lai le
>   One/some/several people come ASP
>   'One/some/several people have come'

In such cases an existential verb *you* 'there be' has to introduce the sentence:

> b   You yige/yixie/jige ren lai le

Given this, consider the examples in (2) below taken from the same piece of writing by a native speaker of Chinese (Cantonese) which discusses the merits of teaching deaf children lip reading as opposed to sign language. What account would you give of the use of *there* in these sentences?

> 2a   In Hong Kong, most of the deaf schools use the teaching of lip reading instead of sign language because there are less teachers have been trained how to use sign language.
> b   There are still some schools use the teaching of sign language.
> c   There are some signs are the same between different sets of sign language.

  d   In this activity, time limit is very important because we forget the
      things easily after a period of time and there may have something
      happened that attract our attention.
  e   It is true that even a Chinese deaf child who has learned lip reading
      for many years, there are still some words he cannot guess.

Is this speaker's use of expletive *it*, as illustrated in (3), different from her use
of *there*? Why might this be?

  3a   It is difficult for parents to find out their children are deaf.
   b   It is best for them to learn lip reading.
   c   Though they are deaf, it does not mean they are dumb.
   d   It is essential for them to learn the skills in this preparation stage.
   e   After having sense training, it is much easier for deaf children to
       go on to have the learning lip reading.

Exercise 6: Considering the role of the Empty Category Principle in the L2 acquisition of Spanish (sections 5.5.3, 5.6)

(Material used in this exercise is reprinted with the permission of Monica Sopher)
Sopher (1995) gave a Spanish grammaticality judgement task relating to properties of the pro-drop parameter to (i) 31 intermediate-level L2 speakers of Spanish
(L1 English); (ii) 40 advanced-level L2 speakers of Spanish (L1 English); (iii) a
control group of 38 native speakers of Spanish.
   In Spanish it is possible to extract a subject across an overt complementizer as
in (1a) (example from Sopher's test):

  1a   ¿Qué jugador de fútbol consideras que completaría nuestro
       equipo?
       *Which football player do you think that will join our team?

But it is not possible to delete the complementizer *que*, as it is in English:

  b   *¿Qué jugador de fútbol consideras ___ completaría nuestro
      equipo?
      Which football player do you think ___ will join our team?

The reason why extraction is possible across *que* in (1a) is claimed to be that the
subject has moved from a postverbal position – its trace is governed by the verb
and therefore licensed. Hence there is no violation of the Empty Category Principle
(ECP).

Twelve of the sentences in Sopher's judgement task tested knowledge of these properties in Spanish. Six of them were grammatical like (1a), and six were ungrammatical like (1b). Her results, given in the box below, show the proportions of responses of 'accept' and 'reject' to the grammatical sentences like (1a), and the proportions of responses of 'accept' and 'reject' to the ungrammatical sentences like (1b) (results do not add up to 100% because there were some responses of 'don't know', which are not included here):

Proportions of responses (%) of 'accept' and 'reject' to grammatical and ungrammatical sentences involving subject extraction (based on Sopher 1995)		
	'Accept' grammatical sentences	'Reject' grammatical sentences
Intermediate	49.7%	37.3%
Advanced	31.4%	56.9%
Native	78.9%	15.4%
	'Accept' ungrammatical sentences	'Reject' ungrammatical sentences
Intermediate	41.0%	43.7%
Advanced	29.3%	62.7%
Native	20.4%	76.5%

Do you think that this evidence bears on the question of whether learners can reset parameters in second language acquisition (section 5.6)?

5.10 Further reading

The acquisition of the syntactic realization of theta roles and argument structure in a second language, and the influence of the L1 in that process, is a relatively underexplored area. For recent discussion see Juffs, A. 1996: *Learnability and the Lexicon: Theories and Second Language Acquisition Research*. Amsterdam: John Benjamins; Montrul, S. 1997: The L2 acquisition of dative experiencer subjects. *Second Language Research* 13, 264–28; Juffs, A. 1998: Some effects of first language argument structure and morphosyntax on second language sentence processing. *Second Language Research* 14, 406–24.

Divergence between L2 speakers and native speakers of the target language (including some studies of advanced/near-native speakers) is the subject of issue 14(4) (1998) of the journal *Second Language Research*.

For recent discussion of issues relating to null subjects and the pro-drop parameter see Liceras, J. and Díaz, L. 1999: Topic-drop versus pro-drop: null subjects and pronominal subjects in the Spanish L2 of Chinese, English, French, German and Japanese speakers. *Second Language Research* 15, 1–40; Roebuck, R., Martínez-Arbelaiz, M. and Pérez-Silva, J. 1999: Null subjects, filled CPs and L2 acquisition. *Second Language Research* 15, 251–82.

Notes

1 How the NPs *three men, a stranger* are assigned Case in this construction is a matter of current controversy. On one account (Chomsky 1986a) nominative Case is transmitted from *there* to *three men, a stranger*. On another account two Cases are assigned, nominative Case to *there* and a 'partitive Case' to *three men, a stranger* (Belletti 1988; Lasnik 1995).

2 There are some restrictions on the appearance of *there* with unaccusative verbs. The THEME argument has to be non-specific, so that while *There arrived a stranger* is grammatical, *?There arrived the stranger* is less so. Not all unaccusative verbs allow *there* to occur with equally grammatical results: *Once upon a time there lived a witch . . .* I*?Once upon a time there died a witch . . .* These restrictions will not be of concern here.

3 The one case where unaccusative and unergative verbs are distinguished syntactically in English is with *there*, as we have seen: *There arrived three men*. But the presence of constructions like these in English cannot 'explain' the Japanese speakers' use of postverbal subjects only with unaccusative verbs. To realize that *there*-constructions only involve unaccusative verbs, one has to know the unaccusative–unergative distinction in advance.

4 Although languages which permit null subjects have overt subject pronouns which are used in stressed environments, as discussed above, they do not have expletive pronouns equivalent to English *it, there*.

5 The Empty Category Principle will be discussed in chapter 7. Rizzi's (1997: 276) version of it is

Empty Category Principle: t must be properly head-governed

where proper head government means 'government by a head X within its immediate projection X' and where the head is lexical or has agreement or tense features'.

6 The French informants might have been expected to perform better on this construction on the assumption that French and English have the same parameter setting. However, as White notes, the way French avoids *that*-trace is by using the form *qui*, 'who': *Qui crois-tu qui va téléphoner?* (lit. 'Who do you think who will telephone?'). Since *who* and *that* are interchangeable under some circumstances in English (*The man that/who phoned . . .*), and assuming that French *qui* has an [agreement] feature,

some French speakers may wrongly have assumed that English *that* has an [agreement] feature licensing the trace.

7 Huang actually treats them as 'variables'. The difference is that variables are not necessarily the result of movement. For the purposes of discussion here, we will assume that the empty categories in Chinese topic constructions are traces.

6 The Second Language Acquisition of Nominal Phrases

6.1 Introduction

In section 2.5 we referred to an accuracy profile which Andersen (1978) found in the written L2 English of a group of 89 Spanish speakers. On noun-related morphology (that is, the articles *the*, *a*, plural *-s*, possessive *'s*) implicational scaling revealed that his subjects used *the* (e.g. *the book*) more frequently in target-like contexts than *a* or plural *-s* (e.g. *a book*, *books*), and they used *a/* plural *-s* more frequently in target-like contexts than possessive *'s* (e.g. *John's book*). In this chapter we will consider this descriptive generalization in more detail, asking whether it is another manifestation of second language learners constructing mental grammars in systematic ways. Interest will focus in particular on the factors which have emerged in earlier chapters: the role of lexical projections in initial-state grammars; the incremental development of the specification of functional categories; the influence of the L1. In view of the discussion of final-state grammars in chapter 5, we will also be interested in discovering whether there are any areas where L2 learners persistently differ from native speakers of the target language.

The discussion in this chapter will proceed as follows. First, two studies of the acquisition of articles in L2 English will be described. Then, a recent proposal in theoretical syntax will be outlined which claims that noun phrases are part of a more articulated structure involving two functional categories, 'Number' and 'Determiner', and that nominal phrases like *the book* are in fact determiner phrases (DPs). An assessment will be made of the extent to which second language learners build this structure over time in their L2 mental grammars. It will be argued that there are striking similarities between the way L2 learners of English build representations for the DP and the way that they build representations for

IP, as described in chapter 2. Finally, a property of DPs which appears to cause learners persistent difficulty will be described, and the implications of this for a theory of final-state L2 syntactic knowledge will be discussed.

6.2   Studies of the second language acquisition of the English articles *the, a, φ*

Section 6.2 describes an analysis of the English articles which several L2 researchers have used to interpret the acquisition of them by second language learners; the results from two such studies are then discussed.

6.2.1   The distribution and interpretation of English articles

English has three so-called **articles**, *the, a* and *φ* (zero) illustrated in (1):

   1a   I should take **the** rabbit to the vet
     b   I saw **a** rabbit in the garden yesterday
     c   I saw *φ* rabbits in the garden yesterday[1]

The articles appear to have different, but overlapping, distributions. The definite article *the* can potentially be used with all types of noun: count nouns like *rabbit* in both singular and plural, mass nouns like *porridge, evidence*, and abstract nouns like *truth, understanding*:

   2a   I saw **the** rabbit/**the** rabbits   (count)
     b   He made **the** porridge for us/She presented
          the evidence   (mass)
     c   **The** understanding they reached was shortlived   (abstract)

The indefinite article *a* can be used with singular count nouns and abstract nouns, but not with plural count nouns, and not usually with mass nouns (unless they can be interpreted as singular count nouns: *They bought a cheese with a smokey flavour*):

   3a   I saw **a** rabbit/*a rabbits   (count)
     b   They reached **an** understanding   (abstract)
     c   *She presented **an** evidence/*He made **a** porridge   (mass)

The *φ* article can be used with plural count nouns, mass nouns and abstract nouns, but not usually with singular count nouns (unless they can be interpreted as mass nouns: e.g. *She doesn't eat rabbit*):

Table 6.1 Co-occurrence possibilities of the articles *the*, *a*, *φ* and types of noun

Article	Noun types	Examples
the	N [+count, +singular]	the rabbit
	[+count, −singular]	the rabbits
	[−count, +mass]	the porridge
	[−count, −mass]	the truth
a	N [+count, +singular]	a rabbit
	[−count, −mass]	a (home) truth
φ	N [+count, −singular]	φ rabbits
	[−count, +mass]	φ porridge
	[−count, −mass]	φ truth

4a I saw *φ* rabbits/*φ* rabbit in the garden (count)
  b She presented *φ* evidence for her claims (mass)
  c The situation calls for *φ* understanding (abstract)

The types of nouns with which the articles co-occur are summarized in table 6.1.

In addition to their different distributional properties, the articles also have different interpretations. Bickerton (1981) suggests that these differences can be captured in terms of two binary features: whether the article and associated noun phrase refer to a specific entity [±specific referent], and whether the article and associated NP are already known, from the previous discourse or from context, to the person who is listening to or reading the sentence [±hearer knowledge]. Since these distinctions have been used by a number of L2 researchers as the basis for interpreting the L2 acquisition of English articles (e.g. Huebner 1985; Parrish 1987; Chaudron and Parker 1990), I shall briefly illustrate them.

+Specific Referent [+SR], −Hearer Knowledge [−HK]

When an NP refers to a specific entity which the hearer cannot identify from what has already been said or from the context, *a/φ* are used:

5 Speaker A: How will you get a ticket for the England–France match?
    Speaker B: I have a contact/I have *φ* contacts

Here 'my contact(s)' are specific, but this is the first time they have been introduced into the discourse.

–Specific Referent [–SR], –Hearer Knowledge [–HK]

When an NP refers to a non-specific entity which the hearer cannot identify from what has already been said, or from the context, *a/ϕ* are again used:

    6 Speaker A: What does she want to do when she's married?
          Speaker B: Have **a** baby/Have *ϕ* babies

Here, since 'having a baby' is only a plan, there is no specific baby that the speaker has in mind, and it is the first time that this topic has been introduced into the discourse, so is not known to the hearer.

+Specific Referent [+SR], +Hearer Knowledge [+HK]

When an NP refers to a specific entity which the hearer can identify from what has been said before or from the context, *the* is used:

    7a Speaker A: How will you get a ticket for the England–France match?
          Speaker B: I have a contact
          Speaker A: Is that **the** same contact who failed to get you tickets for Wimbledon?

     b Speaker A: What does she want to do when she's married? .
          Speaker B: Have a baby
          Speaker A: What will they do with **the** baby when they go to Africa?

Two special cases within this category are worthy of note:

(a) NPs which are specific and known from the speaker's and hearer's 'shared general knowledge' are [+SR, +HK], for example *the Sun, the Moon, the North Pole*.

(b) Partitive and locative NPs can be determined as 'known' by virtue of being a part of another NP with which they are associated. In the following examples, although the main NP is [–HK] (*a ship, an old shirt, an envelope*), the accompanying partitive or locative NP is in some sense 'known' by virtue of being a part of the main NP: *The bow of a ship came into view* (partitive); *Cut **the** collar off an old shirt* (partitive); *Write your name on **the** back of an envelope* (locative).

Table 6.2 Interpretation of English articles in relation to the features [±specific referent] and [±hearer knowledge]

	+SR	−SR
+HK	She had **the** baby at home Goldilocks ate **the** porridge She presented **the** evidence	**The** rabbit is a nuisance A rabbit is a nuisance φ Rabbits are a nuisance φ Theories must always be supported by φ evidence
−HK	I have a contact I have φ contacts They reached an understanding She presented φ evidence	She hopes to have a baby She wants to write φ books

−Specific Referent [−SR], +Hearer Knowledge [+HK]

When an NP refers to a non-specific entity or entities identified by the hearer from general knowledge of the entity itself, we have a case of a generic interpretation. For example, if someone says, *The holidaymaker will find lots to do in Wales*, no specific holidaymaker is referred to, but we can identify a reference to a type of person whose general characteristics we know from our own experience. All three articles *the/a/φ* can be used with nouns to produce a generic interpretation; but in the case of *the* the noun must be a count noun and singular:

8   Speaker A: I saw a rabbit eating my carrots yesterday
    Speaker B: The rabbit can cause problems for **the** gardener
                 A rabbit can cause problems for a gardener
                 φ Rabbits can cause problems for φ gardeners

The way in which the features [±Specific Referent] and [±Hearer Knowledge] determine the interpretation of the English articles is summarized in table 6.2.

So there is a complex interplay in English between the co-occurrence possibilities of articles and nouns, determined by properties of the noun like [±count], [±singular] and [±mass], and the interpretation given to the whole noun phrase in terms of whether it is specific or not, and whether it is known to the hearer from the discourse, from the context of utterance or from general knowledge.

6.2.2   Two studies of the second language acquisition of English articles

Parrish (1987) collected data on the use of *the*, *a* and ϕ in the L2 English of an L1 Japanese speaker. The subject was 19 years old and had been living in the United States for just three weeks when data collection began. Although the subject had received six years of English instruction prior to arrival in the US, Parrish assessed her to be at the 'beginning level'. Data were collected every ten days over a four-month period from structured interactions with the researcher (storytelling and description of a place).

Parrish scored her results as follows. She took every context in the transcripts of her informant's productions where a native speaker of English would have used an article, and classified each context according to the two features [±specific referent] and [±hearer knowledge]. She then counted the number of tokens of each type of article used by the informant in a given context, and compared that usage with what a native speaker would have used in the same context. The results are presented in table 6.3 (based on Parrish's table 1 (1987: 368)).

To illustrate how the results should be interpreted, consider the [+SR, +HK] cell. This tells us that there were 193 contexts where nouns were used which a native speaker would have interpreted as [+specific referent, +hearer knowledge]. A native speaker would only have used the article *the* in these contexts. Parrish's informant, however, used *the* in 131/193 (67.9%) of cases. She used no article in the remaining 62/193 (32.1%) of cases.[2]

There are several things to note about the results in table 6.3. Firstly, the informant makes a lot of use of the zero article: 228/436 (52.3%) of article contexts produced over the four-month period involve ϕ. And it is clear from the [+SR, +HK] cell that some of these are cases where a native speaker would use an overt article. Secondly, the [+SR, −HK] cell tells us that there are some cases where the informant has overgeneralized *the* to contexts where it is ungrammatical for native speakers.

What table 6.3 does not tell us is the extent to which *a* and ϕ are used with the appropriate type of noun: [±count, ±singular, ±mass]. For example, as Parrish observes, from the [+SR, −HK] cell we cannot tell whether ϕ is being used in a target-like way such as *I need ϕ money*, or a non-target-like way such as *I have ϕ brother*. To provide such information, Parrish further analysed the results in terms of the accuracy of each article in obligatory contexts. Unfortunately, the results are not presented in a way which can be directly compared with the results in table 6.3. However, her discussion of one of the data collection samples – sample 11 (the penultimate data collection point in the study) – is indicative. Out of a total of 32 contexts in this sample where *a* would have been obligatory for a native speaker, Parrish's informant used *a* only 6 times (i.e. only 19% of

Table 6.3 Distribution (number of tokens) in four contexts of *the*, *a*, ϕ produced by a Japanese speaker over a four-month period

+SR +HK contexts Example: *She had the baby/the babies at home*			−SR +HK contexts Example: *The rabbit/A rabbit/ϕ rabbits can cause problems for gardeners*		
Article	*Tokens*	%	*Article*	*Tokens*	%
¶the	131	67.9	¶the	4	9.5
a	0	0.0	¶a	0	0.0
ϕ	62	32.1	¶ϕ	38	90.5
Total	193	100	Total	42	100

+SR −HK contexts Example: *I have a contact/ϕ contacts*			−SR −HK contexts Example: *She wants to have a baby/ϕ babies*		
Article	*Tokens*	%	*Article*	*Tokens*	%
the	13	9.4	the	0	0.0
¶a	37	26.8	¶a	23	36.5
¶ϕ	88	63.8	¶ϕ	40	63.5
Total	138	100	Total	63	100

¶ indicates the article or articles a native speaker of English would use in the context in question. The use of the zero article is only possible for native speakers when the N is plural, mass or abstract: ϕ *rabbits/ ϕ porridge/ ϕ understanding*. Parrish's subject, however, produced zero articles everywhere.
Source: Based on Parrish 1987: 368

target-like use). By contrast, out of a total of 50 contexts where *the* would have been obligatory for a native speaker, Parrish's informant used *the* 37 times (i.e. 74%). Of the 13 contexts where a native speaker would have used ϕ, the informant used ϕ 12 times (i.e. 92%). Where the informant used an article in a non-target-like way, this was typically ϕ; *a* was never used in contexts where *the* or ϕ are required by native speakers.

This indication of the relative accuracy of each article, coupled with the findings in table 6.3, seems to suggest the following: *the* is typically being used to mark

NPs with specific reference. These are also mostly NPs which are known to the hearer, but there are some cases where they are not (Parrish 1987: 365). Where *a* is used it categorically marks the fact that the NP is not known to the hearer. However, the relative degree of suppliance of *a* in obligatory contexts is much lower than the suppliance of *the*, suggesting that it emerges later than *the*. The ϕ article is widely overgeneralized, and appears to function as a 'default' article (i.e. used in all contexts, even where it is not possible in the target language).

While Parrish's informant was in the early stages of acquiring English, she was not a complete beginner. Nevertheless, given the profile of the results, one might speculate that when she was in the initial state, either only *the* (but not *a*) was present alternating with ϕ, or even that there were no articles in her grammar; in either case, *a* is a later development. The idea that at least some L2 learners of English start out without a representation for articles is not without support in the literature. Two Punjabi-speaking subjects reported in Klein and Perdue (1992: 61–88) show an article-less stage more clearly. These subjects had been resident in the UK for 13 and 20 months respectively at the time data were first collected from them, and they had little instruction in English prior to that period. Hence they had considerably less exposure to English than Parrish's Japanese subject, who had had six years of instruction prior to her arrival in the United States. In both cases it is noted that while, at the first cycle of testing, there is a good range of nouns in their productions, in the case of one informant 'there is no definite article' (1992: 68) and in the case of the other 'bare N is the most frequently used referential device' (1992: 83). However, evidence bearing on the question is sparse in the literature, so little can be said.

Huebner (1985) had already found a pattern in the use of *the* and *a* similar to that of Parrish's subject in the L2 English of a Hmong speaker from Laos. In this case, though, a developmental disjunction in the appearance of *the* and *a* is much clearer. Huebner conducted a longitudinal one-year study with this subject who was acquiring English in an untutored setting in the United States, and undertook a follow-up study 20 months later. In the one-year study data were collected approximately every three weeks from free conversation. Initially, this subject's article usage consisted of a contrast between *da* (a phonological approximation to native *the*) and ϕ – that is, there was no contrast between *da* and *a*. Then, after six weeks, Huebner reports that *da* flooded all contexts. However, around week 21 of the study the subject started to drop *da* from [−SR −HK] contexts, and, from about week 27, to drop it from [+SR −HK] contexts. In other words, the subject was dropping *da* from precisely those contexts where *a*, but not *the*, is possible in native English. But at this stage *a* is not present: there is just a binary contrast between *da*/*the* [+HK] and ϕ *[−HK]*. In the follow-up study 20 months later, Huebner found that *a* had begun to appear in the [+SR, −HK] contexts. The results from this follow-up study are given in table 6.4, where percentage scores for Huebner's subject are compared with those of Parrish's subject.

Table 6.4   Use of *da*, *ϕ*, *a* by an untutored Hmong-speaking L2 learner of English after several years in the US, compared with Parrish's Japanese-speaking subject

	+SR +HK			+SR –HK			–SR –HK		
	Score	*%*	*(Parr.) (%)*	*Score*	*%*	*(Parr.) (%)*	*Score*	*%*	*(Parr.) (%)*
da/the N	64	94.1	(67.9)	7	18.9	(9.4)	7	22.6	(0.0)
ϕ N	4	5.9	(32.1)	20	54.1	(63.8)	20	64.5	(63.5)
a N	0	0.0	(0.0)	10	27.0	(26.8)	4	12.9	(36.5)

Source: Based on Huebner 1985

Although they are not equal in the absolute proportions of articles used in each context, Parrish's and Huebner's informants show a similar pattern: *da/the* used frequently and predominantly in [+SR, +HK] contexts, but also used in [–HK] contexts (impossible for native speakers); *a* used much less frequently, but restricted (in a target-like way) to [–HK] contexts.

The results from these longitudinal case studies of speakers of Asian languages show a similar pattern to the accuracy profile that Andersen found in a cross-sectional study of Spanish speakers: *a* was used less frequently in appropriate contexts than *the*. All three studies suggest that L2 learners of English acquire the properties encoded by the English article system incrementally. If Andersen's further finding that possessive *'s* is less accurate than *a* is generalizable, and if the speculation that the initial state may be characterized as lacking articles is at least worth considering, then we have a possible descriptive generalization about how knowledge of English noun-related morphology develops in the mental grammars of L2 learners:

(bare NP)

↓

specificity in the NP (marked by *the/da*)

↓

hearer knowledge in the NP (marked by *a/ϕ*)

↓

possessive *'s*

We now need to ask whether this pattern of development is the effect of systematic grammar building, and whether there is any L1 influence on the process: in other words, whether development in this domain can be characterized as 'modulated structure building'. To do this we need to have an understanding of the structure of phrases involving NPs. This is considered in the next section.

6.3 The structure of English determiner phrases

Section 6.3 draws a parallel between the properties of Infl and the properties of the category 'determiner', and suggests that what we have been calling NP up to now involves a functional category, D, which selects NP as its complement. It is claimed that D is interpreted by reference to a D-Operator, just as Tense is interpreted by reference to a Tense Operator, and that the structure of possessives is similar to the structure of passives.

In discussing the structure of clauses in chapter 2, I presented some of the arguments for postulating an Infl category. In English, Infl realizes tense and the agreement relation which exists between the verb and the subject in finite clauses. We have since seen a range of phenomena in second language acquisition which receive an interesting account if the existence of such a category is assumed. Abney (1987), noting parallels between the structure of clauses and the structure of nominal phrases, has proposed a similar sort of analysis for nominal phrases. Consider the similarity between the pair of sentences in (9):

9a John refuses to leave
 b John's refusal to leave

Suppose we assume that the possessive 's of (9b) is the nominal equivalent of the tense/agreement -s of the clause in (9a). If we say that possessive 's is a morpheme realizing the category **determiner,** or D, then by analogy with IP the structure of (9b) is as illustrated in (10)[3]:

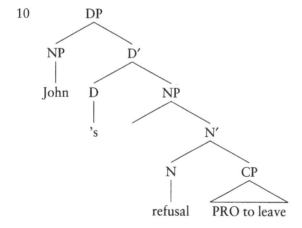

Abney's proposal is that the articles *the, a, φ*, pronouns like *my, your, her*, etc., and demonstratives like *this, that*, etc., belong to the class D. So, many of the phrases which I have been referring to as NPs up to now are in fact DPs on this proposal, and NPs are the projection of determiner-less Ns:

11

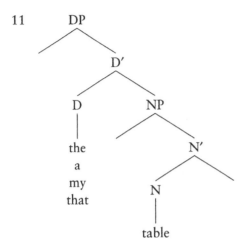

It could be claimed that there are at least two parallels between the properties of D and the properties of Infl. Recall that in section 2.10 we assumed that the tense feature of Infl must be **bound** by reference to a tense operator heading the clause, so that the clause is given an appropriate time reference with respect to the rest of the discourse. D would also appear to need to be linked to discourse. As we saw above, an NP whose referent has already been introduced into the discourse, and hence is known to the hearer, takes a different article (*the*) from one which has not (and with which *a* or *φ* is appropriate). Where an NP has a referent which is known to the hearer this is presumably because it is bound in its reference to something which has either already been mentioned, is present at the time of speaking, or is part of the knowledge shared by the speaker and hearer. Where it is not known, the NP is free of any such references.

One way of capturing this notion is to suggest that clauses are headed by a **D-Operator** which binds the D morphemes in the clause, as well as the Tense Operator which binds tense morphemes (see section 2.10):

12 [DO$_i$ [$_{IP}$ I saw D$_i$/D$_j$ rabbit in the garden yesterday]]

If a determiner is not co-indexed with the D-Operator (i.e. it is D$_j$) its interpretation will be 'unknown referent', and *a/φ* will be selected (*I saw a rabbit in the garden yesterday*). If a determiner is co-indexed with the D-Operator (i.e. it is D$_i$) its interpretation will be 'known referent', and a number of determiners will be possible: *the* (*I saw **the** rabbit in the garden yesterday*); *a/ϕ* in their generic use (*A rabbit can be a nuisance to gardeners*); *this*, *that*; and others. See Hyams (1996: 110–16) for some discussion of a D-Operator in child and adult grammars.

A second parallel between the properties of D and the properties of Infl is in the structure of possessive DPs and passive IPs (see section 5.4.1 for some discussion of the passive construction in English). There are two ways of potentially realizing a possessive construction in English, illustrated in (13):

13a The old man's friend
  b The friend of the old man

Old man and *friend* appear to bear the same thematic relation to one another in both constructions, *old man* being the 'experiencer' or GOAL, in some sense, of the friendship of the other participant. Recall that by Baker's Uniformity of Theta Assignment Hypothesis which I discussed in section 5.3.2, identical thematic relationships between items are represented by identical structural relationships at the start of the derivation. This means that both phrases in (13) have the same initial structure. Suppose that this structure is along the lines of (14):

14

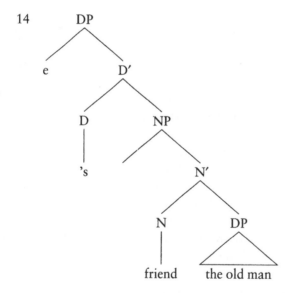

This structure is parallel to the initial structure of passives in English. In passive constructions the *be* + V-*en* morphology turns two-argument transitive verbs into one-argument unaccusatives which cannot assign Case to their argument (see section 5.3.3). This forces the argument to raise to the specifier of IP to satisfy its need for Case, as illustrated in (15):

15

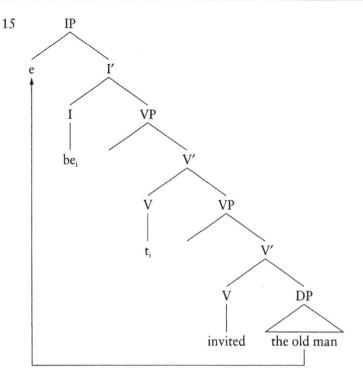

Nouns and adjectives in English are not able to assign Case: *the story his life,* *proud her achievements,* *fond his brother.* Given the proposed analysis in (14), to receive Case the DP complement of *friend – the old man –* could raise to the specifier of the topmost DP, if it is assumed that *'s* assigns genitive Case to its specifier. This would be directly parallel to the raising of a DP from the complement position of the verb to the specifier of IP in the case of passives:

16

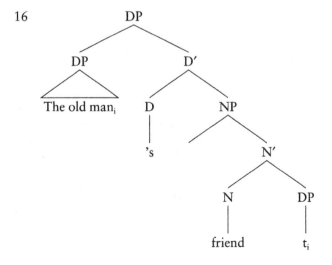

Alternatively, English has another option for assigning Case to the complements of Ns and As, and that is to introduce the preposition *of*: *the story of his life, proud of her achievements, fond of his brother*. If we assume that *of*, like all prepositions, is a Case assigner, but unlike other prepositions is thematically transparent allowing the thematic relationship between *friend* and *the old man* to continue, we will have captured the relation between the two constructions in (13). (The topmost D in (13b) is realized by the article *the*, a non-Case-assigning form which selects an empty specifier):

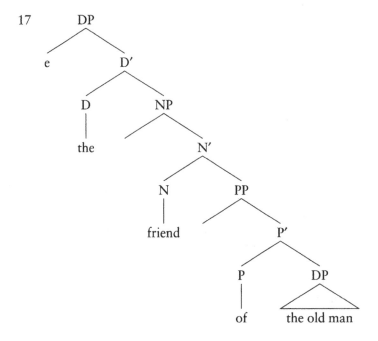

6.4 Grammar-building in the second language acquisition of DPs

In section 6.4 it is claimed that *the* emerges before *a* in the grammars of L2 speakers because it is a less specified determiner than *a*, and possessive *'s* appears later still because it involves a specifier–head relation. The effect of the L1 on the development of L2 learners' knowledge of the functional category D is discussed.

6.4.1 Incremental development in the acquisition of DP

Let's return now to the descriptive generalization of section 6.2.2. There we speculated that a possible way in which determiner phrases develop in L2 English is as follows:

(bare NP)

↓

specificity in the NP (marked by *the/da*)

↓

hearer knowledge in the NP (marked by *a/φ*)

↓

possessive *'s*

Surprisingly, this sequence of development shares some similarities with the kind of sequence of development found in the acquisition of English IP. In that case we argued that learners started with a bare V, and its projection VP. In acquiring copula *be* they established a minimally specified Infl which became subsequently specified for aspect, and then for tense and agreement. The initial 'bare NP' phase, if it exists, is reminiscent of the bare VP phase. The appearance of *the* signals the establishment of the category D. A possible reason for its emergence before *a* is that it requires the lesser specification of the two. Firstly, *the* places minimal restrictions on the type of NP complement it selects; the NP can be count or non-count, singular or plural: *the egg, the porridge, the eggs* (the complement cannot, however, be a proper noun: **The George has arrived*). Secondly, the early use that L2 speakers make of *the* appears to be to mark the specificity of the accompanying NP. Specificity is a local modification of the meaning of the NP (in contrast to distinguishing whether the NP is known to the hearer or not, which involves the D-Operator). Thus the acquisition of *the* is reminiscent of the acquisition of copula and auxiliary *be*.

The introduction of *a* into a learner's grammar establishes a contrast with *the* in terms of [± hearer knowledge]. This requires a more highly specified D. First, *a* is more selective in the NP complements it can take. It can only select a singular, count NP (*an egg, *an eggs, *a porridge*). Learners have to acquire the complementary distribution of *a* and *φ* in these environments. Second, [±HK] is a non-local relation, involving co-indexation or contra-indexation with the D-Operator. The appearance of *a* after *the* in the sequence of development is reminiscent of the appearance of tense marking after the acquisition of copula *be* and auxiliary *be* in the acquisition of IP.

Finally, possessive *'s* is a morpheme on which Andersen's Spanish-speaking subjects were least accurate. Is this difficulty parallel to the difficulty of subject–verb agreement in the acquisition of IP? Given the account of possessive *'s* constructions in 6.3, a specifier–head relation is involved, and I speculated before that the specifier–head relation is at the root of the difficulty of subject–verb agreement. Therefore I would predict the same difficulty here. All this suggests that L2 learner knowledge of English DPs may develop incrementally in the same way as it appears to develop incrementally in the case of IP. In fact, just as we found L1 influence in this area in the acquisition of IP (Spanish speakers were more accurate earlier on subject–verb agreement than Japanese speakers) similar

L1 influence appears to arise in the case of DP. This is considered in the next section.

6.4.2 L1 influence on the building of grammatical representations for DP

In section 2.4.2 a study by Makino (1980) was described in which it appeared that Japanese-speaking learners of L2 English were comparatively more accurate in using possessive 's than Dulay and Burt's (1973, 1974) Spanish-speaking learners. This finding has been replicated by Shirahata (1988) who, using the implicational scaling technique of Andersen (1978), also found that Japanese speakers performed more accurately on possessive 's than Andersen's Spanish speakers. It is possible that this is the result of L1 influence on grammar building. If true, since possessive 's is a morpheme belonging to the functional category D, it would be further evidence that the L1 can influence the development of functional categories.

Japanese has a construction involving a genitive Case-assigning particle which is similar to English 's:

  18   tookyoo-no hoteru
        Tokyo-Gen hotels
        'Tokyo's hotels'

In Spanish, by contrast, possession is realized syntactically only by a construction equivalent to English *of*-possessives:

  19   los hoteles de Madrid
        the hotels of Madrid

Note that in (18) the 'possessor', *Tokyo*, precedes the thing possessed, while in (19) the 'possessor', *Madrid*, follows. Spanish speakers learning English therefore have to acquire both the syntactic operation which moves *Madrid* into the specifier of DP and the morpheme 's which marks the possessive relation between the specifier and the complement in *Madrid's hotels*. By contrast, Japanese speakers have a D morpheme in their L1 which marks the same relationship as 's in English. It would seem plausible to assume that their L1 influences development in the L2.

A similar influence of the L1 appears to arise in the case of a property included in Andersen's accuracy profile which I have not touched on yet: the plural inflection -s which attaches to N. In Andersen's study, plural -s was of the same order of accuracy as the article *a*. There is evidence, however, that plural -s may be more difficult for speakers of a language like Japanese than for speakers of a language like Spanish. Wakabayashi (1997) compared the performance of two groups of advanced learners of English, 15 Japanese speakers and 15 Spanish speakers, students or researchers in Cambridge, in the UK, on a computer-generated grammaticality judgement task. Thirteen types of sentences were included in the test, one type relating to the marking of plural on the N, as in (20a), and another type relating to the use of *a* in a [–HK] context, as in (20b) (examples from Wakabayashi 1997: 166):

20a Jack went to the market yesterday. He bought *five apple* and one big pineapple to make a dessert

b Yesterday Mike saw *tall, handsome man* in the class. He was their new headmaster

Wakabayashi performed a rank-ordering analysis on his results which showed that the Japanese subjects found it more difficult to detect the ungrammaticality of these two types of sentences than the Spanish subjects, but that in each case plural *-s* and *a* clustered together. This is consistent with Andersen's original clustering of these two forms in the accuracy profile for Spanish speakers but also indicates that there could be an L1 influence on the rate of development.

Wakabayashi argues that a parameter of variation allowed within Universal Grammar which is set differently between D in Japanese and D in English and Spanish is at the root of this difference in development. Whereas in English and Spanish the category D is always obligatory, and always marks a contrast between singular and plural where count nouns are involved, in Japanese D is optional. For example, the noun *ringo*, 'apple', can appear in a sentence like (21a) with no determiner, but with the range of interpretations indicated (examples from Wakabayashi 1997: 309):

21a Taroo-ga mise-de ringo-o katta
Taro-Nom shop-at apple-Acc bought
'Taro bought an apple/apples/the apple/the apples at the shop'

Optionally, a numeral can be used which is accompanied by a classifier and which indicates that the N is plural, although no plural inflection attaches to the N:

b Taroo-ga mise-de san-ko ringo-o katta
Taro-Nom shop-at three-CL apple-Acc bought
'Taro bought three apples at the shop'

Wakabayashi claims that it is only when a numeral is present that DP is projected to host it. This absence of D in the absence of numerals means that Japanese speakers must acquire the specification of English D 'from scratch', so that the appearance of *a/-s* comes later than for Spanish speakers. Since D is a functional category, this again would be evidence that the L1 can influence the development of functional categories.[4]

More Advanced Discussion

6.5 L1 influence and the functional category Num(ber)

Parodi et al. (1997) have also argued that the nature of functional categories associated with NP in the L1 influences the development of these categories in the L2. To understand their results, we need to elaborate a little on the structure of DP. Several linguists have proposed that in addition to D and N there is a Num(ber) category which appears between them. By X'-theory, Num projects to Num' and to NumP. Num is a functional category to which number morphemes like [+singular] and [–singular] (i.e. plural) belong. In English [+singular] is realized by a zero inflectional morpheme, or possibly absence of a morpheme, (e.g. *table-ø*); [–singular] is realized by a regular inflection *-s* (*table-s*) or, in a handful of cases, by irregular forms (e.g. *foot → feet, child → children*, etc.). One argument to support the proposal of a category Num is the location of adjectives. Adjectives normally precede nouns in English, but in other languages, for example the Romance languages, many follow the noun and have the same interpretation as the English prenominal equivalents. This similarity in interpretation associated with different syntactic positioning can be captured if adjectives are generated as specifiers in NP, and if in the Romance languages, but not in English, nouns move from NP to Num (Bernstein 1991; Ritter 1993), as illustrated in (22):

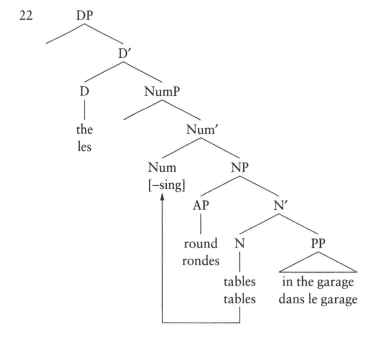

N movement to Num is like verb movement to Infl, which was claimed to be the effect of strong inflections under Infl (see sections 3.3.3 and 3.6). In a parallel way, it might be suggested that in the Romance languages, the inflections under Num are strong and this forces the noun to move. By contrast, in languages which have prenominal adjectives, like English, the inflections under Num are weak and lower from Num to N.[5]

Parodi et al. assume such an analysis for German, involving both the functional categories D and Num. German is like English in having prenominal adjectives and overt plural inflections which contrast with a zero inflection for singular (or absence of inflection). It differs, however, in that determiners and adjectives agree in number with the noun, and are inflected for Case (nominative, accusative, genitive, dative) and gender (masculine, feminine, neuter). For example, compare the articles and adjectives in a simple phrase in English and German:

23a The interesting book
  b The interesting book-s

24a **Das** interessant-**e** Buch
  b **Die** interessant-**en** Büch-er[6]

To account for these properties, Parodi et al. assume that the syntax of (24) is something like (25):

25

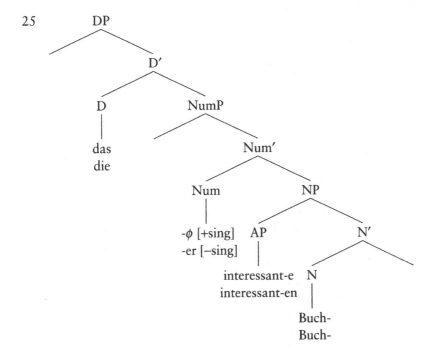

Here, not only do the [±singular] inflections appear under Num, but also there is some form of agreement which matches the forms that appear in D, Num and AP.

Parodi et al. studied the acquisition of German DPs by three different L1 groups: speakers of Korean, Turkish and Romance languages. Korean is rather like Japanese in that it has no articles (although it does have demonstratives equivalent to *this*, *that*). Adjectives and numerals precede the noun, as in German. Unlike Japanese, there is a plural inflection on the noun, but it is not obligatory, and its absence is preferred if there is a numeral. In Turkish there are no articles either (but there are demonstratives). Adjectives and numerals precede the noun, but numerals can also follow the noun. There is a plural inflection which attaches to the noun, and this is obligatory except when a numeral is present, when the inflection is usually absent. In the Romance languages articles are typically obligatory; numerals precede the noun, but most adjectives follow it. The noun typically inflects for plural, and articles and adjectives also agree with the noun in number (and gender).

Given these L1 differences, speakers of these languages could face potentially different tasks in learning German. Speakers of Korean and Turkish would have to acquire obligatory articles where their L1 does not have them. If these belong to D, they have to establish a new specification for a functional category. By contrast, articles are obligatory in the Romance languages, as in German. If the properties of L1 functional categories influence L2 grammar building, speakers of Romance languages should find it easier to acquire German articles than Korean/Turkish speakers.

Secondly, Romance languages have N movement (to strong inflections under Num) but Korean and Turkish do not, and neither does German. Here is a case where speakers of Romance languages have to 'lose' a property of a functional catgeory in their L1 to perform in a target-like way. Recall that 'modulated structure building', like 'minimal trees', assumes that in the initial state L2 learners' grammars involve lexical projections in principle. If this is correct, we should see no evidence of movement of N above adjectives in any of the L2 speakers' early grammars, in spite of L1 differences. This is because N movement is forced by inflections in Num, a functional category, and Num should in principle be absent from initial state L2 grammars.

In their investigation, Parodi et al. used both cross-sectional and longitudinal data from informal interviews with speakers of Korean, Turkish and Romance languages. To simplify consideration of their results, we will look only at the longitudinal data from one of their Turkish-speaking informants, Ilhami, one Spanish-speaking informant, Ana, and the cross-sectional data from two groups of Korean speakers, classified by Parodi et al. into level I (elementary), and level II (more advanced). None of the subjects had received intensive language instruction in German. The Korean speakers had been resident in Germany for periods ranging from 9 months to 18 years at the time of data collection; data were

Table 6.5 Acquisition of the German DP by three sets of subjects: L1 Korean, Turkish and Spanish

1 *Subjects*	*2* *Overt D element* *(versus no D* *element)*		*3* *Absence of* *plural inflection* *on N*		*4* *Proportion of* *postnominal* *adjectives*	
Korean	*Score*	*%*	*Score*	*%*	*Score*	*%*
Level I	65/252	25.8	20/34	58.8	(both groups)	
Level II	425/793	53.6	35/113	31.0	1/102	1.0
Turkish	*Score*	*%*	*Score*	*%*	*Score*	
Ilhami I (10 m)	98/116	84.5	3/7	42.9	There were	
Ilhami II (18 m)	67/79	84.8	0/1	0	103 tokens of	
Ilhami III (29 m)	114/132	86.4	0/2	0	adjectives in the Turkish data overall – all were prenominal	
Spanish	*Score*	*%*	*Score*	*%*	*Score*	*%*
Anna I (5 m)	69/110	62.7	6/17	35.3	7/28	25.0
Anna II (24 m)	64/66	97.0	2/4	50.0	0/10	0

m = months
Source: Based on Parodi et al. 1997

collected from Ilhami at three points (at 10 months, 18 months and 29 months after arrival) and from Anna at two points (at 5 months and 24 months after arrival). None of the subjects, then, were complete beginners when data were first collected.

The results are presented in table 6.5. In column 2, scores for the number of overt D elements (definite and indefinite articles, demonstratives and so on) produced by the informants, as opposed to absence of a D element, are given as a proportion of the contexts where they would be obligatory for native speakers of German. Column 3 shows the absence of plural inflections on plural nouns. Column 4 shows the number of adjectives used in (non-target-like) postnominal position (as a proportion of all cases of adjective use).

Parodi et al. first point out that the results in column 2 show that there is an L1 influence on the rate of omission of determiner elements in obligatory contexts. The Spanish speaker omits fewer determiners than the level I Korean speakers, even after just 5 months of exposure to German. And by the time she has been resident for 24 months there are almost no omissions. By contrast, the elementary level Korean speakers supply only a quarter of required D elements, and even in the more advanced group this rises to only a half. Parodi et al. suggest that 'these differences challenge the minimal trees hypothesis, since the interlanguages of all (adult) L2 acquirers are said not to generate DPs initially and therefore D-omission rates should be similar at especially early stages of development' (1997: 38).

Certainly the results are consistent with L1 influence on the rapidity with which a D category emerges in the learner's L2 grammar, and that is incompatible with 'minimal trees', which claims that functional categories are not L1 influenced but develop only in response to positive evidence from the L2. But the results are not inconsistent with the possibility that initial L2 grammars consist of lexical projections 'in principle', but allow the establishment of functional categories from early on if there is appropriate evidence for them – the view taken by the 'modulated structure building' hypothesis. If properties transferred from the L1 have the effect of sensitizing L2 learners to the existence of functional categories in the L2, the early appearance of a D category in the Spanish speaker's grammar would be the effect of an obligatory D in Spanish. The later appearance of D in the grammars of Korean speakers would be the effect of their constructing a grammar for the German D system on the basis of target language input alone.[7]

Some evidence to support the view that although the Spanish speaker establishes a D projection early on, the initial grammar of this speaker (and speakers of Romance more generally) is essentially lexical, comes in relation to column 3. Column 3 shows informants' use of plural inflections on N. In all three L1s nouns have plural inflections (although they are not obligatory in Korean and Turkish). Given this, one might expect L1 influence to assist learners in constructing representations for plural in German. Yet the proportion of omissions of plural inflections in German are quite high for all subjects (although there are few tokens in some samples, making it difficult to draw conclusions). Assuming that plural inflections belong to Num, a functional category, the L2 speakers do appear to be having some difficulty establishing the appropriate specification of this category for plural marking in German, in spite of a similar specification in their L1s. Interestingly, Parodi et al. note that 'at early levels of L2 acquisition, there is a high incidence of expressing plurality via lexical means, as measured by the proportion of quantifiers and numerals to other D-elements' (1997: 27). In other words, in the early stages learners are using lexical categories to signal plurality rather than the inflections belonging to the functional category Num.

This is consistent with learners constructing initial-state L2 grammars where lexical categories are preferred over functional categories.

Finally, in column 4, the interesting result is that the Spanish speaker uses postnominal adjectives in German in 25% of cases at the first recording. Since this pattern is almost entirely absent from the Korean- and Turkish-speaking informants, this suggests some initial L1 influence. Since postnominal adjectives are assumed to be the result of N moving to Num, a functional category, as Parodi et al. note, this poses some difficulty for the view that functional categories are in principle absent from initial-state L2 grammars (predicted by both 'minimal trees' and 'modulated structure building'), and that there is no L1 influence on the development of functional categories (predicted by 'minimal trees', but not by 'modulated structure building'). However, observe that the results in column 2 argued for the presence of D early on in the Spanish speaker's grammar for German. If D is present early on, Num (which occurs between D and NP) should be present too. If the L1 influences properties of the L2 at the point when they develop (see the discussion in section 2.10) it might be that Spanish Num, which requires N movement, initially influences this speaker's grammar for German. This would be consistent with the kind of pattern we found when French speakers acquired English IP: they continued to allow thematic verbs to raise over adverbs, as in French. What is surprising here is that the Spanish speaker appears to have eliminated such influence after 24 months in an immersion environment.

So, the results from the Parodi et al. study of the L2 acquisition of the German DP seem to point to L1 influence on the development of D and Num, both functional categories. The speakers investigated all appeared to have initial-state or transitional-state grammars. In the next section we will consider a case where a property associated with Num – gender marking – appears to pose persistent difficulty, even into advanced stages for speakers of L1s which do not mark gender.

More Advanced Discussion

6.6   A persistent difficulty for L2 speakers in constructing a representation for the DP

The results from the study of Parodi et al. generally show that, with increasing exposure to German, speakers of Korean, Turkish and Spanish are approximating to target-like use of overt D elements, plural inflections and prenominal adjectives. One particularly striking finding is the speed with which the Spanish speaker appears to establish that German does not allow postnominal adjectives. A similarly rapid elimination of postnominal adjectives was also found by Parodi et al. in the performance of the other speakers of Romance languages in their sample. This would appear to be a counter-example to the claim of Tsimpli and Roussou (1991) discussed in the previous chapter (5.5.3) that adult L2 speakers cannot reset L1 values of parameters associated with functional categories. If strong inflections in Num are one value of a 'number parameter' (forcing the N to move to Num), and weak inflections in Num are the other value (with the inflections lowering to N), speakers of Romance languages would appear to be able to acquire a different parameter value in the L2. It is possible that this is the case; below we will consider evidence from English learners of French which suggests that they can successfully acquire N movement to Num in French. If correct, the claim that L2 learners cannot acquire *any* parameter values associated with functional categories which are not realized in their L1s would be too strong. But recall also that Tsimpli and Roussou's claim allows for the possibility that L2 learners 'misanalyse' L2 input, making it look on the surface as if they have reset parameters when they haven't. Since the Romance languages do allow prenominal adjectives (see note 5), it is possible that speakers of these languages learning German place all German adjectives in a position higher than Num. If this were the case, speakers might still be raising the N to Num, but this would be invisible. It is not entirely clear what evidence would enable us to test for this possibility, although adjectives in prenominal position in Romance are usually associated with slightly different interpretations from those in postnominal position; investigating the interpretation that speakers of Romance languages assign to prenominal adjectives in German might be a way into the problem. I leave the question open here.

There is another parameter associated with Num, however, which does seem to cause L2 speakers persistent difficulty: a gender-marking parameter. Romance languages typically mark a grammatical distinction between masculine and feminine nouns (a contrast which we will represent as ±masculine). In French, for instance, all nouns have to be either masculine or feminine, and this determines the form that both determiners and adjectives take, for example:

26a   **le/un** bois[+masc] vert   'the/a green wood'
   b   **la/une** forêt [−masc] verte   'the/a green forest'

According to Ritter (1993), [±masc] is a feature which belongs to the category Num in French. Although there are no overt 'gender inflections' associated with this feature, it controls agreement between the morpheme under D, the noun and any adjectives present. The presence or absence of a gender feature in nominal phrases appears to be a parameter of variation allowed by UG; for example, it is present in the Romance languages, but not in English. Furthermore, Ritter argues that its location is also parametrized: in French it belongs to the category Num, but in Hebrew it is only associated with the category N.

Child L1 learners of French appear to acquire the gender-agreement-controlling feature of Num early in development, and make few errors in their choice of determiners (Clark 1985). Karmiloff-Smith (1979) has even found that French children as young as three years two months are consistently able to choose an appropriate determiner with nonsense words like *bicron* [+masc] and *plichette* [−masc]. Since these words, and hence their genders, are unknown to the children, alternative behaviours are imaginable: they could simply not produce a determiner when faced with such nouns, or they could use a 'default' determiner (i.e. a form used when the gender of a noun is unknown). The fact that they make a gender-sensitive choice which is consistent with similar nouns which they presumably do know (e.g. *citron* [+masc] 'lemon', *fourchette* [−masc] 'fork') suggests that the gender feature of Num needs to be satisfied.

In contrast, English speakers learning Romance languages appear to have a different way of acquiring gender distinctions which suggests that they may have long-term difficulty with the gender feature under Num (i.e. in acquiring a parameter value not set in their L1). Andersen (1984) studied the spontaneous Spanish of a 12-year-old L1 English speaker, Anthony, after 2 years of peer interaction with Spanish speakers in Puerto Rico. Spanish has a gender-marked determiner system similar to French:

27   el/un [+masc]   la/una [−masc]   'the/a'

In a sampled set of 100 DPs, Anthony used only *la* for the definite article, and only *un* for the indefinite article. In other words, Anthony was making no gender distinctions in the DP at all – he had a single form for the definite and indefinite articles, just as English does.

In an unpublished comparison of L2 speakers of French at a more advanced stage of development than Anthony was in Spanish, R. Hawkins (1998) found that although learners were drawing a distinction between masculine and feminine nouns, they were doing so in an asymmetrical way. The informants were ten university students in the final year of a degree course in French in the UK who had spent at least six months in France as part of their studies, and ten university students in Canada who had experienced a French immersion programme in secondary school (data collected by Bazergui et al. 1990). In both cases subjects were asked to watch an animated film and then describe what had happened. The oral productions were transcribed, and unambiguous uses of definite and indefinite articles were scored, together with tokens of prenominal and postnominal adjectives. The results show that for each individual informant, one of the pair of definite article forms *le/la*, and one of the pair of indefinite article forms *un/une* is almost always used correctly with nouns of the appropriate target-language gender, but this use does not extend to all nouns of that gender. The other member of the pair is typically used with nouns of both genders. To

Table 6.6 Accuracy in using definite/indefinite articles of the appropriate gender, and accuracy in placing adjectives pre- and postnominally

Subjects	Definite article		Indefinite article		Noun-Adjective order		
	Target-like form	Over-generalized form	Target-like form	Over-generalized form	N–Adj	Adj–N	*Adj–N
UK	88/88 (100%)	117/133 (88%)	73/76 (96.1%)	109/135 (80.7%)	39/39 (100%)	109/109 (100%)	0 (0%)
Canada	90/99 (90.9%)	84/103 (81.6%)	55/59 (93.2%)	58/96 (60.4%)	33/33 (100%)	75/79 (94.9%)	4/79 (5.1%)

illustrate with a hypothetical example: in (28) non-native speaker 1 (NNS1) uses *la* correctly with a noun of feminine gender (*forêt*), but *le* with both masculine and feminine nouns; non-native speaker 2 (NNS2) uses *le* correctly with the masculine noun *bois*, but *la* with both feminine and masculine nouns:

28   Native speaker   NNS1   NNS2
        le bois, 'the wood'   *le bois*   *le bois*
        le village, 'the village'   *le village*   *la village*
        la ville, 'the town'   *le ville*   *la ville*
        la forêt, 'the forest'   *la forêt*   *la forêt*

I will refer to the *la* form of NNS1 and the *le* form of NNS2 as the 'target-like form', and the other article in each case as the 'overgeneralized form'. The overall group results are presented in table 6.6.

One interpretation of the results is that informants have a default form of definite and indefinite article (the 'overgeneralized form' in table 6.6) which they use when they are not sure about the gender of a noun. This is suggested by the fact that the overgeneralized form is not necessarily the same across individuals; for one informant it is *le*, for another it is *la*. It is also suggested by the fact that for the same speaker it is not necessarily the case that the definite and indefinite overgeneralized forms match for gender; so the same speaker may use *le* as the overgeneralized definite article and *une* as the overgeneralized indefinite article. This variability across individuals and lack of matching of overgeneralized definite/indefinite articles in the same individual's grammar suggests that there is no underlying gender feature in Num controlling gender agreement between D and N, as there is in native French.

How, then, do English speakers come to make considerable target-like use of the non-default forms? One possibility is that because the informants have had relatively long exposure to French, they have learned a list of exceptions to their default forms. To illustrate, let us return to the hypothetical example of (28). A speaker who has *le* as the default form might, in early stages of development, produce *le village, le ville, le forêt* (in contrast to the native set *le village, la ville, la forêt*). But then at some later point this speaker learns that *forêt* is an exception. Thereafter the set *le village, le ville, la forêt* are produced where *la* is now used in a target-like way (but undergeneralized), while *le* continues to be overgeneralized. This interpretation of the results in table 6.6 would be consistent with a view that at an earlier point in development, these L1 English learners of French might have had a grammar which was like Anthony's grammar for Spanish.

If this interpretation of the results is correct, it suggests that L1 English speakers may not acquire the gender feature of Num in L2 French and Spanish, even into advanced stages when their L2 grammars are perhaps close to their final-state. On the surface, of course, it looks like they have acquired the gender feature of Num. But if they have learned a set of exceptions to the default article, and stored these in the lexicon, this would conceal the fact that the gender feature of Num has not been established. Such an account would be consistent with Tsimpli and Roussou's (1991) claim that parameter values of functional categories not already fixed in the L1 cannot be acquired in the L2.

At the same time, the performance of these English speakers in relation to noun–adjective order in French suggests precisely the opposite: that English speakers can acquire the strong inflections of French Num which force the N to raise. In French, adjectives typically appear in postnominal position, although there is a set of very frequent adjectives which normally appear prenominally. As can be seen from table 6.6, the informants in the present study produced almost no cases of non-target-like *adjective + noun* order; adjectives in their productions appeared almost always in target positions. This is difficult to explain without assuming that they have acquired N movement to Num to produce adjectives in postnominal position. Unlike the case of the speakers of Romance languages learning German where it was possible to claim that they might be placing adjectives in a position higher than Num and still raising Ns (without visible surface effect), in the case of English speakers learning French there is no obvious position in which they could place adjectives to avoid raising N to Num; N movement to Num seems to be the only option. We therefore appear to have evidence which suggests that L2 learners have difficulty establishing a parametrized gender feature on Num where it is not present in their L1, but also evidence which suggests that they can acquire another parameter value associated with Num: strong inflections. This raises the intriguing possibility that some kinds of parameter values associated with functional categories are difficult or impossible for L2 learners to acquire, while others are acquirable. If correct, the reason why this may be so is an open question.

6.7   Summary of chapter 6

The main points made in chapter 6 are the following:

- There are syntactic similarities between nominal phrases and clauses. While clauses have a CP–IP–VP structure, nominal phrases have a DP–NumP–NP structure. Assuming that articles belong to the category D, and singular/plural inflections belong to the category Num, the results of studies of L2 learners acquiring English suggest that they acquire the structure of nominal phrases incrementally, just as it was argued in chapters 2 to 4 that they acquire the structure of clauses incrementally. Although it is not clear from the studies examined in this chapter whether there is an initial phase of development where functional categories are absent, when D emerges it is at first underspecified. Typically, the presence of D in a learner's grammar is signalled by the morpheme *the* used to indicate the specificity of the accompanying NP; thus, *the* fulfils a local function, modifying the meaning of the NP. When *a* begins to be used, apparently later, it signals that the L2 learner has established a non-local contrast between NPs which are known to the hearer from the discourse or the context of utterance, and those which are not.
- There is evidence that properties of the L1 influence the development of both functional categories D and Num. Speakers of Japanese acquire the English possessive *'s* morpheme more quickly than Spanish speakers. Assuming that genitive Case assignment is a feature of D, and that Japanese has such a feature but Spanish does not, this finding suggests that a property of a functional category in the L1 influences development of the same property in the L2. By contrast, speakers of Spanish are quicker to establish plural inflections on N in English than Japanese speakers. Spanish has plural inflections, but Japanese does not. If [±singular] is a feature of the functional category Num, the presence of such a feature in Spanish would appear to allow Spanish speakers to establish this feature more quickly in their grammars for English than Japanese speakers. A similar pattern emerged in the acquisition of overt determiners in German by speakers of Romance languages and speakers of Korean. In the Romance languages articles are typically obligatory, but not in Korean, so the faster establishment of D in German by Romance speakers is consistent with L1 influence. These cases are counter-examples to the 'minimal trees' theory which claims that that there is no L1 influence on the representation of functional categories in L2 learners' mental grammars.
- The acquisition of properties of the functional category Num raised some interesting problems for the 'no-parameter-resetting' proposal of Tsimpli and Roussou (1991) discussed in chapter 5. Speakers of Korean, Turkish and Romance languages learning German, and English speakers learning French,

all appear to acquire the appropriate 'strength' of inflections under Num which determines whether the N raises to Num or not. If strong and weak inflections are different values of a parameter, it seems that L2 learners can acquire parameter values in the L2 which are fixed differently from the L1. At the same time, it was argued that English speakers have persistent difficulty with a gender feature belonging to Num in Romance languages like French and Spanish. They appear to acquire gender marking differently from native speakers of these languages. If the presence versus absence of the gender feature is a parameter of variation allowed by UG, learners appear not to be resetting the parameter. This raises the possibility that some parameter values associated with functional categories which differ between the L1 and the L2 may be acquirable, while others are not.

6.8 Exercises

Exercise 1: Analysing the non-native use of *the* in English (section 6.2.1)

The following two sentences were written by a Chinese (Cantonese) speaker on the topic of teaching English as a foreign language in the primary school:

> In the other words, the cooperation between the teachers, the parents and the pupils also play the crucial parts in this matter. The effort is indeed necessary.

Which uses of *the* are non-native like? On the basis of the account given in section 6.2.1 of the distribution and interpretation of English articles, explain why they are non-native-like.

Exercise 2: Analysing the non-native use of English articles with generic nominal phrases (sections 6.2.1, 6.2.2)

The following is an (unaltered) extract from a sample of writing by a native speaker of Chinese (Cantonese). (This is not the same writer as in exercise 1, but data from this informant were also used in chapter 5, exercise 5.) The writer is discussing the merits of teaching lip reading as opposed to sign language to deaf children.

Assume that all the expressions in bold are cases where the writer intended to use nominal phrases generically, i.e. as cases of [−SR, +HK]. How does this informant's use of articles in these cases differ from that of a native speaker? Does she have a systematic underlying grammar for generic nominals from which her use of articles follows?

> ϕ **lip-reading** is a kind of ϕ **media** of ϕ **communication** used by some deaf people. They get the messages from looking at the movement of the speaker's lips and the speaker's facial expression. Not all **the deaf children** can receive the education of ϕ lip-reading because it depends on the deafness of the deaf chidden. ϕ **deafness** can be divided into four groups. The first group is dealing with the deaf children who are profoundly deaf, that means there is little or no response to ϕ **sound**, no response to ϕ **human voice**. The second group is dealing with the deaf children who are severely deaf. They response to ϕ voice but limited to ϕ situations. The third group is dealing with the deaf children who are moderately deaf. They only response to ϕ voice in ϕ favourable situations. The last group is dealing with the deaf children who are partially deaf. They remain a little residual hearing and can response to ϕ voice nearly as the same as **the normal children** though ϕ **hearing loss** constitutes a handicap.

Exercise 3: Evaluating the claims in the text about the development of articles and the role of the L1 against new data (sections 6.4.1, 6.4.2)

(Material used in this exercise is reprinted with the permission of Cambridge University Press)

Using a picture description task, Thomas (1989) collected information about the use of *the, a, ϕ* in spontaneous production by 30 adult L2 learners of English. Twenty-three informants spoke L1s lacking articles (e.g. Japanese, Chinese), and seven spoke L1s with articles (e.g. French, German). Thomas classed the informants into three proficiency levels: low (n = 11), mid (n = 9), high (n = 10).

Recall that the features [±Specific Referent] and [±Hearer Knowledge] divide the contexts for article use in English into 4 basic types:

[+SR, −HK] e.g. Mary had **a** baby.
[+SR, +HK] e.g. She called **the** baby Antonia.
[−SR, −HK] e.g. She should move to **a** bigger house.
[−SR, +HK] e.g. **A** baby takes up a lot of space.

Consider the proportions of *the, a, ϕ* supplied by Thomas's informants in contexts like the above where native speakers would use *the* or *a* (we exclude all of the contexts where ϕ would have been possible for a native for the purposes of this exercise):

Proportions of English articles produced by 30 non-native speakers in contexts where *the* or *a* would be required by native speakers: percentages given in brackets (based on Thomas 1989)

		No. of tokens produced					
		Total contexts	*a*	%	*the* %	ϕ	%
[+SR, −HK]	a	831	517	(62.2)	124 (14.9)	190	(22.9)
[+SR, +HK]	the	1023	20	(2.0)	873 (85.3)	130	(12.7)
[−SR, −HK]	a	140	105	(75.0)	7 (5.0)	28	(20.0)
[−SR, +HK]	a	11	10	(90.9)	1 (9.1)	0	
	the	0	0		0	0	

Is the pattern here consistent with the claim made in section 6.4.1 about the development of *the* and *a*? Compare this with the distribution of articles (in percentages) by L1 background (L1 without articles versus L1 with articles) across all *the* and *a* target contexts:

Comparison of proportion (%) of use of articles by speakers from different L1 backgrounds in contexts where natives would require *the* or *a* (based on Thomas 1989)

Target form	L1 with articles (n = 7)			L1 without articles (n = 23)		
	the %	*a* %	ϕ %	*the* %	*a* %	ϕ %
the	96.7	0.3	3.0	80.9	2.5	16.6
a	8.5	77.9	13.6	15.5	59.0	25.5

Thomas notes that the use of *the* and *a* in appropriate contexts by speakers of L1s with articles is significantly greater, statistically, than by speakers of L1s without articles. Are these results consistent with the claims about L1 influence made in section 6.4.2?

The results presented here conflate the performance of speakers at different proficiency levels (low, mid, high). Does this matter in assessing the influence of the L1 on L2 learners' knowledge of the properties of D?

Exercise 4: Considering whether the emergence of plural -s in
L2 English reflects the emergence of the functional category
Num (section 6.4.3)

In section 6.4.3 it was suggested that plural inflections belong to the functional category Num. Since English and German both have plural inflections, this means that they both instantiate the category Num.

Wode (1981) collected spontaneous L2 English data from four German-speaking children in the early stages of learning English naturalistically in the United States. He identified what seem to be three stages in the development of the use of English plurals (although recall that stages are idealizations, and what you normally find in development is a continuum):

(I)   The children used just one form of a noun in both singular and plural contexts. Although these forms mostly corresponded to what would be a bare N for native speakers, e.g. *egg*, sometimes the form used ended in an *s*, e.g. *eggs*. The presence of *s*-final nouns in the child's grammar appeared to be accidental, since one child might have an *s*-final noun and another not. Wode gives the following example where one child, Lars, used the form *eggs* for both singular and plural, and another child, Heiko, *egg*:

> Lars: Who want this eggs?
>   You give me one eggs?
> Heiko: How many egg you have?
>   I want two egg.

(II) A variant of the first N appears in the children's productions alongside the original N. Mostly this is a form ending in *s*, if the original was a bare N, but is a bare N if the original ended in *s*. New *s*-final Ns are restricted to use in plural contexts, but at first not all plural contexts. The original bare N continues to be used both in singular and plural contexts. Crucially, where the N in stage (I) had a final *s*, this does NOT continue to be used in both singular and plural contexts. Instead, the new bare N form is used in both, and the (original) *s*-final form is now restricted to a subset of plural contexts.

(III) The *s*-final N is generalized to all plural contexts, and the bare N is restricted to singular contexts (i.e. the native pattern).

What do you infer from this about the role that the functional category Num plays in the development of a representation for plural in these children's L2 English grammars? What influence does the L1 have?

Exercise 5: Designing a study to test knowledge of the case-assigning properties of D in English (sections 6.3, 6.4.2)

English has two ways of expressing possession within nominal phrases:

1a   Ralph's new car
 b   The brother of Peter

In section 6.3 is was argued that in (a) 's belongs to the category D, and assigns genitive Case to its specifier position (to which *Ralph* has moved in (1a)).

German also allows both possibilities, suggesting a similar underlying construction, although there are some differences between the two languages in the distribution of each construction (irrelevant for the purposes of this exercise):

2a   Rolfs neuer Wagen
 b   Der Bruder von Peter

French only has a construction equivalent to the (b) examples of (1)–(2); there is nothing corresponding to the (a) examples:

3a   La nouvelle voiture de Rodolphe
 b   Le frère de Pierre

Suppose that you wanted to test whether constructions like (1a–b) emerge at the same time in the L2 English grammars of speakers of German and French, or whether there is an order of emergence, and what influence the L1 has. What kind of test design would you employ? Consider the following factors in developing your design:

- the kind of informants required (age, experience of learning English)
- the proficiency of informants
- the type of elicitation task (what kinds of data will give you the best chance of drawing inferences about underlying competence?)

Assuming you obtain results which reflect properties of underlying competence, what would you infer about the acquisition of the genitive Case-assigning properties of English D if

- (1b) emerged significantly earlier than (1a) in both groups of learners;
- (1a–b) emerged at the same time in both groups of learners;
- (1b) emerged significantly earlier in the French speakers than (1a), but (1a–b) emerged simultaneously in the German speakers?

Exercise 6: Considering the implications of different native speaker/non-native-speaker interpretations of a syntactic operation (section 6.4.4)

In section 6.4.4 evidence was presented which suggests that English speakers do not find it difficult to acquire N raising to Num in L2 French. In the spontaneous description of an animated film, informants correctly located prenominal and postnominal adjectives to a high degree of accuracy.

Coppieters (1987) has found, however, that in discussing the interpretation of prenominal and postnominal adjectives in French with highly proficient near-native speakers who speak L1s without N movement, and with native speakers, an interesting difference emerges. While the native speakers' comments on the interpretation of these adjectives 'are relatively stable and repetitive' (1987: 559), by contrast many of the non-native speakers 'exhibited very limited mastery over the expressive resources available to N[ative]S[peaker]s through adjective placement' (1987: 559).

To illustrate, examples like the following (from Coppieters) differ considerably in meaning. While native speakers interpreted the differences consistently, the non-natives often had idiosyncratic interpretations:

1a Voilà une triste histoire. 'That's a story that makes you cry'
 b Voilà une histoire triste. 'That's an embarrassing problem'

2a Hier ce honteux journaliste est encore venu chez nous. 'Yesterday that shameful journalist came to our house again'
 b Hier ce journaliste honteux est encore venu chez nous. 'Yesterday that journalist who is ashamed of what he did came to our house again'

If speakers of L1s without N raising can acquire N raising in an L2, yet have difficulty assigning native-like interpretations to adjectives which appear both prenominally and postnominally, does this pose any problems for the claim that they have acquired the appropriate strength of inflections in Num in the L2?

6.9 Further reading

One of the best discussions of English articles in the L2 context can be found in Thomas, M. 1989: The acquisition of English articles by first- and second-language learners. *Applied Psycholinguistics* 10, 335–55. There is, though, very little work on the acquisition of DPs by L2 speakers. For discussion of the DP hypothesis itself, see Giusti, G. 1997: The categorial status of determiners. In L. Haegeman (ed.) *The New Comparative Syntax*, London: Longman, and chapter 4 (sections 7 and 8) of Radford, A. 1997: *Syntactic Theory and the Structure of English: A Minimalist Approach*. Cambridge: Cambridge University Press.

Notes

1   An alternative to the claim that English has a zero article is to say that the article is simply absent in examples like (1c). However, since the contexts where no overt article is permitted are, as we shall see in this section, syntactically restricted and give rise to specific interpretations, it is more likely that a zero article is involved.
2   In note 1 a justification was given for assuming a zero article in native English. It is less clear whether an L2 informant like the one studied by Parrish is using a zero article, or whether the article is simply absent. For the purpose of exposition I will refer to cases where there is no overt article as 'zero article', but the reader should be aware that this usage may conceal an underlying difference between non-native and native speakers.
3   Abney's proposal for possessive *'s* is not quite the same as (10). He claims that *'s* is a Case inflection attached to *John*, and that D is filled by an abstract determiner which assigns Genitive Case to its specifier, giving rise to the Case inflection. We won't explore the merits of this alternative proposal here.
4   In view of what was said about (18), it would have to be assumed that D is present in Japanese both when a numeral is present, and when the NP is involved in a possessive construction.
5   The Romance languages also have prenominal adjectives, e.g. *les petites tables rondes*, 'the small round tables'. It has been argued that these are derived in a higher position in the tree:

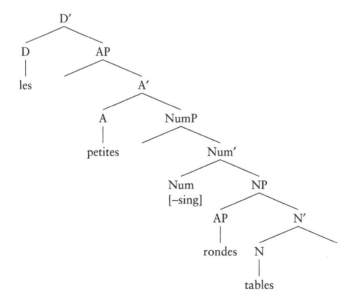

See Radford (1993) for discussion.

6   The quality of the stressed vowel in some nouns also changes, as indicated here by a change from *u* to *ü*. This will not be of concern here.

7   Note that the Turkish speaker does not omit D elements as much as the Korean speakers. However, the first sample of his speech was not collected until he had been resident in Germany for ten months, so he may already have had sufficient exposure to German to have established the appropriate specification for D. But Turkish, like Korean, does not have articles, so it is not clear why his use of articles is much greater than even the more advanced Korean speakers.

7 Constraints on Syntactic Representations and Second Language Acquisition

7.1 Introduction

In section 1.4 several reasons were given for thinking that human beings have an innate language faculty which guides and facilitates the way mental grammars for native languages are constructed. Chapters 2–6 have been concerned with establishing the extent to which that innate language faculty might be involved in the establishment of mental grammars for second languages. The position argued for so far, briefly, is that principles of Universal Grammar underlie the development of knowledge; initial-state grammars consist primarily of lexical projections, but we have encountered a number of cases where functional projections are apparently present from early on; knowledge of syntax develops incrementally in transitional-state grammars, with learners initially constructing representations for local syntactic relations with underspecified functional categories; L1 influence may occur at points of development where the L1 property is relevant; parameters associated with functional categories which are set differently in the L2 from the L1 may be unresettable for older L2 learners, with learners 'misanalysing' input data from the target language (although we encountered an apparent counter-example to this claim in section 6.4.4).

An argument given in section 1.4 in support of an innate language faculty operating in native language acquisition was that the syntactic knowledge of a mature native speaker is greater than anything that could have been inferred from the input (i.e the samples of language that are encountered). This is often called the **underdetermination** of syntactic knowledge by the input, or the **poverty** of the stimulus (Hornstein and Lightfoot 1981; Lightfoot 1991; 1999; White 1989). For example, native speakers know that while some arrangements of syntactic constituents produce grammatical sentences, others, which are just as interpretable and are of no greater complexity, are nevertheless ungrammatical. Yet there is nothing in the input to indicate this. Consider the following. We have seen that information questions are normally formed in English by the movement of a *wh*-phrase to the specifier position of a clause-initial CP, leaving a trace in the position from which the *wh*-phrase has moved (see section 4.8.1):

> 1a [$_{CP}$ Who$_i$ e [$_{IP}$ t$_i$ bought an electric guitar]]?
> b   [$_{CP}$ What$_i$ did$_j$ [$_{IP}$ Janice t$_j$ buy t$_i$]]?

Such movement or **extraction** of *wh*-phrases can also take place from embedded clauses:

> 2a [$_{CP}$ Who$_i$ did$_j$ [$_{IP}$ Freda t$_j$ discover [$_{CP}$ e [$_{IP}$ t$_i$ bought an electric guitar]]]]?
> b   [$_{CP}$ What$_i$ did$_j$ [$_{IP}$ Freda t$_j$ discover [$_{CP}$ e [$_{IP}$ Janice bought t$_i$]]]]?

Information questions can even be formed by turning two of the constituents in a clause into *wh*-phrases, but in this case one of them does not move, as in (3):

> 3   [$_{CP}$ Who$_i$ did$_j$ [$_{IP}$ Freda t$_j$ discover [$_{CP}$ e [$_{IP}$ t$_i$ bought what]]]]?[1]

Children learning English as a first language will come across examples of grammatical sentences like these in the input they receive. They subconsciously convert the facts of movement of *wh*-phrases in questions into a productive grammar which enables them to produce and to understand information questions they have never come across before. They must be able to do this to explain the following: every native speaker of English recognizes that while the sentences of (4) may be nonsensical (because the questions are bizarre) or unintelligible (because the words are invented) they are nevertheless grammatical:

> 4a What did your goldfish discover the television ate?
> b   Who did the snazzle discover primped the torlab?

So, exposed to examples like (1)–(3) speakers of English will learn that *wh*-phrases are extracted in information questions, and that they may be extracted from embedded clauses. Once learned, they will be able to use this knowledge productively to determine the grammaticality of novel sentences, as (4) illustrates.

Given such productivity, however, how is it that native speakers know immediately that while sentences like (3) are grammatical, the sentences of (5) are ungrammatical?

5a *[_CP_ What_i_ did [_IP_ Freda discover [_CP_ who_j_ e [_IP_ t_j_ bought t_i_]]]]?

b *[_CP_ Who_i_ did [_IP_ Freda discover [_CP_ what_j_ e [_IP_ t_i_ bought t_j_]]]]?

(5a–b) are as easy to interpret as (3), and appear to be no more complex. And yet we feel strongly that they are ungrammatical. The inevitable conclusion is that there is a constraint on the movement of _wh_-phrases in English. Native speakers know this unconsciously without benefit of evidence in the input (and it is unlikely that native speakers are ever taught about the ungrammaticality of sentences like (5)). There must therefore be principles of UG which constrain (i.e. put limits on) the movement of constituents in syntax.

One purpose of this chapter is to outline, briefly, some of the constraints on syntactic operations which linguists have uncovered, and to consider how those constraints might follow from principles of UG. They appear to fall into two basic types: constraints on the movement of constituents (like _wh_-phrases) and constraints on the interpretation of pronouns and anaphors (pronouns are forms like _she/her, he/him, they/them_, etc.; anaphors are '-self' forms like _herself, himself, themselves_, and so on). The way that linguists have attempted to account for both of these types of constraint has changed over time. We will try to give a flavour in this chapter both of the early attempts at explanation and of more recent ones.

A second purpose of the chapter is to assess the extent to which such constraints are operative in the mental grammars of second language speakers. Since we have already seen evidence supporting the involvement of principles of UG in other areas of L2 grammar construction, we might expect to see evidence for the principles governing constraints on movement and interpretation, even where they are not manifest in an L2 speaker's native language. However, for such principles to operate, learners typically have to have highly developed L2 grammars which are capable of productively generating complex sentences. This engages the question of final-state L2 grammars more directly than has been the case up to now.

Because constraints on syntactic operations provide evidence that grammatical knowledge cannot be wholly inferred from properties of input, they have been an important focus for L2 researchers working within the principles and parameters approach to L2 syntax. If it can be established that older L2 learners show knowledge of constraints, where evidence for these is absent both in samples of the target language and in the speaker's L1, this would suggest the involvement of UG in second language acquisition. The results, so far, have been mixed though, as we shall see. The position that will be argued for in this chapter is that principles which determine constraints are fully operative in L2 acquisition, but that older L2 speakers can differ from native speakers in their reactions to violations of constraints for two reasons: either their ability to process complex sentences in the L2 in real time declines with age; or they have difficulty with parameter settings in the L2 which are different from the L1.

7.2   The early treatment of constraints on the movement of constituents: subjacency and bounding nodes

Section 7.2 explains a proposed principle of UG called 'subjacency' which requires constituents extracted from embedded clauses to move in short steps. Some constructions which force constituents to move over longer stretches of syntactic structure, giving rise to ungrammaticality, are then described.

There are three types of syntactic movement, and each is subject to different kinds of constraint. Head movement is one kind, for example when V moves to I (see section 3.3.3), or N moves to Num (see section 6.4.3). Another kind is the movement of an argument DP to another argument position, as in the case of the movement of postverbal arguments with unaccusative verbs (see section 5.3.4). A third kind of movement, which we will be concerned with here, involves moving a *wh*-phrase, or *wh*-phrase-like operator (see note 4) from an argument position like subject, direct object or object of a preposition to a non-argument position at the front of the clause: in English, the specifier position of CP.

Compare the structure of sentence (3) and the sentences in (5) in more detail, repeated here as (6):

6a $[_{CP1}$ Who$_i$ did $[_{IP1}$ Freda discover $[_{CP2}$ e $[_{IP2}$ t$_i$ bought what]]]]?
 b   *$[_{CP1}$ What$_i$ did $[_{IP1}$ Freda discover $[_{CP2}$ who$_j$ e $[_{IP2}$ t$_j$ bought t$_i$]]]]?
 c   *$[_{CP1}$ Who$_i$ did $[_{IP1}$ Freda discover $[_{CP2}$ what$_j$ e $[_{IP2}$ t$_i$ bought t$_j$]]]]?

In section 4.8.1 it was proposed that a Q morpheme belonging to the category C(omplementizer) indicates that a clause is a question. In English, if there is a *wh*-phrase present, Q requires that the *wh*-phrase move into the specifier position of CP. In the sentences of (6), which are all direct questions, the Q morpheme is located under the C of CP1. This means that the questioned phrase – either the subject *who* or direct object *what* of the embedded clause – must move out of the lower clause to the specifier of the CP in the main clause. This is in order to satisfy a principle of Universal Grammar which requires that *wh*-phrases be in a specifier–head relation with a head specified for Q. In (6a), where the embedded subject moves and the embedded direct object remains *in situ*, this yields a grammatical result. In (6b–c), where one of the *wh*-phrases moves to the specifier position of CP2, movement of the other *wh*-phrase to CP1 is impossible. And yet movement of a *wh*-phrase to CP2 is not in principle impossible, as (7) shows:

7a   Freda discovered $[_{CP}$ who$_i$ e $[_{IP}$ t$_i$ bought an electric guitar]]]]
 b   Freda discovered $[_{CP}$ what$_i$ e $[_{IP}$ Janice bought t$_i$]]]]

The difference between (6a) on the one hand, and (6b–c) on the other, appears to be precisely the fact that when the specifier of CP2 is filled, a *wh*-phrase from the embedded clause cannot move to the higher CP1. This suggests that when *wh*-phrases move in English, they have to move to the specifier position of the **nearest CP**. And to do that the specifier position has to be empty.

A *wh*-phrase does not have to stay there, however. If there is an empty CP specifier higher up, and if there are reasons for doing so, the *wh*-phrase can carry on moving, for example if there is a Q morpheme under the C of CP1. So in (6a) *who* moves first to the specifier of CP2, and then on up to the specifier of CP1. This is known as step-by-step or **cyclic** movement. A trace is left by the moved *wh*-phrase in the specifier of CP2:

8   [$_{CP1}$ **Who**$_i$ did [$_{IP1}$ Freda discover [$_{CP2}$ t$_i'$ e [$_{IP}$ t$_i$ bought what]]]]?

The reason why (6a) is grammatical, then, is that the *wh*-phrase has moved in two local steps, in each movement going to the specifier position of the nearest CP. The reason why (6b)–(6c) are ungrammatical is that *wh*-phrases already fill the specifier position of CP2, forcing the other *wh*-phrase to make a long movement up to CP1. This movement is just too long.

The early account of this requirement for the cyclic movement of *wh*-phrases was to propose a principle of Universal Grammar called **subjacency** (Chomsky 1973, 1977). Subjacency requires that a constituent move only a short distance from its trace (the trace must be 'subjacent to' the moved constituent) where distance is measured in terms of structural domains called **bounding nodes**. A node is a point in a tree diagram (or a labelled bracketing) representing a maximal projection, like IP. The principle of subjacency is usually expressed along the following lines:

Subjacency
A constituent may cross only one bounding node in a single movement.

It was then stipulated that IP is a bounding node in English, but CP is not. Consider how this accounts for the grammaticality of (6a) and the ungrammaticality of (6b–c). In (9), the bounding nodes are marked by a #.

9a   [$_{CP1}$ Who$_i$ did [$_{IP1\#}$ Freda discover [$_{CP2}$ t$_i'$ e [$_{IP2\#}$ t$_i$ bought what]]]]?[2]
 b   *[$_{CP1}$ What$_i$ did [$_{IP1\#}$ Freda discover [$_{CP2}$ who$_j$ e [$_{IP2\#}$ t$_j$ bought t$_i$]]]]?
 c   *[$_{CP1}$ Who$_i$ did [$_{IP1\#}$ Freda discover [$_{CP2}$ what$_j$ e [$_{IP2\#}$ t$_j$ bought t$_i$]]]]?

In (9a) *who* moves first to the specifier of CP2. In doing so it crosses IP2, but this is the only bounding node it crosses in that movement, and so the trace t$_i$ is subjacent to the moved *who*. In a second step *who* moves to the specifier of CP1, leaving another trace, t_i', in the specifier of CP2, and in doing so again crosses just one bounding node, IP1, and so there is no violation of subjacency. In (9b–c), however, because there are *wh*-phrases already occupying the specifier of CP2, to get to the specifier of CP1 *what* and *who* have to move directly from the embedded clause, and in doing so cross two IP nodes (IP2 and IP1). The traces of *what* in (9b) and *who* in (9c) are therefore not subjacent to their *wh*-phrase antecedents, and the principle of subjacency is violated.

7.2.1 Constructions which give rise to violations of subjacency

Various types of construction can give rise to subjacency violations. The case considered in the previous section is an example of a **wh-island**. A clause headed by a *wh*-phrase blocks the grammatical extraction of some other constituent (like a castaway, a constituent cannot escape from the island – the imagery, and discovery of most of the constructions which give rise to subjacency violations are due to Ross 1967).

Complex DPs

DP, as well as IP, is a bounding node in English. This means that when a DP takes a clausal complement, any extraction of a *wh*-phrase from that clausal complement will cross two bounding nodes – DP and a higher IP – and give rise to a subjacency violation. Compare (10a) and (10b):

10a $[_{CP1}$ Which film star$_i$ did $[_{IP1\#}$ Bob hear $[_{CP2}$ t_i' that $[_{IP2\#}$ Jerry had married $t_i]]]]$?

   b *$[_{CP1}$ Which film star$_i$ did $[_{IP1\#}$ Bob hear $[_{DP\#}$ the news $[_{CP2}$ t_i' that $[_{IP2\#}$ Jerry had married $t_i]]]]]$?

In both sentences *which film star* moves first from the embedded clause to the specifier of CP2, crossing only one bounding node, IP2. In the second step, while *which film star* in (10a) again crosses only one bounding node, IP1, in (10b) it crosses DP and IP1 on its way to the specifier of CP1; these are two bounding nodes, and there is a subjacency violation.[3]

A similar, but more perceptible, violation occurs in extracting *wh*-phrases from relative clauses, where three bounding nodes are crossed, as in (11b):

11a Bob met $[_{DP\#}$ a journalist $[_{CP}$ who$_i$ e $[_{IP\#}$ t_i writes detective stories]]]

   b *$[_{CP1}$ What$_i$ did $[_{IP1\#}$ Bob meet $[_{DP\#}$ a journalist $[_{CP2}$ who$_j$ e $[_{IP2\#}$ t_j writes $t_i]]]]]$?

Here *what* has not been able to move into the specifier of CP2 because it is filled by the relative pronoun *who*, and has to move directly to CP1. In doing so it crosses three bounding nodes: IP2, DP and IP1. Thus DPs with clausal complements – **complex DPs** – constitute islands.

Complex subjects

Subjects which are themselves clauses are often analysed as DPs with empty D heads, and hence create domains out of which movement is impossible:

> 12a [$_{IP1\#}$ [$_{DP\#}$ e [$_{CP}$ That [$_{IP2\#}$ he invited his boss for lunch]]] was surprising]
>
>   b *[$_{CP1}$ Who$_i$ was [$_{IP1\#}$ [$_{DP\#}$ e [$_{CP2}$ t$'_i$ that [$_{IP2\#}$ he invited t$_i$ for lunch]]] surprising]]?

Contrast this with *wh*-phrase movement from a clause in object position in similar sentences (and where it is assumed that the clause is not a DP):

> 13a [$_{IP1\#}$ It was surprising [$_{CP}$ that [$_{IP2\#}$ he invited his boss for lunch]]]
>
>   b [$_{CP1}$ Who$_i$ was [$_{IP1\#}$ it surprising [$_{CP2}$ t$'_i$ that [$_{IP2\#}$ he invited t$_i$ for lunch]]]]?

In (13b) the second movement of *who* crosses only one bounding node, IP1, and the sentence is grammatical.

By the same token, extraction from any lexically overt DP subject with a complement causes a violation of subjacency:

> 14a [$_{IP\#}$ [$_{DP\#}$ An invitation to lunch] is accepted by most people]
>
>   b *[$_{CP\#}$ What$_i$ is [$_{IP\#}$ [$_{DP\#}$ an invitation to t$_i$] accepted by most people]]?

Thus subjects constitute islands for subjacency.

7.2.2 Subjacency is only a constraint on movement

Subjacency is a property which is only activated by the movement of constituents in syntactic structure. If constituents do not move they cannot give rise to subjacency violations. For example, sometimes subjacency violations in English can be 'rescued' to a certain extent by the introduction of a **resumptive pronoun**. This is a pronoun inserted in the position where a *wh*-phrase would have left a trace if it had moved. The presence of a resumptive pronoun means that the *wh*-phrase has not moved, but is inserted directly into the specifier position of CP. Compare:

15a *[CP1 Which book_i did [IP1# she wonder [CP2 when e [IP2# he read t_i]]]]?

  b ?[CP1 Which book did [IP1# she wonder [CP2 when e [IP2# he read it]]]]?

The reason why (15b) feels less ungrammatical is that nothing has moved. Instead of a *wh*-phrase moving from a position inside an embedded clause to CP1 leaving a trace behind, it is generated directly in CP1 and binds the pronoun in IP2 (see section 7.6 for binding). The reason why sentence (15b) nevertheless still feels odd is because English *wh*-phrases do not naturally bind pronouns – they are constituents which seem to need to bind traces.

Similarly, in languages where there is no overt syntactic movement there are no subjacency violations. Huang (1982) was one of the first to show that Chinese, which does not have overt syntactic *wh*-phrase movement, allows constructions which would violate subjacency in English where *wh*-phrases move. To illustrate, (16a) involves an interrogative *wh*-phrase inside a complex DP (example from Lasnik and Uriagereka 1988) and (16b) an interrogative *wh*-phrase inside a complex subject (example from Huang). In Chinese, complements to DPs are to the left of the N within that DP, the opposite to English:

16a *Complex DP*
     Ni   xiangxin [[[Lisi mai-le   shenme _{IP}] de _{CP}] shuefa _{DP}]?
     You believe   Lisi buy-ASPECT what   C   claim
     '*What_i do you believe [the claim [that Lisi bought t_i]]?'

  b *Complex subject*
     [_{IP} [_{DP} [_{CP} [_{IP} Wo mai shenme]]] zui   hao]?
                  I   buy what   most good
     '*What_i is [that I buy t_i] best?'

(16a–b) are direct questions in Chinese and fully grammatical. English allows similar constructions only as 'echo' questions (i.e. where there is emphatic stress on the *wh*-phrase, and either the speaker has failed to hear what someone has said, or expresses surprise at it):

17a You believe the claim that Lisi bought WHAT?
  b That I buy WHAT is best?

In both the Chinese and the English cases, because the *wh*-phrase has not moved in the syntax, there is no violation of subjacency.

7.3   The investigation of subjacency in second language acquisition

Section 7.3 outlines the conditions which must be met in order to investigate whether subjacency is operative in second language acquisition. Three studies are described which have attempted to assess whether the L2 English grammars of speakers whose first languages do not have *wh*-phrase movement are subject to subjacency. Findings appear to suggest that the older speakers are when they are first immersed in English, the less likely they are to be sensitive to subjacency.

Because languages differ in whether they have syntactic *wh*-phrase movement or not, this area has been of considerable interest to L2 researchers investigating whether Universal Grammar guides the construction of L2 mental grammars. Subjacency is a principle which is claimed to constrain all such movement. If UG is involved in second language acquisition, evidence for subjacency should be found in cases where the L2 involves *wh*-phrase movement, even in the grammars of speakers whose L1s do not have such movement.

7.3.1   Establishing that L2 speakers are sufficiently advanced to test for subjacency

One has to be quite careful in testing the question of whether L2 learners are sensitive to the constraints which subjacency imposes on movement operations. As Schachter (1989) and White (1989) have pointed out, because the structures in question are relatively complex and because they require speakers' intuitions about types of sentences they do not normally encounter – ungrammatical ones – test design must incorporate two controls:

(a)   It has to be established that subjects have indeed acquired the kinds of structure in which movement occurs. For example, if L2 learners treated sentences like (18a) as ungrammatical, we could not conclude that this was the result of subjacency if they did not also recognize a sentence of the same structural complexity, like (18b), as fully grammatical:

> 18a   *What$_i$ did she wonder [$_{CP}$ when e [$_{IP}$ John would buy t$_i$]]?
>   b   She wondered [$_{CP}$ when e [$_{IP}$ John would buy a new car]]

(b)   It has to be established that subjects have acquired the type of movement involved. For example, if again L2 learners treated sentences like (18a) as ungrammatical, we could not conclude that this was a result of subjacency unless they also treated (19) as fully grammatical:

19 What$_i$ did she expect [$_{CP}$ t$_i'$ e [$_{IP}$ John would buy t$_i$]]?

If L2 learners treated both (18b) and (19) as grammatical, but treated (18a) as ungrammatical, then that finding would be compatible with the claim that they are sensitive to a subjacency violation, and hence have built a grammatical representation in which movement is constrained by that principle. If L2 learners failed to recognize either (18b) or (19) as grammatical, no conclusion could be drawn about the reason for their treating (18a) as ungrammatical, since it would not be clear that they had the relevant syntactic representations in their grammars.

7.3.2 Early studies of the involvement of subjacency in the construction of L2 mental grammars

There have been a number of studies of whether L2 learners are sensitive to subjacency or not. Results have not always been clearly interpretable, though, because the necessary conditions described in 7.3.1 for determining whether a speaker has acquired the structural prerequisites have not always been established. An early attempt to design a study which takes account of these conditions is that of Schachter (1989). Schachter devised a test which incorporated both a measure of subjects' sensitivity to subjacency violations and a measure of their knowledge of parallel fully grammatical sentences (a 'syntax test'). She chose four construction types which induce subjacency violations in English (from Schachter 1989: 79–80 – bounding nodes are indicated by #):

> *wh*-island violations
> *Who$_i$ did [$_{IP\#}$ the senator ask the President [$_{CP}$ where e [$_{IP\#}$ he would send t$_i$]]]?

> Complex DP violations (called 'complex NP violations' in Schachter's study)
> *Who$_i$ did [$_{IP\#}$ the police have [$_{DP\#}$ evidence [$_{CP}$ t$_i'$ that [$_{IP\#}$ the mayor murdered t$_i$]]]]?

> Combined *wh*-island and complex DP violations (relative clauses)
> *What$_i$ did [$_{IP\#}$ Susan visit [$_{DP\#}$ the store [$_{CP}$ Op$_j$ that [$_{IP\#}$ t$_j$ had t$_i$ in stock]]]]?[4]

> Complex subject violations
> *Which party$_i$ did [$_{IP\#}$ [$_{DP\#}$ [$_{CP}$ t$_i'$ for [$_{IP\#}$ Sam to join t$_i$]]] shock his parents]?

For each construction type Schachter devised 6 sentences, so that there were 24 ungrammatical sentences in the test. Alongside these she had 4 parallel grammatical construction types which did not involve *wh*-phrase movement to the CP of the main clause, and again she devised 6 test sentences for each construction type:

wh-island
The dorm manager asked me [$_{CP}$ who$_i$ e [$_{IP\#}$ I wanted [$_{CP}$ t$_i'$ e [$_{IP\#}$ to have t$_i$ as a roommate]]]]

Complex DP
There is [$_{DP\#}$ a good possibility [$_{CP}$ that [$_{IP\#}$ we can obtain the information elsewhere]]]

Combined *wh*-island and complex DP
[$_{DP\#}$ The theory [$_{CP}$ Op$_i$ e [$_{IP\#}$ we discussed t$_i$ yesterday]]] will be on the exam next week

Complex subject
[$_{DP\#}$ e [$_{CP}$ That [$_{IP\#}$ oil prices will rise again this year]]] is nearly certain

Finally, 18 distractor sentences were added to the test.[5] The sentences were then randomized, and subjects in the test were required to judge the grammaticality of the sentences. There were three groups of experimental subjects:

20 Chinese speakers
21 Korean speakers
20 Indonesian speakers

All the subjects were students at the University of Southern California, and had begun English at the age of 12 or later. They were 'all highly proficient speakers of English' (1989: 80) who had on average lived in the United States for the following periods of time: Chinese subjects (four years); Korean subjects (three years one month); Indonesian subjects (two years three months). There was also a control group of 19 native speakers.

Schachter chose to include speakers of Chinese and Indonesian alongside Korean speakers in the test because she assumed that while no *wh*-phrase movement to CP occurs in Korean, there is limited movement in Chinese and Indonesian. In Chinese, although *wh*-phrase movement is not possible in questions, Schachter followed Huang (1982) in assuming that movement occurs in topicalized and relative clause constructions. In Indonesian she assumed that *wh*-phrase movement

Table 7.1 Possible outcomes for individual subjects on a given construction type in a test of knowledge of subjacency

		Syntax test	
		Pass	*Fail*
Subjacency test	Pass	A	B
	Fail	C	D

Source: Schachter 1989: 79

occurs in questions, but only from subject position (so that *Who$_i$ [t$_i$ ate the cake]?* is grammatical, while *What$_i$ did [Sheila eat t$_i$]?* is not).[6] By including speakers of languages with some movement, but more restricted movement than in English, Schachter hoped to test whether this would have any effect on subjects' ability to detect violations of subjacency.

In her analysis of the results, Schachter compared subjects' performance on the 'syntax test' component with their performance on the 'subjacency violation' part. She determined that a subject had passed the syntax test if that subject judged 5/6 of the sentences as grammatical for each construction type, and that a subject had passed the subjacency test if that subject judged 5/6 of the sentences as ungrammatical for each construction type. She then tabulated the results to check, for each subject and for each construction type, the relationship between performance on related grammatical and ungrammatical sentences. Given this approach to analysing the results, a particular subject could fall into any one of the cells A–D in table 7.1 for a given construction type.

It is expected that the majority of native speaking controls would fall into cell A: that is, they will accept the grammatical sentences and reject the ungrammatical subjacency violations. Providing that the experimental subjects have acquired the relevant syntactic properties, if they have access to Universal Grammar in building syntactic representations they should also fall into cell A. If their results are such that they fall into cell C, this would indicate that they have acquired the relevant syntactic properties, but are not sensitive to subjacency, and would call into question whether they have access to UG. If the results of the subjects fall into either cell B or cell D, nothing can be inferred from them about whether UG plays a role in the construction of L2 mental grammars because subjects have not yet acquired the relevant syntactic properties.

On the basis of this partitioning of the results, table 7.2 compares, on each construction type, those subjects from each of the four groups in the experiment who fell into cell A (i.e. the numbers from each L1 group who passed both the

Table 7.2 Comparison of the number of subjects who passed both the syntax test and the subjacency test with those who failed one or both of the tests

	wh-*island*			*Complex DP*			*Relative clause*			*Complex subject*		
	A	C	BD	A	C	BD	A	C	BD	A	C	BD
Korean	3	13	5	2	15	4	5	8	8	3	7	11
Indonesian	8	6	6	8	11	1	6	9	5	6	11	3
Chinese	7	9	4	11	9	0	10	6	4	7	7	6
English controls	14	3	2	10	7	2	17	0	2	15	1	3

A = subjects who passed both the syntax and subjacency tests
C = subjects who passed the syntax test but failed the subjacency test
BD = subjects who failed the syntax test
Source: Based on Schachter 1989

syntax test and the subjacency test, suggesting that they have access to UG) with those who fell into cell C (i.e. the numbers from each L1 group who passed the syntax test but failed the subjacency test, suggesting that they may not be sensitive to this principle of Universal Grammar) and with those who fell into either of cells B or D (suggesting that they have not acquired the syntactic properties from which an inference can be drawn).

The native speakers perform as expected on *wh*-islands, relative clauses (that is a combination of a *wh*-island and a complex DP) and complex subjects; the majority of them accept the sentences they were expected to accept as grammatical, and reject the sentences containing subjacency violations. The less clear-cut performance of the native speakers on the sentences involving complex DPs may possibly indicate that the subjacency violation induced by the sentences used in the test is weaker than in other cases. (See section 7.5 for discussion of the more recent treatment of constraints on movement, and in particular the notion of 'strong' and 'weak' islands.)

Note that the number of Korean speakers who pass both the syntax test and the subjacency test (i.e. those who fall into cell A) is smaller than the number of Indonesian and Chinese speakers; however, even in the latter two groups fewer subjects, proportionately, are successful than in the group of native speakers. Schachter found, on the basis of a statistical measure (the 'chi-square' test) that the proportion of subjects in each of the three non-native speaker groups who were successful was significantly lower than the proportion of subjects in the native speaker group. Fewer of the Koreans were successful than the Chinese and Indonesians, but not significantly so.

The conclusion that Schachter draws is that the results 'constitute a major difficulty for . . . those who believe that all the principles of UG are available and accessible to postpuberty language learners' (1989: 85). She also suggests that they partially support the view which says that adult second language learners are only able to access properties of UG which are instantiated in their L1. Korean lacks evidence of subjacency (because there is no movement), and as expected few Korean subjects who have acquired the relevant constructions in L2 English are sensitive to subjacency. Indonesian and Chinese speakers have subjacency in a limited form, and while more of them appear to be sensitive to subjacency in L2 English, a substantial number of them are not: 'It would appear that these subjects had difficulty either in generalizing their knowledge to new cases, or in accessing their knowledge reliably' (1989: 85). Notice, however, that what these results show is that *some* speakers from all of the non-native speaker groups are fully successful in establishing mental grammars for English which obey subjacency constraints. The difference is that the number of those who are fully successful varies from one language group to another.

Schachter pursued her investigation of the influence of the L1 in a subsequent study (1990) by introducing a comparison group of L1 Dutch-speaking learners of L2 English. It was assumed that *wh*-movement and bounding nodes are alike in Dutch and English. We then have four groups of L2 learners of English whose L1s would appear to represent a spectrum of divergence from English in relation to how the principle of subjacency is realized. At the extremes are Dutch (which has movement and bounding nodes as in English) and Korean (which has no movement, and hence no role for subjacency to play). In between are Chinese and Indonesian, which have movement but of a more restricted kind than in English. If L2 learners' mental grammars are constrained by UG, and assuming that they have acquired the property of syntactic movement of *wh*-phrases, we would expect to see similar intuitions about the ungrammatical cases across all the learners. If, however, learners do not have direct access to UG, we might expect to see some influence of the L1. The subjects in this second study were:

18 Dutch speakers
21 Indonesian speakers
20 Chinese speakers
20 Korean speakers
19 native speaker controls

The Indonesian, Chinese, Korean and English-speaking controls were, as in the 1989 study, students at the University of Southern California; the Dutch subjects were first year undergraduate students in a language and linguistics programme at the Catholic University of Nijmegen. The Indonesian, Chinese and Korean subjects were classed by Schachter as 'highly proficient speakers of English',

Table 7.3 Mean correct responses of L2 learners to three types of sentence in English: (a) 24 grammatical declarative sentences; (b) 24 ungrammatical sentences involving subjacency violations; (c) 6 grammatical sentences involving *wh*-phrase movement

	24 grammatical sentences treated as grammatical	24 ungrammatical sentences treated as ungrammatical	6 grammatical sentences with wh-*movement treated as grammatical*
Native English	21.6	21.2	5.6
Dutch	22.2	21.9	5.8
Indonesian	21.2	15.2	4.3
Chinese	21.2	17.2	4.4
Korean	19.8	12.4	4.6

Source: Based on Schachter 1990

who had begun acquisition of English at the age of 12 or later, and had all lived in the United States for at least two years three months at the time of testing. The Dutch subjects had begun studying English at the age of 11 or 12, and had had at least six years of predominantly classroom instruction; but none of them had studied the property of subjacency. The average length of time the Dutch subjects had spent in English-speaking countries was about one month.

Results of the second study are presented in table 7.3 as accuracy scores for each language group under three headings: (a) mean score for each group in judging as grammatical 24 grammatical declarative sentences involving complex subjects, complex DPs, relative clauses and embedded questions; (b) mean score for each group in judging as ungrammatical 24 sentences where there are subjacency violations involving complex subjects, complex DPs, relative clauses and embedded questions; (c) mean score for each group in judging as grammatical 6 grammatical sentences displaying movement of *wh*-phrases from a direct object position (two cases of movement to the nearest CP, two cases of movement to the next higher CP, and two displaying movement to a yet higher CP).[7]

Schachter found that while there was a high correlation between all subjects' scores on the grammatical declarative sentences and the sentences involving grammatical *wh*-phrase movement, the Dutch speakers were significantly better than all the other groups at detecting the ungrammaticality of the sentences involving subjacency violations, and indistinguishable from the native speaker controls. The Koreans 'performed quite poorly' (1990: 116) on subjacency violations, and the Indonesian and Chinese speakers were better than the Koreans but worse than the Dutch.

Given that the conditions of exposure to English were apparently more favourable for the Indonesian, Chinese and Korean speakers than for the Dutch (much longer residence in an English-speaking environment), the results are very striking. It would appear that unless specific properties of UG are instantiated in one's L1, access to them in later SLA is difficult. Dutch has *wh*-phrase movement and bounding nodes like English. Because of that, Dutch speakers can deploy that knowledge in acquiring L2 English. Korean has no parallel movement, hence the bounding status of nodes is irrelevant in Korean, and there are no subjacency effects. Although exposure to English input enables Korean speakers to acquire the appropriate locations for *wh*-phrases in English, they appear to have great difficulty in determining the constraints on those locations. Schachter comments:

> the learner can identify certain sentences with *wh*-movement as being possible English patterns . . . But there is no external evidence . . . which would lead the learner to conclude that subjacency violations . . . are *not* grammatical. For this, the learner of English must access an internal knowledge source – and if one's internal knowledge source is lacking in this area, the learner is at a loss. (1990: 116–17)

Schachter's interpretation of this 'lack' in the internal knowledge source is that the principle of subjacency itself becomes inaccessible after the development of the L1. In a more recent review of these issues (Schachter 1996: 163) she argues that UG is not available to older L2 learners outside the L1, and that there is a maturational schedule in early life before and after which certain principles of UG cannot be incorporated into a developing grammar.

Johnson and Newport (1991) adopt a similar view to Schachter, proposing that 'whatever the nature of the endowment that allows humans to learn language, it undergoes a very broad deterioration as learners become increasingly mature' (1991: 215–16). The evidence for their view comes from a study which, like Schachter, investigates the acquisition of *wh*-phrase movement in L1 Chinese-speaking L2 speakers of English and the sensitivity of learners to the principle of subjacency. Their study is designed to incorporate a number of controls to ensure the validity of the results, and it also introduces an additional variable not investigated by Schachter: the effect of the age at which subjects were first immersed in English on their sensitivity to subjacency violations.

The test instrument was a grammaticality judgement task focusing on three structural domains which potentially give rise to subjacency violations if *wh*-phrases are extracted:

(a) complex DPs with clausal complements: . . . *[the fact [that Janet liked maths]]*
(b) complex DPs which are relative clauses: . . . *[the policeman [who found Cathy]]*
(c) *wh*-islands: . . . *[how [Mrs Gomez makes her cookies]]*

On the basis of each of these structural domains, Johnson and Newport constructed four sentence types:

(i)   **A declarative sentence**
The teacher knew the fact that Janet liked maths

(ii) **A sentence involving grammatical *wh*-phrase extraction**
What$_i$ did [the teacher know [t$_i'$ [that Janet liked t$_i$]]]?

(iii) **A subjacency violation**
*What$_i$ did [the teacher know [the fact [t$_i'$ that [Janet liked t$_i$]]]]?

(iv) **An ungrammatical sentence involving lack of S–V inversion**
*What the teacher did know that Janet liked?

Sentence type (i) tests whether subjects have acquired the kinds of structure from which *wh*-movement gives rise to a subjacency violation. Sentence type (ii) tests whether subjects have acquired the kind of cyclic movement of *wh*-phrases necessary to examine their sensitivity to subjacency. Sentence type (iii) actually tests sensitivity to subjacency. Sentence type (iv) acts as a control to test subjects' ability to detect ungrammaticality generally in a task of this sort. Thus the task met the requirement described in 7.3.1 that subjects should be tested on their knowledge of the structural domains and the operation of *wh*-movement alongside, and independently of, testing of awareness of subjacency violations.

This procedure produced 12 basic sentence types (4 for each of the 3 structural domains), for which 12 test sentence tokens were constructed, producing a total of 144 sentences. To these were added 12 simple main clause *wh*-questions, and 24 unrelated 'filler' sentences (12 grammatical/12 ungrammatical) to produce a test of 180 items. These were presented to subjects aurally as a tape recording, each read twice by a native speaker of American English at a slow to moderate speed. Subjects were required to circle, on a piece of paper, 'yes' if they thought a sentence was grammatical, and 'no' if they thought it was not. They were asked to respond to every sentence, guessing if they were not sure.

The subjects who participated in the test were all native speakers of Chinese. For 23 of the subjects immersion in English occurred at age 18 or later (the age range of the group was 18–38). By 'immersion' Johnson and Newport mean arrival in the United States and exposure to natural English on a daily basis. Although all of the subjects had received tutored instruction before arrival (on average 6.8 years of instruction) earlier research (Johnson and Newport 1989) had led them to conclude that 'whatever natural endowment youth confers upon the language-learning process, it is limited to the natural learning situation (i.e. immersion)' (1991: 228). The subjects had been resident in the United States for a minimum period of 5 consecutive years at the time of testing (the range of years of residence being 5–12), and they were all graduate students, postdoctoral researchers or teaching staff at an American university, using English on a daily basis at work (although the married subjects tended to use Chinese at home with their families). Type and length of exposure to English, then, would appear to be optimal for testing whether learners are able to acquire *wh*-phrase movement in English, and are sensitive to subjacency.

A second group of 21 subjects had arrived in the United States between the ages of 4 to 16. They had also had a minimum of 5 consecutive years of residence (range 5–15). They were undergraduate students (with the exception of two who were graduates) at an American university. Like the older learners, they typically spoke Chinese at home and English at school/university, although once at university they mostly spoke English. They had received no tutored instruction in English prior to arrival in the United States. Note that in terms of length of exposure to English, this group is similar to the older informants of the first group; the intention was to make the two groups as comparable as possible, varying only the age at which immersion in English first occurred. In addition to the experimental groups, a control group of eleven native speakers of American English (undergraduate students) took the test. Johnson and Newport eliminated any subject who failed to respond to the grammaticality of simple *wh*-questions in main clauses above chance level. This resulted in one of the post-18-year-old arrivals being eliminated from the results.

The group results for the older, late immersion group and the native-speaker control group are presented in figure 7.1 (Johnson and Newport's figure 3 – results from the younger, early immersion group are considered below). Construction types are indicated along the horizontal axis. 'Simple' appears to refer to the 12 simple main clause *wh*-questions plus the 24 'fillers';[8] 'control' refers to grammatical sentences like (ii) above which involve cyclic *wh*-phrase movement and are structurally parallel to the subjacency violation cases. The results show that in judging the grammaticality of declarative sentences of comparable complexity to subjacency violations, and in judging simple *wh*-questions, both the non-native speakers and the native speakers are highly accurate: the native speakers score 36/36 on the simple questions and close to 34/36 on the declaratives, while the non-natives score close to 34/36 and 32/36 respectively. (We return to the control sentences below.) However, on the subjacency violation sentences there is a wide discrepancy in accuracy. While the native speakers correctly reject 35/36 sentences on average, the non-natives only reject 22/36 sentences on average. This is a statistically significant difference (on the basis of a t-test). The non-native speakers find many of the subjacency violations grammatical. They also perform quite inaccurately on the ungrammatical sentences involving no S–V inversion, although subjects are more accurate at detecting these errors than the subjacency violations.

Figure 7.1 Mean number of correct responses to five sentence types in English: comparison of native speakers and the late immersion group of L1 Chinese speakers (figure 3 in Johnson and Newport 1991)

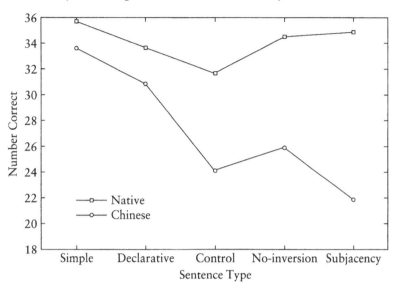

Reprinted from Johnson, J. and Newport, E. 1991: Critical period effects on universal properties of language: the status of subjacency in the acquisition of a second language. *Cognition*, 39, 215–58, with permission from Elsevier Science.

Breaking down subjects' performance on the subjacency violations by type – DP with a clausal complement, DP which is a relative clause and *wh*-island – Johnson and Newport found that the performance of the non-native speakers was significantly above chance level on DPs which were relative clauses, but not significantly above chance in the other two cases. Recall that this contrasting performance on different types of subjacency violations was found by Schachter (1989) in her native English-speaking control subjects, who were less likely to reject extractions out of complex DPs with a clausal complement than out of relative clauses or *wh*-islands. I take up this issue in section 7.5.

Finally, Johnson and Newport ran one further test with a subset of seven of the non-native speakers and six of the native speakers to see whether the non-native speakers were interpreting the moved *wh*-phrases in the subjacency violation sentences appropriately; for example, if in a sentence like *What did the policeman know where the thief hid?* the subjects were interpreting *what* as somehow not the object of *hid*, but of *know* (e.g. as in the equivalent declarative *The policeman knew **something** about where the thief hid*) then one couldn't tell whether they were constrained by subjacency or not because movement from the object position of *know* does not violate subjacency.

Table 7.4 Mean responses of subjects in interpreting *wh*-phrases on a subjacency comprehension test

Type of island	Correct	Other interpretation	Don't know
DP-complement clause			
Chinese	3.57	0.14	0.28
English	3.83	0.0	0.16
DP-relative clause			
Chinese	2.57	0.14	1.28
English	1.16	0.0	2.83
wh-island			
Chinese	3.28	0.28	0.43
English	3	0.0	1

Note: 4 is the maximum potential correct for each type of island
Source: Adapted from Johnson and Newport 1991: 242

Informants were presented with written sentences like *The policeman knew where the thief hid the jewels*. They were then asked questions like *What did the policeman know where the thief hid?* Their responses were scored as 'correct' (*jewels* would be the correct answer in this case), as 'other interpretation' (if they gave some other response) or as 'don't know'. The results are presented in table 7.4. The crucial scores are in the middle column 'other interpretation'. If subjects scored 2 or more here, they would be assigning a different interpretation to the moved *wh*-phrase from the one intended, and as can be seen they do not. An interesting and unexpected result, however, emerges in the case of the interpretation of the moved *wh*-phrase in subjacency violations involving relative clauses. The native speaker controls have considerable difficulty assigning an interpretation to such *wh*-phrases, hence the score of 2.83 in the 'don't know' column. By contrast, the non-native speakers, as Johnson and Newport observe, appear to be better than the natives at understanding questions which contain relative clause subjacency violations. We will return to this observation in section 7.5.

Turning now to a comparison of the results on the subjacency violation sentences of the non-native-speaker group who arrived in the United States after the age of 18 with the group who arrived before the age of 17, there is a considerable difference (figure 7.2). The subjects whose first immersion in English occurred between the ages of 4 to 7, although slightly less accurate than the native speakers, are not significantly different from them. Arrival after the age of 7, by contrast,

Figure 7.2 Comparison of the number correct on subjacency and no-inversion test items by native speakers of English and L1 speakers of Chinese whose immersion occurred at different ages (figure 7 in Johnson and Newport 1991)

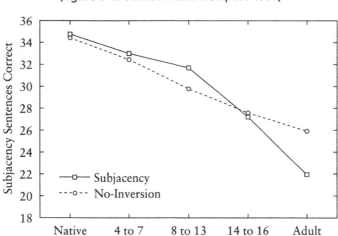

Reprinted from Johnson, J. and Newport, E. 1991: Critical period effects on universal properties of language: the status of subjacency in the acquisition of a second language. *Cognition*, 39, 215–58, with permission from Elsevier Science.

does give rise to significant differences between the native and non-native groups, and these differences become more marked with increasing age.

The results show that the test used is a valid measure of sensitivity to subjacency (both the native speaker controls and the youngest age-of-arrival non-native speaker group perform highly accurately) and that Chinese speakers immersed in English beyond the age of 17 are very different in the way they treat subjacency violations in English from native speakers or other Chinese speakers who experienced immersion at a younger age. Older learners reject subjacency violations above chance level in the case of DP-relative clause islands, but at chance level in the case of DP-complement clause islands and *wh*-islands. Since they are accurate on simple sentences involving grammatical *wh*-questions and grammatical declarative sentences of comparable complexity to the islands, Johnson and Newport conclude that they have partial access to a principle of UG: 'It may seem odd to suggest that adult learners have partial access to subjacency . . . however, this odd probabilistic status is what the empirical data suggest. How this partial knowledge should ultimately be characterised is unknown at this time' (1991: 244).

However, one aspect of the results from the older learners which Johnson and Newport do not take fully into account is the rather poor performance of informants on the 'control' sentences in figure 7.1. These are grammatical *wh*-questions which are structurally equivalent to the subjacency violation cases (rather than simple *wh*-questions). The group accepts only two-thirds of these. This could either mean that every individual is only accepting two-thirds of the sentences, or that there is a profile more like the one found in Schachter's (1989) study, where some speakers accept all the control sentences, while others do not. Since accuracy on the subjacency violations in figure 7.1 is just under two-thirds, there is the possibility that those speakers who are inaccurate on subjacency violations just haven't acquired *wh*-phrase extraction in complex sentences. This might cast doubt on whether the results really show that speakers are not sensitive to subjacency. What still requires explanation, if this is the case, is why older speakers with long exposure to the L2 like these have difficulty with *wh*-phrase movement in complex sentences, whereas younger speakers apparently do not.

Nevertheless, both Schachter (1990, 1996) and Johnson and Newport (1991) question the availability of principles of UG to guide the construction of mental grammars in older L2 learners, arguing that there is a sensitive period during which such principles are available (hence the success of the younger group of learners) but which declines as an effect of increasing maturity. In Schachter's case she argues that principles become unavailable; in Johnson and Newport's case, they propose that principles remain partially available, but in a way which is unclear.

These views are obviously a strong challenge to the view I have been adopting up to now that grammar-building by all L2 learners, including older L2 learners, is constrained by the principles of UG (even if parametric options are difficult for learners to access) and for which considerable evidence has been presented in chapters 2–6. In the next section we will consider more recent proposals in linguistics concerning how constraints on movement are determined within Universal Grammar, and then in section 7.5 how this might offer the potential for an alternative interpretation of results like those of Schachter and Johnson and Newport.

More Advanced Discussion

7.4 More recent accounts of constraints on movement

In this section it will be shown that the notion of 'bounding node' is not sufficient on its own to explain different degrees of ungrammaticality which arise when different types of constituents are moved in sentences. Rather, it is necessary to consider the nature of the structural position from which a constituent has moved, and the type of constituent it is. Once this has been done, constraints on movement can be defined in a way which does not require reference to specific bounding nodes. This section illustrates the notion of a 'barrier', and explains the 'Empty Category Principle' and 'Relativized Minimality'.

7.4.1   Degrees of ungrammaticality induced by moving constituents too far

The early account of constraints on the movement of *wh*-phrases and operators treated all movements of constituents as equal, and attempted to identify the structural domains, or bounding nodes, which would give rise to ungrammaticality if a moved constituent crossed more than one of them in a single step. However, it was soon noticed that different kinds of constituent extracted across the same two bounding nodes can give rise to different degrees of ungrammaticality (Huang 1982; Chomsky 1986b). Compare the ungrammaticality of the examples in (20b–c), both of which involve extraction out of a *wh*-island of the same type:

> 20a   They wondered [$_{CP}$ whether e [$_{IP\#}$ she could mend the puncture very quickly]]
>
> b   ?[$_{CP1}$ What$_i$ did [$_{IP1\#}$ they wonder [$_{CP2}$ whether e [$_{IP2\#}$ she could mend t$_i$ very quickly]]]]?
>
> c   *[$_{CP1}$ How quickly$_i$ did [$_{IP1\#}$ they wonder [$_{CP2}$ whether e [$_{IP2\#}$ she could mend the puncture t$_i$]]]]?[9]

While both (20b) and (20c) are ungrammatical, many speakers feel that (20b) involves a 'milder' kind of ungrammaticality than (20c). The bounding nodes in (20b–c) remain the same in both cases; what differs is that in (20b) an **argument** (a direct object) is extracted, while in (20c) an **adjunct** (an adverbial), is extracted (see section 5.3.1 for arguments and adjuncts).

Such differences in degree of ungrammaticality between an extracted direct object and an extracted adjunct also arise where other types of island are involved – for example, complex DPs with clausal complements: extraction of the embedded direct object in (21b) causes a milder kind of ungrammaticality for many speakers than extraction of the embedded adjunct adverbial in (21c):

> 21a   Bob heard [$_{DP}$ the news [$_{CP}$ that [$_{IP}$ Mary had bought a house very cheaply]]]
>
> b   ?[$_{CP1}$ Which house$_i$ did [$_{IP1\#}$ Bob hear [$_{DP\#}$ the news [$_{CP2}$ t$_i'$ that [$_{IP2\#}$ Mary had bought t$_i$ very cheaply]]]]]?
>
> c   *[$_{CP1}$ How cheaply$_i$ did [$_{IP1\#}$ Bob hear [$_{DP\#}$ the news [$_{CP2}$ t$_i'$ that [$_{IP2\#}$ Mary had bought a house t$_i$]]]]]?

In a similar way, some types of construction allow the fully grammatical movement of direct objects, but give rise to mild ungrammaticality when adverbial adjuncts move. Sentential negation (Ross 1967), 'factive' verbs (Cinque 1990) and impersonal constructions (Culicover 1997) are such cases. Compare (22) and (23):

22a What$_i$ didn't she mend t$_i$ very quickly?

  b What$_i$ does he regret that they left t$_i$ so early?

  c What$_i$ was it obvious that they bought t$_i$ too cheaply?

23a ?How quickly$_j$ didn't she mend the puncture t$_j$?

  b ?How early$_j$ does he regret that they left the party t$_j$?

  c ?How cheaply$_j$ was it obvious that they bought the painting t$_j$?

Finally, Huang (1982) observed that although movement of a direct object, providing that it crosses no other *wh*-phrases, normally gives rise to fully grammatical sentences, movement of a direct object is impossible when it is within a clause which is itself an adjunct. More generally, extraction from a complex adjunct always produces ungrammaticality. In (24a) the bracketed clause is an adjunct:

24a Tom left [before Bill finished the lecture]

  b *[$_{CP}$ What$_i$ did [$_{IP1\#}$ Tom leave [$_{PP}$ before [$_{CP}$ t$_i'$ e [$_{IP2\#}$ Bill finished t$_i$]]]]]?

These examples make it clear that to explain constraints on movement properly, it is necessary to consider the type of constituent being moved and the position in the structural configuration from which it is moving, as well as how far it can move. Moving an adjunct 'too far', or extracting from an adjunct, appears to give rise to greater ungrammaticality than moving an argument 'too far'. And this appears to have something to do with the way that the relation between a moved constituent and its trace are interpreted. Roberts (1997: 200) points out that cases like the (b) examples of (20)–(21) are 'awkward . . . [but] . . . intelligible', while in the (c) examples of (20)–(21) it is difficult to see what interpretation is intended. This suggests that the (b) examples simply violate a constraint on how far *wh*-phrases can move, but the (c) examples violate a constraint on interpreting the moved *wh*-phrase/trace relation. By the same token, the examples of (23) and (24b) are awkward by virtue of the difficulty of interpreting the *wh*-phrase as having moved from the position occupied by its trace.

There have been various proposals in the linguistic literature for refining the principle of subjacency to deal with these cases (Chomsky 1986b; Rizzi 1990; Manzini 1992). A proper consideration of each would go beyond the scope of this book (see Roberts (1997: chapter 4) for a clear exposition of their strengths and weaknesses). Here two of the proposals, those of Chomsky (1986b) and Rizzi (1990), which have been influential in L2 research will be briefly presented before we return to consider the L2 results.

The basic insight which underlies both proposals is that constructions where 'milder' ungrammaticality effects occur involve the movement of arguments which are governed by (i.e. are complements to) lexical categories. Constructions where stronger ungrammaticality effects occur either involve the movement of a non-argument – an adjunct – or involve the movement of an argument which is not governed by a lexical category. Consider the declarative sentence in (25), and the effect of moving various of its constituents in (26):

25 Sue wondered [$_{CP}$ whether [$_C$ e [$_{IP}$ John had [$_{VP}$ [$_{VP}$ delivered the package to their customers] quickly]]]]

In (25) *John* is an argument (the AGENT of *had delivered*) but it is governed by the non-lexical category C. *The package* is an argument (the THEME of *had delivered*) which is governed by the verb *delivered*, a lexical category, and so too is *her customers* (the GOAL of *had delivered*) which is governed by the pre-position *to*, a lexical category. *Quickly* is neither an argument nor is it governed by a lexical category – it is adjoined to VP and hence governed by Infl, a non-lexical category:

26a ?[$_{CP1}$ What$_i$ did [$_{IP1}$ Sue wonder [$_{CP2}$ whether e [$_{IP2}$ John had delivered t$_i$ to their customers quickly]]]]?

b ?[$_{CP1}$ Who$_i$ did [$_{IP1}$ Sue wonder [$_{CP2}$ whether e [$_{IP2}$ John had delivered the package to t$_i$ quickly]]]]?

c *[$_{CP1}$ Who$_i$ did [$_{IP1}$ Sue wonder [$_{CP2}$ whether e [$_{IP2}$ t$_i$ had delivered the package to their customers quickly]]]]?

d *[$_{CP1}$ How quickly$_i$ did [$_{IP1}$ Sue wonder [$_{CP2}$ whether e [$_{IP2}$ John had delivered the package to their customers t$_i$]]]]?

On the basis of this insight, Chomsky's idea is that any maximal projection (DP, VP, IP, CP, etc.) is a potential **barrier** to movement unless it is an argument which is governed by a lexical category. This does not require that specific projections be stipulated as 'bounding nodes' as the earlier proposal did, but instead suggests that particular structural configurations are islands from which extraction is not possible. Constraints on movement can now be defined in terms of barriers. Where a constituent k moves leaving a trace, no more than one barrier may intervene. Ungrammaticality gets stronger the more intervening barriers there are:

27a ? . . . k$_i$ . . . [$_B$ . . . [$_B$ . . . t$_i$ . . .]]
b * . . . k$_i$ . . . [$_B$ . . . [$_B$ . . . [$_B$ . . . t$_i$ . . .]]]

Consider (26) again in terms of this. In (26a) and (26b) *what* and *who* are arguments of *had delivered* and are extracted from DP positions which are governed by lexical categories (*delivered* and *to* respectively), hence not barriers. They cross two IPs in one step, IP2 then IP1. Since IP is governed in both cases by

C, a non-lexical category, IP is a barrier. Hence two barriers are crossed and the sentences are ungrammatical. In (26c) *who* is an argument of *had delivered*, but being the subject it is in the complement of C, hence governed by C, a non-lexical category; in (26d) *how quickly* is not an argument and it is in the complement of Infl, another non-lexical category. *Who* and *how quickly* therefore not only cross two IP barriers, but they are also extracted from their own maximal projections (DP in the case of *who*, AdvP in the case of *how quickly*) which are themselves barriers because they are not governed by lexical categories. So they cross three barriers and a stronger violation of grammaticality results.

While capturing a number of descriptive generalizations which were not captured by the earlier bounding node account, Chomsky's proposal unfortunately also requires additional stipulations to eliminate some unwanted consequences. Firstly, as things currently stand, in the configuration CP–IP–VP, both IP and VP are barriers because IP is the complement of C, and VP the complement of Infl, and neither C nor Infl are lexical categories. This would wrongly predict that simple sentences like the following are ungrammatical:

28 $[_{CP}$ Who$_i$ did $[_{IP}$ John $[_{VP}$ see $t_i]]]$?

To avoid this problem, Chomsky has to stipulate that Infl is not an inherent barrier, as other maximal projections are, but inherits barrierhood; under certain conditions (which need not concern us here) it is not a barrier to movement. This is the case of (28).

Secondly, further stipulation is required to explain why subject extraction across the complementizer *that* gives rise to ungrammaticality, while extraction across an empty complementizer does not:

29a Who$_i$ do $[_{IP1}$ they think $[_{CP}$ t$_i'$ e $[_{IP2}$ t$_i$ met Sue]]]$?
　b ?Who$_i$ do $[_{IP1}$ they think $[_{CP}$ t$_i'$ that $[_{IP2}$ t$_i$ met Sue]]]$?

In both cases *who* crosses the same number and type of barriers, so the difference in grammaticality cannot result from barrierhood alone.

Thirdly, it is difficult to account for the mild ungrammaticality of extraction from a DP with a clausal complement, as in (30):

30 ?Who$_i$ does $[_{IP1}$ he believe $[_{DP}$ the story $[_{CP}$ t$_i'$ e $[_{IP2}$ Sue met $t_i]]]]$?

Here CP is not a barrier to extraction because it is governed by the lexical N *story*, and DP is not a barrier because it is governed by the lexical V *believe*. *Who* therefore crosses only one barrier in each of its two movements: IP2 in the first movement, IP1 in the second. So again, the mild ungrammaticality cannot result from barrierhood alone. The refinements required to handle these cases are beyond the scope of this book. Instead, we will move on to the second proposal for handling constraints on movement in which examples like (29) have a central place.

7.4.2   The Empty Category Principle and Relativized Minimality

Whereas Chomsky's 'barriers' proposal focuses on those properties of structural configurations which create islands to block the movement of constituents, Rizzi's (1990) account focuses on the conditions under which the traces left behind by movement are licensed and identified (in parallel fashion to the licensing and identification of null pronoun subjects – see section 5.5.1). Ungrammatical movement results in traces being in positions where they are either not licensed, not correctly identified, or both.

The main criterion for the licensing of a trace of a moved constituent is that it be in a configuration like the following where the trace is a sister to a head X, and X is a lexical category or Infl[10]:

31

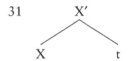

So while the trace t_i in (32a) is licensed because it is a sister to the verb *met*, and the sentence is grammatical, the trace t_i in (32b) is a sister to C, not one of the licensing categories, and the sentence is ungrammatical by virtue of containing an unlicensed trace:

32a   Who$_i$ do they think [$_{CP}$ t'_i [$_C$ that] [$_{IP}$ John [$_{VP}$ met [t_i]]]]?
  b   ?Who$_i$ do they think [$_{CP}$ t'_i [$_C$ that] [$_{IP}$ t_i [$_{VP}$ met John]]]?

Rizzi refers to this licensing requirement as 'proper head-government': traces must be properly head-governed (i.e. sisters to lexical heads, Agr or T).

But consider (29a) again. Why is this sentence grammatical if, like (32b), the trace is head-governed by C, which is not one of the licensing heads? Rizzi's answer is that while the category C in the normal case is not a licensing head, this is an area where UG allows some variation. Particular languages may allow specific morphemes belonging to the category C to have features which turn them into licensing heads. In English, while the complementizer [$_C$ *that*] does not have such features, in (29a) the empty complementizer is in fact a zero complementizer, [$_C$ ϕ], which according to Rizzi has an agreement feature, Agr. The agreement feature forces agreement between the trace of *who* in the specifier of CP and [$_C$ ϕ], and this activates [$_C$ ϕ] as a head-governor for the immediately following trace in the subject position.

The identification of traces is achieved in one of two ways. If the trace is a sister to a θ-role assigner (like a verb) and is assigned a θ-role, this is sufficient to identify it. If the trace is in an adjunct position, or is a subject (hence not a sister to a θ-role assigner, even though it may have a θ-role) it does not receive an interpretation in that position and so must be identified by its antecedent (the moved constituent). Rizzi then suggests that antecedent identification is a very local phenomenon: moved adjuncts or subjects may not cross another constituent *of the same type*. The reason is that because adjunct or subject traces are dependent on an antecedent for their interpretation, any intervening constituent of the same type will bind the trace and give it the wrong interpretation. So questions like (33b) seem very ungrammatical because a *wh*-phrase, *what*, intervenes between the *wh*-phrase *how cheaply* and the trace which it should identify: *How cheaply ... what ... t*:

33a   Bill said that they bought the house very cheaply
   b   *How cheaply$_j$ did Bill say what$_i$ they bought t$_i$ t$_j$
   c   ?What$_i$ did Bill say how cheaply$_j$ they bought t$_i$ t$_j$

By contrast, (33c) is less ungrammatical. There is still the unwanted intervening *wh*-phrase, but the trace t$_i$ is a sister to the θ-assigner *buy* and is identified by its θ-role. So all that is involved is *what* having failed to move through the specifier of the lowest CP.

The licensing and identification requirements on traces are captured in a proposed invariant principle of Universal Grammar, the **Empty Category Principle** (ECP) (Rizzi 1990: 32):

34   **The Empty Category Principle (ECP)**
     A nonpronominal empty category must be
     (i) properly head-governed (Formal Licensing)
     (ii) antecedent-governed or theta-governed (Identification)

To capture the requirement that antecedents must be very close to adjunct or subject traces for proper identification, Rizzi first distinguishes three types of constituent: maximal projections (XPs) which move to non-argument positions (like *wh*-phrases), maximal projections which move to argument positions (e.g. THEME arguments of unaccusative verbs which move to the specifier of IP, e.g. *The letter$_i$ arrived t$_i$ yesterday*) and heads (for example verbs moving to Infl, or Ns moving to Num). He then shows that for grammaticality, the distance between the antecedent and the trace must be minimal. So configurations in which the following occur:

35   *wh-phrase$_1$ ... wh-phrase$_2$ ... t$_1$
     (maximal projections in non-argument positions)

$$*DP_1 \ldots DP_2 \ldots t_1$$
(maximal projections in argument positions)
$$*X_1 \ldots X_2 \ldots t_1$$
(head categories)

Where there are categories of the same type intervening between the antecedent and its trace are difficult to interpret and therefore give rise to strong ungrammaticality. Because the minimal distance required for grammaticality between a moved constituent and its trace can only be violated by a category of the same type as the antecedent, such violations are relative, hence the theory is known as **Relativized Minimality**.[11]

In both Chomsky's 'barriers' account and Rizzi's ECP/Relativized Minimality proposal the movement of constituents in syntactic derivations is not constrained by absolute restrictions. Rather, the grammaticality of movement is a function of the type of constituent involved, the status of the position from which it moves and the distance the constituent has to travel in a single movement. This means that some violations of grammaticality involving only one of these factors are relatively weak (like extraction of object arguments from *wh*-islands, extraction of subjects across *that* (*that*-trace effects), extraction of arguments from DPs with clausal or prepositional complements), while others involving more than one of these factors, or the same factor more than once, are relatively strong (like extraction from adjuncts, from DPs with relative clause complements, or from sentential subjects).

Recent L2 research on constraints on movement has focused on whether L2 learners whose L1s do not have movement can detect relative differences in the strength of ungrammaticality. The idea is that even though L2 learners may be significantly less accurate than native speakers at detecting ungrammatical movement, if they show sensitivity to the different degrees of ungrammaticality caused by UG-determined strong versus weak violations, then that would suggest that they are constructing mental grammars constrained by principles like barrierhood or the ECP/Relativized Minimality. This approach is discussed in the next section.

More Advanced Discussion

7.5 Reconsidering whether L2 speakers' mental grammars are sensitive to constraints on movement

In this section three features of the data collected by Schachter (1989) and Johnson and Newport (1991) are discussed which might lead one to question the inaccessibility of constraints on movement to post-childhood L2 learners. Two alternative views are then discussed. The first proposes that if L2 learners are sensitive to the 'strong' and 'weak' constraints on movement determined by UG, this shows that principles must be involved in grammar-building. The second proposes that learners may only appear to be having trouble with constraints on movement; in fact, they are having difficulty with the parameter setting which triggers movement.

Both Schachter (1989, 1990, 1996) and Johnson and Newport (1991) suggest that access to the principles of UG which constrain movement deteriorates beyond childhood (fully, according to Schachter, so that principles not activated in the L1 are inaccessible; partially, according to Johnson and Newport). The evidence which supports these claims is that older L2 learners, despite considerable exposure to the target language, are significantly less successful than native speakers at detecting constraints on movement.

However, there are three features of the data on which they base these claims which might lead one to question the conclusions. First, in Schachter's (1989) study, *some* of the Korean informants (the language group with the least accurate scores) performed like native speakers. That is, there were individuals who passed both the syntax and subjacency tests, where 'pass' was determined by a stringent criterion: 5/6 answers needed to be correct in both cases. This indicates that some speakers can achieve native-like intuitions, which is inconsistent with the idea that principles of UG are partially or fully inaccessible – some speakers clearly can access them.

Secondly, in the Johnson and Newport (1991) study, the older Chinese informants (those immersed in English for the first time at age 18 or later) showed different reactions to different types of subjacency violations. While they were not significantly above chance level in detecting the ungrammaticality of movement out of *wh*-islands and across DPs with clausal complements, they were significantly above chance level in detecting the ungrammaticality of movement out of relative clauses. Since under the 'barriers' and 'ECP/Relativized Minimality' approaches to constraints on movement, extraction from relative clauses gives rise to stronger ungrammaticality than extraction from *wh*-islands and DPs with clausal complements, it appears that Johnson and Newport's older informants are sensitive to this UG-determined contrast, even though their performance in absolute terms is worse than that of native speakers.

Third is the surprising finding in Johnson and Newport's (1991) 'interpretation of subjacency violations' task, reported in table 7.4. They found that while native speaker controls had difficulty interpreting extraction from relative clauses like * *What$_i$ did they congratulate the policeman [who$_j$ [t$_j$ found t$_i$]]?*, the Chinese speakers were considerably more successful in providing appropriate interpretations. Relative clauses are often treated as adjuncts to the DP which heads them (*[who$_j$ [t$_j$ found t$_i$]]* being an adjunct to *the policeman* in the above example). Recall that Roberts (1997) suggested that subjacency violations involving arguments are awkward but interpretable, while those involving adjuncts are difficult even to interpret. The performance of the native speakers in Johnson and Newport's task is consistent with this idea. But the performance of the Chinese speakers suggests that they are not treating such examples as if they were extractions from adjuncts.

In the light of considerations like these, there have been two recent alternative accounts of older L2 learners' ability to detect constraints on syntactic movement in the L2 where such constraints are not activated in the L1, neither of which require the claim that the principles of UG are inaccessible in late L2 acquisition. The first, while recognizing that speakers of languages like Chinese, Korean and Japanese do not reject subjacency violations to the same degree as native speakers, nevertheless points to the differential sensitivity within groups to different degrees of ungrammaticality. This view argues that it is a mistake to compare non-native speakers with native speakers directly – the less accurate performance of non-native speakers in absolute terms may be for a variety of reasons unconnected with the accessibility of principles of UG (for example, a reduced ability for on-line language processing in older L2 learners which makes it difficult for them to analyse complex sentences in tests – Martohardjono, 1998). But what is crucial is whether learners can discriminate relative ungrammaticality. The second view suggests that while the principles of UG remain fully operative in second language acquisition beyond childhood, if particular movement operations are not realized in the L1, L2 learners will have difficulty establishing the appropriate parameter value which forces movement in the L2. In particular, they may opt for alternative analyses where the representations they construct are not subject to constraints in the same way. We will look at both views in turn.

7.5.1   Findings showing that L2 learners are sensitive to 'strong' and 'weak' constraints on movement

Martohardjono (1993, also summarized in Epstein et al. 1996: 688–9) constructed a grammaticality judgement task where sentences involving several kinds of movement violation were included alongside grammatical sentences: 'strong violations' (extractions from relative clauses and adjunct clauses) and 'weak violations' (extractions from *wh*-islands and DPs with clausal complements). She administered the task to L1 speakers of Chinese, Indonesian and Italian, as well as a control group of native speakers of English. All the non-native speakers were deemed to be 'advanced'. The results (presented in table 7.5) show that while overall the mean rate at which non-native informants rejected grammatical sentences differed between the language groups, the relative rejection of strong versus weak violations is consistent across all groups. On the basis of these results, Epstein et al. (1996: 688) argue that 'although L2 learners may lag behind native speakers with regard to accuracy rates, their judgements of *wh*-structures may still derive from their knowledge of UG principles'.

Table 7.5 Relative rejection rates of 'strong' and 'weak' constraints on movement in English by speakers of different L1s

Language group	Strong violations %	Weak violations %
English	99	78
Italian	91	62
Indonesian	88	46
Chinese	75	44

Source: Based on Martohardjono 1993

X. Li (1998) develops a similar idea. This study investigates whether L1 Chinese-speaking learners of L2 English are differentially sensitive to the extraction of *wh*-phrases from 'strong' and 'weak' islands, and whether they find violations involving *wh*-phrases which are adjuncts worse than violations involving *wh*-phrases which are arguments. The prediction is that 'even if L2 learners fail to keep pace with the English speakers in the experiment, they can still demonstrate [the same] sensitivity pattern across different structure types' (1998: 95). The informants were a group of 180 L1 Chinese-speaking students of English at university in China (the 'China group'), 16 L1 Chinese-speaking graduate students and visiting scholars who had been in the United States for at least three years (the 'Graduate group'), and 25 native English-speaking controls. All the Chinese speakers had typically started learning English at the age of 14 or 15, and none of the China group had been immersed in an English-speaking environment.

To test sensitivity to strong and weak islands, Li used a 34-item grammaticality judgement task in which there were 11 'strong' island violations (*wh*-phrases extracted from relative clauses and sentential subjects), 11 'weak' islands (*wh*-phrases extracted from *wh*-islands and DPs with PP complements like *?What$_i$ are you interested in [his articles on t$_i$]?*) and 12 control sentences, 6 of which involved grammatical *wh*-phrase extractions from structurally parallel sentences. The results are given in table 7.6.

It can be seen from table 7.6 that the China group, with less exposure to English than the graduate group, perform less well overall than the native speaker controls. However, they reject strong island violations to a greater extent than weak island violations, suggesting that the principles of UG involved are nevertheless operative. The graduate group appear to be native-like, with the exception that the native controls reject *wh*-islands more strongly. These results, of course, conflict with the earlier findings of Schachter (1990) and Johnson and Newport (1991) who found a significant difference between Chinese speakers

Table 7.6 Mean accuracy (%) of three groups of informants in rejecting sentences with ungrammatical *wh*-phrase movement

Subjects	'Strong' islands		'Weak' islands	
	Relative clause %	Sentential subject %	wh-island %	DP-island %
China group (N = 180)	71.6	70.1	52.1	61.1
Graduate group (N = 16)	87.8	88.0	70.0	80.0
Native speakers (N = 25)	92.8	90.4	89.3	79.2

Source: Based on X. Li 1998

with comparably long immersion in English and native speaker controls. It is not clear why there is this difference.

An interpretation task was used to test whether informants find violations involving adjunct *wh*-phrases worse than violations involving argument *wh*-phrases. Informants read short stories of four or five sentences in length and were then asked questions in which a *wh*-phrase could have been extracted from more than one position. For example, one story was about a boy who had forgotten his grandmother's birthday and who asked his mother if she would telephone his grandmother with him. Following the story informants were asked: *Who did he ask ___ [to call ___]?* where there are two possible responses: *his mother* (corresponding to the object gap after *ask*) and *his grandmother* (corresponding to the object gap after *call*). Some of these ambiguous questions involved ungrammatical *wh*-island violations, but Li varied both the status of the extracted *wh*-phrase and the intervening *wh*-phrase. We will focus here on just two of the types of sentence investigated by Li and illustrated in (36):

36a Who$_i$ did the boy ask __a$_i$_ [how to help __?b$_i$_]?
  b When$_i$ did John know __a$_i$_ [how to fix his bike __*b$_i$_]?

In (36a) an argument *wh*-phrase has either been extracted from the complement of *ask* grammatically, or from the complement of *help* ungrammatically, but this is a weak violation because the trace is licensed and θ-governed: the mild ungrammaticality arises because *who* could not pass through the lower specifier of CP which is filled by *how*. In (36b) an adjunct *wh*-phrase has been extracted either from the higher sentence grammatically, because it is licensed and antecedent governed, or ungrammatically from the embedded clause because although the

Table 7.7 Informant responses to the interpretation of argument *wh*-phrases and adjunct *wh*-phrases extracted from a *wh*-island

(I) Sentence type: *Who*$_i$ *did the boy ask* __a$_i$__ *[how to help* __?b$_i$__ *]?*

	only a	both a and b	only b
China group (N = 180)	51.9% (187/360)	43.9% (158/360)	1.7% (6/360)
Native controls (N = 25)	56% (28/50)	34% (17/50)	8% (4/50)

(II) Sentence type: *When*$_i$ *did John know* __a$_i$__ *[how to fix his bike* __*b$_i$__ *]?*

	only a	both a and b	only b
China group (N = 180)	59.4% (214/360)	30% (108/360)	5.8% (21/360)
Native controls (N = 25)	78% (39/50)	14% (7/50)	2% (1/50)

Source: Based on Li 1998

trace is licensed, *how* interferes with the antecedent government of the trace by *when*. This is a strong violation. Since responses that informants can give to the questions are potentially ambiguous on the basis of the stories they have heard, examples like (36) involve a conflict between what is interpretively possible (both gaps) and what is syntactically possible (only the first gap gives rise to clear grammaticality). Li scored the results in terms of informants' acceptance of just the interpretation associated with the (a) gaps, acceptance of both interpretations (a) and (b), and acceptance only of interpretation (b). The results comparing the China group and the native speaker controls are given in table 7.7. (There were two tokens of each sentence type, hence the total possible number of responses for each interpretation is 360 for the China group (180 × 2) and 50 for the native controls (25 × 2).)

Although the China group show a greater tendency to accept the interpretation of the *wh*-phrase associated with the gap in the embedded clause than the native speakers, they are less likely to do so when it is an adjunct (the type (II) sentence) than when it is an argument (the type (I) sentence). This suggests that they are sensitive to the difference in status of the two traces and the means by which they are identified. Again, this is consistent with the principles of UG being involved in the way that L2 speakers construct mental grammars.

7.5.2 An argument that L2 learners may be having difficulty with parameter settings

Notice that table 7.7 also shows that the Chinese speakers are actually *interpreting wh*-phrases extracted from the embedded position indicated by 'b' more successfully than native speakers of English. This is similar to the findings in Johnson and Newport's interpretation test where Chinese speakers interpreted extractions from relative clauses more successfully than native speakers. A possible explanation for this is offered by the second of the recent alternative accounts of L2 speakers' knowledge of constraints on movement which does not require that principles of UG are inaccessible. On this view older L2 learners differ from native speakers in detecting constraints on movement not because principles fail to constrain grammar building but because the L2 learners have difficulty acquiring the parameter value in the L2 which determines movement.

Recall that Schachter (1989) assumed that Korean lacks *wh*-phrase movement. Related to this is Rizzi's (1996) claim that there is a principle of UG which requires *wh*-phrases to appear in a local specifier–head agreement relation with a head specified for Q (this head usually being the functional category C). This principle allows a parameter of variation, however: in some languages agreement must occur in surface syntax (like English), in others it occurs at the point where questions are interpreted (a level of representation known as Logical Form – see section 4.8.1) – this is the case in Korean, and for some constructions in Chinese and Indonesian. Speakers of Korean, Chinese and Indonesian learning L2 English will have to learn that *wh*-phrase/Q 'agreement' occurs in surface syntax in English. Suppose that 'agreement' (i.e. the matching of an interrogative feature on the *wh*-phrase with the Q of the functional head) is the trigger for movement, and is in fact distinguishable from the mere presence of a *wh*-phrase in the specifier of CP. *Wh*-phrases could appear as the specifier to a C specified for Q, but unless agreement between the two occurs, the *wh*-phrase will not have moved there from a position lower in the clause. Instead, it will have been inserted directly from the lexicon and can only be interpreted if it is co-referential with a pronoun in the complement to C (see the discussion of resumptive pronouns in section 7.2.2). One possibility is that when speakers of Korean, Chinese and Indonesian learn English, they acquire the surface location of *wh*-phrases, but have not reset the parameter which requires agreement (and hence movement) in surface syntax. White puts the case for this clearly:

> Instead of presuming that L2 learners have the same representation [for sentences where there are island violations like: *?Which bike did Mary wonder whether she should mend?*[12]] as native speakers of English (i.e. *wh* . . . t) but no access to subjacency, we should consider other possible representations for such sentences consistent with their linguistic behaviour . . . I propose that, when they appear to accept subjacency violations, they analyse the English sentences as containing a base-generated *wh*-phrase, with a base-generated null resumptive *pro* in the gap. (1992c: 457–8)

That is, speakers essentially have a representation like:

37   *Which bike* did Mary wonder whether she should mend *it*?

Here *which bike* is inserted directly into the specifier of CP and not moved there, and a pronoun is inserted directly in the object position of *mend*. The two are then interpreted in the same way as any other antecedent–pronoun dependency, for example: *John_i wondered whether Mary would speak to him_i*. The only difference is that the pronouns are null in this case.

One may now propose that what Schachter's (1989) results show is that speakers of languages without overt movement or only partial movement have more difficulty establishing that fronted *wh*-phrases in English result from movement than speakers of languages which have movement, like Dutch. This would be consistent with L1 influence on the way learners construct a representation for interrogative C. Dutch has *wh*-phrase movement, and when speakers encounter English *wh*-phrases they assume movement. Chinese, Korean and Indonesian have only partial or no movement, and this influences the construction of a specification for interrogative C – it seems to be particularly difficult for speakers of these languages to 'hit on' the right parameter setting (agreement in surface syntax), although some appear to do so, as Schachter's (1989) results show. On this view, the principles of UG could still be fully operational in constraining L2 grammar-building, but differences between L2 and native speakers would arise as the result of lack of parameter resetting.

This proposal is also consistent with the findings in Johnson and Newport's interpretation test. The native speakers in the test had particular difficulty interpreting extractions from relative clauses like:

38   *Who should the policeman who found get a reward?

But the Chinese speakers appeared to have more success. One can see why they might find these sentences relatively comprehensible if they were interpreting such sentences as involving a *wh*-phrase binding a pronoun, as in:

39   For which person, the policeman who found **her** should get a reward?

In section 5.5.3 the 'no parameter resetting' claim (Tsimpli and Roussou 1991) was discussed in relation to the pro-drop parameter. The results here from studies of constraints on movement suggest that 'no parameter resetting' may be too strong, and that 'difficulty in establishing the correct parameter setting' may be a more appropriate characterization, since some older L2 speakers apparently do acquire the appropriate parameter values.

7.5.3   Summary of the findings of studies of L2 learners' knowledge of constraints on movement

- The most informative studies of whether L2 learners' mental grammars are sensitive to constraints on movement (and hence to the principles of UG which constrain movement) are those involving speakers of L1s which differ in movement possibilities from the L2. Since evidence for constraints on movement is not plausibly provided in L2 input, if speakers are aware of constraints not operative in their L1, they must have constructed grammars which obey principles of UG.
- Two controls are required to ensure that data obtained on island violation sentences are reliable: (a) L2 learners must treat grammatical sentences of the same structural complexity as the island violations as grammatical; (b) they must accept grammatical *wh*-phrase movement in complex sentences.
- Early studies comparing native speakers of Korean, Chinese, Indonesian (with long exposure to English in an immersion environment) with Dutch speakers and native controls (Schachter 1989, 1990; Johnson and Newport 1991) found: (a) strong L1 influence in those immersed beyond childhood, in that speakers of languages without movement (Korean) or with partial movement (Chinese, Indonesian) were less likely to detect island violations than speakers of languages with similar movement possibilities to English (Dutch); (b) an age effect, in that L1 Chinese speakers immersed in English in childhood performed like native speakers in detecting island violations; (c) evidence that some speakers, of whatever age at first immersion and L1 background, are sensitive to island violations. The conclusions researchers drew from these studies were that either UG is not available to older L2 learners outside their L1 (Schachter 1996) or that there is partial access to the principles of UG (Johnson and Newport 1991).
- More recent studies have assumed that constraints on movement are a function of the type of constituent involved, the status of the position from which it moves and how far it has to move in a single step – hence that violations of constraints can vary in strength.
- Given this assumption, one account of the results from L2 studies suggests that if L2 learners show differential sensitivity to strong and weak islands, then their grammars are constrained by principles of UG, even if their ability to detect island violations is significantly worse than that of native speakers; differences between L2 speakers and native speakers are the result of other factors, for example difficulty with processing language in real time (Martohardjono 1998).
- A second account suggests that L2 speaker/native speaker differences arise because older L2 speakers have difficulty setting the parameter value which

triggers movement in surface syntax, if it is not realized in their L1. Although learners might locate *wh*-phrases in the right position for English, this does not necessarily mean that movement is involved. L2 speakers differ from native speakers because they have not analysed *wh*-phrase constructions as involving movement.

More advanced discussion

7.6   Binding constraints on anaphors

Section 7.6 describes the syntactic conditions which determine how anaphors like *herself, myself, ourselves*, etc., are interpreted in English. The proposed principle of UG which gives rise to these conditions – 'principle A' of the 'binding principles' – is then described. An early proposal for a parameter of variation associated with 'principle A' is discussed and rejected in favour of more recent claims which link the morphological structure of anaphors to their interpretive possibilities. The extent to which L2 learners are able to construct appropriate representations for anaphor binding in the L2 are then discussed in relation to results from several representative studies.

In sections 7.2 to 7.5 I discussed the constraints which put limits on how far constituents can move grammatically, and how these constraints are involved in the way L2 learners construct mental grammars. Similarly, there are constraints on the interpretations that can be assigned to pronouns and anaphors. Pronouns (in English, forms like *she/her, they/them, we/us*, etc.) and anaphors (reflexives like *herself, themselves* and the reciprocal expression *each other*) do not have a fixed meaning, but depend for their reference on being linked to DPs which do. The dependency relation is known as **binding**: the DP with the fixed meaning (the 'referring' DP) is the antecedent for, or **binds**, the pronoun or anaphor. Since most L2 work up to now has focused on the binding of anaphors, I will concentrate on these in this section, and set aside the binding of pronouns.

7.6.1   The descriptive facts of the binding of anaphors in English

Not every DP in a sentence is a potential binder for an anaphor; there are constraints on binding relationships. Consider some typical cases from English:

Antecedents for anaphors in tensed clauses

In tensed clauses anaphors can be bound by a subject or object DP, or both:

40a   June$_i$ blamed herself$_i$
       (bound by the subject)
   b   Charles talked to June$_i$ about herself$_i$
       (bound by a prepositional object)
   c   Gemma$_i$ talked to June$_j$ about herself$_{ij}$
       (bound by either the subject or object)

But an anaphor cannot be the subject of a tensed clause, nor can it be bound by a DP outside a tensed clause:

41a   *Herself$_i$ blamed June$_i$
   b   *June$_i$ thought [that Charles blamed herself$_i$]
   c   *June$_i$ believed [that herself$_i$ was to blame]

Antecedents for anaphors in non-finite clauses

Where non-finite clauses are involved, the subject is usually null (represented by PRO, called 'big PRO' to distinguish it from 'little *pro*'), and its interpretation is controlled by an argument in the main clause:

42a   Charles forced June$_i$ [PRO$_i$ to talk]
   b   June$_i$ promised Charles [PRO$_i$ to talk]

Anaphors within the non-finite clause can be bound by PRO or by an object, but cannot be bound by a DP outside the non-finite clause:

43a   Charles forced June$_i$ [PRO$_i$ to talk about herself$_i$]
   b   Charles forced Tony$_j$ [PRO$_j$ to talk to June$_i$ about herself$_i$]

44a   *June$_i$ forced Charles$_j$ [PRO$_j$ to talk about herself$_i$]
   b   *Charles$_j$ promised June$_i$ [PRO$_j$ to talk about herself$_i$]

There is a special class of verbs including *believe, expect, consider*, which select non-finite clausal complements with an overt subject marked for accusative Case ('Exceptional Case Marking' verbs). Anaphors can occur in the subject position of such complements:

45   June$_i$ believed [herself$_i$ to be in danger]

Antecedents for anaphors in DPs

When anaphors occur inside a complex DP, they can be bound by an antecedent outside, providing that there is no specifier present. When a specifier is present, it blocks binding from outside:

46a Julie$_i$ showed Tom [$_{DP}$ e [$_D$ a [$_{NP}$ picture of herself$_i$]]]
  b *Julie$_i$ showed Tom [$_{DP}$ Eric [$_D$'s [$_{NP}$ picture of herself$_i$]]]
  c Julie$_i$ showed Tom [$_{DP}$ June$_j$ [$_D$'s [$_{NP}$ picture of herself$_{*i/j}$]]]

Antecedents must c-command anaphors

Finally, an antecedent DP must be in a particular structural relationship to the anaphor it binds known as **c-command** ('constituent command'). Although in the following the anaphors and antecedent DPs are within the same tensed clause, a binding relationship is not possible because *June* does not c-command *herself*:

47a *June$_i$'s brother blamed herself$_i$
  b *Charles talked to herself$_i$ about June$_i$

A constituent X c-commands another Y under two conditions: either X and Y are sisters, e.g.:

48

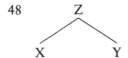

(Here X c-commands Y, and Y c-commands X); or X is higher in the tree structure than Y, does not directly dominate Y (where 'dominate' means that every branch in the tree connecting the two is a descending branch), and every category which dominates X also dominates Y. To illustrate, consider the structure of (49):

49

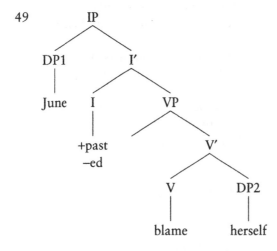

In (49) V', VP, I', IP, I and DP1 are all higher in the tree than DP2, but only I and DP1 do not dominate DP2 because in the other cases every branch connecting V',

VP, I′, IP to DP2 is a descending branch. Both I and DP1 c-command DP2 because every category dominating them (I′ and IP in the case of I, just IP in the case of DP1)) dominates DP2 as well. Since DP1 c-commands DP2, it is a possible antecedent for DP2. Contrast this with the structure of (50):

50

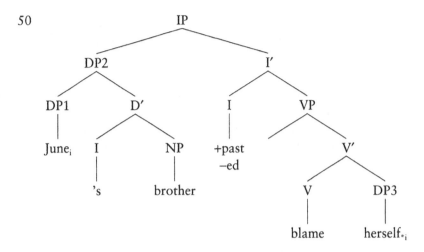

Here, although DP1 is higher in the tree than DP3, and does not dominate DP3, not every category which dominates DP1 dominates DP3; in particular, DP2 dominates DP1, but does not dominate DP3. The failure of *June* to c-command *herself* in both examples of (47) means that it is not a possible antecedent for the anaphor. A standard definition of c-command is the following (from Roberts 1997: 27):

51 **c-command**
       α c-commands ß if and only if α does not dominate ß and every
       category dominating α dominates ß.

7.6.2 Binding domains and binding principle A

The complex distribution of binding possibilities for anaphors illustrated in section 7.6.1 indicates that there are certain structural domains within which anaphors must be bound. The crucial elements defining these domains appear to be:

(a)   The presence of a subject: anaphors must be bound within a projection which contains a subject (examples 40, 43, 46a, 46c).
(b)   The presence of an Infl which assigns nominative Case: anaphors must be bound within a projection where nominative Case is assigned, so cannot appear as the subjects of tensed clauses (example 41).

There are various formulations of these two requirements on binding domains in the linguistic literature. For the purposes of exposition we will use the one proposed in Roberts (1997: 142):

> 52 **Binding domain**
>   The binding domain of α is the smallest XP containing α and either: a subject (distinct from α and which does not contain α) or: the Infl that assigns nominative Case

The principle which governs the binding of anaphors can now be stated. It forms one of three 'binding principles' and is conventionally known as 'principle A'. For completeness, the other two binding principles are also given: the principle governing pronoun binding (principle B), and the principle which determines that DPs which have specific conceptual content ('referring expressions') cannot be bound by an antecedent:

> 53 **Binding principles**
>   A: An anaphor must be bound in its binding domain
>   B: A pronoun must be free in its binding domain
>   C: A referring expression must be free

The binding principles are invariant properties of human language. But it seems that languages vary in the way they determine binding domains. The definition of binding domain given in (52) works for English, but in other languages anaphors can be bound by DPs in positions which would give rise to ungrammaticality in English. In Russian, an anaphor can be bound across the PRO subject of an infinitive, but not across the nominative subject of a finite clause (example from MacLaughlin 1998):

> 54a Sasha$_i$ poprosila Marinu$_j$ [PRO$_j$ narisovat' sebja$_{i/j}$]
>   Sasha$_i$ asked Marina$_j$ [PRO$_j$ to draw herself$_{i/j}$]
>   b Sasha$_i$ preset, [shtoby Marina$_j$ narisovala sebja$_{*i/j}$]
>   Sasha$_i$ requests [that Marina$_j$ draw herself$_{*i/j}$]

In Chinese, anaphors can even be bound across the nominative subject of a finite clause (example from Roberts 1997):

> 55 Zhangsan$_i$ renwei [Lisi$_j$ hai-le ziji$_{i/j}$]
>   Zhangsan$_i$ thinks [Lisi$_j$ hurt himself$_{i/j}$]

In early research, Wexler and Manzini (1987) argued that there are five different binding domains that can be found cross-linguistically, illustrated for convenience

Table 7.8   Illustration of the five different possible domains relevant for the binding principles which constitute five settings of a parameter of variation

Domain	Illustrative example
Contains a subject	(a) Kate said that Alice wished that Mary would persuade Helen to see [June$_i$'s portrait of herself$_i$]
Contains an Infl (finite or non-finite)	(b) Kate said that Alice wished that Mary would persuade Helen [PRO$_i$ to see [June's portrait of herself$_i$]]
Contains a finite Infl (of any kind)	(c) Kate said that Alice wished that [Mary$_i$ would persuade Helen [PRO to see [June's portrait of herself$_i$]]]
Contains an indicative Infl*	(d) Kate said that [Alice$_i$ wished that [Mary would persuade Helen [PRO to see [June's portrait of herself$_i$]]]]
Contains the matrix Infl	(e) [Kate$_i$ said that [Alice wished that [Mary would persuade Helen [PRO to see [June's portrait of herself$_i$]]]]]

*In some languages the clause complement to verbs like *wish* would contain a verb in a subjunctive form – for this setting of the binding domain parameter such a form would not count, only the clause containing the tensed form of *wish* itself.
Source: Wexler and Manzini 1987

from English in table 7.8. These are different values of a binding domain parameter (i.e. languages opt for one of these as the 'smallest XP' in which anaphors must be bound).

The idea that structural configurations define how distant a potential antecedent for an anaphor can be, independently of the properties of the anaphor itself, is similar to the early research on constraints on movement, where it was assumed that bounding nodes limit how far a *wh*-phrase can move, independently of the status of the *wh*-phrase. Just as more recent research on movement has shifted emphasis to the status of the constituent moved, and the position it moves from, recent work on binding has shifted attention to the nature of the anaphor itself, and whether this plays a role in determining potential antecedents.

First, it has been observed that in languages where anaphors can be bound non-locally, as in examples (b)–(e) of table 7.8, they are morphologically simple forms, unlike the morphologically complex forms of English which consist of a *pronoun + self* (*him-self*, *her-self*, etc.). Moreover, in these 'long-distance' binding relationships, the antecedent DP is typically a subject (P. Pica 1987; Cole et al.

1990). Second, it has been observed that in some languages the long-distance binding of morphologically simple anaphors can occur across the subjects of DPs and non-finite clauses, but cannot occur across the subject of a tensed clause. For example, binding would be possible up to *Mary* in the following sentence, but could go no higher: *Kate said that Alice wished that [Mary$_i$ would persuade Helen [PRO$_i$ to see [June$_i$'s portrait of herself$_i$]]]*. Those languages where this is the case are precisely those where tensed Infl has agreement inflections (e.g. the Slavic languages – Bennett and Progovac 1998). In languages where tensed Infl does not have agreement inflections, *Alice* and *Kate* in the illustrative sentence would also be possible antecedents for the anaphor (e.g. Chinese and Japanese).

These observations have led to the idea that potential antecedents for anaphors can be predicted to a large extent on the basis of whether the anaphor is morphologically complex (**polymorphemic**) like English *her-self*, *him-self*, etc., or morphologically simple (**monomorphemic**) like the Chinese *ziji*, 'self', or Japanese *zibun*, 'self', linked to the observation that a **subject** is crucially involved in defining the binding domain. For example, Progovac (1992, 1993) proposes that polymorphemic anaphors are structurally DPs whose binding domain is defined by a DP subject, while monomorphemic anaphors are structurally D heads whose binding domain is defined by a subject which is also a head category. In practice this is Infl because it is the head which selects the subject of the clause (we put the technical details to one side here). In English, the polymorphemic DP anaphors can be bound only by other DPs up to, but not beyond, a subject DP. So we get the distribution illustrated in (56):

56a Julie$_j$ saw [June$_i$'s picture of herself$_{i/*j}$]
  b Julie$_j$ thought that [June$_i$ liked herself$_{i/*j}$ too much]
  c Julie$_k$ hoped that [June$_j$ would talk to Mary$_i$ about herself$_{i/j/*k}$]

In languages where anaphors are monomorphemic (like Russian and Chinese), the binding domain is determined by Infl. Only subjects are possible antecedents and binding is possible up to, but not beyond, an Infl with agreement inflections. If a language does not have agreement inflections (like Chinese), an anaphor can be bound by every subject up to the matrix subject (Russian and Chinese examples from Bennett and Progovac 1998):

57a Professor$_j$ poprosil assistenta$_i$ [PRO$_i$ tchitat' svoj$_{i/j}$ doklad
      professor asked assistant [PRO to-read self's report]
      'The professor asked his assistant to read his own report'
  b Vanja$_j$ znaet [shto Volodja$_i$ ljubit svoju$_{i/*j}$ sestru]
      'Vanja knows [that Volodja loves self's sister]'
      'Vanja knows that Volodja loves his own sister'

c Zhangsan$_k$ renwei [Lisi$_j$ zhidao [Wangwu$_i$ xihuan ziji$_{i/j/k}$]]
Zhangsan think Lisi know Wangwu like self
'Zhangsan thinks that Lisi knows that Wangwu likes himself'

Because DP subjects determine the binding domain for DP anaphors, and because a head subject (in the form of Infl) determines the binding domain for D anaphors, Progovac refers to the proposal as the 'relativized subject' approach to determining binding domains, similar to Rizzi's 'relativized minimality' approach to constraints on movement. It is unnecessary (and descriptively inadequate) to have parameters for binding domains defined independently of the anaphors themselves, as in the Wexler and Manzini (1987) account. A justification for the proposal is that in some languages there are both monomorphemic and poly-morphemic anaphors, for example Chinese. If Progovac is correct, in these lan-guages we would expect polymorphemic anaphors to behave like English anaphors, and this appears to be the case. The Chinese polymorphemic *taziji*, 'he-self/she-self', can only be bound by *Wangwu* in a sentence parallel to (57c) (again from Bennett and Progovac 1998):

58 Zhangsan$_k$ renwei [Lisi$_j$ zhidao [Wangwu$_i$ xihuan taziji$_{i/*j/*k}$]]
Zhangsan think Lisi know Wangwu like he-self
'Zhangsan thinks that Lisi knows that Wangwu likes himself'

7.6.3 Anaphor binding in second language grammars

Because the conditions under which the binding of anaphors is possible display both invariant design features of language (an anaphor must be bound by a c-commanding antecedent within a domain defined by a DP subject or a D subject) and cross-linguistic variation (the relevant subject domain is defined by the morphological status of the anaphor (poly- or monomorphemic) and in the case of monomorphemic anaphors whether Infl has agreement inflections or not), there is potential for investigating issues related to those which have preoccupied us throughout the book: how knowledge of anaphor binding develops over time, the extent to which the binding principles constrain grammar building, the role the L1 plays, and the extent to which binding differences between the L1 and L2 are acquirable.

Unfortunately, a number of problems have arisen in trying to interpret data from L2 learners in relation to these issues which make it difficult to draw firm conclusions at present. Firstly, one has to be certain that learners have distinguished anaphors from pronouns in the L2. If L2 speakers of English allow the inter-pretations for an anaphor indicated in (59), is it because they are allowing long-distance binding of a polymorpheme (and hence have a grammar which falls outside UG), or because they are treating *herself* as a pronoun?

59 Mary$_i$ told Sue$_i$ that Ann liked herself$_i$ too much

Both *Mary* and *Sue* are potential antecedents if *herself* has been misanalysed as a pronoun.

Secondly, one has to be certain that learners have determined whether an anaphor is a monomorpheme or a polymorpheme. If L2 speakers of English allow the binding relation indicated in (60), is it again because they have failed to establish the appropriate binding domain for a polymorpheme (and hence have a grammar which is not UG-determined) or because they have misanalysed *herself* as a monomorpheme?

60 Mary$_i$ told Sue that Ann$_i$ liked herself$_i$ too much

Thirdly, one has to be certain what status the L2 learner has assigned to Infl – whether it is marked for agreement inflections or not. If L2 speakers of English (correctly) allow the binding relation indicated in (61), is it because they have acquired the polymorphemic status of *herself*, or because they are treating *herself* as monomorphemic and Infl as inflected for agreement (in which case binding would be subject-oriented, but would be restricted to the embedded tensed clause)?

61 Mary$_i$ told Sue that Ann$_i$ liked herself$_{i/*i}$ too much

Fourthly, in experimental studies where learners have to make decisions about binding relationships, researchers have found it extremely difficult to establish whether their responses reflect the full range of their competence rather than preferred interpretations of an anaphor in a given context (White et al. 1997). For example, if speakers of an L1 with long-distance binding only accept the local binding relation in (61), is this really because their L2 grammars only allow local binding, or because in processing complex English sentences in real time they prefer the closest antecedent to the anaphor?

All of these factors make it difficult to draw firm conclusions currently about how performance data from L2 learners might relate to underlying knowledge of binding and to what extent UG, the L1 and the ability to reset parameters are involved. Below we describe three studies in this domain, but the conclusion will be in agreement with Hamilton's (1998) assessment that results are ambiguous, and that to date the best one can say is that no study conclusively shows that principles of UG are *not* involved in the way L2 learners construct representations for anaphor binding.

Finer (1991) reports two studies of anaphor binding by L2 learners of English. The first was an earlier study by Finer and Broselow (1986) of L1 Korean speakers. Korean is apparently a language with a monomorphemic anaphor, *caki*, 'self', which therefore only accepts subjects as antecedents. Furthermore Infl in Korean does not have agreement inflections, and so long-distance binding up to the matrix subject is possible. Finer and Broselow gave six adult Korean speakers in intensive ESL programmes in the United States a picture identification task. This involved a set of cartoons and associated sentences like the following:

62a Mr Fat thinks that Mr Thin will paint himself
b Mr Fat wants Mr Thin to paint himself

(62a) involves a tensed embedded clause, while (62b) involves a non-finite embedded clause. For each sentence there were two cartoons, only one of which matched the possible interpretation of the sentence for native speakers. For example, in the case of (62a), one cartoon showed Mr Fat with a 'thought bubble' coming out of his head depicting Mr Thin applying paint to his own body (the locally bound interpretation appropriate for English). The other cartoon showed Mr Fat with a thought bubble depicting Mr Thin painting Mr Fat (the long-distance interpretation which is inappropriate for English). Informants had to choose the appropriate picture for the sentence. The results, calculated for the group as a whole, showed that for sentences with tensed embedded clauses like (62a), 22/24 choices were for the picture showing (correct) local binding, while for sentences like (62b) 14/24 choices were for the picture showing local binding, but 9/24 choices were for long-distance binding (with 1/24 accepting both pictures). At least some of the informants, then, appear to accept non-local binding when the verb in the embedded clause is non-finite, but require local binding when it is not. This would be potentially consistent with learners having a grammar for L2 English where the anaphor is monomorphemic, but tensed Infl is inflected for agreement – a possibility which is realized neither in Korean nor English. Thus learners would have adopted a possibility allowed by UG, but which is present neither in the L1 nor the L2 – an example of underdetermination of knowledge (which is how Finer and Broselow interpret it).

In the second study, Finer used the same method with 30 L1-Korean and also 20 L1-Japanese speaking learners of English and found very similar results. Since Japanese is like Korean in having a monomorphemic anaphor, *zibun*, 'self', and Infl lacks agreement inflections, it suggests that the pattern found was not an idiosyncratic function of the earlier small group of informants. At the same time, one cannot rule out the possibility that these informants have not acquired the agreement features of English Infl, but strongly prefer local binding in embedded tensed clauses for some reason.

One way to begin to tease these possibilities apart is to investigate how speakers of languages like Korean/Japanese learning English treat cases of the local binding of anaphors by non-subjects, as in *Charles talked to June$_i$ about herself$_i$*. If L2 learners are treating English anaphors as monomorphemes, they should not allow them to be bound by local non-subjects like *June*. Hirakawa (1990) examined this in the L2 English of native speakers of Japanese. Hirakawa's informants were 65 primarily tutored learners who had started learning English typically at the age of 12. Although they were divided initially into different proficiency groups, it turned out, somewhat surprisingly, that there was no significant difference in their performance, so they can be treated as a single group. There was also a control group of 20 native speakers of English, and a comparator group of 22 native speakers of Japanese who took a Japanese version of Hirakawa's test.

The test was a multiple-choice grammaticality judgement task in which informants were asked to decide who *himself* or *herself* referred to in contexts like the following:

63 John said that Bill hit *himself*
  a. John
  b. Bill
  c. either John or Bill
  d. someone else
  e. don't know

The test sentences involved embedded finite and non-finite clauses as in the Finer studies, but Hirakawa also included one-clause sentences where the anaphor could be bound either by a subject or a non-subject, e.g. *Bob talked to Paul about himself*. There were five tokens of each type of sentence in the test.

The results on the one-clause sentence type were as follows:

64 Sentence type: *Bob talked to Paul about himself*
  (a) **L2 learners' choices**
     Bob: 73.9%
     Paul or both Bob/Paul: 25.9%
  (b) **English native speaker choices**
     Bob: 67%
     Paul or both Bob/Paul: 32%

The Japanese comparator group, on equivalent sentences in Japanese, chose the (a) answer, i.e. 'Bob' alone, in 95.5% of cases. This shows two things. Firstly, Japanese speakers' responses to anaphor binding in English are different from their responses to anaphors in their native Japanese; secondly, that although the Japanese speakers choose the subject in sentences like (64) as the antecedent in higher proportions than the prepositional object, this may well reflect a preference rather than the fact that they have not acquired the polymorphemic status of the anaphor. This is because native speakers of English themselves prefer subject antecedents in this kind of test.

On two- and three-clause sentence types, responses differ between native and non-native speakers of English:

65   Sentence type: *John said that Bill hit himself*
   (a)   **L2 learners' choices**
         Bill: 77%
         John or both John/Bill: 23%
   (b)   **English native speaker choices**
         Bill: 99%
         John or both John/Bill: 1%

66   Sentence type: *Mary asked Ann to introduce herself*
   (a)   **L2 learners' choices**
         Ann: 55.1%
         Mary or both Mary/Ann: 44.2%
   (b)   **English native speaker choices**
         Ann: 98%
         Mary or both Mary/Ann: 2%

These results are very similar to those found by Finer, in the sense that whether the clause is tensed or not has a significant effect on the extent to which the L2 speakers allow non-local binding. But since these informants respond to sentences like (64) as if they had realized that English anaphors are polymorphemic, they should not allow long-distance binding in cases like (65)–(66) at all.

Does this mean that these L2 speakers have constructed grammars which do not fall within the constraints imposed by the principles of UG? While this may seem possible on the face of it, two other observations which have been made recently confuse the matter. It has been discovered that in some languages the same anaphors apparently behave like polymorphemes when they are locally bound (i.e. they can be bound both by subjects and non-subjects) but behave like monomorphemes when they are bound outside the local domain (i.e. they can be bound only by subjects). This is apparently the case for Norwegian *seg*, 'self', and Icelandic *sig*, 'self' (Thomas 1993, citing studies by Maling 1986; Reuland and Koster 1991). Thomas further reports that child L1 learners of English, during development, apparently also allow non-local antecedents to bind English anaphors, perhaps for reasons connected with developing language processing capacities rather than with underlying competence. So the results obtained by Hirakawa could be consistent either with Japanese speakers assuming that English anaphors have the properties of those in Norwegian and Icelandic (options allowed by UG), or with their having language processing problems of the kind L1 speakers have.

Thomas (1995) argued that the one kind of binding of anaphors that should not be allowed by UG, even in languages like Norwegian and Icelandic, is long-distance binding by a non-subject, as in:

67   John told Mary$_i$ Bill liked herself$_{*i}$

Here, if *herself* allows long-distance binding, it is being treated as monomorphemic, but in that case it can only be bound by the subject of the matrix clause. To test this, Thomas investigated the L2 acquisition of a language which allows long-distance binding of anaphors: Japanese. There were 58 learners of L2 Japanese in her study, 32 L1 English speakers, and 26 speakers of other L1s (including languages which also allow long-distance binding like Chinese and Korean). Informants were divided into two groups, high and low proficiency, and there was a control group of 34 native speakers of Japanese. The test involved judging whether a sentence was a true reflection of a brief story presented in words and pictures. For example, one story depicts two characters, A and B, playing base-ball; A gets hit on the head, and later A's father asks, 'What happened?', to which A replies, 'B hit me.' The sentence informants then had to assess (in Japanese) was *A said that B hit self*. If informants allow *self* to be bound by *A* the sentence is a true reflection of the story, but if they only allow *self* to be bound by *B* it is not.

Thomas found that there was a significant difference for the high-proficiency group between the way they treated long-distance subject antecedents in such sentences and the way they treated long-distance objects. Fewer than 20% of objects were accepted, but nearly 60% of subjects. While the preference for subjects was stronger in native speakers, this nevertheless suggests that the L2 learners' grammars were consistent with UG. By contrast, the low-proficiency L2 learners allowed long-distance binding by both subjects and objects in around 50% of cases; there was no significant difference. Thomas suggests that these results may be the effect of the low proficiency learners misanalysing the Japanese anaphor *zibun* as a pronominal. The results obtained from the high-proficiency learners suggest that at some point in development they come to realize that *zibun* is a monomorphemic anaphor.

7.6.4 Summary of section 7.6

It can be seen from this brief consideration of just some of the studies of binding properties operating in L2 grammars that results are difficult to interpret because of the number of variables involved: whether a form is an anaphor or pronoun, whether an anaphor is mono- or polymorphemic, whether Infl has agreement features or not, whether specific tasks promote preferences in performance and whether processing is a problem for speakers at low proficiency levels. It seems that the best that can be concluded at present is that 'there is no compelling evidence of L2 interlanguage grammars of binding that are illicit with respect to Universal Grammar', and that L2 learners perform in ways which suggest that their knowledge is underdetermined both by the L1s they speak and by the L2 input they encounter (Hamilton 1998: 317).

7.7 Summary of chapter 7

We have covered a lot of ground, including considerable technical linguistic detail, in this chapter. The main points made were the following:

- L2 researchers have been interested in constraints on the movement of constituents and the interpretation of anaphors because of the potential they offer for investigating whether principles of UG are directly involved in L2 grammar-building. Where speakers acquire an L2 which differs from the L1 in the types of movement or binding possibilities allowed, evidence that they can determine limits on those possibilities could only be explained on the basis of an innate language faculty; neither the L1 nor input from the target language are plausible sources for that knowledge (section 7.1).
- Results from studies of L2 speakers' intuitions about violations of constraints on movement present a complex picture. They are only valid if it can be shown that informants recognize the grammaticality of sentences of equal structural complexity to the ungrammatical sentences, and the grammaticality of cyclic movement (section 7.3.1). Even where these criteria are met, L2 speakers are not necessarily as successful as native speakers at detecting violations of constraints. Speakers of L1s with very different movement possibilities from English are typically less likely to be successful than speakers of L1s with similar kinds of movement (section 7.3.2). It was argued that this is not because speakers have difficulty accessing principles of UG – their ability to differentiate 'strong' from 'weak' islands suggests otherwise (section 7.5.1). Rather, it seems that they have difficulty either with processing language in real time, which affects their capacity to perform like native speakers in tests, or in 'hitting on' the parameter setting which gives rise to movement (agreement between the *wh*-phrase and the Q morpheme of C) (section 7.5.2).
- Studies of L2 speakers' interpretations of anaphor binding suggest that they construct grammars which are not necessarily determined by the L1 they speak or by target language input. However, given the current state of our knowledge, it is difficult to determine whether this is an effect of the morphological status of the anaphor (mono- versus polymorphemic), the features of Infl (whether it has agreement), whether learners have preferred interpretations in given contexts, or whether they have processing problems (section 7.6.3).

7.8 Exercises

Which of the following sentences do you find grammatical and which ungrammatical? In the ungrammatical cases, explain what kind of violation is involved: *wh*-island, complex DP (with clausal complement), complex DP (which is a relative clause), or complex subject.

1. Who did Sally tell Ben that she had met?
2. What did Sally ask when Bill would buy?
3. Who did Bert's liking Sue seem to annoy?
4. Who did Brian know why Tom met?
5. What did Bob say when he met Carol?
6. What did Sue go to the shop that sells?
7. What did Paul notice that the inspector was wearing?
8. What did Sharon believe the story that Tim stole?
9. To whom did Chris explain the story that Jill had told?
10. Who did Bert's liking seem to annoy Sue?

Indonesian is a language which can form questions either by leaving *wh*-phrases in situ or by starting a sentence with a *wh*-phrase immediately followed by the interrogative complementizer *yang*:

> 1   Ahmad men-ulis   laporan itu
>   Ahmad active-wrote report   the
>   'Ahmad wrote the report'
>
> 2a   Ahmad men-ulis   apa?
>   Ahmad active-wrote what?
>   b   Apakah yang Ahmad di-tulis?
>   What   Q   Ahmad passive-wrote
>   'What did Ahmad write?'

However, questions like (2b) are only possible where the questioned constituent is the subject, hence the need for a passive verb in (2b) which has moved the questioned constituent (the object) into the subject position. Schachter (1989, 1990) assumes that *wh*-phrase movement is involved in (2b), but that movement is only possible from subject position in Indonesian.

Making this assumption yourself (not all linguists do – see Martohardjono (1993) for a non-movement account) consider the following results from a study by Mirizon (1998). Mirizon gave an English grammaticality judgement task to two groups of native speakers of Indonesian, five learners classed as intermediate and five as advanced, together with a control group of native speakers. The L2 speakers were all adults who had started English in the classroom at the age of 12–13, and had spent about a year in the UK as graduate students. Some of the sentences in the test involved grammatical and ungrammatical *wh*-phrase movement. The proportions of responses of 'accept' to specific sentence types are given below (there were at least two tokens of each type in the test):

(i)   Grammatical *wh*-phrase movement from embedded subject and embedded object position (percentages of responses of 'accept'):

What did Sue ask Bob [φ [t was on sale in the Union Shop]]?
Intermediate	Advanced	Native speaker
67.5%	72.5%	90%

Who does the journalist believe [φ [Tom saw t]]?
Intermediate	Advanced	Native speaker
67.5%	72.5%	90%

(ii)   Ungrammatical *wh*-islands (percentages of responses of 'accept'):

*What did the chairman say [when [t would take place]]?
Intermediate	Advanced	Native speaker
33.7%	32.5%	5%

(iii)   Ungrammatical complex DPs with a clausal complement (percentages of responses of 'accept'):

*What does the government deny the claim [t that [the minister said t]]?
Intermediate	Advanced	Native speaker
55%	40%	12.5%

Do these results provide any evidence that Indonesian speakers have acquired *wh*-phrase movement in English from positions not possible in Indonesian (as opposed to having recognized that *wh*-phrases are clause-initial in English, but without *moving* the *wh*-phrases there)? Give reasons for your answer.

Exercise 3: Distinguishing cases of 'strong' and 'weak' violations of constraints on movement (section 7.4.1)

Which of the following sentences do you find grammatical and which ungrammatical? Which of the ungrammatical sentences can be classified as 'weak' violations, and which as 'strong'? In section 7.4.1 it was argued that 'weak' violations involve the movement of arguments governed by lexical categories; 'strong' violations involve either the movement of an adjunct, or the movement of an argument not governed by a lexical category:

1. To whom did Tom forward the message that a new vaccine had been discovered?
2. What was Jim angry with Mo after she had bought?
3. Where did Tom deny the fact that a new vaccine had been discovered?
4. What did the police ask the man who was singing?
5. What did the police arrest the man who was carrying?
6. What did John believe how Jim repaired?
7. What is Anne taking her complaint to the police going to achieve?
8. What is Anne finishing by the deadline very unlikely?
9. What did Eric say to Steve after the Thompsons left?
10. What did Bob say that had happened last week?
11. How did John know what Jim repaired?
12. Who did she say was staying for several days in Paris?

Exercise 4: Deciding whether L2 learners are having difficulty with the Empty Category Principle or with properties of complementizers (section 7.4.2)

In section 7.4.2 it was argued that the category C cannot in general license a following trace, but that certain morphemes belonging to the category C may have features which override this principle: for example, the English complementizer $[_C \phi]$ in examples like: *What did Sue say $[t' \phi [t$ would look nice in the kitchen]]*? (Rizzi 1990). Mirizon (1998), in the study described in exercise 2, included sentence tokens relating to the extraction of embedded subjects, both in the presence of $[_C that]$ and in the presence of $[_C \phi]$. Responses were as follows:

(i) Grammatical *wh*-phrase movement from embedded subject position (percentages of responses of 'accept'):

> What did Sue ask Bob [t' ϕ [t was on sale in the Union Shop]]?
>
> | Intermediate | Advanced | Native speaker |
> |---|---|---|
> | 67.5% | 72.5% | 90% |

(ii) Ungrammatical *wh*-phrase movement from embedded subject position (percentages of responses of 'accept'):

What did Sue tell Bob [t' that [t would look nice in his office]]?

Intermediate	Advanced	Native speaker
55.2%	50%	17.5%

Comparing these results with the others reported in exercise 2, is there evidence here to suggest that these informants' grammars violate the Empty Category Principle? If you conclude that there is no evidence for this claim, what explanation might be offered for the non-native/native differences evident in the responses to type (ii) sentences?

Exercise 5: Determining possible antecedents for pronouns and anaphors (section 7.6.1)

In the following sentences, determine which of the DPs in each sentence are possible antecedents for the pronoun or anaphor in bold. Then explain why these are possible antecedents:

1. Maria thought that Nicoletta had written to Irene about **herself**
2. John's brother spoke about **himself**
3. Tom read Tony's story about **himself** to Bill
4. Tom read a story about **himself** to Bill
5. June thought that Mary believed **herself** to be innocent
6. June thought that Mary had promised to treat **herself**

Exercise 6: Considering whether L2 speakers have acquired the polymorphemic status of English anaphors (section 7.6.3)

Bennett and Progovac (1998) investigated the interpretation of anaphors in the L2 English of native speakers of Serbo-Croatian. In Serbo-Croatian, the anaphor *sebi*, 'self', is monomorphemic, which means that it must be bound by a subject. But in addition, tensed Infl in Serbo-Croatian has agreement features, so *sebi* can only be bound by subjects up to the point where there is a tensed Infl. For example, in the Serbo-Croatian equivalent of (1), the binding possibilities are as indicated:

1 $Mary_k$ knew that [$Susan_j$ heard [Ann_i's description of $self_{i/j/*k}$]]

Bennett and Progovac administered an English multiple-choice comprehension test to two groups of native speakers of Serbo-Croatian – classed as 'low' (n = 44) and 'high' (n = 29) proficiency L2 speakers of English – and a control group of native speakers of English (n = 47). In this task informants were given sentences like:

2   Bobby likes Peter's story about himself

They were asked to choose which of the DPs are possible antecedents for *himself*: *Peter, Bobby*, both or none.

Informants' choices (in percentages) on two of the sentence types included in the test are given below (I exclude figures for the choice 'none' which was hardly chosen at all):

(i)   Choices (in percentages) of antecedents in one-clause sentences:

Bobby$_2$ likes Peter's$_1$ song about himself

Choice	Native speaker	Low proficiency	High proficiency
1	91.5%	65.9%	65.5%
2	4.3%	21.6%	8.6%
1 and 2	4.3%	12.5%	25.9%

(ii) Choices (in percentages) of antecedents in two-clause sentences:

Michael$_3$ says that Peter$_2$ read John's$_1$ letter about himself

Choice	Native speaker	Low proficiency	High proficiency
1	81.9%	51.1%	60.3%
2	3.2%	20.5%	6.9%
3	4.3%	8.0%	1.7%
1 and 2	5.3%	11.4%	19.0%
1, 2, 3	3.2%	2.3%	5.2%

On the basis of these results, can one say that the L2 speakers have acquired the polymorphemic status of English anaphors like *himself*?

If sentences like the following were included in the test, which choices would you predict these L2 speakers to make: *Gemma talked to June about herself*.

7.9 Further reading

For accessible discussion of constraints on movement see Haegeman, L. 1994: *Introduction to Government and Binding Theory* (2nd edn). Oxford: Blackwell, chapter 8; Roberts, I. 1997: *Comparative Syntax*. London: Arnold, chapter 4; Culicover, P. 1997: *Principles and Parameters: An Introduction to Syntactic Theory*. Oxford: Oxford University Press, chapters 6–7.

In the L2 context, a good discussion of how to interpret results from studies of L2 speakers' intuitions about constraints on movement can be found in White. L. 1992c: Subjacency violations and empty categories in second language acquisition. In H. Goodluck and M. Rochemont (eds), *Island Constraints: Theory, Acquisition and Processing*, Dordrecht: Kluwer. A recent cluster of articles on the topic makes up part II of Flynn, S., Martohardjono, G. and O'Neil, W. (eds) 1998: *The Generative Study of Second Language Acquisition*. Mahwah, NJ: Lawrence Erlbaum Associates. A study which argues that adult L2 speakers can construct L2 grammars which are target-like in terms of constraints on movement is White, L. and Genesee, F. 1996: How native is near-native? The issue of ultimate attainment in adult second language acquisition. *Second Language Research* 12, 233–65.

Accessible discussion of pronoun/anaphor binding can be found in two of the texts referred to above: Roberts (chapter 3) and Culicover (section 8.3).

In the L2 context, part III of Flynn et al. (1998) is a cluster of papers on binding. For some recent discussion of yet another complicating factor in the investigation of binding in SLA, see Hamilton, R. 1998: Underdetermined binding of reflexives by adult Japanese-speaking learners of English. *Second Language Research* 14, 292–320.

Notes

1 In examples (1)–(3) the traces of both *wh*-phrase movement and I-to-C movement (i.e. movement of *did*) have been indicated. In subsequent examples, for ease of exposition, only the traces of *wh*-phrase movement will be shown.
2 The reader may be wondering why *what* can remain *in situ* in (9a). Normally, a single *wh*-phrase in a clause in English must raise to the specifier of CP. If it is left *in situ* it gives rise to a stylistically marked construction known as an 'echo question', which expresses a kind of disbelief:

> i – What did John do?
>   – He bought a piranha.
>   – He did what?

But when there are two *wh*-phrases in the same clause, since both cannot move to the specifier of CP (**Who what bought? *What who bought?*), one of them stays where it is. It seems that the one higher in the structure to start with is the one which moves:

iia   [$_{CP}$ Who$_i$ [$_{IP}$ t$_i$ bought what]]?
  b   *[$_{CP}$ What$_i$ did [$_{IP}$ who buy t$_i$]]?

This is known as a 'superiority effect' (Chomsky 1973).

3   The early accounts of subjacency assumed that phrases like *the news, the story, rumours* were NPs, rather than DPs, as they are treated in current work (see section 6.3). The early accounts therefore called NP the bounding node. For consistency with chapter 6, I will treat DP as the bounding node.

4   In English relative clauses it is usually assumed that either an overt *wh*-phrase or a null operator, Op, is moved from an argument position in the clause to the specifier of the CP which is the complement to a DP (also see section 4.9.1):

  i   The store [$_{CP}$ which$_i$ e [t$_i$ had the new Sting album in stock]]
  ii   The store [$_{CP}$ Op$_i$ that [t$_i$ had the new Sting album in stock]]

Although Op is null, it still fills the specifier position of CP, and stops other *wh*-phrases landing there, giving rise to subjacency violations.

5   The distractor sentences were made up of nine grammatical *wh*-questions (e.g. *Who$_i$ did the President say [t$_i'$ e [he planned to appoint t$_i$ as an advisor]]?*) and nine ungrammatical cases of rightward movement (e.g. **[That [a new book t$_i$] has just appeared t$_i'$] is very exciting [on SLA]$_i$.*).

6   Others have argued that Indonesian is like Chinese in not having *wh*-phrase movement in questions; the gap which occurs in the subject position when the subject is questioned is in fact a null pronoun (Martohardjono and Gair 1993).

7   As White (1992c) observes, although Schachter's (1989) study included, alongside sentences testing subjacency violations, other sentences which test whether subjects accept grammatical sentences of the same structural complexity, and sentences involving grammatical *wh*-phrase movement, the *wh*-phrase movement sentences only formed part of the distractors, and were not scored in the results. It is possible, then, in theory that the subjects tested might have been having difficulty with *wh*-phrase movement generally, which would mean that they would not be accurate in detecting subjacency violations. Schachter rectifies this in her (1990) study by scoring responses to grammatical sentences involving *wh*-phrase movement. The results (the third column in table 3) show that although the Indonesian, Chinese and Korean speakers are slightly less accurate than the Dutch or native English speakers, there is no significant difference in accuracy between them.

8   Johnson and Newport are unclear in their description of this. In their text they say that the 'fillers' were not counted for the purpose of analysis. But the mean score here could only be out of 36 if the 12 simple *wh*-questions and 24 fillers were counted together.

9   In (20c) I am assuming that *how quickly* is intended to modify the verb *mend*, as the location of the co-indexed trace indicates, and not the verb *wonder*. If *how quickly* modifies *wonder* the sentence is grammatical, although pragmatically odd since 'wondering' is not really compatible with a manner adverb like *quickly*.

10   Rizzi in fact assumes the split-IP account of Pollock (1989) (see section 3.6), so the set of licensing heads are the lexical heads N, V, P, A, plus Agr and T.

11   Rizzi (1990: chapter 3) in fact proposes some further modifications to this account of the ECP/Relativized Minimality which will not be dealt with here.

12   The material in parentheses is mine.

8 The Construction of a Theory of Second Language Syntax: Some Issues and Controversies

8.1 Introduction

Throughout this book we have been concerned with understanding the kind of syntactic knowledge that second language learners develop as the result of contact with the target language. This enterprise involves constructing theories for two phenomena. First, a theory of the mental architecture that must be present in the mind of learners from the outset to enable them to convert samples of language encountered into a productive grammar for the L2. To the extent that constructed L2 grammars go beyond information found either in input from the target language or in the learner's L1, this constitutes the **logical problem** of second language acquisition: how can L2 speakers come to know what they do on the basis of random samples of language (Bley-Vroman 1990; Gregg 1996; White 1989; forthcoming)? The kinds of grammatical knowledge for which L2 input or the L1 provide little or no evidence include the ability to produce and understand L2 sentences not encountered before, the ability to distinguish grammatical from ungrammatical sentences where there is no direct evidence bearing on such decisions, and the systematic construction of representations which are found neither in the L1 nor the L2, but are found in other human languages. Second, a theory of the growth of L2 syntactic knowledge over time. Such a theory must be able to account for how L2 syntactic representations change from an initial state, through transitional states and into the final state (when learners' grammars appear to have stopped evolving). This is commonly referred to as the second language **developmental problem** (Felix 1984; White 1989; Gregg 1996).

The logical problem could in principle be addressed in a variety of ways. For example, it might be supposed that second language acquisition is no different in its essentials from the acquisition of other kinds of skill, like the ability to do arithmetic, play the guitar or drive a car. If this were the case, the mental architecture underlying each of these would be the same – some kind of general learning mechanism – but applied to knowledge acquisition in a number of different domains. Some second language researchers have taken this view (Wolfe-Quintero 1992; Klein and Perdue 1992; Skehan 1998; see Mitchell and Myles 1998, for a comparison of theories). However, this has not been the view taken here. From the outset the choice was made to assume that second language acquisition, like first language acquisition, is a special ability different from the ability to learn other things, and for which there is specially dedicated neural architecture in the brain, commonly referred to as the 'language faculty'. At the core of the language faculty we have assumed that there is a Universal Grammar (UG) which provides humans with the tools for constructing mental grammars for particular human languages. The particular version of UG adopted here involves principles of grammar construction which determine the range and type of possible grammatical representations that language learners can form, but which also allow variation along certain dimensions: 'parameters' of variation (Chomsky 1981, 1986a, 1995).

When evaluating theories of the logical problem, it is important to keep in mind that they are just theories, formulated by individuals or groups of researchers, and not established fact. As theories, they evolve in the light of new findings or new insights, and they can be wrong. The 'best' theory will probably emerge ultimately as a function of factors like the range of phenomena it is capable of predicting, its 'elegance' and 'simplicity', its plausibility in relation to what is known about the human mind more generally, and so on. Given that we hardly have more than the most basic understanding of even descriptive facts from the SLA research which has been undertaken up to now, it is difficult at present to undertake a comparison of theories in these terms. What can be said is that by adopting a principles-and-parameters theory (P&P) approach, understanding can be advanced in a number of concrete ways, as I hope has been demonstrated in the preceding chapters. There are at least four reasons why P&P is a good candidate theory for addressing the logical problem in L2 syntax:

(a)   Because proposals about syntactic structure are explicit within P&P, they allow the formulation of specific testable hypotheses about the nature of L2 syntactic knowledge. The ability to test a hypothesis empirically is important because while results which are consistent with it can never prove that the hypothesis is correct (there may be other, as yet undiscovered, data which are incompatible with it), results which do not match predictions suggest that the hypothesis is wrong, or wrongly formulated. Such findings allow researchers to avoid blind alleys, and narrow the search space for future enquiry.

(b) Because P&P has not been formulated specifically with SLA in mind – it has been developed primarily as a theory about the properties of mature *native* grammars – it is independently justified. Theories which provide explanations for some phenomenon A, when they were originally formulated to explain a different phenomenon B, are usually more interesting than theories which only explain phenomenon A.

(c) If the P&P approach to explaining second language syntax is the correct one, it will be theoretically parsimonious. Many linguists believe that only the postulation of an innate language faculty with a P&P-type UG at its core can explain the capacity that children have to acquire L1s. If the same properties of UG can explain the construction of L2 grammars, it is unnecessary to postulate an additional and different mechanism for acquisition: the account of L1 and L2 acquisition is parsimonious.

(d) Some linguists regard first language acquisition and disordered native competence (which arises, for example, as the result of brain trauma) as important 'windows' on the structure of linguistic knowledge in the mind. These complement the more general enquiry of linguistics into the nature of normal competence. If the P&P approach to second language acquisition is the correct one, it provides a further 'window' from a different perspective. The convergence of evidence from these different sources should in time lead to a comprehensive model of human linguistic ability.

As for the developmental problem, we have encountered a number of competing theories in the course of discussion. In chapter 2 'minimal trees', 'valueless features' and 'full access to UG' theories were introduced. But it was argued that each leaves a residue of problems when confronted with empirical data from studies of L2 learners. As a result, I adopted a tentative 'working theory' referred to as 'modulated structure building' which was tested against other data as I proceeded. Modulated structure building turned out to have its own residue of problems.

Since each of these theories assumes a P&P approach to the logical problem of L2 syntactic knowledge, a question that may be asked is why competing theories of the developmental problem should arise. There appear to be two main reasons. The first is that researchers have adopted different views, not always explicitly articulated, of the way that modules of the language faculty interact with each other, and with other, non-language-faculty components of mind. The second is that, amid the relative messiness of performance data collected from L2 learners, researchers have differed in what they regard as significant and insignificant properties. In sections 8.3 to 8.5 I will examine in detail how these factors might combine to raise issues and generate controversy in attempts to account for the three elements of the developmental problem: the nature of initial-state, transitional-state and final-state L2 grammars. As a prologue to that discussion, I briefly describe the modularity of the language faculty and how it is that linguists can hold different hypotheses about the way the modules interact (section 8.2.1), I discuss how a different interpretation of the relation between syntax and lexicon can affect the interpretation of L2 development (8.2.2), and then illustrate how the same L2 data can be treated as significant in one theory and insignificant in another (section 8.2.3).

8.2   Modularity and the interpretation of L2 performance data

> Section 8.2 describes the components (modules) which are generally assumed to constitute the language faculty, and how these relate to other modules of the brain. Two different conceptions of the way that syntax and the lexicon can interact are discussed, and it is suggested that these different conceptions may give rise to different ways of interpreting the development of L2 syntactic knowledge, and the significance attributed to performance data.

8.2.1   The modularity of the language faculty

It is generally assumed that the language faculty consists of at least the following components or **modules** (although different linguistic theories make different assumptions about the internal organization of these modules, and the range of phenomena each deals with):

A lexicon

The lexicon is the module where all the morphemes, words formed from combinations of morphemes, idioms (like *spill the beans, take to the cleaners*) and clichés (like *a breath of fresh air*) of a language are stored (Jackendoff 1997: Chapter 7). Each stored item includes a specification for how it is pronounced, what it means and what its syntactic properties are. The syntactic specification includes at least an indication of what category the entry belongs to (e.g. N, V, Infl, D, etc.) and, where appropriate, what it can select as a complement and as a specifier when it projects into a phrase. So the lexical entry for a morpheme like *hit* would include the feature [V], and a specification that it takes a DP complement, while the entry for *cry* would include the feature [V], but would specify that it takes no complement.[1]

A computational device – the syntax

The syntactic module of the language faculty is a computational device which takes items from the lexicon, combines them into larger phrases, and then performs different operations on those phrases (moving constituents around, associating affixes and free morphemes). The phrases created by the syntax are known as **phrase markers,** and the sequence of phrase markers that the syntax creates in order to construct a sentence is known as a **derivation.**

A phonological module

The phonological module determines the range of sounds and possible combinations of sounds which can be used to specify the sound structure of individual morphemes in the lexicon. It also specifies how combinations of morphemes in derivations produced by the syntax are pronounced.

A morphological module

The morphological module determines how individual morphemes combine with others to form complex lexical items.

An interpretive module – Logical Form

'Logical Form' is the module which specifies how the individual meanings of morphemes combine in a derivation to produce complex propositional meanings. It operates on the output of the syntax.

A standard view is that the modules of the language faculty interact with other modules of the brain at specific points called **interfaces** (Chomsky 1995). For example, the lexicon is assumed to have an interface with modules of the brain which deal with visual stimuli, auditory stimuli, beliefs, knowledge, etc. So the morpheme {red} has a meaning specification which may be linked to a specific kind of visual perception (in those with normal vision); the morpheme {queen} has a meaning specification which may be linked to a module where knowledge about social organization (and in particular the nature of monarchies) is stored. The output of the phonological module interfaces with the sensori-motor module of the brain which deals with the physical production and perception of speech. Logical Form interfaces with a module or modules of the brain which deal with propositional thinking. (For discussion of the modularity of the language faculty and other components of the mind/brain see Fodor 1983; Smith and Tsimpli 1995; Smith 1999: Chapters 1–2.)

Crucially for the discussion in this chapter, linguists have taken different views about the way in which modules within the language faculty interact with each other. We will focus specifically on the relation between the lexicon and the syntax here (see Jackendoff 1997: Chapter 4, for brief discussion of different views of the lexicon–syntax relation). In early work on generative grammar, including early versions of the P&P approach, the dominant view was that the syntactic module constructs phrase markers independently of the lexicon, into which lexical items are subsequently inserted. In other words, the syntax provides a 'structural template' and then fills it with morphemes drawn from the lexicon. To illustrate, consider the trivial sentence *Jo liked tomatoes*. The syntax would construct an initial phrase marker for this sentence approximately like (1a) (with some irrelevant details ignored), into which the lexical items in (1b) would then be inserted, to form the phrase marker (1c):

1a

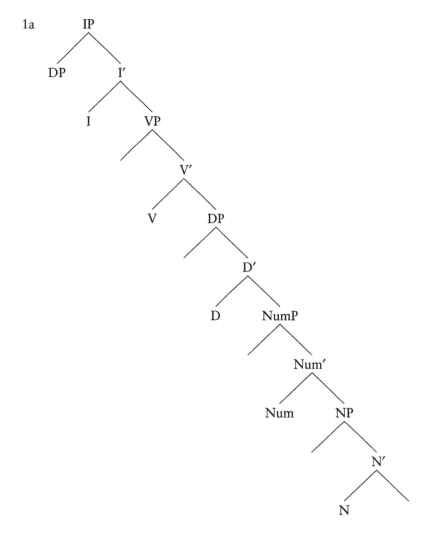

b [N Jo] [V like] [N tomato]
   [I -ed] [Num -s] [D ∅]

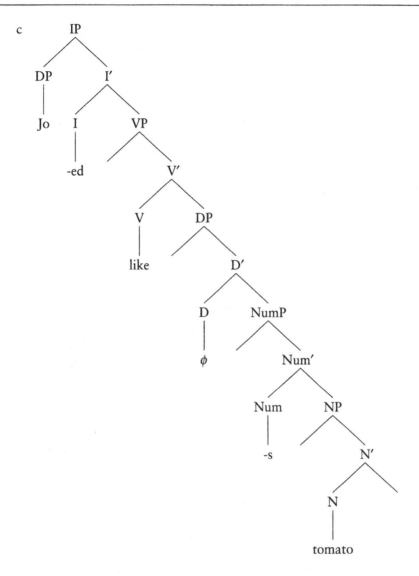

Having constructed (1c), the syntax then proceeds to transform it, e.g. by associating *-ed* and *like*, *-s* and *tomato* (by lowering the inflections, I have assumed up to now). For convenience, I will refer to this conception as the 'structural template' view from now on.

A more recent view, however, discussed explicitly in Chomsky (1995), holds that the syntax does not construct structural templates independently of the lexicon. Instead, the syntax selects arrays of lexical items directly from the lexicon and 'merges' them into an initial phrase marker. On this view, (1a) is not a step in the derivation; (1b) is the starting point, and the syntax takes the items of (1b) and projects them into the structure (1c). The necessary constraints to prevent the syntax from merging the wrong constituents are built into the specification for each item in the lexicon: each morpheme belongs to a category, and there is a statement of the categories it can combine with (its selectional requirements). I will refer to this second conception as the 'lexical array' view.

The 'structural template' view has the advantage that general syntactic properties affecting whole classes of items can be removed from the lexicon and built into the procedure for constructing the template. For example, English and French differ in the strength of inflections belonging to Infl and Num. In French, thematic verbs and nouns raise to tensed Infl and Num respectively as we have seen (*Jo n'aime$_i$ pas t$_i$ les tomates*, 'Jo doesn't like tomatoes'; *un tomate$_i$ vert t$_i$*, 'a green tomato'). In English, we have assumed that inflections lower from tensed Infl and Num to V and N. These strength properties do not have to be specified in the lexical entry for every inflection, given the 'structural template' view. Instead, the generalization that every finite verbal inflection and every nominal inflection is either strong or weak can be captured by marking Infl and Num in the template as strong or weak.

There are also disadvantages to the 'structural template' view, however. One is that the lexicon and the template duplicate a lot of information. The template necessarily contains category labels and information about what each category selects as a complement and as a specifier. But each entry in the lexicon also must contain the same information, otherwise *like* might be inserted wrongly under an N in the template, or an intransitive verb like *arrive* might be wrongly inserted into a VP with a DP complement. Another disadvantage is that it is not clear how the 'structural template' view can handle optional constituents (adjuncts) efficiently. Since adjuncts can be added to any sentence, must the syntax generate every possible adjunct phrase that might be added to a sentence just in case lexical items are drawn from the lexicon to fill these slots? But this is in fact impossible since the use of adjuncts is potentially infinitely recursive; no matter how many adjuncts a sentence has, it is always possible to add one more: *John liked the girl [who he met] [who wore a red scarf] [who didn't show any interest in him] . . . [yesterday] [on a bus] [in a rainstorm] . . .* and so on. On the other hand, if the syntax generates a projection for an adjunct only when lexical items are drawn from the lexicon to be inserted into that projection, it may as well take all items directly from the lexicon and merge them into phrase markers without constructing an independent template.

One advantage of the 'lexical array' view, where structure is projected from items taken directly from the lexicon, is that neither of these problems arises. The syntax need project no more structure than is required by the selected lexical items, and there is no duplication of categorial and selectional information. A possible disadvantage is that properties affecting whole classes of lexical items are not now captured independently from the lexicon, but have to be specified as features of every lexical entry affected. On the other hand, this allows one to make an interestingly strong claim about the syntactic-computational component: it is universally invariant, and any parametric variation between languages is located in the feature specification of lexical items and not in the syntax. This is a position taken by Chomsky in current work (1995, 1998). We will return to consider this in more detail in section 8.5.

8.2.2 How different interpretations of the syntax–lexicon relation can affect the interpretation of L2 development

Consider how these different views of the relation between the syntax and the lexicon may affect how L2 researchers interpret the same L2 performance data. In chapter 4, L2 German production data collected by Vainikka and Young-Scholten (1994, 1996a, 1996b) from speakers of Korean and Turkish (SOV languages) and speakers of Romance languages (SVO languages) were described. It appears that Korean and Turkish speakers' productions are predominantly of the OV type in early stages, while those of Romance speakers are predominantly VO, changing quickly to OV. Vainikka and Young-Scholten argue, from the fact that there is almost no overt evidence for an Infl category (informants' utterances typically lack auxiliaries and modals, subject–verb agreement and thematic verb raising), that these learners' initial-state L2 grammars have a VP projection but no IP projection, and that speakers of Romance languages quickly change the headedness of the VP from head-initial to head-final. By contrast, Schwartz and Sprouse (1996), and Epstein et al. (1998) argue, on the basis of the same data, that although there may be little overt morphological evidence for Infl, nevertheless it is present.

The Vainikka and Young-Scholten analysis is consistent with a 'lexical array' view of the relation between the syntax and the lexicon: where there is little or no evidence for inflections/auxiliaries, these have simply not yet been acquired as lexical entries in the lexicon. Since the syntax takes arrays of lexical items from the lexicon to merge into phrase markers, if no items belonging to Infl are present, only VPs will be projected. Functional projections are only constructed by the syntax in later development once morphemes belonging to functional categories have been acquired. By contrast, the Schwartz and Sprouse and Epstein et al. analysis is consistent with a 'structural template' view of the syntax–lexicon relation. If the syntax constructs phrase markers independently of the lexicon, then it is not necessary for an L2 speaker to have acquired lexical items belonging to the categories that the syntax projects. The 'structural template' may be present because UG determines that the syntax always projects a functionally complete initial Phrase Marker, or because it is transferred from the L1. In the L2 German case Infl is present even though there may be no overt evidence for it in the productions of early-stage L2 learners.

8.2.3 Significant and insignificant properties of performance data

The second reason why competing theories of the developmental problem have arisen seems to be that researchers have differed in what they regard as significant and insignificant properties in the performance data collected from informants. Whatever the type of data (whether collected from free production, guided production, judgement tasks, interpretation tasks, and so on) they are always examples of an individual speaker's performance and may only indirectly reflect that speaker's underlying grammatical competence. Speakers may know more than is present in the data – or the data may make it look like they have knowledge when in fact they do not. Moreover performance data are mostly complex, with any given sample simultaneously involving more than one grammatical property. As a result researchers usually have to make a decision about which features of the data bear significantly on the aspect of competence under investigation, and relegate others to the sidelines as insignificant 'noise'. Different theories arise when a phenomenon treated as 'noise' by one researcher is foregrounded as significant by another.

To illustrate from the case of the L2 acquisition of German again, Vainikka and Young-Scholten (1998: 22) argue that speakers of Romance languages learning German are still at a 'lexical projection only' phase of development (i.e. they project VP but not IP) when their productions *predominantly lack* auxiliaries and modals, subject–verb agreement and verb raising; this in spite of the fact that their informants do produce subject–verb agreement '11% to 36% of the time', and some of them produce auxiliaries and modals. Vainikka and Young-Scholten are treating this as 'noise' in the data. By contrast, Epstein et al. (1998: 61) argue that even slight performance evidence like this for functional categories suggests that 'L2 learners have knowledge of the full inventory of both lexical and functional syntactic categories provided by Universal Grammar'. They treat the presence of subject–verb agreement and auxiliaries/modals as significant evidence, and the fact that such forms are not always present or are used in non-target-like ways as the effect of learners failing to acquire language-specific idiosyncratic properties of 'morphophonetics'.

In the remainder of this chapter I will discuss some currently controversial issues like these in the construction of a theory of L2 syntactic development. We will try to consider how different conceptions of the interaction of modules of the language faculty with each other and with other components of the brain, together with the significance attributed to types of performance data, may affect views held. The range of observations collected in earlier chapters will be brought to bear on this discussion. The theories which have been discussed so far – 'minimal trees', 'valueless features', 'full access', and 'modulated structure building' – will be reconsidered, along with some recent refinements. For the purpose of exposition, issues will be discussed in relation to three stages of L2 development: initial-state grammars, transitional-state grammars and final-state grammars. As with other categorizations of this type, they represent analytical idealizations.

More Advanced Discussion

8.3 Issues concerning initial-state L2 grammars

Section 8.3 asks how much grammatical information initial-state L2 grammars may contain, and outlines different positions that can be taken on this issue: (a) only some of the categories that will eventually be required for mature competence are present in the initial state; (b) all of the categories required for mature competence are potentially available, but are only realized if there is positive evidence from the L2 for them; (c) all of the categories required for mature competence are already present in the initial state. We consider which theories adopt which position, and assess which may be a candidate for 'best' theory of the initial state. Given certain assumptions, 'full access' theories look promising, but a problem with them is that they may be unfalsifiable.

One of the main issues to resolve about initial-state L2 grammars is how much grammatical information they contain. Are early-stage L2 learners capable of generating phrase markers with the same range of categories and phrase projections as mature speakers of the target language (even though they obviously have not yet established all the language-particular specifications required)? Or do they have grammars which generate only a subset of the categories and projections which will eventually be acquired? A positive response to the first question is often described as a **strong continuity** approach to the problem; since the same categories and properties are present from the initial state through development to final-state competence, grammatical knowledge is 'continuous', with changes occurring only in language-specific detail. A positive response to the second question is a **weak continuity** approach to the problem; although some categories and projections are present in the initial state, others appear later.

A priori, the simplest assumption would seem to be strong continuity, since this requires no theory of development beyond what is required to explain the acquisition of language-specific properties; weak continuity would, in addition, require a theory of why some categories and projections are initially absent, and what triggers their later appearance. Let us therefore start with the less simple case, and consider what may lead researchers not to make the simplest assumption.

8.3.1   Weak continuity and 'bootstrapping' accounts of the initial state

A basic question to ask is what the acquisitional advantage for an L2 learner would be in initially constructing a grammar which consists of fewer categories than are required for mature competence; say a grammar which initially consisted of just lexical categories and their projections (but not functional categories), as 'minimal trees' and 'modulated structure building' propose. Assuming a 'lexical array' view of the relation between syntax and the lexicon, one advantage may be that it facilitates the learnability of the L2. An L2 learner is initially faced with strings of undifferentiated sounds (or orthographic symbols). The task is to turn this continuum into discrete lexical entries from which the syntax can construct derivations for use in the production and comprehension of the L2. As a way into this undifferentiated continuum, suppose learners at first focus (unconsciously) on detecting morphemes which have most 'perceptual prominence'. Morphemes belonging to substantive categories like N, V, A and so on are good candidates for perceptual prominence (in contrast to morphemes belonging to functional categories). They are typically free forms which are phonologically strong (having word stress) and are associated with stable conceptual meanings. By contrast, morphemes belonging to the functional categories are typically phonologically weak (they are either inflections or, if they are free forms, are usually unstressed) with variable meanings, encoding either grammatical relational information (like agreement, Case) or non-local dependencies (like tense, binding).

If the L2 learner isolates substantive morphemes first, and stores them in the L2 lexicon, the syntax (which is innately given, and assumed to be universally invariant under the 'lexical array' conception) will automatically construct derivations just on the basis of these stored categorized morphemes. Once such lexical entries are established, they can be used by the syntax in 'parsing' new incoming L2 data. Although parts of the input are still unknown, the volume of what is unknown has been reduced by the already established categories in the lexicon, and the detection problem reduced in proportion.

Given this account, perceptual prominence will determine that early L2 derivations consist of lexical projections. This does not mean that functional projections are by definition absent from initial-state L2 grammars; only that the presence of functional projections is dependent on learners detecting evidence for them in the input, and this may be perceptually difficult at the beginning. It potentially allows the full availability of UG from the start, but the derivations produced are determined by what is in the lexicon. This kind of weak continuity account has been given the name **bootstrapping** by some L1 acquisition researchers (Pinker 1987; Gleitman 1990; Hirsh-Pasek and Golinkoff 1996: 33–41). Learners latch on to some elements of the input as a way into constructing a grammar.

One argument against 'bootstrapping' is the presence of subjects in L2 speakers' early utterances. Subjects appear to be present from the beginning, in utterances like *She read book*, and we have been assuming that they are located in the specifier of IP. But this requires that an Infl category is already present in the lexicon, suggesting that it is unnecessary for learners to acquire it.

This argument can be countered, however, given recent proposals that subjects are generated in the specifier of VP (a lexical projection) in initial phrase markers, and subsequently moved to the specifier of IP in languages like English (Koopman and Sportiche 1991). If this is correct, in early L2 utterances Infl need not be present to explain why learners' grammars generate subjects. There are at least three reasons justifying VP-internal subjects. Firstly, the proposal allows a more direct mapping between argument structure and initial syntactic structure, because all arguments can be assigned to structural positions within the VP projection. Secondly, it takes account of cross-linguistic variation in the surface location of subjects. In some languages AGENT arguments appear to be able to remain in a VP-internal position. For example, in passive constructions in Malay, the AGENT can remain in such a position, whereas in English AGENTs cannot and must be introduced as prepositional adjuncts (Guilfoyle, Hung and Travis 1992). The structure of the Malay passive in (2a) is shown in (2b). The corresponding English structure, with *John* remaining in the specifier of VP, is ungrammatical:

2a   Buku itu di + baca John
     book the PASS + buy John
     'The book was bought by John'

 b $[_{IP} [_{DP} \text{Buku itu}]_i \text{ di + baca}_j [_{VP} \text{John } [_{V'} t_j [t_i]]]]$
     $*[_{IP} [_{DP} \text{The book}]_i \text{ was}_j [_{VP} \text{John } [_{V'} t_j \text{ bought } [t_i]]]]$

Thirdly, it resolves a technical problem that the 'floating' of quantifiers from the specifier of IP to the specifier of VP gives rise to: *All journalists love a star* → t_i *Journalists all$_i$ love a star*. Here a trace left by the quantifier is in a position where it is not licensed by a governing lexical category, and where its antecedent (*all*) is not in a c-commanding position, and yet the sentence is grammatical. However, if subjects are generated VP-internally, and *journalists* raises to the specifier of IP, the trace is licensed by Infl (see section 7.4.2) and identified by the c-commanding *journalists*: *Journalists$_i$ all t_i love a star*. Given this account of VP-internal subjects, VP adverbs – which we have been assuming up to now are generated in the specifier of VP – must be accounted for differently. A standard analysis treats them as adjoined to the VP: $[_{VP} \text{Adverb } [_{VP} \text{ARGUMENT } [_{V'} \text{V ARGUMENT}]]]$.

Two of the theories we have already considered – 'minimal trees' and 'modulated structure building' – propose that the initial state may not involve functional categories: that is, adopt weak continuity views. Do either of them make such a claim from a 'bootstrapping' perspective? It is not clear that they do. Vainikka and Young-Scholten (1998: 18) argue that of the possible core projections that constitute clauses in mature grammars – CP, IP and VP – L2 learners initially analyse utterances 'as consisting of the smallest possible subtree consistent with the data'. This seems to imply that *by hypothesis* L2 learners' early grammars only project VP, and not that the absence of functional projections is a consequence of how learners perceive input. In other words, learners impose a VP analysis on L2 input, whether there is any evidence for functional categories in that input or not. Moreover, the strictly circumscribed influence of the L1 that Vainikka and Young-Scholten assume – only lexical projections are L1-influenced, functional projections are not – suggests that they regard the early lexical phase as an internal feature of the grammar: L2 learners transfer the L1 properties of Vs, Ns, As and Ps as the starting point, prior to contact with the L2.

'Modulated structure building', as it has been formulated up to now, is rather ambivalent about the relation between the syntactic module and the lexicon. It proposes that initial-state L2 grammars consist in principle of lexical projections, but that functional projections can be established early if there is appropriate evidence; this is consistent with the 'bootstrapping' variant of weak continuity. However, in those cases discussed in earlier chapters where functional categories appear early – for example, the projection of Infl to host thematic verbs moved over negation in L2 French (section 3.6) – their appearance is not driven by the acquisition of morphemes belonging to Infl. Rather, the selectional requirements of the sentential negator *(ne) pas* in French force thematic verbs to raise above Neg to an underspecified Infl category, present in the derivation only to host the moved thematic verb. But this seems to presuppose that Infl is established in a 'structural template' which is generated by the syntax just in order to provide a position for a thematic verb to move to when a sentential negator is present. Infl in this case is not established as the result of a learner noticing a morpheme in the input which she assigns to the category Infl, and stores in the lexicon. However, as in the case of the status of subjects, recent proposals in linguistics about the relation between functional categories and overt functional morphology offer a way of resolving this problem. I discuss these proposals in section 8.3.2.

8.3.2 Strong continuity and 'full access' accounts of the initial state

'Full access' theories of the initial state like those of Schwartz and Sprouse (1994, 1996) and Epstein et al. (1996, 1998) not only assume that all lexical and functional categories are available in the initial state, but propose that they are also *present* in the L2 grammar (transferred from the L1 according to Schwartz and

Sprouse; provided by UG according to Epstein et al.: a strong continuity view).[2] They also appear to adopt a 'structural template' conception of the function of syntax. For example, Epstein et al. (1998: 64), discussing Vainikka and Young-Scholten's claim that CP is absent in the early L2 German of their informants because the complementizer *dass* is absent, conclude that 'it is altogether possible that the absence of the complementizer *dass* in some of the utterances of the L2 learners in the Vainikka and Young-Scholten data . . . is due simply to the failure to acquire the lexical entry'. This seems to draw a clear distinction between items in the lexicon and phrase markers generated by the syntax, suggesting a 'structural template' view. Schwartz (1998), assuming both a full access to UG and a full transfer of L1 syntactic properties view of the initial state ('the starting point [for the L2 grammar is] the entirety of the L1 grammar' (1998: 36)) also appears to adopt a position compatible with a syntax which forms structural templates:

> Can the absence of verbal inflection and overt complementizers be considered sufficient for concluding that the *categories* Infl and C themselves are non-existent? It seems equally plausible to say that the functional categories are indeed there – and even fully specified as in the L1 grammar – but just not overtly filled . . . initially. (1998: 44)

What kinds of evidence might support claims that both lexical and functional categories are present in the initial state L2 grammar? Interestingly, because 'full access' accounts seem to require a 'structural template' view of the syntax–lexicon relation, some of the same evidence that 'minimal trees' and 'modulated structure building' would treat as 'noise' is regarded as supporting evidence. Vainikka and Young-Scholten (1998: 22–3) argue that nine of their Korean, Turkish and Romance-language-speaking L2 learners of German are still at a 'lexical projection' phase of development because:

(a) They only produce correct subject–verb agreement on thematic verbs in 11% to 36% of cases (depending on the individual).
(b) They rarely raise thematic verbs over adverbs and the sentential negator.
(c) Only five out of the nine informants produce tokens of auxiliaries and modals, and do so infrequently.

Nevertheless, in all these cases there is *some* overt evidence consistent with the presence of functional categories. Although 'full access' theories do not require that learners have acquired overt morphology to have functional categories in their grammars, the fact that they have is support for the position. More generally, if we reconsider the studies discussed over the course of the book, it is difficult to find cases where either overt morphology or evidence for movement of constituents to functional categories is entirely absent from initial state grammars; and this is expected if functional categories are present in the initial state.

Is it possible, then, to make a reasoned choice between theories which assume weak continuity, 'bootstrapping' or strong continuity as candidates for providing the best explanation of the initial state? On one level one might point to the theoretical problems associated with the 'structural template' conception of how the syntax operates: i.e. duplication of categorial information between the lexicon and the syntax, and difficulties in dealing with adjuncts. If strong continuity theories presuppose a 'structural template' view, then weak continuity and 'bootstrapping' theories might be preferred over them because they assume the 'lexical array' view which avoids such problems. Against this, however, is the fact that strong continuity is the simplest assumption one can make about the initial state grammar and does not require an additional explanation for why some categories and projections are at first absent. Moreover, recent proposals by Chomsky (1995) about the relation between functional categories and the overt morphology which realizes them, renders strong continuity theories fully consistent with a 'lexical array' view of the syntax–lexicon relation. If Chomsky's proposals are correct, strong continuity theories of the L2 initial state not only make the simplest assumption but can also claim that functional categories are present in the lexicon in the absence of overt morphological exponents of those categories.

Contrary to what we have assumed up to now, Chomsky has argued that inflectional morphology is not associated with substantive categories as part of syntactic derivations; rather, the association between inflections and substantive categories takes place in the lexicon. Inflections are therefore separate from the functional categories which determine their interpretation. To illustrate, verbal inflections like third person {-s} or past tense {-ed} in English are associated directly with the verb in the lexicon. (There are different ways in which this association could be achieved which will not be of concern here.) So, the lexical entry for an ordinary regular verb like *walk* has a number of morphological variants: {walk}, {walk + s$_{+tense, -past, 3ps}$}, {walk + ed$_{+tense, +past}$}, and so on. Functional categories essentially consist of sets of abstract syntactic features whose function is to 'check' that inflected substantive categories which appear in syntactic derivations are the correct ones. To continue the illustration, Infl in a particular derivation might have the features [$_{Infl}$ +tense, +past, V] and in another the features [$_{Infl}$ +tense, −past, 3ps, V]. The purpose of Infl now is to 'check' that the inflected verbs which the syntax takes from the lexicon to construct a derivation match the features of Infl. So, if the syntax constructs derivations like (3a) and (3b) (simplified) they will be grammatical because the features of Infl and V match (the derivation 'converges' in Chomsky's terms):

3a   [$_{IP}$ John [$_{Infl}$ +tense, +past, V] [$_{VP}$ [$_V$ {walk + ed$_{+tense, +past}$}]]]

  b   [$_{IP}$ John [$_{Infl}$ +tense, −past, 3ps, V] [$_{VP}$ [$_V$ {walk + s$_{+tense, -past, 3ps}$}]]]

By contrast, if the syntax constructs a derivation like (4), there is a clash between the feature that Infl must have to check the third person plural feature of the subject, and the feature it needs to check the third person singular inflection on the verb:

4 $*[_{IP} [They_{3p \ plur} [_{Infl} +tense, -past, 3p \ plur, V] [_{VP} [_V \{walk + s_{+tense, -past, 3ps}}]]]]$

The clash of features renders the derivation ungrammatical (it 'crashes' in Chomsky's terms).

One of the interesting consequences of this account is that 'affix lowering', which until now we have regarded as a major property of English syntax, and thematic verb raising to 'pick up' the inflections of Infl as in French, are no longer possible grammatical operations. Instead, in all languages that have verb morphology, this is licensed by the matching of features between Infl and the inflected verb. The difference between English and French is that thematic verbs in French must raise to have their inflections checked, while thematic verbs in English do not raise – their inflections are checked where they are, in the VP. What we have been calling 'strong inflections' in French and 'weak inflections' in English up to now are, on this account, strong and weak 'features' of Infl.

Given this conception, the presence of functional categories in the lexicon with null phonological content is expected – their main purpose is to check that the features of inflected substantive categories match the requirements of the derivation.[3] This solves one of the problems that the 'bootstrapping' view of 'modulated structure building' gives rise to in early L2 grammars. If functional categories with abstract features and null phonological content are normal in the lexicon, then it is not necessary for L2 learners to acquire overt morphology belonging to those categories to establish the presence of a functional category. Evidence of thematic verb raising above Neg in L2 French could trigger the establishment of Infl in the lexicon; i.e. the movement of lexical constituents to functional positions is just as likely to trigger the establishment of a functional category in the lexicon as overt morphology.

But if this is accepted, it undermines the rationale for weak continuity or 'bootstrapping' views of the initial state. If it is normal for functional categories stored in the lexicon to have no overt phonological exponent, it is just as conceivable that the lexicon in initial-state grammars contains both lexical and functional categories, the functional categories having little or no phonological content, even where the same categories in the target language do have such content. This makes it very difficult to imagine what kind of empirical evidence might distinguish between a 'bootstrapping' view of the initial-state lexicon, which primarily contains lexical categories and only admits that functional categories are present where the complement selectional requirements of lexical categories provide triggering evidence, and a 'full access' view of the initial-state lexicon, where a full set of lexical and functional categories are present, even though there may be no language-specific morphological or syntactic distributional evidence for them.

Since overt morphological and syntactic distributional evidence are no longer required, 'bootstrapping' is unnecessary. But another problem now arises. If empirical evidence is unnecessary for the initial-state grammar to construct derivations involving a full set of categories and features, the 'full access' claim is unfalsifiable; we have no way of testing for the presence of functional categories in the initial state.

8.3.3   Summary of section 8.3

- Although, a priori, strong continuity might be the simplest assumption to make about initial-state L2 grammars (all lexical and functional categories needed for the construction of a mature grammar are already present in the grammar), there may be a 'learnability' advantage for learners in constructing initial grammars which consist primarily of lexical categories and their projections: they provide a foothold into the undifferentiated continuum of L2 sounds (or orthographic symbols) enabling learners to 'bootstrap' their way into an L2 grammar. If the syntax constructs derivations by merging arrays of lexical items (and not by constructing a separate 'structural template' into which lexical items are inserted), once lexical categories have been acquired, the grammar can partially parse new input, reducing the volume of what is unknown, and reducing the acquisition task in proportion.
- An argument that may be made against early lexical-projection-based grammars is the presence of subjects; if these are located in the specifier of IP, as we had been assuming before, then IP must be present. However, acceptance of the more recent proposal that subjects are initially generated in a VP-internal position eliminates this problem.
- 'Minimal trees' appears not to be compatible with a 'bootstrapping' account, since functional categories are initially absent by hypothesis. 'Modulated structure building' is compatible with a 'bootstrapping' view, if it is accepted that both overt morphology and syntactic distributional evidence can trigger the establishment of functional categories in the lexicon; the latter is possible if a 'feature checking' view of the role of functional categories is adopted.
- 'Full access' theories of initial state L2 grammars are incompatible with a 'bootstrapping' view because they assume that lexical and functional categories are present independently of evidence for such categories in the target language input. Since it is not clear what empirical evidence would distinguish 'modulated structure building' from 'full access' under a 'feature checking' view of functional categories (given the current state of our knowledge) 'full access' theories should be preferred on conceptual grounds because they make the simplest assumption: strong continuity between initial- and final-state grammatical knowledge. However, since no overt morphological or syntactic

distributional evidence is required to justify the presence of functional categories in initial-state L2 grammars, 'full access' theories are themselves difficult to falsify.

More Advanced Discussion

8.4   Issues concerning transitional-state L2 grammars

Section 8.4 considers what may give rise to change in L2 learners' mental grammars, and why their productions are characterized by optionality. I discuss the significance that different theories accord to overt morphology and the properties of the L1 in triggering change. It is argued that there is a connection between the significance accorded to overt morphology in L2 development, and the view that a theory takes of how modules of the language faculty function in development.

8.4.1   Two aspects of transitional-state grammars in need of explanation

Two of the questions raised by transitional-state grammars in need of answers are: what causes development, and why are transitional-state grammars characterized by optionality (the use of two or more constructions or forms when the target language has only one)? The various theories of the developmental problem we have considered share some assumptions about how to explain development and optionality, but differ on others. All theories appear to assume that development is the effect of conflict between the derivations that the current grammar is capable of generating and properties of the L2 input which cannot be accommodated within those derivations. This gives rise to internal UG-constrained change. It is what Schwartz (1999) has called 'failure driven' development: when the grammar fails to 'parse' (that is, 'assign a structural description to') the input, a new category, or a new specification of an existing category, is established. Most theories also appear to assume that one kind of trigger for internal change is conflict between word order in the input and the word order determined by the current grammar. ('Valueless features' does not make this assumption, however – see below.) For example, most theories would assume that when L2 speakers of German move from a basic OV grammar to a VO grammar (as in the data of Vainikka and Young-Scholten, 1994, 1996a, 1996b) this is a consequence of learners noticing that the surface distribution of verb and object in German main clauses conflicts with the OV derivations their early grammars generate (although theories disagree about what effect this change has on the grammar). By contrast, theories differ in the significance they attach to the evidence provided by overt morphemes belonging to functional categories in triggering development (whether free forms or bound forms), and the influence that the L1 has on development. They also differ in what they regard as giving rise to optionality.

8.4.2 Theories which highlight the significance of overt morphology in transitional-state grammars

For 'minimal trees', the initial-state L2 grammar consists just of lexical projections, by hypothesis, as we have seen. Development is the introduction into the grammar of functional categories when learners observe that the lexically based initial-state grammar cannot parse all the input. 'Minimal trees' appears to assume that learners first notice failure to parse in relation to syntactic distributional properties and free morphemes instantiating functional categories in the L2; the noticing of parsing failure in relation to inflections comes later. For example, in the case of Korean, Turkish and Romance-language-speaking learners of German, Vainikka and Young-Scholten argue that when they notice that surface VO order in main clauses conflicts with the OV orders generated by their initial-state grammars, this syntactic distributional information triggers the establishment of a functional projection above VP for the verb to move to. They call this an underspecified Finite Phrase (FP):

5   $[_{VP}\ OV] \rightarrow [_{FP}\ V_i\ [_{VP}\ O\ t_i]]$

In the acquisition of English as an L2, they argue (1994, 1998) that learners move from VP-based derivations to FP-based ones when they notice that the free morphemes copula *be* and auxiliary *be* cannot be parsed by their grammars, for example:

6   $[_{VP}\ she\ singing] \rightarrow [_{FP}\ she\ 's_i\ [_{VP}\ t_i\ singing]]$

The functional category initially established in both cases is an FP, rather than an IP, because 'the learner at this stage has not yet determined exactly which features are represented in the F[inite] position' (1998: 27). Having established FP, when learners notice that inflections cannot be parsed by the current FP-based grammar, this triggers the more detailed specification of F to include features for tense, person, number, etc.; i.e. F becomes Infl.

L1 influence, according to 'minimal trees', only affects the initial lexical projection phase. The development of functional projections is triggered by overt distributional/morphological evidence and is uninfluenced by the properties of L1 functional categories. This suggests that 'minimal trees' has a 'lexical array' view of how the grammar operates in the initial state, which switches to a 'structural template' view once functional projections emerge. The dichotomy in L1 influence can then be explained if it is supposed that L1 influence is essentially lexical; entries in the L2 lexicon are potentially influenced by features of cognate entries in the L1 lexicon. 'Minimal trees' can now draw a distinction between properties of lexical entries (L1-influenced) and the structure of phrase markers (not L1-influenced).

This radical distinction that 'minimal trees' draws between lexical projections and functional projections is consistent with the explanation that Vainikka and Young-Scholten offer for optionality. Optionality is the effect of 'competing grammars' within the same individual: 'the grammar of an earlier stage *competes* with the grammar of a later stage, and signs of both stages can be observed in the data' (1996a: 13). Here the idea seems to be that the syntax alternates between constructing a phrase marker from items in the lexicon and producing a template, or alternates between different structural templates.

'Modulated structure building' shares with 'minimal trees' the assumption that both syntactic distributional information and overt morphology are significant triggers for development. However, 'modulated structure building' differs because it assumes that the initial state consists of lexical projections not by hypothesis, but for learnability reasons ('bootstrapping'). Development occurs by the addition of new items to the lexicon – not only new items belonging to substantive categories like N, V, A, but new items belonging to functional categories (detected in the input either from syntactic distributional evidence or overt morphological evidence) – or by changing the specification of existing lexical items (again from evidence in the input). Since the assumption is that the syntactic module is an invariant component of the language faculty, operating the same way whatever the language, only the addition of new functional items to the L2 lexicon (or new specifications of existing functional items) will give rise to new kinds of derivation. If the L1 influences the L2 through association between cognate entries in the lexicons for each language, this would explain not only why L1 influence affects both lexical and functional categories, but also why the L1 only becomes influential at appropriate points of development. Consider an example discussed in section 2.8. The fact that Spanish has subject–verb agreement, while Japanese does not, does not appear to affect the development of Spanish and Japanese learners' knowledge of English verb morphology until agreement begins to be acquired. At that point Spanish speakers have a considerable advantage. This is explicable if L1 influence occurs only when the person and number features of Infl begin to be specified.

Whereas 'minimal trees' proposes that learners establish (initially underspecified) functional categories first on the basis of syntactic distributional information and free functional morphemes, and only later establish other functional properties on the basis of bound functional morphemes, with 'modulated structure building' we were led to the view that learners represent functional categories and their features first on the basis of the most local dependencies. They acquire features which determine less local dependencies progressively. Local head–complement relations (such as copula + complement, auxiliary *be* + V-*ing*, *the* + NP) are represented before non-local relations (like tense binding, *wh*-phrase binding of variables, definiteness binding of articles), which are represented before some kinds of specifier–head relation (like subject–verb agreement). Under the 'lexical array' view, this means that *lexical entries* encoding local head–complement relations are stored in the lexicon before lexical entries encoding non-local relations, which in turn are stored before lexical entries encoding specifier–head relations.

However, the notion of 'locality' in 'modulated structure building' is vague. It is currently not clear if it can be defined formally in terms of natural classes within the grammar; e.g. whether the early emergence of copula *be* and the triggering of Infl in English, the early emergence of *the* and the triggering of D in English, and the acquisition of Neg and the triggering of Infl in French can be deemed to involve the same kind of local relation. Alternatively, the particular functional morphemes which appear early in L2 acquisition may reflect another kind of 'bootstrapping', where learners could in principle establish, say, subject–verb agreement relations from early on, but do not do so in L2 English because the 3rd person -*s* is low in perceptual prominence. One should note, though, that if the empirical observation is correct that morphemes realizing different kinds of syntactic relation emerge consistently in L2 grammars at different points of development, explaining such developmental patterns is a problem facing every theory of transitional state grammars, and not just 'modulated structure building'.

Optionality has not been considered within the 'modulated structure building' theory up to now, which offers no obvious mechanism for handling it. One possibility is that it is a consequence of the way in which inflected substantive categories are stored in the lexicon. To illustrate, consider the point at which L2 learners of English begin to notice (unconsciously) that past tense morphology in the input fails to be parsed by the current grammar. They may begin then to store forms in the lexicon like {walk + {ed}}, {sang = {sing + past}}. On the 'lexical array' view, this would necessarily trigger the specification of Infl as having the features [+tense, +past] because these are required by UG to license the past-tense inflections on the verbs (through 'checking'). However, learners may not yet have learned the fact that other verbs must be similarly inflected for past tense. So although Infl is now specified for [+tense, +past] when a sentence refers to past events, verbs selected from the lexicon will not necessarily have inflected past tense forms. Verbs will appear to inflect optionally for past tense in the productions of L2 learners. (For a similar account of optionality in the context of 'full access' theories, see section 8.4.3.)

'Valueless features' in its original version (Eubank 1993/94), and in contrast to 'minimal trees' and 'modulated structure building', appears to incorporate no specific theory of development. Learners notice overt morphology in L2 input which is not parsed by the current grammar, and this causes features of functional categories to become specified. But in principle different learners could notice different morphemes at different times. To explain systematic patterns across learners in the development of morphology, 'valueless features' would have to appeal to the frequency of particular morphemes in the input, or some notion of phonological salience, as in 'minimal trees'. In more recent work (1996), where Eubank allows for the possibility that the initial state is characterized by lexical projections, the theory of development becomes indistinguishable from that of 'minimal trees'.

On the other hand, the explanation of optionality is the main goal of 'valueless features'. The inertness of the features of functional categories, it is claimed, causes learners not to know whether constituents raise to those functional categories or not, or whether substantive categories are inflected or not. And this persists through developmental stages until full overt morphological paradigms are acquired. At that point the features of functional categories which check inflected substantive categories are fixed and optionality should cease. (Although for a recent variant of this theory claiming that the 'strength' features of functional categories which control movement give rise to permanent optionality, see section 8.5.)

There are, however, some empirical problems for this account. As Schwartz (1999) notes, any evidence of L1 influence on functional categories in initial or transitional states, or any evidence of lack of optionality involving functional categories, would be difficult to reconcile with 'valueless features'. She cites the study of Parodi et al. (1997) discussed in section 6.4.3, where speakers of Romance languages and speakers of Korean and Turkish are compared in their acquisition of the adjective–noun order of German. If the 'valueless features' theory is correct, speakers of both Romance languages and Korean/Turkish would initially be expected to allow optional Adj–N/N–Adj orders in German. This is because it is assumed that a 'strength' feature of Num determines the possibility of N raising. This feature should be inert, so speakers will not know whether raising is possible or not. However, the study shows that there was only one token of N–Adj order out of 205 cases of adjective–noun combinations in the productions of the Korean and Turkish speakers (i.e. less than 0.5%). By contrast tokens of N–Adj order were found in the productions of the Romance speakers in proportions ranging from 13% to 37.5%. This suggests that the extent to which optionality is present in initial-state/transitional state grammars is affected by features of functional categories in the L1, contrary to what 'valueless features' predicts. Similarly, the robust evidence we considered in section 5.7.2 for the contrast in the acquisition of obligatory subjects in English between speakers of Chinese-type languages and Greek-type languages (the former seem to acquire obligatory subjects from very early on, while the latter allow optional null subjects for a considerable period) should not occur according to 'valueless features'. If the choice between null subjects and obligatory subjects is deter-mined by a licensing feature belonging to Infl, both groups should show optionality until they have acquired the agreement paradigm in English.

8.4.3   Theories which question the significance of overt morphology in transitional-state grammars

Proponents of 'full access' theories of L2 syntactic competence – whether they assume transfer of L1 properties as Schwartz and Sprouse (1996) and Grondin and White (1996) do, or whether they do not, as in Epstein et al. (1996, 1998) – have highlighted a potential problem for 'minimal trees', 'modulated structure building' and 'valueless features' in the role they attribute to overt morphology in triggering development. They point out that L2 speakers are not only required to detect overt morphology in the input, in order to trigger the introduction of functional categories/functional features into their L2 grammars, but implicitly make the stronger claim that such categories/features are not established *until speakers show significant productive use of that morphology* in their utterances. This is in fact true. For example, Vainikka and Young-Scholten (1994) require that L2 learners of German use subject–verb agreement morphology in 60% or more of their utterances before they allow that IP has been projected (or rather 'AgrP' in their account). Before the 60% 'productive use' criterion is reached, 'minimal trees' claims that learners have an unspecified F(inite) P(hrase), and that tense and agreement morphology appearing on verbs is just 'noise'. Similarly, with 'modulated structure building' there is an implicit assumption that use of morphemes in production is the criterion by which functional categories or their features are deemed to be established. The objections that supporters of 'full access' theories raise are, firstly, that whatever proportion of use is chosen as the criterion for marking the emergence of a functional category or feature in the grammar, it will be arbitrary; secondly, that the use of overt morphology in production is not necessarily a reliable indicator of underlying competence: 'When categories fail to show up in production data, one should be wary of concluding that they are altogether absent' (Grondin and White 1996: 30).

While these are valid points, it is nevertheless the case that there appears to be robust, cross-learner systematicity in the appearance over time of syntactic distributional/morphological properties in L2 speakers' productive use of the L2, as we have seen in earlier chapters. Some properties are used earlier and more frequently than others by all speakers. Any full theory of transitional-state L2 grammatical knowledge needs to explain these developmental disjunctions in production. 'Minimal trees' and 'modulated structure building' attempt to do so by assuming that all modules of the language faculty are available for grammar building and are functioning normally. But the construction of fully target-like derivations is not possible until overt evidence allows the establishment of the lexical entries and their features on which the modules operate; and the detection of these is controlled by perceptual factors.

'Full access' theories assume that all categories and features required for fully grammatical derivations are present in the lexicon from the outset, and just not mapped onto the right morphological/phonological material yet. Given this, two properties of development would be expected to follow: (a) minimal exposure to samples of the L2 should be sufficient to establish the appropriate triggering of morphological/phonological material onto categories and features; i.e. a long period of development would be unexpected; (b) individuals would vary one from another in developmental profiles depending on the particular samples of language each has been exposed to; e.g. one learner might encounter agreement morphology before tense morphology, while another encounters tense morphology before agreement morphology. If categories and features are already present in the lexicon, it would be expected that agreement would appear before tense in the first speaker's productions, and tense before agreement in the productions of the second.

Since most 'full access' theories recognize the need to explain cross-learner systematicity in the development of L2 production ability, they typically claim that one (or more) of the non-syntactic modules of the language faculty is not operating normally in SLA.[4] An illustration of this kind of 'full access' account of developmental disjunctions in production is provided in a recent analysis by Lardiere (1998a, 1998b) of the grammatical competence of an L1 Chinese-speaking near native speaker of English. Lardiere's informant – Patty – had arrived in the United States at the age of 22, and was recorded in informal conversational situations after ten years of continuous residence, and twice more eight-and-a-half years later. During this period she obtained BA and MA degrees at US universities, and between the first and second/third recordings her immersion in English was near total, including marriage to a native speaker. So the amount of naturalistic exposure to English she had had was considerable. Lardiere investigated in particular Patty's use, on obligatory occasions, of nominative Case-marked pronouns (*she, I, we*, etc.), whether she raised thematic verbs over negative *n't* and VP adverbs, her use of past-tense morphology, and her use of the 3rd person present singular inflection -*s*. The results are given in table 8.1, where sample 1 represents tokens collected after 10 years of residence, and samples 2 and 3 represent tokens collected after 18-and-a-half years of residence.

These results show that in her use of correct nominative Case-marked pronouns and in not raising thematic verbs, Patty was already performing in a native-like way at the first sampling after ten years of residence. In the case of past tense, however, she fails to mark verbs on around two-thirds of required occasions, and the appropriate 3rd person -*s* on thematic verbs is almost entirely absent from her productions. This shows a striking developmental disjunction in the productive

Table 8.1 Proportions of correct use on obligatory occasions of four grammatical properties by an advanced L2 speaker of English

Sample	Correct nominative Case	Tokens of thematic V raising over Neg	over Adv
1	49/49 (100%)	0/42 (0%)	0/27 (0%)
2	378/378 (100%)	0/46 (0%)	1/77 (1.3%)
3	76/76 (100%)	0/24 (0%)	0/18 (0%)

Sample	Correct past-tense morphology	Correct 3ps morphology (on thematic verbs)
1	24/69 (34.8%)	2/42 (4.8%)
2	191/548 (34.9%)	0/4 (0%)
3	46/136 (33.8%)	1/22 (4.5%)

Source: Based on Lardiere 1998a, 1998b

use of the Case-assigning and strength features of Infl, compared with tense and agreement morphology.

The point that Lardiere makes is that if one used Vainikka and Young-Scholten's criteria for acquisition, it could be proposed, on the basis of Patty's performance on overt morphology, that she has not acquired Infl. Yet her performance in correctly using nominative Case-marked pronouns indicates that Infl must be present (recall that nominative Case is assigned by Infl); and her performance in (correctly) not raising thematic verbs suggests that she must know that Infl has a 'weak' feature in English. So Lardiere's claim is that Patty has acquired all the appropriate abstract parametrized features associated with English Infl. But she clearly has considerable, and long-term, problems in producing appropriate inflectional morphology in English. This leads Lardiere to argue: '[that] as L2 acquisition proceeds . . . the courses of syntactic and morphological development are independent; that the mapping between them is indirect, and that it may be this mapping itself – in the morphology or PF [= phonological] component – which is imperfectly acquired' (1998a: 2).

So on this account the developmental disjunction found in Patty's productive use of Case-marked pronouns and no thematic verb movement on the one hand, and tense- and agreement-inflected verbs on the other, is the effect of the morphological (or phonological) modules failing to function normally to map lexical entries, fully specified with appropriate abstract features, onto overt phonological forms in English.

Another 'full access' proposal argues that the morphological module may fail to associate substantives successfully with their inflections in the first place (in contrast to Lardiere's account which assumes that the association has occurred). This is an argument developed by Prévost and White (2000) who treat optionality in the productions of L2 speakers as a problem of selecting the appropriately inflected item from the lexicon. Prévost and White looked at longitudinal production data collected in interviews with two L1 Arabic-speaking learners of L2 French, and two Romance-language-speaking L2 learners of German. The French data were collected as part of the European Science Foundation project on L2 acquisition by adult immigrants (Perdue 1993). Subjects were interviewed from a year after arrival in France roughly every month over a three-year period. The German data were collected as part of the ZISA project (Clahsen et al. 1983) where interviews began roughly three months after arrival in Germany and continued at regular intervals over two years.

Prévost and White found a lot of alternation between finite and non-finite verb forms over the period of data collection in contexts where native speakers would use only a finite verb form or a non-finite one; hence optionality. Crucially, though, this optionality was asymmetrical. While non-finite verb forms occurred both in non-finite and finite contexts, finite verb forms largely occurred only in finite contexts, and on the whole agreed appropriately with the subject. For example, the L2 learners of German produced utterances like (examples from Prévost and White):

7a   Er sagt (finite) der Herr   (Anna)
     He says the man
  b   Er kaufe (non-finite) ein Blume   (Anna)
     He buy a flower
  c   tausend ich nich können (non-finite) (Zita)
     thousand I not can

But they were very unlikely to produce a finite verb form in a non-finite position, for example following the negator in a main clause in the equivalent to (c) above:

7d   *tausend ich nich kann

This leads Prévost and White to adopt the following theory of morphology in their account of the L2 observations (a theory known as 'distributed morphology' (Halle and Marantz 1993) which is, interestingly, clearly formulated from a 'structural template' conception of the syntax–lexicon relation):

> For lexical insertion to take place, the features of the vocabulary item must be consistent with the features of the terminal node in the syntax where it is to be

inserted. While the features of a syntactic node will be fully specified, features of a lexical item may be partially specified (or underspecified), in that some features may be lacking. The features of the lexical item do not need to exactly match all the features of the hosting node: it is sufficient that they form a proper subset of the feature bundle of that node. (2000: 23)

This means that as the result of acquiring forms like *sagt*, Infl will be specified for [+tense, −past, 3p sing]. This specification is necessary to license the inflected form of the verb *sagen*, 'say'. But learners may not yet have acquired inflections corresponding to these features on other verbs. Until they do, substantive entries which are already in the lexicon will be selected as 'default' forms. Observe that this account is not incompatible with a 'modulated structure building' view of optionality, as discussed above.

Returning to the original problem which started this section: it is true that 'minimal trees' and 'modulated structure building' require significant morpho-syntactic evidence in the production data of L2 speakers to justify the claim that the underlying grammatical properties have entered L2 speakers' mental grammars. However, the advantage of this is that it allows both theories to give some account of systematic cross-learner developmental disjunctions, while maintaining that all modules of the language faculty are functioning normally. By contrast, 'full access' theories argue that evidence of distributional patterns/morphology in L2 speakers' productions under-represents their competence; UG-determined categories and features are present in their grammars throughout development, whether there is evidence in production data for them or not. However, to explain developmental systematicity 'full access' theories must propose that non-syntactic modules of the language faculty are not functioning normally. We see, then, that the theory of development a researcher adopts depends crucially on the significance attributed to certain types of performance data.

8.4.4 Summary of section 8.4

- All theories of transitional-state L2 grammars seem to assume that development is 'failure-driven' (Schwartz 1998): change occurs when the current grammar fails to parse L2 input. Theories differ in what effects they claim change has on learners' mental grammars.
- Most theories assume that syntactic distributional properties of the input can trigger change (but 'valueless features' does not). They differ in the role that overt morphology is assumed to play in giving rise to change. 'Minimal trees' and 'modulated structure building' claim that learners noticing overt functional morphemes in the input causes change through the addition of new categories/features to the lexicon. 'Valueless features' claims that change occurs when L2 speakers acquire complete morphological paradigms; at that point

optionality in the grammar should cease. 'Full access' theories argue that the full range of categories and features is present in the lexicon from the outset; L2 learners need to learn overt morphology only to map it onto already existing syntactic representations.

- 'Minimal trees' and 'modulated structure building' have an account for systematic cross-learner developmental disjunctions in production which maintains that all modules of the language faculty function normally. 'Full access' theories claim that developmental disjunctions in production are the result of one (or more) of the modules of the language faculty not functioning normally.

More Advanced Discussion

8.5 Issues concerning final-state L2 grammars

Section 8.5 asks whether the possibility of attaining target-like grammatical competence in an L2 is affected by a critical period. I explain what a critical period is, and how it might be interpreted in the context of the language faculty. Given the assumptions made about how the modules of the language faculty interact, if a critical period does affect UG it would have to affect features of functional categories in the lexicon. Not all researchers, however, accept this view.

8.5.1 A critical period for language acquisition?

One question which has been central in the debate between researchers about the nature of final-state L2 grammatical competence (when L2 speakers appear to show no further development – sometimes known as the 'steady state' or 'endstate') is the following:

> Is the possibility of acquiring target-like grammatical competence in a second language affected by a critical period? That is, are learners who are first exposed consistently to an L2 in early life more likely to achieve target-like competence than those who encounter the L2 in their teens or beyond?

Critical periods for the development of cognitive abilities appear to arise when there is interaction between innately determined, but unconfigured, brain cell structure and external stimuli; that is, a part of the brain is specifically designed for, say, vision, but for the neurons in that area to connect up, visual stimuli from the outside are required. So in mature humans the ability to interpret visual information coming from the eyes is partly the effect of dedicated brain structure, and partly the result of experience. The period during which experience can trigger the establishment of connections is often time-limited, and this is the 'critical period'. In the case of vision, the critical period appears to last from birth to around the age of six. Children not exposed to visual stimuli during this early period of life whose sight is restored later (e.g. through corneal transplants) sadly often do not recover the ability to see, although their eyes may be in working order.

Greenfield (1997: 114) provides a striking example of the impact that the critical period can have on the development of visual perception. An Italian child had one of his eyes bandaged for two weeks during infancy as treatment for a minor infection. The treatment cleared the infection, but apparently coincided with the period of development when connections were being fixed between nerves in the eyes and neurons in the visual area of the brain. Because one eye was covered, preventing visual stimuli reaching the brain from that eye, the connection was not fixed. When the bandage was removed, the boy was left with a healthy eye, but he couldn't 'see' anything through it because it was no longer connected to the brain. Because the critical period had passed, there was no possibility of re-establishing the connection.

One may ask why the brain should have evolved in such a way as to require critical periods in some domains (and in fact critical periods are not limited to humans, but found throughout the animal world for a variety of cognitive functions). One possible answer is that while in the mature state organisms require fixed and stable cognitive structures to enable them to survive in their particular environments, some flexibility in how those structures are established in early life allows the brain to adapt to local conditions. For example, it is known that in those who are born with normal auditory areas in the brain, but are deaf as the result of defects in the ears, the auditory areas take over some visual functions giving enhanced peripheral vision. (See Eubank and Gregg (1999) for discussion of critical periods in cases like these, and specifically in relation to language.)

If there is an area of the brain which has dedicated neural architecture for use in constructing mental grammars (the language faculty) but which needs to be exposed to external linguistic stimuli for grammatical knowledge to develop, it is conceivable that it too is subject to a critical period. If this part of the brain is not exposed to linguistic stimuli during early life, this might lead to difficulty or even impossibility in acquiring a grammar in later life. There is, in fact, evidence that delayed exposure to a first language may give rise to such problems (Curtiss 1988). However, because the conditions under which children are deprived of linguistic stimuli are often accompanied by other psychological or physical privations, it is difficult to separate the effects of each. For example, in a well-known case (Curtiss 1977; 1988) a child called Genie was isolated by a disturbed father between the ages of 20 months and 13 years 7 months, confined to a small bedroom, fed only infant food, and given little visual, tactile or auditory stimulation. When she was discovered she couldn't walk, chew or bite, and didn't speak. Genie subsequently failed to develop English normally. Whereas she acquired vocabulary, with knowledge of the selectional requirements of substantive categories, and was able to understand and produce sentences expressing propositions, as well as distinguish different types of question, she showed little productive use of grammatical morphemes, even after eight years. She produced sentences like *I like hear music ice cream truck; Like kick tyre Curtiss car* (Curtiss 1988). At the same time, Genie's general non-linguistic cognitive skills (spatial awareness, logical sequencing and drawing skills) developed considerably after she was discovered. It is possible, therefore, that a critical period for constructing a grammar is involved here, and Genie had gone beyond that critical period when she was discovered, making it impossible for her to acquire a full native-like grammar. On the other hand, it is also possible that the resources of the language faculty were potentially fully available, but her deprived childhood gave rise to other psychological problems affecting her ability to use them.

Deciding whether a critical period affects second language acquisition is even more difficult because there is already a language in place. Even if there is a critical period for first language acquisition, it could be argued that the establishment of an L1 triggers the neurological connections required for further language acquisition. Such a view of the critical period has been called the 'exercise hypothesis' (Johnson and Newport 1991; Bialystok 1997). By exercising the language faculty in early life, it remains active. At the same time, many older L2 learners do not appear to acquire the same competence as native speakers, even after long exposure to the language, which may suggest that there is a critical period affecting some aspects of the ability to construct mental grammars.

In discussion in previous chapters I have taken it as axiomatic that the principles of UG constrain grammar-building, even in second language acquisition which occurs in later life. This means that I have accepted that no critical period affects the principles of UG. Moreover, if the 'lexical array' view of the syntax–lexicon relation is adopted, the syntactic module is universally invariant in the way it operates. It is therefore not dependent on external stimuli to fix options and is unlikely to be subject to a critical period. The interpretive module of the language faculty – Logical Form – is also generally assumed to be universally invariant (Chomsky 1995). This means that if there is a critical period for second language acquisition, it would have to affect the features of lexical entries, or the morphological module, or the phonological module. Differences in accounts of non-native-speaker/native-speaker divergence have often been along these lines.

8.5.2 Differing views on a critical period for UG-determined knowledge in second languages

The 'no-parameter-resetting' claim of Tsimpli and Roussou (1991) discussed in section 5.5.3 is a claim that a critical period affects certain features of lexical entries: the features of functional categories which determine parametrized options. If the syntactic module is universally invariant, parametric differences between languages must be located in the feature values of functional categories stored in the lexicon, and which are selected as part of the 'lexical array' on which the syntax operates. For example, the parametric difference between English and Chinese in the fronting of *wh*-phrases (section 4.8.1) is a difference in the choice of values of the feature [wh] of an interrogative complementizer: English has chosen [+wh], which forces a *wh*-phrase to move overtly to satisfy feature checking, while Chinese has chosen [–wh], which does not force the *wh*-phrase to move overtly. Or consider the pro-drop parameter in Spanish and Greek-type languages. This is the effect of a feature of Infl which licenses *pro* in its specifier position (with concomitant identification by the person and number features) (section 5.5.1).

Tsimpli and Roussou's claim is that where speakers of such languages learn an L2 which does not have the features of C or Infl set in the same way, resetting is impossible. When learners become aware of properties of the input which their current L2 grammar cannot parse, they cannot change the L1 parameter setting, although they may analyse that input in ways which render it compatible with the L1 values. So Tsimpli and Roussou proposed that Greek speakers misanalyse English subject pronouns as either agreement inflections on the verb, or as sentential topics identifying the *pro* subject.

This kind of account can be extended to other areas where L2 learners who have developed advanced, and possibly final-state, grammars behave differently in performance tasks from native speakers. The divergence in performance on subjacency tests discussed in chapter 7 could be the effect of speakers whose L1s do not have overt *wh*-phrase movement having difficulty with the parametrized feature of C – [+wh] – which triggers movement in English. If speakers have not reset the parameter, but recognize that *wh*-phrases must appear in the specifier of CP, they may adopt a non-movement analysis where the *wh*-phrase is base-generated and binds a null pronoun.

The evidence we considered in chapter 7 also suggested another, but related possibility: that learners have available the parametric options allowed by UG, but cannot determine whether a different parameter setting from the one present in their L1 is correct or not. This would be consistent with Schachter's (1989) finding that some speakers of Korean appeared to have 'hit on' the right parameter setting for English, while the majority had not. A recent variant on the idea that beyond a critical period language learners are no longer able to decide which value of a parametrized feature of a functional category is the correct one can be found in Beck (1998a). Beck argues that the 'strength' of features associated with functional categories like Infl and Num which force substantive heads (V, N) either to raise or not, ceases to operate properly beyond a critical period, leaving learners in a permanent state of uncertainty about whether heads move or not:

The morphosyntactic features that require or prohibit [head] raising become impoverished during the course of maturation and this local impairment results in L2 grammars that effectively overgenerate (i.e. allow optional raising) when compared to mature, adult-state N[ative] L[anguage] grammars. (1998a: 316)

The difference between this account and Tsimpli and Roussou's is that it postulates a state of permanent uncertainty in the L2 learner's grammar about the appropriate value of a parametrized feature (whereas in Tsimpli and Roussou's account learners retain the L1 value and cannot access the L2 value), and it is restricted to 'strength' – i.e. it is extremely local.

Many researchers do not accept, however, that a critical period exists for the acquisition of UG-determined knowledge, either in relation to the principles *or* the parameters, and propose alternative explanations for why adult L2 speakers with final-state grammars might differ on performance tasks from native speakers. Schwartz and Sprouse (1996) and Schwartz (1999) argue that adult L2 learners have full access to the range of options allowed by UG, but attribute possible final-state performance differences to the initial full transfer of the grammatical properties of the L1. The presence of L1 features in the grammar, including parametrized features fixed in specific ways, may make it difficult for learners to interpret positive evidence from target-language input for different settings. In other words, the triggering properties of linguistic stimuli which lead to the appropriate setting of parameter values in first language acquisition may be hindered in second language acquisition by the presence of already established knowledge structures. Consider a study discussed by Schwartz (1999), and which figured in exercise 2 of chapter 4: the acquisition of L2 French by L1 speakers of Dutch (Hulk 1991).

Modern French is a language which is not verb second, so that when a non-subject is moved to the front, the verb cannot move into second position:

8a   Jean mangeait des fraises hier
     Jean eat-Imperf some strawberries yesterday
     'Jean ate strawberries yesterday'
 b   Hier Jean mangeait des fraises
 c   *Hier mangeait Jean des fraises

Child L1 learners of French will never hear examples like (8c) and so will not construct a verb-second grammar. Dutch is a verb-second language like German, so that the equivalent sentences to those of (8) show a different distribution of grammaticality:

9a   Jan at aardbeien gisteren
     'Jan ate strawberries yesterday'

b *Gisteren Jan at aardbeien
c Gisteren at Jan aardbeien

Hulk gave a French grammaticality judgement task involving various grammatical and ungrammatical word orders to four groups of native speakers of
Dutch at different stages of learning, from beginners in secondary school to first
year majors in French at university. She found that the tendency to accept Dutch
word orders which are ungrammatical in French declined steadily with the proficiency of the groups, so that the university students rejected nearly all ungrammatical orders and accepted all possible French word orders. The one case where
the university students persistently allowed both Dutch and French word orders
involved sentences like (8b–c): 10% of responses accepted the (c)-type sentences.
In other words, they were allowing adverbials adjoined to IP as in (8b) and
adverbials moved to the specifier of CP to co-occur in their grammars. This kind
of co-occurrence, though, is a possibility allowed by UG. For example, it existed
(as Hulk points out) in Middle French (Adams 1987). Schwartz's argument is
that the initial presence in Dutch speakers' grammars for L2 French of a transferred verb-second property means that although positive evidence for adverbs
adjoined to IP is available from French, no positive evidence will tell them that
they cannot also have verb second, because UG allows this possibility. Thus
Dutch speakers are likely to differ from native speakers of French for reasons not
connected with a critical period for UG.

Other research which acknowledges that there are clear performance differences between adult L2 speakers with final-state grammars and native speakers
attributes those differences to non-syntactic properties of the language faculty.
Lardiere (1998a, 1998b) for example, whose study we discussed in section 8.4.3
in relation to transitional-state grammars argues that the problem for Patty is in
mapping the abstract feature specifications of lexical items onto their morphological realizations. So whereas Infl has [+tense, +past, V] features and presumably checks a verb drawn from the lexicon with abstract past tense features {V
+tense, +past}, the problem arises in mapping these abstract features onto an
inflected verb form in the phonological module. Prévost and White (2000), whose
study was also discussed in section 8.4.3 argue that the problem is one of lexical
access – when the lexical array is selected for computation by the syntax, the
mechanism that performs this operation 'misses' the required inflected verb form,
and pulls out a stem or a default form.

Much current research into L2 final-state grammars is focusing on how to
obtain evidence to decide between these alternatives. For example, if it can be
shown that L2 speakers who were first immersed in the L2 beyond childhood can
acquire the syntactic consequences associated with a feature of a functional
category in the L2 which is either set differently from or not realized at all in the
L1, this would constitute evidence against the 'no-parameter-resetting' claim. But
it would be necessary to show that *all* the syntactic consequences have been

acquired; the acquisition of only some consequences would be insufficient. Even if it can be shown that all the syntactic consequences associated with a particular feature are part of an L2 speaker's mental grammar, this does not mean that all features with parametrized values are acquirable. It may be that some are subject to a critical period and some are not, raising interesting questions about what the function of a critical period may be. If it can be shown that there is no critical period affecting the parametric options made available by UG, then the question becomes why other operations of the language faculty, like the ability to map syntactic representations onto morphological forms or to access lexical items, should deteriorate in later L2 acquisition. Such questions promise some interesting empirical investigations over the next few years.

8.5.3 Summary of section 8.5

- A critical period arises where brain cells designed for a specific cognitive purpose need to interact with external stimuli during a certain period of an organism's life for appropriate connections to be established. It has been argued that a critical period exists for first language acquisition. It is not clear whether a critical period exists for second language acquisition; the 'exercise hypothesis' claims that the acquisition of an L1 triggers the neurological connections required for further language acquisition, hence there is no critical period for SLA.
- If there is a critical period affecting SLA, given a 'lexical array' view of the syntax–lexicon relation, there are only three areas of the language faculty which could be affected: the morphological module, the phonological module or the features of lexical entries. Other modules of the language faculty are invariant and do not depend on external stimuli to fix options.
- Theories about why L2 speakers with final-state grammars should diverge from native speakers in performance have differed in whether they claim that there is a critical period beyond which parametrized features of functional categories become inaccessible, or whether they claim that differences arise because learners have difficulty interpreting L2 input, mapping derivations onto morphological forms or accessing lexical items.

8.6 Summary of chapter 8

The main points made in chapter 8 are the following:

- Although there are a variety of ways in which the logical problem of second language acquisition could be addressed, the principles and parameters (P&P) version of UG was adopted because it offers the potential to advance our understanding of the nature of second language acquisition and human linguistic ability in concrete ways. At the same time, the P&P perspective has given rise to competing theories of the developmental problem: 'minimal trees', 'modulated structure building', 'valueless features' and 'full access to UG'. It was argued that these are products of different conceptions of how modules of the language faculty interact, and differing views of what are significant and insignificant aspects of L2 performance data (sections 8.1–8.2).

- A 'strong continuity' view of initial-state L2 grammars holds that they contain all the lexical and functional categories necessary to develop final-state grammars; a 'weak continuity' view holds that only some categories are present. A rationale was given for a weak continuity view in terms of learners 'bootstrapping' their way into representations for the L2 (section 8.3).

- L2 grammars undergo development when they fail to parse L2 input. 'Minimal trees', 'modulated structure building' and 'valueless features' argue that development is visible in performance data. In particular, where a surface syntactic or morphological property is not present in an L2 speaker's productions in some specifiable proportion, it is not yet represented underlyingly in the grammar. 'Full access' theories argue that L2 syntactic development is not necessarily linked to surface morphosyntactic realizations. L2 speakers may know more than they can produce (section 8.4).

- L2 researchers have adopted different approaches to explaining why the final-state L2 grammars of older learners may differ from those of native speakers. One view is that there is a critical period affecting the parametrized features of functional categories – options not instantiated in the L1 are difficult to access in second language acquisition. Another view is that because L1 properties are transferred into L2 grammars, this makes it difficult for learners to interpret L2 input appropriately. A third view is that L2 learners have difficulty either mapping syntactic representations onto morphological forms or accessing the lexicon.

8.7 Conclusion

The syntactic properties of natural languages are complex – so complex that the construction by linguists of a full explicit theory of the underlying principles and permissible language-specific variation is still some way off. Nevertheless, learners of second languages can develop unconscious knowledge of a good deal of that complexity, and do so in ways which are systematic and often independent of the L1s they speak or the conditions under which they acquire L2s. This is strongly suggestive of the involvement of 'an internal knowledge source' (Schachter 1990: 117). I have taken this knowledge source to be the language faculty, an innate biological endowment specific to human beings.

In its essentials, the hypothesis I have tried to develop proposes that in order to construct mental grammars, L2 learners need to detect physical exponents of lexical and functional categories present in the L2 input, and store a representation for those categories in their mental lexicons. Once they have done so, the language faculty uses the lexical entries to construct derivations within constraints imposed by UG. I have argued that the representation of categories in the lexicon is developmentally selective, so that not all possible categories present in the input are initially available in the learner's lexicon for computation; and I have also claimed that properties of L1 lexical entries may influence representations in the L2 lexicon throughout development. This line of argument has been based on patterns found in performance data. Other researchers disagree, arguing that performance data under-represent the richness of the grammatical knowledge that L2 speakers have, even in the earliest stages of development. They also disagree about the extent of L1 influence.

Where people start learning an L2 beyond childhood and apparently fail to develop the same ability to use grammatical knowledge as native speakers of the target language, I have suggested that this may be because certain parametrized features of functional categories are difficult to reset from the value present in the L1; either the L2 value is unavailable, or it is available but learners are unable to determine whether the L1 or L2 value is appropriate. Again, others disagree, suggesting that where divergence between native and non-native speakers occurs, it is not because of incomplete knowledge of parametrized features, but because of problems non-native speakers have in learning or using language-specific realizations of those features. In the first case the implicit assumption is that there is a critical period for the acquisition of input-determined options allowed by UG. In the second case the assumption is that there is no critical period, and the neural architecture of the language faculty is unaffected by physical changes in the brain which accompany growth, although the capacity to deploy the language faculty may change.

Controversies like these generate further empirical research to find evidence which may disconfirm one or other hypothesis. A consequence is that our understanding of the nature of L2 syntactic knowledge deepens, and issues become clearer. One of the reasons why work in this area is exciting is that it has only just begun, leaving many things to be discovered.

8.8 Exercises

Discussion topics

1. How do theories of L2 syntactic development differ in the importance they attach to the first language a person speaks?

2. What view have you formed of the role that functional categories (C, Infl, D, Num, and perhaps others) play in second language acquisition?

3. '[Adult L2 learners] progressively build an interlanguage grammar that resembles human language grammar and not some random concatenations of words' (Herschensohn 2000). Discuss.

4. 'The thesis that at least some invariant principles of the language organ remain active after the critical period appears to be a highly plausible one . . . On the other hand, the thesis that adults are capable of parameter fixing in the process of language acquisition after puberty . . . does not appear to be plausible' (Strozer 1994: 209). What evidence could you cite to support this position? What evidence could you cite to argue against it?

5. 'In SLA, there is often a confusion between competence (in the sense of underlying linguistic representation) and performance (use of that representation to understand and produce language). People often look at L2 performance, note that it differs from native speakers, and argue that this demonstrates essential defects in competence . . . But it is in fact possible that L2 learners' underlying competence is to some extent hidden by performance factors, such as the demands of processing or parsing' (White, forthcoming). Can you give examples of performance data which might hide L2 learners' underlying competence? Is it ever possible to use performance data as reliable evidence of underlying competence? Do you see any dangers in constructing theories of L2 development which do not directly predict performance?

6. 'It is perfectly reasonable for particular theories to discount or ignore certain supposed empirical findings in the field because they lie outside a theorist's domain of interest . . . Nevertheless, a theory must account for at least some of the major accepted findings within its scope if it is to be useful' (Long 1995). What kinds of observations about initial-, transitional- and final-state L2 grammars do you consider it important for a theory of L2 syntax to provide an explanation for?

8.9 Further reading

Three books are in preparation at the time of writing which deal in greater depth with issues raised in chapter 8: Herschensohn, J. 2000: *The Second Time Around: Minimalism and L2 Acquisition*. Amsterdam: John Benjamins; White,

L. Forthcoming: *Universal Grammar in the Second Language: From Initial to Steady State*. Cambridge: Cambridge University Press; Carroll, S. Forthcoming: *Input and Evidence: The Raw Material of Second Language Acquisition*. Amsterdam: John Benjamins.

Recent collections of research papers of relevance are Beck, M.-L. (ed.) 1998b: *Morphology and its Interfaces in Second Language Knowledge*. Amsterdam: John Benjamins; Klein, E. and Martohardjono, G. (eds) 1999: *The Development of Second Language Grammars: A Generative Approach*. Amsterdam: John Benjamins.

An exchange of views between proponents of 'minimal trees', 'valueless features' and 'full access' theories can be found in volume 12 (1) of the journal *Second Language Research* (1996), and in Flynn, S., Martohardjono, G. and O'Neil, W. (eds) 1998: *The Generative Study of Second Language Acquisition*. Mahwah, NJ: Lawrence Erlbaum Associates.

A collection which has recently appeared on the critical period is Birdsong, D. (ed.) 1999: *Second Language Acquisition and the Critical Period Hypothesis*. Mahwah, NJ: Lawrence Erlbaum Associates.

The main journal for research articles on L2 syntax from a UG perspective is *Second Language Research*, but articles can also often be found in *Studies in Second Language Acquisition*, *Language Acquisition* and *Language Learning*.

Notes

1 Up to now we have assumed that the specifier position of VP hosts verb-phrase adverbs like *often, quickly*, and so on. A more recent proposal is that the specifier of VP is where the subject of a clause is initially generated, with the subject moving to the specifier of IP subsequently (Koopman and Sportiche 1991). See section 8.3.1 for more discussion. If this is correct, the lexical entry for V would specify that it takes a DP specifier.

   Some linguists (for example Pesetsky 1982) have argued that the selectional properties of morphemes in the lexicon can be derived from their meaning. In the case in question, from the argument structure of the two verbs. The single argument of a verb like *cry* is converted into a syntactic specifier, while one of the two arguments of a verb like *hit* is converted into a syntactic specifier and the other into a syntactic complement.

2 It should perhaps be pointed out that although 'minimal trees' adopts a weak continuity view of the initial state, it is nevertheless a 'full access' theory because it assumes that L2 learners will eventually have full access to UG.

3 It is nevertheless the case that while a major purpose of the functional categories is to license inflections on substantive categories, there are some free morphemes which

instantiate the functional categories directly. For example, modal verbs in English like *will, can, may*, etc., appear to instantiate the features of Infl, and the verbal complements to these modals have no inflectional properties to be checked.

4   Paradoxically, this means that 'minimal trees' and 'modulated structure building' have a strong continuity view of the functioning of the language faculty (all modules functioning as they do in mature native speaker grammars), while 'full access' theories have a weak continuity view (some module(s) not functioning in the same way).

References

Abney, S. 1987: The English noun phrase in its sentential aspect. Unpublished doctoral dissertation, MIT.

Adams, M. 1987: Old French and the theory of pro-drop. *Natural Language and Linguistic Theory* 5, 1–32.

Adiv, E. 1984: Language learning strategies: the relationship between L1 operating principles and language transfer in L2 development. In R. Andersen (ed.).

Alexiadou, A. and Anagnostopoulou, E. 1998: Parametrizing Agr: word order, V-movement and EPP-checking. *Natural Language and Linguistic Theory* 16, 491–539.

Allan, D. 1992: *The Oxford Placement Test*. Oxford: Oxford University Press.

Andersen, R. 1978: An implicational model for second language research. *Language Learning* 28, 221–82.

Andersen, R. 1984: What's gender good for, anyway? In R. Andersen (ed.).

Andersen, R. (ed.) 1984: *Second Languages: A Cross-Linguistic Perspective*. Rowley, Mass.: Newbury House.

Aoun, J. and Li, Y. 1993: *Wh*-elements in situ: syntax or LF? *Linguistic Inquiry* 24, 199–238.

Atkinson, M. 1992: *Children's Syntax: An Introduction to Principles and Parameters Theory*. Oxford: Blackwell.

Bailey, N., Madden, C. and Krashen, S. 1974: Is there a 'natural sequence' in adult second language learning? *Language Learning* 24, 235–43.

Baker, M. 1988: *Incorporation: A Theory of Grammatical Function Changing*. Chicago: University of Chicago Press.

Balcom, P. 1997: Why is this happened? Passive morphology and unaccusativity. *Second Language Research* 13, 1–9.

Bardel, C. 1997: Negation in Swedish L2 learners of Italian. In L. Diaz and C. Pérez (eds), *Views on the Acquisition and Use of a Second Language: Proceedings of EUROSLA 7*, Barcelona: Universitat Pompeu Fabra.

Bazergui, N., Connors, K., Lenoble, M. and Majkrak, B. 1990: *Acquisition du français (L2) chez des adultes à Montréal*, 2 vols. Québec: Office de la langue française.

Beck, M.-L. 1997: Regular verbs, past tense and frequency: tracking down a potential source of NS/NNS competence differences. *Second Language Research* 13, 93–115.

Beck, M.-L. 1998a: L2 acquisition and obligatory head movement: English-speaking learners of German and the local impairment hypothesis. *Studies in Second Language Acquisition* 20, 311–48.

Beck, M.-L. (ed.) 1998b: *Morphology and its Interfaces in Second Language Knowledge*. Amsterdam: John Benjamins.

Belletti, A. 1988: The Case of unaccusatives. *Linguistic Inquiry* 19, 1–34.

Belletti, A. and Rizzi, L. (eds) 1996: *Parameters and Functional Heads: Essays in Comparative Syntax*. Oxford: Oxford University Press.

Bennett, S. and Progovac, L. 1998: Morphological status of reflexives in second language acquisition. In S. Flynn, G. Martohardjono and W. O'Neil (eds).

Bernstein, J. 1991: DPs in French and Walloon: evidence for parametric variation in nominal head movement. *Probus* 3, 101–26.

Besten, H. den 1983: On the interaction of root transformations and lexical deletive rules. In W. Abraham (ed.), *On the Formal Syntax of the Westgermania*, Amsterdam: John Benjamins.

Bialystok, E. 1997: The structure of age: in search of barriers to second language acquisition. *Second Language Research* 13, 116–37.

Bickerton, D. 1981: *Roots of Language*. Ann Arbor: Karoma Press.

Birdsong, D. 1989: *Metalinguistic Performance and Interlanguage Competence*. New York: Springer.

Birdsong, D. (ed.) 1999: *Second Language Acquisition and the Critical Period Hypothesis*. Mahwah, NJ: Lawrence Erlbaum Associates.

Bley-Vroman, R. 1990: The logical problem of foreign language learning. *Linguistic Analysis* 20, 3–49.

Braidi, S. 1999: *The Acquisition of Second Language Syntax*. London: Arnold.

Brown, R. and Hanlon, C. 1970: Derivational complexity and order of acquisition in child speech. In J. Hayes (ed.), *Cognition and the Development of Language*, New York: Wiley.

Cancino, H., Rosansky, E. and Schumann, J. 1978: The acquisition of English negatives and interrogatives by native Spanish speakers. In E. Hatch (ed.), *Second Language Acquisition: A Book of Readings*, Rowley, Mass.: Newbury House.

Cardinaletti, A. 1997: Subjects and clause structure. In L. Haegeman (ed.).

Carroll, S. forthcoming: *Input and Evidence: The Raw Material of Second Language Acquisition*. Amsterdam: John Benjamins.

Chaudron, C. and Parker, K. 1990: Discourse markedness and structural markedness: the acquisition of English noun phrases. *Studies in Second Language Acquisition* 12, 43–64.

Chomsky, N. 1957: *Syntactic Structures*. The Hague: Mouton.

Chomsky, N. 1965: *Aspects of the Theory of Syntax*. Cambridge, Mass.: MIT Press.

Chomsky, N. 1973: Conditions on transformations. In S. Anderson and P. Kiparsky (eds), *A Festschrift for Morris Halle*, New York: Holt, Rinehart and Winston.

Chomsky, N. 1977: *Essays on Form and Interpretation*. Amsterdam: Elsevier Publications.

Chomsky, N. 1981: *Lectures on Government and Binding*. Dordrecht: Foris.

Chomsky, N. 1982: *Some Concepts and Consequences of the Theory of Government and Binding*. Cambridge, Mass.: MIT Press.

Chomsky, N. 1986a: *Knowledge of Language*. New York: Praeger.

Chomsky, N. 1986b: *Barriers*. Cambridge, Mass.: MIT Press.

Chomsky, N. 1995: *The Minimalist Program*. Cambridge, Mass.: MIT Press.

Chomsky, N. 1998: Minimalist inquiries: the framework. *MIT Working Papers in Linguistics* 15, 1–56.

Cinque, G. 1990: *Types of A'-dependencies*. Cambridge, Mass.: MIT Press.

Clahsen, H. 1984: The acquisition of German word order: a test case for cognitive approaches to L2 development. In R. Andersen (ed.).

Clahsen, H. and Hong, U. 1995: Agreement and null subjects in German L2 development: new evidence from reaction-time experiments. *Second Language Research* 11, 57–87.

Clahsen, H., Meisel, J. and Pienemann, M. 1983: *Deutsch als Zweitsprache: Der Spracherwerb ausländischer Arbeiter.* Tübingen: Gunter Narr.

Clahsen, H. and Muysken, P. 1986: The availability of Universal Grammar to adult and child learners: a study of the acquisition of German word order. *Second Language Research* 2, 93–119.

Clark, E. 1985: The acquisition of Romance, with special reference to French. In D. Slobin (ed.), *The Cross-Linguistic Study of Language Acquisition*, vol 1, Hillsdale, NJ: Lawrence Erlbaum Associates.

Cole, P., Hermon, G. and Sung, L.-M. 1990: Principles and parameters of long-distance reflexives. *Linguistic Inquiry* 21, 1–22.

Cook, V. and Newson, M. 1996: *Chomsky's Universal Grammar.* Oxford: Blackwell.

Coppieters, R. 1987: Competence differences between native and near-native speakers. *Language* 63, 544–73.

Crain, S. and Lillo-Martin, D. 1999: *An Introduction to Linguistic Theory and Language Acquisition.* Malden, Mass.: Blackwell.

Cromer, R. 1991: *Language and Thought in Normal and Handicapped Children.* Oxford: Blackwell.

Culicover, P. 1997: *Principles and Parameters: An Introduction to Syntactic Theory.* Oxford: Oxford University Press.

Curtiss, S. 1977: *Genie: A Psycholinguistic Study of a Modern-Day 'Wild Child'.* New York: Academic Press.

Curtiss, S. 1988: The special talent of grammar acquisition. In L. Obler and D. Fein (eds), *The Exceptional Brain: Neuropsychology of Talent and Special Abilities*, New York: Guilford.

Davies, W. 1996: Morphological uniformity and the null subject parameter in adult SLA. *Studies in Second Language Acquisition* 18, 475–93.

Devitt, S. 1992: Form and function in the developing verb system of five learners of French as a second language. Unpublished doctoral dissertation, Trinity College Dublin.

Doughty, C. 1991: Second language instruction does make a difference: evidence from an empirical study of SL relativisation. *Studies in Second Language Acquisition* 13, 431–69.

Duffield, N. and White, L. 1999: Assessing L2 knowledge of Spanish clitic placement: convergent methodologies. *Second Language Research* 15, 133–60.

Dulay, H. and Burt, M. 1973: Should we teach children syntax? *Language Learning* 23, 245–58.

Dulay, H. and Burt, M. 1974: Natural sequences in child second language acquisition. *Language Learning* 24, 37–53.

Dulay, H., Burt, M. and Krashen, S. 1982: *Language Two.* Oxford: Oxford University Press.

DuPlessis, J., Solin, D., Travis, L. and White, L. 1987: UG or not UG, that is the question: a reply to Clahsen and Muysken. *Second Language Research* 3, 56–75.

Ellis, R. 1984: Can syntax be taught? A study of the effects of formal instruction on the acquisition of *wh*-questions by children. *Applied Linguistics* 5, 138–55.

Ellis, R. 1985: *Understanding Second Language Acquisition.* Oxford: Oxford University Press.

Ellis, R. 1989: Are classroom and naturalistic acquisition the same? A study of the classroom acquisition of German word order rules. *Studies in Second Language Acquisition* 11, 305–28.

Ellis, R. 1990: *Instructed Second Language Acquisition.* Oxford: Blackwell.

Ellis, R. 1994: *The Study of Second Language Acquisition*. Oxford: Oxford University Press.

Emonds, J. 1978: The verbal complex V'-V in French. *Linguistic Inquiry* 9, 49–77.

Epstein, S., Flynn, S. and Martohardjono, G. 1996: Second language acquisition: theoretical and experimental issues in contemporary research. *Brain and Behavioural Sciences* 19, 677–714.

Epstein, S., Flynn, S. and Martohardjono, G. 1998: The strong continuity hypothesis: some evidence concerning functional categories in adult L2 acquisition. In S. Flynn, G. Martohardjono and W. O'Neil (eds).

Eubank, L. 1987: The acquisition of German negation by formal language learners. In B. VanPatten, T. Dvorak and J. Lee (eds), *Foreign Language Learning: A Research Perspective*, Cambridge, Mass.: Newbury House.

Eubank, L. 1990: Linguistic theory and the acquisition of German negation. In B. VanPatten and J. Lee (eds), *Second Language Acquisition – Foreign Language Learning*. Clevedon: Multilingual Matters.

Eubank, L. (ed.) 1991: *Point Counterpoint: Universal Grammar in the Second Language*. Amsterdam: John Benjamins.

Eubank, L. 1993: Sentence matching and processing in L2 development. *Second Language Research* 9, 253–80.

Eubank, L. 1993/94: On the transfer of parametric values in L2 development. *Language Acquisition* 3, 182–208.

Eubank, L. 1994a: Optionality and the initial state in L2 development. In T. Hoekstra and B. Schwartz (eds).

Eubank, L. 1994b: Discussion paper: towards an explanation for the late acquisition of agreement in L2 English. *Second Language Research* 10, 84–93.

Eubank, L. 1996: Negation in early German-English interlanguage: more 'valueless features' in the L2 initial state. *Second Language Research* 12, 73–106.

Eubank, L. and Gregg, K. 1999: Critical periods and (second) language acquisition: divide et impera. In D. Birdsong (ed.), *Second Language Acquisition and the Critical Period Hypothesis*, Mahwah, NJ: Lawrence Erlbaum Associates.

Fabb, N. 1990: The difference between English restrictive and non-restrictive relative clauses. *Journal of Linguistics* 26, 57–78.

Felix, S. 1984: Maturational aspects of Universal Grammar. In A. Davies, C. Criper and A. Howatt (eds), *Interlanguage*, Edinburgh: Edinburgh University Press.

Finer, D. 1991: Binding parameters in second language acquisition. In L. Eubank (ed.).

Finer, D. and Broselow, E. 1986: Second language acquisition of reflexive binding. *Proceedings of the North Eastern Linguistic Society* 16, 154–68.

Flynn, S., Martohardjono, G. and O'Neil, W. (eds) 1998: *The Generative Study of Second Language Acquisition*. Mahwah, NJ: Lawrence Erlbaum Associates.

Fodor, J. 1983: *The Modularity of Mind*. Cambridge, Mass.: MIT Press.

Fuller, J. and Gundel, J. 1987: Topic prominence in interlanguage. *Language Learning* 37, 1–18.

Gass, S. and Schachter, J. (eds) 1989: *Linguistic Perspectives on Second Language Acquisition*. Cambridge: Cambridge University Press.

Gass, S. and Selinker, L. 1994: *Second Language Acquisition: An Introductory Course*. Hillsdale, NJ: Lawrence Erlbaum Associates.

Gavruseva, L. and Lardiere, D. 1996: The emergence of extended phrase structure in child L2 acquisition. In A. Stringfellow, D. Cahana-Amitay, E. Hughes and A. Zukowski (eds), *Proceedings of the 20th Annual Boston University Conference on Language Development*, Somerville, Mass.: Cascadilla Press, 225–36.

Giacomi, A. and Véronique, D. (eds) 1986: *Acquisition d'une langue étrangère*. Aix-en-Provence: Université de Provence.

Giusti, G. 1997: The categorial status of determiners. In L. Haegeman (ed.).

Gleitman, L. 1990: The structural sources of verb meanings. *Language Acquisition* 1, 3–55.

Goodluck, H. 1991: *Language Acquisition: A Linguistic Introduction*. Oxford: Blackwell.

Green, G. 1974: *Semantics and Syntactic Regularity*. Indiana: Indiana University Press.

Greenfield, S. 1997: *The Human Brain: A Guided Tour*. London: Weidenfeld and Nicolson.

Gregg, K. 1996: The logical and developmental problems of second language acquisition. In W. Ritchie and T. Bhatia (eds).

Grondin, N. and White, L. 1996: Functional categories in child L2 acquisition of French. *Language Acquisition* 5, 1–34.

Guéron, J. and Hoekstra, T. 1995: The temporal interpretation of predication. In A. Cardinaletti and M.-T. Guasti (eds), *Small Clauses (Syntax and Semantics Series, Vol 28)*, New York: Academic Press.

Guilfoyle, E., Hung, H. and Travis, L. 1992: Spec of IP and Spec of VP: two subjects in Austronesian languages. *Natural Language and Linguistic Theory* 10, 375–414.

Haegeman, L. 1990: Understood subjects in English diaries. *Multilingua* 9, 157–99.

Haegeman, L. 1994: *Introduction to Government and Binding Theory* (2nd edn). Oxford: Blackwell.

Haegeman, L. 1995: *The Syntax of Negation*. Cambridge: Cambridge University Press.

Haegeman, L. (ed.) 1997: *The New Comparative Syntax*. London: Longman.

Haegeman, L. and Guéron, J. 1999: *English Grammar: A Generative Perspective*. Oxford: Blackwell.

Hakuta, K. 1976: A case study of a Japanese child learning English as a second language. *Language Learning* 26, 321–51.

Hale, K. and Keyser, S. 1993: On argument structure and the lexical expression of syntactic relations. In K. Hale and S. Keyser (eds), *The View from Building 20: Essays in Honor of Sylvain Bromberger*, Cambridge, Mass.: MIT Press.

Halle, M. and Marantz, A. 1993: Distributed morphology and the pieces of inflection. In K. Hale and S. Keyser (eds), *The View from Building 20: Essays in Honor of Sylvain Bromberger*, Cambridge, Mass.: MIT Press.

Hamann, C., Rizzi, L. and Frauenfelder, U. 1996: On the acquisition of subject and object clitics in French. In H. Clahsen (ed.), *Generative Perspectives on Language Acquisition*, Amsterdam: John Benjamins.

Hamilton, R. 1995: The noun phrase accessibility hierarchy in SLA: determining the basis for its developmental effects. In F. Eckman, D. Highland, P. Lee, J. Mileham and R. Rutkowski Weber (eds), *Second Language Acquisition Theory and Pedagogy*, Mahwah, NJ: Lawrence Erlbaum Associates.

Hamilton, R. 1998: Underdetermined binding of reflexives by adult Japanese-speaking learners of English. *Second Language Research* 14, 292–320.

Hammerly, H. 1991: *Fluency and Accuracy: Toward Balance in Language Teaching and Learning*. Clevedon: Multilingual Matters.

Hawkins, J. 1980: On implicational and distributional universals of word order. *Journal of Linguistics* 16, 193–235.

Hawkins, R. 1987: Markedness and the acquisition of the English dative alternation by L2 learners. *Second Language Research* 3, 20–55.

Hawkins, R. 1998: Explaining the difficulty of French gender attribution for speakers of English. Paper presented at the 8th annual EUROSLA conference, Paris.

Hawkins, R. and Chan, C. 1997: The partial availability of Universal Grammar in second language acquisition: the 'failed functional features hypothesis'. *Second Language Research* 13, 187–226.

Hawkins, R., Towell, R. and Bazergui, N. 1993: Universal Grammar and the acquisition of French verb movement by native speakers of English. *Second Language Research* 9, 189–233.

Herschensohn, J. 2000: *The Second Time Around: Minimalism and L2 Acquisition.* Amsterdam: John Benjamins.

Hertel, T. and Pérez-Leroux, A. 1998: The role of the lexicon in the second language acquisition of Spanish word order. Paper presented at the Generative Approaches to Second Language Acquisition conference, Pittsburgh.

Hirakawa, M. 1990: A study of the L2 acquisition of English reflexives. *Second Language Research* 6, 60–85.

Hirakawa, M. 2000: L2 acquisition of Japanese unaccusative verbs by speakers of English. In K. Kanno (ed.), *The Acquisition of Japanese as a Second Language*, Amsterdam: John Benjamins.

Hirsh-Pasek, K. and Golinkoff, R. 1996: *The Origins of Grammar: Evidence from Early Language Comprehension.* Cambridge, Mass.: MIT Press.

Hoekstra, T. and Schwartz, B. (eds) 1994: *Language Acquisition Studies in Generative Grammar.* Amsterdam: John Benjamins.

Hornstein, N. and Lightfoot, D. (eds) 1981: *Explanation in Linguistics: The Logical Problem of Language Acquisition.* London: Longman.

Huang, C.-T. 1982: Logical relations in Chinese and the theory of grammar. Unpublished doctoral dissertation, MIT.

Huang, C.-T. 1984: On the distribution and reference of empty pronouns. *Linguistic Inquiry* 15, 531–74.

Huang, C.-T. 1995: Logical form. In G. Webelhuth (ed.), *Government and Binding Theory and the Minimalist Program*, Oxford: Blackwell.

Huebner, T. 1985: System and variablity in interlanguage syntax. *Language Learning* 35, 141–63.

Hulk, A. 1991: Parameter setting and the acquisition of word order in L2 French. *Second Language Research* 7, 1–34.

Hyams, N. 1996: The underspecification of functional categories in early grammar. In H. Clahsen (ed.), *Generative Perspectives on Language Acquisition*, Amsterdam: John Benjamins.

Hyltenstam, K. 1984: The use of typological markedness conditions as predictors in second language acquisition: the case of pronominal copies in relative clauses. In R. Andersen (ed.).

Jackendoff, R. 1972: *Semantic Interpretation in Generative Grammar.* Cambridge, Mass.: MIT Press.

Jackendoff, R. 1997: *The Architecture of the Language Faculty.* Cambridge, Mass.: MIT Press.

Jaeggli, O. and Safir, K. (eds) 1989: *The Null Subject Parameter.* Dordrecht: Kluwer.

Johnson, J. and Newport, E. 1989: Critical period effects in second language learning: the influence of maturational state on the acquisition of English as a second language. *Cognitive Psychology* 21, 60–99.

Johnson, J. and Newport, E. 1991: Critical period effects on universal properties of language: the status of subjacency in the acquisition of a second language. *Cognition* 39, 215–58.

Juffs, A. 1996: *Learnability and the Lexicon: Theories and Second Language Acquisition Research*. Amsterdam: John Benjamins.

Juffs, A. and Harrington, M. 1995: Parsing effects in L2 sentence processing: subject and object asymmetries in *wh*-extraction. *Studies in Second Language Acquisition* 17, 483–512.

Juffs, A. and Harrington, M. 1996: Garden path sentences and error in L2 processing. *Language Learning* 46, 283–326.

Kageyama, T. 1993: *Bunpoo to Gokeisei*. Kasukabe: Hituji Syoboo.

Karmiloff-Smith, A. 1979: *A Functional Approach to Child Language: A Study of Determiners and Reference*. Cambridge: Cambridge University Press.

Kayne, R. 1994: *The Antisymmetry of Syntax*. Cambridge, Mass.: MIT Press.

Klein, E. and Martohardjono, G. (eds) 1999: *The Development of Second Language Grammars: A Generative Approach*. Amsterdam: John Benjamins.

Klein, W. and Dittmar, N. 1979: *Developing Grammars*. Berlin: Springer.

Klein, W. and Perdue, C. 1992: *Utterance Structure*. Amsterdam: John Benjamins.

Koopman, H. and Sportiche, D. 1991: The position of subjects. *Lingua* 85, 211–58.

Koster, J. 1978: Why subject sentences don't exist. In S. Keyser (ed.), *Recent Transformational Studies in European Languages*, Cambridge, Mass.: MIT Press.

Krashen, S. 1977: Some issues relating to the monitor model. In H. Brown, C. Yorio and R. Crymes (eds), *On TESOL '77: Teaching and Learning English as a Second Language: Trends in Research and Practice*, Washington, DC: TESOL.

Krashen, S., Madden, C. and Bailey, N. 1975: Theoretical aspects of grammatical sequencing. In M. Burt and H. Dulay (eds), *On TESOL '75: New Directions in Second Language Learning, Teaching and Bilingual Education*, Washington, DC: TESOL.

Krashen, S. and Terrell, T. 1983: *The Natural Approach*. New York: Pergamon.

Lakshmanan, U. 1991: Morphological uniformity and null subjects in child second language acquisition. In L. Eubank (ed.).

Lalleman, J. 1999: The alternation hypothesis revisited: early L2 intuitions about the direction of gapping in Dutch. *Proceedings of the 8th EUROSLA Conference* 2, 157–72. (Special issue of *AILE*, University of Paris.)

Lardiere, D. 1998a: Case and tense in the 'fossilized' steady state. *Second Language Research* 14, 1–26.

Lardiere, D. 1998b: Dissociating syntax from morphology in a divergent L2 end-state grammar. *Second Language Research* 14, 359–75.

Larsen-Freeman, D. 1975: The acquisition of grammatical morphemes by adult ESL students. *TESOL Quarterly* 9, 409–19.

Larsen-Freeman, D. and Long, M. 1991: *An Introduction to Second Language Acquisition Research*. London: Longman.

Larson, R. 1988: On the double object construction. *Linguistic Inquiry* 19, 335–91.

Lasnik, H. 1995: Case and expletives revisited: on greed and other human failings. *Linguistic Inquiry* 26, 615–33.

Lasnik, H. and Uriagereka, J. 1988: *A Course in GB Syntax: Lectures on Binding and Empty Categories*. Cambridge, Mass.: MIT Press.

Levin, B. and Rappaport-Hovav, M. 1995: *Unaccusativity: At the Syntax-Lexical Semantics Interface*. Cambridge, Mass.: MIT Press.

Li, X. 1998: Adult L2 accessibility to UG: an issue revisited. In S. Flynn, G. Martohardjono and W. O'Neil (eds).

Li, Y. 1990: *Order and Constituency in Mandarin Chinese*. Dordrecht: Kluwer.

Liceras, J. 1989: On some properties of the 'pro-drop' parameter: looking for missing subjects in non-native Spanish. In S. Gass and J. Schachter (eds), *Linguistic Perspectives on Second Language Acquisition*, Cambridge: Cambridge University Press.

Lightbown, P. 1977: Consistency and variation in the acquisition of French. Unpublished doctoral dissertation, Columbia University.

Lightbown, P. 1986: Input and acquisition for second language learners in and out of classrooms. *Applied Linguistics* 7, 263–73.

Lightbown, P. and Spada, N. 1993: *How Languages are Learned*. Oxford: Oxford University Press.

Lightfoot, D. 1991: *How to Set Parameters: Arguments from Language Change*. Cambridge, Mass.: MIT Press.

Lightfoot, D. 1999: *The Development of Language: Acquisition, Change and Evolution*. Oxford: Blackwell.

Long, M. 1983: Does second language instruction make a difference? A review of the research. *TESOL Quarterly* 17, 359–82.

Long, M. 1993: Second language acquisition as a function of age: research findings and methodological issues. In K. Hyltenstam and A. Viberg (eds), *Progression and Regression in Language*, Cambridge: Cambridge University Press.

Long, M. 1995: The least a second language acquisition theory needs to explain. In H. Brown and S. Gonzo (eds), *Readings on Second Language Acquisition*, Upper Saddle River, NJ: Prentice Hall Regents.

MacLaughlin, D. 1998: The acquisition of the morphosyntax of English reflexives by non-native speakers. In M.-L. Beck (ed.).

MacWhinney, B. and Snow, C. 1985: The Child Language Data Exchange System. *Journal of Child Language* 12, 271–96.

Makino, T. 1980: Acquisition order of English morphemes by Japanese secondary school students. *Journal of Hokkaido University of Education* 30, 101–48.

Maling, J. 1986: Clause-bound reflexives in modern Icelandic. In L. Hellan and K. Christensen (eds), *Topics in Scandinavian Syntax*, Dordrecht: Reidel.

Manzini, M.-R. 1992: *Locality: A Theory and Some of its Empirical Consequences*. Cambridge, Mass.: MIT Press.

Martohardjono, G. 1993: Wh-movement in the acquisition of a second language: a cross-linguistic study of 3 languages with and without overt movement. Unpublished doctoral dissertation, Cornell University.

Martohardjono, G. 1998: Measuring competence in L2 acquisition: commentary on part II. In S. Flynn, G. Martohardjono and W. O'Neil (eds).

Martohardjono, G. and Gair, J. 1993: Apparent UG accessibility in second language acquisition: misapplied principles or principled misapplications. In F. Eckman (ed.), *Confluence: Linguistics, L2 Acquisition and Speech Pathology*, Amsterdam: John Benjamins.

Mazurkewich, I. and White, L. 1984: The acquisition of the dative alternation: unlearning overgeneralisations. *Cognition* 16, 261–83.

Meisel, J. 1997: The acquisition of the syntax of negation in French and German: contrasting first and second language development. *Second Language Research* 13, 227–63.

Meisel, J., Clahsen, H. and Pienemann, M. 1981: On determining developmental stages in natural second language acquisition. *Studies in Second Language Acquisition* 3, 109–35.

Mirizon, S. 1998: Wh-movement in the acquisition of a second language: an empirical study of native Indonesian speakers at the University of Essex. Unpublished Master's dissertation, University of Essex.

Mitchell, R. and Myles, F. 1998: *Second Language Learning Theories*. London: Arnold.

Morgan, J. and Travis, L. 1989: Limits on negative information in language input. *Journal of Child Language* 16, 531–52.

Müller, G. and Sternefeld, W. 1996: A'-chain formation and economy of derivation. *Linguistic Inquiry* 27, 480–511.

Murphy, V. 1997: The effect of modality on a grammaticality judgement task. *Second Language Research* 13, 34–65.

Myles, F., Mitchell, R. and Hooper, J. 1999: Interrogative chunks in French L2: a basis for creative construction? *Studies in Second Language Acquisition* 21, 49–80.

Oehrle, R. 1976: The grammatical status of the English dative alternation. Unpublished doctoral dissertation, MIT.

Parodi, T., Schwartz, B. and Clahsen, H. 1997: On the L2 acquisition of the morphosyntax of German nominals. *Essex Research Reports in Linguistics* 15, 1–44.

Párraga, E. 1998: Acquisition of English argument structure alternations by Spanish speakers: locative and dative argument structures. Unpublished Master's dissertation, University of Essex.

Parrish, B. 1987: A new look at methodologies in the study of article acquisition for learners of ESL. *Language Learning* 37, 361–83.

Parsons, T. 1995: Thematic relations and arguments. *Linguistic Inquiry* 26, 635–62.

Patkowski, M. 1980: The sensitive period for the acquisition of syntax in a second language. *Language Learning* 30, 449–72.

Pavesi, M. 1986: Markedness, discourse modes, and relative clause formation in a formal and an informal context. *Studies in Second Language Acquisition* 8, 38–55.

Perdue, C. (ed.) 1993: *Adult Language Acquisition: Cross-Learner Perspectives*, 2 vols. Cambridge: Cambridge University Press.

Perlmutter, D. 1978: Impersonal passives and the unaccusative hypothesis. *Proceedings of the Annual Meeting of the Berkeley Linguistics Society* 4, 157–89.

Pesetsky, D. 1982: Paths and categories. Unpublished doctoral dissertation, MIT.

Phinney, M. 1987: The pro-drop parameter in second language acquisition. In T. Roeper and E. Williams (eds), *Parameter Setting*, Dordrecht: Reidel.

Pica, P. 1987: On the nature of the reflexivisation cycle. *Proceedings of the North Eastern Linguistics Society* 17, 483–99.

Pica, T. 1985: The selective impact of instruction on second language acquisition. *Applied Linguistics* 6, 214–22.

Pienemann, M. 1989: Is language teachable? *Applied Linguistics* 10, 52–79.

Pinker, S. 1987: The bootstrapping problem in language acquisition. In B. MacWhinney (ed.), *Mechanisms of Language Acquisition*, Hillsdale, NJ: Lawrence Erlbaum Associates.

Pinker, S. 1989: *Learnability and Cognition: The Acquisition of Argument Structure*. Cambridge, Mass.: MIT Press.

Pollock, J.-Y. 1989: Verb movement, Universal Grammar, and the structure of IP. *Linguistic Inquiry* 20, 365–424.

Prévost, P. and White, L. 2000: Missing surface inflection or impairment in second language acquisition? Evidence from tense and agreement. *Second Language Research* 16, 103–33.

Progovac, L. 1992: Relativised SUBJECT: long-distance reflexives without movement. *Linguistic Inquiry* 23, 671–80.

Progovac, L. 1993: Long-distance reflexives: movement-to-Infl vs. relativised SUBJECT. *Linguistic Inquiry* 24, 755–72.

Puskas, G. 1997: Focus and the CP domain. In L. Haegeman (ed.).

Radford, A. 1993: Head-hunting: on the trail of the nominal Janus. In G. Corbett (ed.), *Heads in Grammatical Theory*, Cambridge: Cambridge University Press.

Radford, A. 1997: *Syntactic Theory and the Structure of English: A Minimalist Approach.* Cambridge: Cambridge University Press.

Reuland, E. and Koster, J. 1991: *Long-Distance Anaphora.* Cambridge: Cambridge University Press.

Ritchie, W. and Bhatia, T. (eds) 1996: *Handbook of Second Language Acquisition.* San Diego: Academic Press.

Ritter, E. 1993: Where's gender? *Linguistic Inquiry* 24, 795–803.

Rizzi, L. 1982: *Issues in Italian Syntax.* Dordrecht: Foris.

Rizzi, L. 1986: Null objects in Italian and the theory of *pro. Linguistic Inquiry* 17, 501–57.

Rizzi, L. 1990: *Relativized Minimality.* Cambridge, Mass.: MIT Press.

Rizzi, L. 1996: Residual verb second and the *wh*-criterion. In A. Belletti and L. Rizzi (eds).

Rizzi, L. 1997: A parametric approach to comparative syntax: properties of the pronominal system. In L. Haegeman (ed.).

Roberts, I. 1997: *Comparative Syntax.* London: Arnold.

Robison, R. 1990: The primacy of aspect: aspectual marking in English interlanguage. *Studies in Second Language Acquisition* 12, 315–30.

Ross, J. 1967: Constraints on variables in syntax. Doctoral dissertation, MIT. Also published (1986) as *Infinite Syntax.* Norwood, NJ: Ablex.

Schachter, J. 1989: Testing a proposed universal. In S. Gass and J. Schachter (eds).

Schachter, J. 1990: On the issue of completeness in second language acquisition. *Second Language Research* 6, 93–124.

Schachter, J. 1996: Maturation and the issue of Universal Grammar in second language acquisition. In W. Ritchie and T. Bhatia (eds).

Schlyter, S. 1986: Surextension et sous-extension dans l'acquisition des verbes de mouvement/déplacement. In A. Giacomi and D. Véronique (eds).

Schumann, J. 1978: The acquisition of English negation by speakers of Spanish: a review of the literature. In R. Andersen (ed.), *The Acquisition and Use of Spanish and English as First and Second Languages*, Washington, DC: TESOL.

Schwartz, B. 1986: The epistemological status of second language acquisition. *Second Language Research* 2, 120–59.

Schwartz, B. 1998: On two hypotheses of 'transfer' in L2A: minimal trees and absolute L1 transfer. In S. Flynn, G. Martohardjono and W. O'Neil (eds).

Schwartz, B. 1999: The second language instinct. In A. Sorace, C. Heycock and R. Shillcock (eds), *Language Acquisition: Knowledge, Representation and Processing*, Dordrecht: Elsevier.

Schwartz, B. and Gubala-Ryzak, M. 1992: Learnability and grammar reorganisation in L2A: against negative evidence-causing the unlearning of verb movement. *Second Language Research* 8, 1–38.

Schwartz, B. and Sprouse, R. 1994: Word order and nominative Case in nonnative language acquisition: a longitudinal study of (L1 Turkish) German interlanguage. In T. Hoekstra and B. Schwartz (eds).

Schwartz, B. and Sprouse, R. 1996: L2 cognitive states and the 'full transfer/full access' model. *Second Language Research* 12, 40–72.

Schwartz, B. and Tomaselli, A. 1990: Some implications from an analysis of German word order. In W. Abraham, W. Kosmeijer and E. Reuland (eds), *Issues in Germanic Syntax*, Berlin: de Gruyter.

Schwartz, B. and Vikner, S. 1996: The verb always leaves IP in V2 clauses. In A. Belletti and L. Rizzi (eds).

Selinker, L., Swain, M. and Dumas, G. 1975: The interlanguage hypothesis extended to children. *Language Learning* 25, 139–52.

Shapira, R. 1976: A study of the acquisition of ten syntactic structures and grammatical morphemes by an adult second language learner: some methodological implications. Unpublished Master's dissertation, UCLA.

Sharwood Smith, M. 1994: *Second Language Learning: Theoretical Foundations*. London: Longman.

Sheen, R. 1980: The importance of negative transfer. *International Review of Applied Linguistics* 18, 105–19.

Shirahata, T. 1988: The learning order of English grammatical morphemes by Japanese high school students. *JACET Bulletin* 19, 83–102.

Shlonsky, U. 1992: Resumptive pronouns as a last resort. *Linguistic Inquiry* 23, 443–68.

Skehan, P. 1998: *A Cognitive Approach to Language Learning*. Oxford: Oxford University Press.

Smith, N. 1999: *Chomsky: Ideas and Ideals*. Cambridge: Cambridge University Press.

Smith, N. and Tsimpli, I.-M. 1995: *The Mind of a Savant: Language Learning and Modularity*. Oxford: Blackwell.

Snow, C. and Hoefnagel-Höhle, M. 1978: The critical period for language acquisition: evidence from second language learning. *Child Development* 49, 1114–28.

Sopher, M. 1995: Resetting the pro-drop parameter: a study of English-speaking adults learning L2 Spanish. Unpublished Master's dissertation, University of Salford.

Sorace, A. 1993: Incomplete vs. divergent representations of unaccusativity in near-native grammars of Italian. *Second Language Research* 9, 22–47.

Sorace, A. 1996: The use of acceptability judgements in second language acquisition research. In W. Ritchie and T. Bhatia (eds).

Stauble, A.-M. 1984: A comparison of a Spanish–English and a Japanese–English second language continuum: negation and verb morphology. In R. Andersen (ed.).

Strozer, J. 1994: *Language Acquisition after Puberty*. Washington, DC: Georgetown University Press.

Swan, M. and Smith, B. (eds) 1987: *Learner English: A Teacher's Guide to Interference and Other Problems*. Cambridge: Cambridge University Press.

Taraldsen, K. 1981: The theoretical interpretation of a class of marked extractions. In A. Belletti, L. Brandi and L. Rizzi (eds), *Theory of Markedness in Generative Grammar*, Pisa: Scuola Normale Superiore.

Tarallo, F. and Myhill, J. 1983: Interference and natural language processing in second language acquisition. *Language Learning* 33, 55–76.

Thomas, M. 1989: The acquisition of English articles by first- and second-language learners. *Applied Psycholinguistics* 10, 335–55.

Thomas, M. 1993: *Knowledge of Reflexives in a Second Language*. Amsterdam: John Benjamins.

Thomas, M. 1995: Acquisition of the Japanese reflexive *zibun* and movement of anaphors in Logical Form. *Second Language Research* 11, 206–34.

Tomaselli, A. and Schwartz, B. 1990: Analysing the acquisition stages of negation in L2 German: support for UG in adult SLA. *Second Language Research* 6, 1–38.

Towell, R. and Hawkins, R. 1994: *Approaches to Second Language Acquisition*. Clevedon: Multilingual Matters.

Trahey, M. 1996: Positive evidence in second language acquisition: some long-term effects. *Second Language Research* 12, 111–39.

Trahey, M. and White, L. 1993: Positive evidence and preemption in the second language classroom. *Studies in Second Language Acquisition* 15, 181–204.

Travis, L. 1984: Parameters and the effects of word order variation. Unpublished doctoral dissertation, MIT.

Trévise, A. and Noyau, C. 1984: Adult Spanish speakers and the acquisition of French negation forms: individual variation and linguistic awareness. In R. Andersen (ed.).

Tsao, F. 1977: A functional study of topic in Chinese: the first step towards discourse analysis. Unpublished doctoral dissertation, University of Southern California.

Tsimpli, I.-M. 1997: Resumptive features and minimalism: evidence from second language acquisition. In *Proceedings of the 21st Annual Boston University Conference on Language Development*, Somerville, Mass.: Cascadilla Press.

Tsimpli, I.-M. and Roussou, A. 1991: Parameter resetting in L2? *University College London Working Papers in Linguistics* 3, 149–69.

Vainikka, A. and Young-Scholten, M. 1994: Direct access to X'-theory: evidence from Korean and Turkish adults learning German. In T. Hoekstra and B. Schwartz (eds).

Vainikka, A. and Young-Scholten, M. 1996a: Gradual development of L2 phrase structure. *Second Language Research* 12, 7–39.

Vainikka, A. and Young-Scholten, M. 1996b: The early stages in adult L2 syntax: additional evidence from Romance speakers. *Second Language Research* 12, 140–76.

Vainikka, A. and Young-Scholten, M. 1998: the initial state in the L2 acquisition of phrase structure. In S. Flynn, G. Martohardjono and W. O'Neil (eds).

Vergnaud, J.-R. 1985: *Dépendances et niveaux de représentation en syntaxe*. Amsterdam: John Benjamins.

Véronique, D. 1986: L'apprentissage du français par des travailleurs marocains et les processus de pidginisation et de créolisation. In A. Giacomi and D. Véronique (eds).

Wakabayashi, S. 1997: The acquisition of functional categories by learners of English. Unpublished doctoral dissertation, University of Cambridge.

Wang, Q., Lillo-Martin, D., Best, C. and Levitt, A. 1992: Null subject vs. null object: some evidence from the acquisition of Chinese and English. *Language Acquisition* 2, 221–54.

Wexler, K. and Manzini, M.-R. 1987: Parameters, learnability and binding theory. *Linguistic Inquiry* 18, 413–44.

White, L. 1985: The pro-drop parameter in adult second language acquisition. *Language Learning* 35, 47–62.

White, L. 1986: Implications of parametric variation for adult second language acquisition: an investigation of the pro-drop parameter. In V. Cook (ed.), *Experimental Approaches to Second Language Learning*, Oxford: Pergamon Press.

White, L. 1989: *Universal Grammar and Second Language Acquisition*. Amsterdam: John Benjamins.

White, L. 1990/91: The verb-movement parameter in second language acquisition. *Language Acquisition* 1, 337–60.

White, L. 1991: Adverb placement in second language acquisition: some effects of negative evidence in the classroom. *Second Language Research* 7, 133–61.

White, L. 1992a: Long and short verb movement in second language acquisition. *Canadian Journal of Linguistics* 37, 273–86.

White, L. 1992b: On triggering data in L2 acquisition: a reply to Schwartz and Gubala-Ryzak. *Second Language Research* 8, 120–37.

White, L. 1992c: Subjacency violations and empty categories in second language acquisition. In H. Goodluck and M. Rochemont (eds), *Island Constraints: Theory, Acquisition and Processing*, Dordrecht: Kluwer.

White, L. 1996: Clitics in L2 French. In H. Clahsen (ed.), *Generative Perspectives on Language Acquisition*, Amsterdam: John Benjamins.

White, L. forthcoming: *Universal Grammar in the Second Language: From Initial to Steady State*. Cambridge: Cambridge University Press.

White, L. and Genesee, F. 1996: How native is near-native? The issue of ultimate attainment in adult second language acquisition. *Second Language Research* 12, 233–65.

White, L., Bruhn-Garavito, J., Kawasaki, T., Pater, J. and Prévost, P. 1997: The researcher gave the subject a test about himself: problems of ambiguity and preference in the investigation of reflexive binding. *Language Learning* 47, 145–72.

White, L., Travis, L. and MacLachlan, A. 1992: The acquisition of *wh*-question formation by Malagasy learners of English: evidence for Universal Grammar. *Canadian Journal of Linguistics* 37, 341–68.

Wode, H. 1976: Developmental sequences in naturalistic L2 acquisition. *Working Papers on Bilingualism* 11, 1–13.

Wode, H. 1981: *Learning a Second Language: An Integrated View of Language Acquisition*. Tübingen: Gunter Narr Verlag.

Wolfe-Quintero, K. 1992: Learnability and the acquisition of extraction in relative clauses and *wh*-questions. *Studies in Second Language Acquisition* 14, 39–70.

Xiao, Y. 1998: An investigation of the syntactic development of school-age Chinese-speaking children learning English: the role of topic prominence. Unpublished doctoral dissertation, University of Hawaii.

Xu, L. 1986: Free empty category. *Linguistic Inquiry* 17, 75–93.

Yip, V. 1995: *Interlanguage and Learnability: From Chinese to English*. Amsterdam: John Benjamins.

Yip, V. and Matthews, S. 1995: I-interlanguage and typology: the case of topic prominence. In L. Eubank, L. Selinker and M. Sharwood Smith (eds), *The Current State of Interlanguage: Studies in Honor of William E. Rutherford*, Amsterdam: John Benjamins.

Yuan, B. 1997: Asymmetry of null subjects and null objects in Chinese speakers' L2 English. *Studies in Second Language Acquisition* 19, 467–97.

Zanuttini, R. 1996: On the relevance of tense for sentential negation. In A. Belletti and L. Rizzi (eds).

Zanuttini, R. 1997: *Negation and Clausal Structure: A Comparative Study of Romance Languages*. Oxford: Oxford University Press.

Zobl, H. 1980: The formal and developmental selectivity of L1 influence on L2 acquisition. *Language Learning* 30, 43–57.

Zobl, H. 1989: Canonical typological structures and ergativity in English L2 acquisition. In S. Gass and J. Schachter (eds).

Zobl, H. 1990: Evidence for parameter-sensitive acquisition: a contribution to the domain-specific versus central processes debate. *Second Language Research* 6, 39–59.

Zobl, H. and Liceras, J. 1994: Review article: functional categories and acquisition orders. *Language Learning* 44, 159–80.

Zwart, J.-W. 1997: The Germanic SOV languages and the universal base hypothesis. In L. Haegeman (ed.).

Index

Lightning Source UK Ltd.
Milton Keynes UK
UKOW06f1100230913

217740UK00002B/56/P

9 780631 191841